The Informal Economy

The Informal Economy

Studies in Advanced and Less Developed Countries

Edited by
Alejandro Portes
Manuel Castells
Lauren A. Benton

The Johns Hopkins University Press
Baltimore and London

This book has been brought to publication with the generous assistance
of the Tinker Foundation.

Originally published in hardcover and paperback, 1989
Second printing, paperback, 1991

The Johns Hopkins University Press, 701 West 40th Street,
Baltimore, Maryland 21211
The Johns Hopkins Press Ltd., London

The paper used in this publication meets the minimum requirements of American
National Standard for Information Sciences—Permanence of Paper for Printed
Library Materials, ANSI Z39.48-1984.

Library of Congress Cataloging-in-Publication Data

The Informal economy : studies in advanced and less developed
    countries / edited by Alejandro Portes, Manuel Castells, and Lauren
    A. Benton.
        p.   cm.
    Bibliography: p.
    Includes index.
    ISBN 0-8018-3735-9 (alk. paper). ISBN 0-8018-3736-7 (pbk. : alk.
paper)
    1. Informal sector (Economics)—Case studies.   2. Informal sector
(Economics)—Government policy—Case studies.   I. Portes,
Alejandro, 1944– .   II. Castells, Manuel.   III. Benton, Lauren A.
HD2341.I534   1989
331.12′51381′092—dc19   88-23004
                                                              CIP

Contents

Acknowledgments

During the years in which the research project on which this book is based was being conducted, we received support from many sources. We would like to acknowledge first those institutions that provided support for the original field studies—in Montevideo, Bogotá, Miami, and Madrid, respectively. The Tinker Foundation deserves special mention, for it made possible the implementation of the Montevideo study under the difficult conditions created by the Uruguayan military regime, and the final conference in which the case studies included in this book were presented. The International Development Research Centre of Canada supported the Bogotá study, and the U.S. National Science Foundation did the same for the analysis of the informal sector of Miami. The study of the Madrid electronics industry was funded by fellowships for Lauren Benton from the U.S. Social Science Research Council, the Wenner-Gren Foundation, and the Commission for Educational Exchange between the United States of America and Spain; the research also received strong support from the Spanish Ministry of Economy.

These four studies comprised the core of the original comparative project, which expanded gradually with the collaboration of others. We wish to acknowledge the participation and support of all the scholars whose work is included in this book, as well as those who, for a variety of reasons, do not figure in the final list of authors. In particular, Larissa Lomnitz, who took part in both project conferences, and Carlos Filgueira, Victor Tokman, and Enzo Mingione, who attended the final one, deserve our recognition for their many contributions to our discussions and to this final product.

At midpoint in the development of the project, a working seminar was held in Baltimore to assess progress and discuss research plans. The Ford Foundation funded this meeting, and we are grateful to it and especially to its Latin America officer at the time, Jeffrey Puryear, for their support. The Johns Hopkins University was the venue for the meeting, and we would like to acknowledge the contribution of two of its officers: George Fisher, dean of the School of Arts and Sciences at the time, gave us enthusiastic support; David W. Cohen, director of the Program in Atlantic History, Culture, and Society, was cosponsor of this seminar and provided requisite supplementary funds as well as unfailing enthusiasm to make it a success.

The final project conference was held in Harper's Ferry, West Virginia, in late 1986. The conference was made possible by grants from the Rockefeller, Tinker, and Wenner-Gren foundations. Mary Kritz of the Rockefeller Foundation and Martha Muse, president of the Tinker Foundation, deserve special mention for their crucial support at that time. Without their assistance and that of project officers in the three foundations, results of the project would not have seen the light of day. The list of participants, discussants, and moderators at both meetings is much too long to include here. We would like to express our sincere recognition to all of them and, in particular, to our colleagues at the Johns Hopkins University. Despite the omission of names, the participation and contributions of each of them are gratefully remembered.

During the last year of the project, we were saddened to learn that Suzana Prates, one of its founding members and coauthor of a chapter in this book, had died in tragic circumstances. Grief at her loss is compounded by the inability to present her with the final product of our collective efforts. Let the following pages stand as a living memorial to her work and the goals to which she dedicated her life.

The task of coordinating revisions and translations of chapters whose authors were based in institutions across the United States and Canada, Latin America, and Europe was daunting. It could not have been implemented without the unwavering support of Anders Richter, senior editor of the Johns Hopkins University Press, who pursued the book from its frail beginnings and made sure that it would be given consideration by the Press. His collaboration and editorial expertise are hereby gratefully acknowledged. Last but not least, Virginia Bailey, Joanne Hildebrandt, and Anna Stoll of the Hopkins sociology department deserve most special recognition. Binnie did marvels juggling funds across grants and countries to finance a complex project; Joanne, first, and Anna, at present, successfully met the challenge of organizing large conferences and then typing and proofing their lengthy proceedings. To each of them, our deepest appreciation.

Introduction

The informal economy, in all the ambiguity of its connotations, has come to constitute a major structural feature of society, both in industrialized and less developed countries. And yet, the ideological controversy and political debate surrounding its development have obscured comprehension of its character, challenging the capacity of the social sciences to provide a reliable analysis. This book takes up the challenge by presenting studies of the structure and dynamics of the informal economy in a variety of social contexts, on the basis of original research. It is also an attempt to provide an initial synthesis of what we know about this phenomenon and of its practical implications for both economic growth and social equity. With the work offered here, we intend to contribute to the clarification of a fundamental, although elusive, reality that, contrary to conventional views in the past, has grown in significance with the development of the modern world.

The book is the outcome of a five-year collaborative project, begun at the University of California, Berkeley, in 1981. In that year, an essay by the first-named editor of this volume attempted to summarize what was then known about the phenomenon of informality in Third World countries and its relationship to the modern, regulated economy.[1] In the process of compiling materials for that essay and during subsequent discussions after its publication, two things became clear: first, that the informal economy represented a central aspect of the economic and social dynamics of less developed countries, despite its notorious absence from official reports; second, that too little was known about this elusive phenomenon, so that characterizations of its structure and functions (including those in the 1981 essay) could only be tentative.

This dearth of information had both a qualitative and a quantitative aspect. First, there were not enough in-depth observational studies that examined the dynamics of informality in different settings or, more important, that traced its linkages with the regulated economy. Second, there were still fewer quantitative estimates of the extent of the informal economy—either in terms of value produced or people employed. In the absence of reliable figures, mainstream economists and others who had neglected these arrangements in the past could argue that the few case studies available represented interesting, but exotic, phenomena of no real economic or social significance. Although we suspected the contrary, there was not enough evidence at that point to sustain more than a tentative alternative position.

For this reason, we decided to launch a multicountry comparative study to meet, at least partially, the existing information gap and test conflicting hypotheses advanced in the literature. The project that evolved from this initiative was based on a series of city studies conducted independently, but with a common conceptual framework and methodological approach. The latter combined a "horizontal" methodology, which attempted to provide quantitative estimates of the relative weight of informal production and employment in each city, with a "vertical" method, which traced the articulation between formal and informal activities in selected sectors of the urban economy. The first, or horizontal, approach was implemented through field surveys or reanalysis of available census reports; the second relied on direct observation and in-depth interviews.[2]

Development of this comparative project required the collaboration of researchers from different disciplines in a number of countries. Originally, the project was to be limited to Latin American and other Third World cities since this was the scope of the original essay and the ensuing discussions. We promptly discovered, however, that activities bearing all the marks of those labeled "informal" in the Third World were present and growing in cities of the United States. This discovery led to the expansion of the original research network and the planned studies to encompass several North American locations: the New York, Miami, Los Angeles, and San Diego metropolitan areas.

As the individual studies progressed and as their early results were examined, it became clear that informalization was very much part of economic reality in a number of Western European countries and that empirical studies had started to delineate its characteristics and dynamics in those areas. This realization prompted the expansion of the comparative project to encompass several Western European case studies.

Finally, it was inevitable that contact would occur between these efforts at investigating the informal sector in capitalist countries and studies that a growing group of scholars were conducting on the "second economy" in the Soviet Union and other Eastern European nations. Although the primary thrust of our comparative project and the research questions that prompted it had to do with informal activities under capitalism, we saw much utility in comparing these results with those coming out of research in centrally planned economies. The basic purpose of this comparison was to discover how activities that possessed many structural characteristics in common—small scale, avoidance of state regulations, flexible sites, use of family labor, among others—could have such different meanings and functions depending on the character of the overarching "formal" economy.

There was much intellectual excitement in bringing together works that revealed the global scope of what was originally thought to be an exclusively Third World phenomenon. During the course of the project, however, several scholars criticized the use of the same concept to encompass such a wide variety of social and economic arrangements. Although a more substantive discussion of the term *informal economy* is reserved for the following chapter, a preliminary methodological reason for our approach can be advanced here. The use of a common term serves to highlight precisely the similiarity of certain social arrangements and economic practices amid very different environments. By identifying such practices as "the same," it becomes possible to investigate systematically the manifold forms that they take and their differing significance for the actors involved and for the society at large.

Thus, without a common term of reference, and its careful prior definition, it would have been impossible to identify commonalities between phenomena inserted in very different political and economic contexts. By bringing such phenomena under the same conceptual umbrella, a comparative study of their characteristics could be initiated on a global scale, rather than remain confined to an exclusively regional or national scope. Selection of the term *informal* to perform this unifying function was due, however, to practical reasons. Our view in this respect is nominalist, and we see no particular difficulty in substituting the term for related ones such as *underground, submerged,* or *secondary.* Several of the ensuing chapters actually employ these terms as synonyms. The reasons for deliberately opting for the concept of informality were the existence of an extensive prior research literature in different world regions under this label and the desire to build on this literature rather than challenge it.

The successive expansion of the original comparative project to new areas created, however, a series of methodological and logistic problems. For one, it became impossible to adhere to a common research design since many case studies were already under way when they were incorporated in later stages of the project. In addition, the conceptualization of the phenomenon and its dynamics—although preserving a common core—became increasingly diversified, in part because of actual empirical differences across research sites and, in part, because of the different intellectual backgrounds and preferences of researchers in a growing network. Finally, there was the problem of finding financial support for an expanding set of studies and the increasingly complex task of their coordination.

Faced with these difficulties, we opted for borrowing a page from the informal artisans and entrepreneurs whom we were studying and adopted a strategy of maximum flexibility. Instead of trying to implement rigidly the same methodological design everywhere or compel the use of the same theoretical definitions and hypotheses, the project evolved—along with its participants— toward increasing diversity of orientations and methodological approaches. Participation in the growing network became primarily a matter of the quality and originality of individual studies focused on common research questions rather than of the specific approaches brought to bear on them. This flexible strategy had also the positive consequence of allowing the incorporation of case studies that were already under way and that could thus produce relevant results in a relatively short period.

In June 1984, a midpoint research planning seminar was held at the Johns Hopkins University to examine progress of individual studies, discuss early findings, and plan the future course of the overall project.³ The final presentation of results took place in a conference at Harper's Ferry, West Virginia, in October 1986. The conference featured three days of presentation of research findings from over twenty countries and extensive discussion of their scope and implications. Chapters in this book are a selection of presentations given at the conference.⁴

Before moving into the substantive topic, a word is in order about the general goals that animated this comparative project and about its place in the landscape of present social research on related issues. The project's broadest aim was to contribute to development of grounded theory on contemporary processes of social change. By *development,* we do not mean the accumulation of abstract models, but rather the renovation of conceptual tools necessary to apprehend an elusive, shifting reality. In this sense, we are less interested in arriving at elegant formalizations than in gaining reliable knowledge about comparable events worldwide.

Similarly, grounded theory refers to the incorporation of this knowledge into statements oriented toward guiding future inquiry and practice. This approach contrasts with frequent attempts to approach present realities deductively on the basis of conceptual frameworks inherited from the past. The social science enterprise can not be justified solely by such inferences. In order to make a contribution that transcends these boundaries, it is necessary to struggle with manifestations of a changing world, abandoning the comfort of familiar definitions and theories, and formulating new and frequently imperfect ones. Although often untidy, such inductive efforts take us closer to the understanding of real events than disquisitions about classic concepts whose empirical referents have often become problematic.

It is for this reason that the research effort reported in the following pages does not culminate in a comprehensive theory of informalization or in a discussion of the place of this concept in the familiar paradigms of social science. Instead, we review the existing literature, present findings from studies in fourteen cities and ten different countries, and analyze the implications of this research for practical attempts to respond to the informal economy. Part 1 presents an overview of the concept and outlines the theoretical basis for much of the recent research on the topic. Subsequent chapters are organized around several themes, each of which simultaneously comprises an independent area of study and focuses on some fundamental aspect of larger questions.

The five chapters of part 2 focus on informalization and its impact on urban economies. Study of the informal sector in Third World countries originated in a critique of the concept of urban marginality, and the chapters reflect this tradition while also moving beyond the earlier debates by placing trends in urban labor markets in historical context and by highlighting linkages between informalization and other transformations. Roberts's chapter offers a novel analysis of the career patterns of workers in the changing informal economy of

Guadalajara, Mexico. The chapter by Fortuna and Prates on Montevideo and that of Lanzetta and Murillo on Bogotá present findings from two major studies that relate changes in the size and composition of the urban informal sector to the trajectory of dependent development in Latin America. The chapters by Sassen-Koob and Stepick offer two different perspectives of informalization and immigration in urban labor markets in North America.

Part 3 presents two contrasting and highly original chapters on the extent and effects of "illicit" activities in very different political and economic settings. Grossman analyzes the nature and consequences of the "black" economy in the Soviet Union. Blanes presents research on the impact of revenues from cocaine exports on the informal and formal sectors of the Bolivian economy. The chapters differ from others in the volume by focusing on circulation rather than production and thus examine in a different light the political and economic importance of informal activities.

Part 4 comprises four works that analyze the role of the informal economy in the process of industrial restructuring. The chapters by Benería, Capecchi, Ybarra, and Benton describe different patterns of "vertical" integration of the informal economy in modern industrial production—ranging from sweatshop labor and homework to high-tech flexible production—and examine the various factors that account for such differences. The four contributions go beyond earlier studies of the informal sector in linking the phenomenon to the accelerated process of industrial restructuring that has been taking place on a global scale since the early 1970s. They characterize informalization as a dynamic process influenced by changing conditions in the world economy, local political factors, and social patterns such as gender roles that affect the allocation of particular industrial tasks.

Part 5 brings together chapters by Fernández-Kelly and García; McGee, Salih, Young, and Heng; and Standing that emphasize the role of the state in shaping the process of informalization. To be sure, nearly all the contributions in this volume address the relationship between politics and the informal economy, some more explicitly than others. But the three chapters gathered here analyze quite specifically the role of the state in creating and controlling, or failing to control, changes in the size and composition of the informal economy. Fernández-Kelly and García challenge our understanding of the state's regulatory functions by examining the behavior of state agencies and their representatives in two North American settings. McGee et al. and Standing analyze the state's contribution to two contrasting trends: decline in the importance of the informal economy in a developing country (Malaysia) and its resurgence in the context of acute crisis and stagnation in an advanced economy (Great Britain).

The above themes are closely interrelated, and many of the chapters would fit easily under more than one heading. Further, several broad issues cross-cut these divisions, since the topic itself requires analysis of the relationship between formal and informal economies and of the role of the state in creating and manipulating that boundary. Because so many of the chapters are eloquent in addressing these larger issues as well as in presenting specific research results, we have chosen to focus in the concluding chapter not on the theoretical significance of findings but rather on their practical implications for local and national communities. This choice recognizes the diversity of conceptualizations in the volume's case studies. The variations are preserved because they reflect actual realities, as well as the complexity of the research tasks involved; above all, they indicate the impossibility of achieving theoretical "closure" on the subject of informalization at the present time.

Substantively, the project belongs to what Evans and Stephens (1987) have termed the "new comparative political economy." The term encompasses an interdisciplinary field concerned with structural processes of transformation worldwide. Its common features are an analytic approach that emphasizes global, rather than exclusively local, causes and effects and a subject matter that is seldom limited to events in a single country.

A large proportion of the research literature identified by Evans and Stephens as part of this field is concerned with events at the "heights" of the polity and the economic system: social revolutions, state transformations, international flows of capital, strategies of multinational corporations, the implementation of national development policies, and the like. This literature stands in contrast with a second approach characterized by attempts to examine closely the substratum of life and work on which larger structures rest. One of the central challenges for the new political economy is to link consistently such ground-level descriptions with broader economic and social processes.

The excitement awakened by the gradual realization of the universal character of the informal economy is based on the opportunity that these activities provide to study global structures and processes of change at a grassroots level. As will be seen in the following chapters, informality is simultaneously part of the daily life of individuals and households and the means through which important production and distribution functions take place. Research on these activities thus affords a unique glimpse into the ways in which individual strategies connect with the broader accumulation process and the superstructures that rely on it.

To be sure, this is not the only ground-level entry point for the study of structural trends. Comparative analyses of the "labor process" in large industrial establishments have served a similar function in recent years (e.g., Edwards 1979; Burawoy 1979, 1985; Sabel and Stark 1982; Stark 1986). However, the informal economy occupies the distinct position in which labor process and family process often become one, and the basic difficulty in observing the activities that promote this convergence is that they are well concealed from public view.

The intellectual journey that this book brings to an end has been one full of challenges and discovery. Aside from realization of the universal character of these activities, a central lesson is that they are not conducted in isolation, but represent a unique entry point for examining the underside of broader structures. The final result is not a tight formal theory, but rather a sourcebook of factual information focused on a common process and highlighting simultaneously its many variants. For many years, social scientists and policymakers in the advanced world proceeded as if the only economy worth studying and acting upon was that recorded in the official statistics. This book will have accomplished its purpose if it helps put to rest such a comforting but dangerous illusion.

Notes

1. "Unequal Exchange and the Urban Informal Sector," chap. 3 in Portes and Walton 1981.

2. This dual design is apparent in several of the chapters below, which describe its implementation in different contexts. See especially the chapters by Lanzetta and Murillo, Fortuna and Prates, and Stepick.

3. The proceedings of the seminar were compiled as "The Urban Informal Sector: Recent Trends in Research and Theory." Department of Sociology, The Johns Hopkins University, Baltimore, 1984. Mimeo. A partial summary is presented in Portes and Benton 1984.

4. Excluded were research-in-progress reports and general commentaries on the state of the field. Both, however, provided useful background materials for the conference and for this volume.

References

Burawoy, M. 1979. *Manufacturing Consent*. Chicago: University of Chicago Press.
————. 1985. *The Politics of Production*. London: New Left Books.
Edwards, R. C. 1979. *Contested Terrain: The Transformation of the Workplace in the Twentieth Century*. New York: Basic Books.
Evans, P. and J. D. Stephens. 1987. "Development and the World Economy." Working Paper no. 8/9. Center for the Comparative Study of Development, Brown University. Mimeo.
Portes, A. and J. Walton. 1981. *Labor, Class, and the International System*. New York: Academic Press.
Portes, A. and L. Benton. 1984. "Industrial Development and Labor Absorption: A Reinterpretation." *Population and Development Review* 10:589–611.
Sabel, C. and D. Stark. 1982. "Planning, Politics, and Shop-Floor Power: Hidden Forms of Bargaining in Soviet-imposed State Socialist Societies." *Politics and Society* 11:439–75.
Stark, D. 1986. "Rethinking Internal Labor Markets: New Insights from a Comparative Perspective." *American Sociological Review* 51:492–504.

1 Overview

1 World Underneath: The Origins, Dynamics, and Effects of the Informal Economy

Manuel Castells and Alejandro Portes

History is full of surprises. Whenever a social fact is believed to be a secular trend, experience reverses it eventually. The growth of the informal economy in different social and economic contexts over the last decade exemplifies this crucial feature of human society. In many contexts self-employment is growing more rapidly than salaried employment. The process of institutionalization of economic activities is slowing down. Horizontal networks, not vertical bureaucracies, seem to be the new models of efficient organizations. Subcontracting prevails over union contracts in various industrial sectors. The cash economy is expanding in the microeconomic realm, while barter is becoming a crucial feature of international exchange. New legions of would-be workers are entering a casual labor market, where a new breed of entrepreneurship is on the make. The informal economy simultaneously encompasses flexibility and exploitation, productivity and abuse, aggressive entrepreneurs and defenseless workers, libertarianism and greediness. And, above all, there is disenfranchisement of the institutionalized power conquered by labor, with much suffering, in a two-century-old struggle.

As with all fundamental social debates, the noise of ideology blurs the profile of the question, thus confusing potential answers. In this chapter, we attempt to outline the principal issues under discussion concerning the informal economy, thus opening the way for their clarification by research conducted in diverse social settings. Our position on these issues does not always agree with those of other authors. However, there is a universe of common concerns addressed by studies of the informal economy throughout the world. Our purpose here is to highlight what these concerns are and offer a general perspective on them as a point of reference for the evaluation of the manifold variants uncovered by empirical inquiries.

What Is the Informal Economy?

The informal economy is a common-sense notion whose moving social boundaries cannot be captured by a strict definition without closing the debate prematurely. This is why we need, first, to refer to the historical realities connoted by the theme, and to understand it as a process, rather than as an object.

In any tentative approach to a confusing and yet significant reality, it is always useful to determine what it is *not,* in spite of the images evoked by the notion in our collective consciousness. The informal economy is not a set of survival activities performed by destitute people on the margins of society. Studies in both advanced industrial and less developed countries have shown the economic dynamism of unregulated income-generating activities and the relatively high level of income of many informal entrepreneurs, sometimes above the level of workers in the formal economy (Lozano 1985; Ferman, Berndt, and Selo 1978; Henry 1978; Portes, Blitzer, and Curtis 1986). Some activities in the informal sector may derive from the desperate need of a worker to obtain the means of subsistence for his or her family. But a similar motivation could lead a worker to accept lower wages in the formal sector. The informal economy is not a euphemism for poverty. It is a specific form of relationships of production, while poverty is an attribute linked to the process of distribution.

At first sight, it would seem inappropriate to use the same concept to embrace such different situations as those of a street seller in Latin America and a software consultant moonlighting in Silicon Valley. And yet, it is precisely because we refer to a specific form of income-generating production relationships that the concept of the informal economy is useful. Thus, we depart from the notions of economic dualism and social marginality which have been so pervasive in the development literature in spite of all empirical evidence accumulated against such notions (see Perlman 1976; Moser 1978).

Although most of the individuals engaged in informal economic activities are poor, particularly in the Third World, informal economic processes cut across the whole social structure. By focusing on the logic of the process, it is possible to look behind the appearance of social conditions (poverty, destitution, blight) to focus on the social dynamics underlying the production of such conditions. Hence, while we do not negate the significance of poverty studies, our interest here is on the analysis of a different subject: the redefinition of production relationships through the articulation of formal and informal activities.

There is strong evidence of the systematic linkage between formal and informal sectors, following the requirements of profitability (Birbeck 1979; Brusco 1982; Roberts, this volume). Individual workers may switch between the two sectors even during the same workday, with a unionized machinist moonlighting as a plumber while a secretary does keypunching at home in her off-duty time (Gershuny 1978; Saba 1980; Mingione 1983). The informal economy is thus not an individual condition but a process of income-generation characterized by one central feature: *it is unregulated by the institutions of society, in a legal and social environment in which similar activities are regulated.*

Any change in the institutional boundaries of regulation of economic activities produces a parallel realignment of the formal-informal relationship.

In fact, it is because there is a formal economy (i.e., an institutional framework of economic activity) that we can speak of an "informal" one. In an ideal market economy, with no regulation of any kind, the distinction between formal and informal would lose meaning since all activities would be performed in the manner we now call informal. At the opposite pole, the more a society institutionalizes its economic activities following collectively defined power relationships and the more individual actors try to escape this institutionalized logic, the sharper the divide between the two sectors.

What is new in the current context is that the informal sector grows, even in highly institutionalized economies, at the expense of already formalized work relationships (Tanzi 1982; Tokman 1986; Sassen-Koob, this volume). Thus, it represents a novel social trend instead of being a mere "lag" from traditional relationships of production. When a modern paper-producing mill in Cali, Colombia, subcontracts the work of providing raw materials to garbage-pickers, this phenomenon cannot be explained as the persistence of survival activities among the urban poor, but rather as a disguised form of wage labor which deprives workers even of the meaning of a proletarian work relationship (Birbeck 1979; Fortuna and Prates, this volume).

Furthermore, it is the expansion of informal activities in a largely regulated context that gives a new historical meaning to the current process of a rising informal economy. It is often argued that uncontrolled, exploitative relationships of production are the oldest story, so that sweatshops represent classical capitalism, not advanced capitalism. But it is precisely the development of sweatshops and of other unregulated activities after a long period of institutional control that causes old forms of production to become new ones. An old form in a new setting is, in fact, new, since all social relationships can only be defined in their specific historical context. This context is defined by the prior existence of institutionalized regulation, by which we understand the explicit, active intervention of the state in the process and outcome of income-generating activities, on the basis of a set of enforceable legal rules.

The absence of institutional regulation in the informal economy may affect various elements of the work process, since each specific situation defines a very distinctive type of activity. It may refer, first of all, to the *status of labor;* for instance, labor may be undeclared, lacking the social benefits to which it is entitled, paid under the minimum wage, or employed under circumstances that society's norms would not otherwise allow. It may refer, second, to the *conditions of work* under which labor is employed. These may involve, for instance, tampering with health conditions, public hygiene, safety hazards, or the location of activities, such as ignoring land-use zoning or placing hazardous manufacturing in the midst of densely populated areas. Third, it may refer to the particular *form of management of some firms.* For instance, a company may engage in systematic fiscal fraud or the generalized use of unrecorded cash-payments as a means of economic transaction. There is no theoretical reason to

I

+ = Licit
− = Illicit

Process of Production and Distribution	Final Product	Economy Type
+	+	Formal
−	+	Informal
+ or −	−	Criminal

II

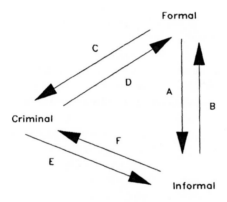

A State interference, competition from large firms, sources of capital and technology
B Cheaper consumer goods and industrial inputs, flexible reserves of labor
C State interference and disruption, supplies of certain controlled goods
D Corruption, "gatekeeper's rents" for selected state officials [1]
E Capital, demand for goods, new income−earning opportunities
F Cheaper goods, flexible reserves of labor

[1] See Blanes, this volume; Grossman, this volume

Figure 1.1. Types of economic activity: *I.* definitions; *II.* relationships.

exclude from the informal economy the unrecorded practices of large corporations, particularly since they have close linkages with the growth of other informal activities. From this perspective, the informal economy is not a marginal phenomenon for charitable social research, but a fundamental politico-economic process at the core of many societies.

Finally, some economic activities may be termed informal because of their very nature, namely, because they are defined as criminal by the institutions of society. Sociologists know, however, that *normal/abnormal* and *legal/criminal* are social categories subject to change. When the laws concerning them are enforced, such categories often represent sources of economic opportunity outside the pale of institutional regulation. Criminal activities possess, however, distinct characteristics that set them apart from those otherwise termed informal. Figure 1.1 attempts to clarify the situation by portraying the relationships between different types of income-earning activities. Those labeled "Criminal" specialize in the production of goods and services socially defined as illicit.

On the other hand, the basic distinction between formal and informal activities proper does not hinge on the character of the final product, but on the manner in which it is produced and exchanged. Thus, articles of clothing, restaurant food, or automobile parts—all perfectly licit commodities—may have their origins in legally regulated or unregulated production arrangements. By distinguishing these different activities rather than combining them into an undifferentiated whole, it is possible to examine their interrelationships in different contexts. Blanes (this volume) analyzes, for example, the influence of the Bolivian drug economy on that country's formal and informal sectors. Other possible influences between these different sectors are illustrated in figure 1.1.

The rest of this chapter focuses on informal activities proper, that is, the unregulated production of otherwise licit goods and services. A central reason for this choice is that these activities, not those conventionally labeled criminal, represent a novel economic trend. As stated above, this novelty lies in the resilience or growth of informal arrangements in contexts in which they were believed to be extinct or in which they were expected to disappear with the advance of industrialization. The following section summarizes evidence of this global trend.

The Reality of the Informal Economy: A Comparative Perspective

The most significant generalizations to be drawn from the existing evidence are, first, that the informal economy is universal, as similar arrangements are found in countries and regions at very different levels of economic development; second, that this sector is heterogeneous, as the forms adopted by unregulated production and distribution vary widely even within single societies; and, third, that there has been an apparent increase of these activities during the last several years.[1]

The evidence for Latin America and other Third World regions is familiar and has been reviewed extensively elsewhere (Tokman 1986, 1982; Bromley 1978; PREALC 1981; Portes and Benton 1984). During the post–World War II period and until 1980, Latin America experienced a rapid and sustained process of industrial development. Table 1.1 contains the relevant empirical evidence for the seven largest Latin American countries, three metropolitan areas, and the region as a whole. Although these data suffer from limitations, discussed below, the pattern that they illustrate is unmistakable.

Between 1950 and 1980, Latin American economies grew at a weighted average of 5.5 percent. As shown in table 1.1, the regional GNP quadrupled during this period. Without exception, individual countries more than doubled their gross national products, although rates of growth were much higher in countries like Colombia, Mexico, and Brazil. Because of rapid population growth, GNP per capita did not grow as fast, but in 1980 it stood at approximately 200 percent of the 1950 figure. The most dynamic element in the growth of this region was, without doubt, the industrial sector. Industry's share of the gross domestic product (GDP) registered an unweighted average annual increase of 6 percent between 1950 and 1975, being much higher in Brazil, Mexico, Peru, and other countries.

The response of labor markets to this accelerated process of industrialization was not what orthodox economic theories of industrial development would have predicted (see Lewis 1959; García 1982). Informal employment, as defined by the United Nations' Regional Employment Program for Latin America (PREALC), declined only from 46 percent to 42 percent of the Latin American labor force (see table 1.1). In 1950, informal activities occupied 30 percent of the urban economically active population (EAP); in 1980, with an industrial plant four times larger, informal employment still stood at 30 percent. Contrary to the experience of the advanced countries, self-employment did not decline with industrialization but remained essentially constant during this thirty-year period.[2]

At this point, it is useful to compare the experience of Latin American countries between 1950 and 1980 with that of the United States at the turn of the century. The two periods are similar in terms of several macroeconomic indicators that point to comparable levels of industrial development (Tokman 1982). Table 1.2 presents data on the relative size of the informal sector in Latin America and the United States during the relevant periods. Not surprisingly, the proportion of informal workers is seen to decline monotonically in the United States. The trend is, after all, one of the empirical underpinnings of the theory of labor absorption under rapid industrial growth. In Latin America, on the other hand, rapid industrial growth during the 1950–80 period led only to a

Table 1.1 Latin America: Segmentation of the Economically Active Population (EAP)

City/Country	Year	GNP[1]	Informal Workers: Urban EAP[2] (%)	Informal Workers: Total EAP[2] (%)	Self-employed[3] (%)
Argentina	1950	12.9	21.1	22.8	7.8
	1980	31.3	23.0	25.7	16.7
Brazil	1950	10.0	27.3	48.3	28.6
	1980	59.2	27.2	44.5	33.7
Chile	1950	3.4	35.1	31.0	22.4
	1980	7.7	27.1	28.9	18.6
Colombia	1950	2.5	39.0	48.3	23.4
	1980	9.5	34.4	41.0	18.9
Mexico	1950	10.0	37.4	56.9	37.4
	1980	44.2	35.8	40.4	23.2
Peru	1950	2.2	46.9	56.3	—
	1980	8.3	40.5	55.8	40.2
Venezuela	1950	2.4	32.1	38.9	28.8
	1980	8.3	20.8	31.5	31.8
Bogotá	1975		33.0 (60.5)[4]		
	1984		34.2 (59.7)		
Montevideo	1968		12.5		
	1983		16.2 (19.3)[5]		
São Paulo	1976		29.7[6]		
	1982		34.4		
Latin America	1950	51.8	30.8	46.5	27.3
	1980	190.9	30.3	42.2 (60.3)[7]	28.3

Sources: Faría 1984, 136; Lopez Castaño 1984, 149; Portes 1985, 22–23; Prates 1984, 557; PREALC 1982, tables 1–3, 4, 8, 9, 19, 23, 24, 33, 34, 62, 63, 77, 78, 96, and 97; Statistical Department of Colombia 1984, table 6; *Statistical Abstracts of Latin America* 1978, tables 2200 and 2201.

[1]Gross national product in billions of 1970 dollars, 1950–1976.

[2]Country figures and those for Latin America are the sum of unpaid family workers, domestic servants, and the self-employed, minus professionals and technicians.

[3]When figures for 1980 were unavailable, those for 1970 were used.

[4]Column figures for Bogotá are the sum of the categories in note 2. Figures in parentheses are the percentage of workers not registered with the national social security system.

[5]Column figures for Montevideo are the sum of unpaid family workers and the self-employed, minus professionals and technicians. The figure in parentheses includes these categories plus wage workers without social security protection for a sample representation of approximately 65.4% of the city's population.

[6]Figures for São Paulo are percentages of "irregular" workers, defined as those receiving less than the legal minimum wage per labor hour.

[7]Figure in parentheses is the sum of the categories in note 2, plus the estimated proportion of informal wage workers.

marginal decline in the size of the informal labor force. Similar conclusions are reached when one considers the category of the self-employed alone—composed, to a large extent, of itinerant odd-jobbers and petty artisans. This category all but disappeared in the industrial sector of the United States during the period of accelerated growth; in Latin America, it remained a stable one-fifth of the industrial labor force (see table 1.2).

There is reason to believe, furthermore, that declines in informal employment, minimal for the region as a whole but significant for a few countries like Mexico and Venezuela, reflect an over-optimistic assessment of actual trends. International agencies, which are the source of these data, have defined informal employment as the sum of the self-employed—excluding professionals and technicians, unremunerated family workers, and domestic servants. Excluded also are informal wage workers, that is, those hired casually and who lack social security protection. According to this definition, therefore, *all* wage workers are part of the formal sector. In Latin America, perhaps with the exception of Argentina and Uruguay, this assumption leads to a gross underestimate of informal employment, since a large proportion of wage laborers are employed in microenterprises that are legally exempted from the existing labor legislation or simply do not observe it.

The figures in table 1.1 indicate the likely size of this underestimate. In Bogotá, for example, informal workers according to the PREALC definition represented about a third of the urban labor force in 1984, the figure being essentially the same as ten years earlier. An alternative and more appropriate definition, based on labor excluded from social security coverage, increases these estimates significantly to about half of the urban EAP in both years.[3] In general, whenever unprotected wage workers are added to the definition of informal employment, the relative size of the latter increases significantly. As shown in table 1.1, this corrected definition leads to a revised estimate of total informal employment in Latin America which exceeds the PREALC figure by approximately 20 percent.

Until a few years ago, the bulk of research on the question of informality was conducted in the Third World because most scholars concluded, on the basis of data such as those in table 1.2, that these arrangements had become extinct in the advanced countries. Thus, the existence of "invented" jobs in the interstices of the modern economy was regarded as a typical reflection of the plight of the poorer countries (Bairoch 1973; Chaney 1979). Labor market analysts in the United States have also suggested that small-scale enterprises and, in particular, those that bypass official regulation, either do not exist or are too insignificant to merit study.[4]

Recent research suggests, however, that this neat division between Third World countries, where the informal sector is large, and advanced ones, where it has nearly disappeared, is wrong. On the contrary, informal arrangements seem to be growing rapidly, at least in some sectors. Research on the

Table 1.2 The Informal Labor Force and Self-employed Workers in Latin America and the United States

	Latin America				United States		
	Informal Workers:				Informal Workers:		
Year	Total[1] (%)	Self-employed[2] (%)	Self-employed in Manufacturing[3] (%)	Year	Total[1] (%)	Self-employed[2] (%)	Self-employed in Manufacturing[3] (%)
1950	46.5	27.3	22.1	1900	50.8	34.0	7.2
1960	44.8	28.1	21.5	1910	41.8	29.3	6.0
1970	44.0	28.3	20.7	1920	34.5	26.1	4.4
1980	42.2	—	—	1930	31.2	23.1	3.0

Sources: PREALC 1982; Tokman 1982, table 4; Lebergott 1964, tables A-3, A-7.

[1]Percentage of total labor force. Informal workers are defined as the sum of the self-employed, unremunerated family workers, and domestic servants.
[2]Percentage of total labor force.
[3]Percentage of total manufacturing labor force.

topic in the United States is more difficult because these activities, clandestine by definition, are more actively persecuted. The first stab at the problem was taken by labor economists whose approach was to estimate the magnitude of "underground" activities on the basis of discrepancies between aggregate monetary indicators. The underlying assumption is that informal transactions take place in cash.

Gutmann (1979), for example, estimated the size of the informal economy by comparing the ratio of outstanding currency to demand deposits in 1978 with the average for the years 1937–41, a period when underground activities were assumed to be close to zero. Increases in the ratio were imputed to growth in these activities. On the basis of this method, Gutmann estimated that the informal economy represented about 10 percent of the currently measured Gross National Product, or $177 billion, in 1978. This approach has been employed with variations by other authors. Spitznas (1981) applied Gutmann's formula to the Second Federal Reserve District, which includes New York City, and estimated the city's underground economy at $16.2 billion in 1978. He also estimated that these activities had been growing rapidly.

Although useful as preliminary indicators of the existence of a previously neglected phenomenon, these indirect methods are flawed in several ways. First, there are no data to demonstrate that informal activities were really zero in selected base years or that informal goods and services are paid for exclusively in cash. Second, these estimates do not provide any clue as to the nature of growth in the "unobserved" economy, the industries in which it is concentrated, or the proportion of the labor force which it employs. Finally, despite the similarity of method, economic estimates vary wildly, raising serious doubts as to their validity. For example, Gutmann calculated that these activities represented about 10 percent of measured GNP in 1978; another analyst increased that figure to 33 percent (Feige 1979); while a third reduced it drastically to 4.4 percent (Tanzi 1980, 1982).

To overcome limitations of the macroeconomic approach, other social scientists have started to engage in firsthand field research. Results of such studies in three U.S. metropolitan areas are presented in this volume (see the chapters by Fernández-Kelly and García; Sassen-Koob; and Stepick). Their findings are supplemented below with data on the evolution of very small establishments (VSEs), defined as those employing less than ten workers.

VSEs are relevant to the question of informality for two reasons. First, by reason of their low visibility, ease of displacement, and other factors, VSEs provide the most appropriate setting for casual hiring, unreporting of income, and other informal practices. Direct observational studies indicate that although many small concerns are forced to obtain licenses (and thus appear in the aggregate statistics), their labor practices are mostly informal. Second, VSEs are easier to convert into totally underground enterprises. While it is generally difficult to informalize a plant employing hundreds of workers, this is not the case for one with only a few employees. Such a firm can close down "officially" one day and reopen the next as an underground concern (Lozano 1985; Green 1983; Siegel and Markoff 1985; Sassen-Koob 1984).

The statistical series in tables 1.3 and 1.4 are drawn from the Census Bureau's *County Business Patterns* for various years. As an estimate of the size of the American informal sector, these data are subject to two opposite biases: first, not all VSEs engage in informal practices, which leads to an overestimate; second, fully informal enterprises escape government record keeping, which leads to the opposite. In this situation, the series are best interpreted as a rough estimate of the evolution of the informal sector, on the basis of those recorded firms that most closely approximate it.

Table 1.3 contains the proportion of VSEs and of their employees in the country as a whole during the period 1965–83. Also included are the proportion of these units and their employees in the states of New York, California, and Florida and of establishments in Queens, Dade (Miami), and San Diego counties. The latter series corresponds to the sites of recent field studies, including those reported in this volume. Number of employees per size-class of enterprise is not available in the county series.

About three-fourths of U.S. establishments counted by the census were VSEs in 1965, and they absorbed approximately one-seventh of the economically active population (EAP). Twenty years later, the figures were almost exactly the same, although the ups and downs along the way are instructive. Between 1965 and 1970, there was a 6-percent decline in the proportion of VSEs and a 2-percent drop in the labor force employed in them. The reversal of this trend between 1970 and 1975 is an artifact of a change in the smaller size-class of establishment reported by the census—from "less-than-8" to "less-than-10" employees. Thereafter and until 1980, there was again a gradual decline in the number of VSEs, but in that year the trend reversed once more so that, by the end of the period, the numbers were about the same as they had been ten years earlier.

State figures follow a similar trend, except that, by 1983, the proportion of VSEs was slightly higher in each state than in the country as a whole. This pattern is still more visible in the three county series: Dade, Queens, and San Diego counties all had average or below-average proportions of VSEs in 1965; two decades later, however, they all exceeded the national average by as much as 4 percent. This evolution supports the conclusion of field studies concerning the growth of a small-business sector with a substantial informal component in these urban areas.

In synthesis, very small economic units are alive and well in the American economy. Their relative number and the proportion of the economically active population employed in them have remained fairly stable over the last decades. A point worth noting is that the recovery in the proportion of VSEs after prior decline occurred in the most recent years. This result is in line

Table 1.3 Relative Number of Units and Employment in Very Small Establishments (VSEs)

Year	U.S. Firms¹ (%)	U.S. Employees² (%)	California Firms¹ (%)	California Employees² (%)	San Diego County Firms¹ (%)	Florida Firms¹ (%)	Florida Employees² (%)	Dade County Firms¹ (%)	New York Firms¹ (%)	New York Employees² (%)	Queens County Firms¹ (%)
1965	76.0	14.1	75.1	14.7	76.9	75.2	17.4	70.8	75.2	13.1	77.0
	(3.5)	(47.7)	(.34)	(4.5)	(.08)	(.12)	(1.3)	(.02)	(.38)	(5.4)	(.05)
1970	70.6	11.9	71.0	12.4	71.2	70.5	14.1	66.7	71.8	11.2	74.8
1975	77.2	16.3	77.0	17.0	78.4	77.8	20.0	77.1	78.9	15.5	80.2
1980	74.1	15.2	73.5	15.2	74.9	75.7	18.7	74.4	76.5	14.8	78.5
1983	76.8	16.4	77.0	16.2	78.5	78.8	19.9	80.8	78.3	15.2	80.1
	(5.3)	(73.0)	(.61)	(8.2)	(.13)	(.28)	(3.2)	(.05)	(.42)	(6.0)	(.06)

Source: U.S. Bureau of the Census, County Business Patterns, various years.

Note: VSEs are defined as firms with less than 10 employees.

¹Figures in parentheses are total number of firms, in millions.
²Figures in parentheses are total number of employees, in millions.

22

with findings of the field studies about the recent growth of urban small businesses and informality.

U.S. immigrant communities, a frequent site for the development of informality, have provided much of the requisite labor for informal activities and even the entrepreneurial drive to initiate them. There is a close association between areas of high immigrant concentration—such as New York, Miami, and San Diego—and those in which the U.S. informal sector seems most vigorous (Waldinger 1985; Lozano 1985; Stepick, this volume). This association has suggested to many that the rise of the informal sector is not the result of any structural requirement of the U.S. economy, but merely the outcome of the survival strategies of immigrants attempting to "make it" in America. Hence, the informalization process can be reversed simply by tightening immigration rules. Before accepting this conclusion, however, it is important to examine the experience of other advanced industrial societies.

Central Italy is probably the best-studied case. Black labor (*lavoro negro*), as informal work is designated in Italy, is common in the central provinces such as Emilia-Romagna, but under vastly different structural arrangements than those found either in Latin America or in the United States. Efforts of large industries to control union power during the 1960s led to a process of decentralization which has acquired its own momentum. In Italy, artisanal enterprises with less than fifteen workers are exempted from certain provisions of the tax code and of the statute of labor (Piore and Sabel 1984, 228). These enterprises increased rapidly in the provinces most affected by the decentralization process. In Modena, they went from 4,970 in 1963 to 21,473 in 1975, a 430-percent increase at a time when the total population grew by just over 10 percent (Sabel 1982, 271). Additional evidence presented in table 1.4 shows that large firms (five hundred employees or more) are only half as common in Emilia-Romagna as in the rest of Italy. Despite the fact that over half of industrial establishments in the province employ less than fifty workers, industrial exports from Emilia-Romagna have increased steadily as a percentage of total Italian exports during the last decade.[5]

Small northern enterprises rarely market finished goods, but instead work under contract for larger formal firms. Cooperatives of informal microproducers under the putting-out system are found in knitwear, clothes, and ceramic tiles around Modena; and in motorcycles and footwear in Bologna. The following description illustrates how these arrangements work:

> The Morini motorcycle plant in Bologna has 100 employees and produces an average of 20 motorcycles per day. Most of the workers in the plant are engaged in assembly. . . . Except for the camshaft and the engine mounting, all of the components are put out: the frame, the tank, the shock absorbers, the handlebars, the brakes, the gears, and the wheels; almost the whole machine is produced by subcontractors. (Brusco 1982, 172)

Table 1.4 Indicators of Informal Sector Production and Employment in Italy and Spain

A. Industrial Employment in Emilia-Romagna

Number of Workers	Emilia-Romagna (%)	Italy (%)
Less than 10	27.8	23.4
Less than 50	25.1	20.9
Less than 250	28.0	23.4
Less than 500	8.4	9.0
500 or more	10.7	23.3
Total	100.0	100.0

B. Industrial Exports from Emilia-Romagna as Percentage of Total Italian Exports

Year	Percentage
1963	6.0
1965	6.3
1967	7.0
1972	8.1
1978	8.8
1980	9.4

C. Employment and Production in the Spanish Footwear Industry

Year	Alicante		Spain	
	Number of Salaried Workers	Value of Production[1]	Number of Salaried Workers	Value of Production[1]
1973	59,767	38,286	417,637	223,965
1975	58,365	46,484	409,992	277,274
1977	50,221	45,857	402,425	321,764
1979	46,942	42,950	355,624	295,020
Percentage Increase, 1970–79	−21	+12	−15	+31

Sources: Brusco 1982; Ybarra 1982a.
[1]Constant prices in millions of 1973 pesetas.

For our purposes, however, the principal lesson from the Italian experience is that a large and diversified informal economy can be sustained without recourse to immigrant labor. Instead, housewives, children, and domestic migrants can be tapped to fill the less-skilled informal jobs, while better-trained and experienced workers frequently become small entrepreneurs. The absence of a direct causal link between foreign labor and informality is confirmed by studies elsewhere in Western Europe, including Great Britain, the Netherlands, and Spain (Pahl and Dennett 1981; Renooy 1984; Ruesga-Benito 1984).

The Spanish case deserves brief mention, as a partial antidote to the optimism emanating from the Italian experience. Since the mid-1970s, many Spanish industries have experienced a process of decentralization quite similar to that of northern Italy. As a result, Spain exports today millions of dollars worth of shoes and other articles produced in factories that do not legally exist. Ybarra (1982a) has presented evidence of this process in the form of employment and production statistics for the footwear industry, centered in the province of Alicante. These data, reproduced in section C of table 1.4, show that the value of production in the industry increased significantly during the seventies at a time when the registered work force was declining precipitously. Since no significant technological innovations were incorporated into production, the decline reflects indirectly the extent to which production was informalized (see Sanchis and Pico 1983; Ybarra, this volume).

Despite the near-sweatshop conditions that appear to be the norm in informal plants, the Spanish experience of decentralization has not been based on immigrant labor, little of which is found in Alicante, but rather on domestic labor reserves. In the footwear industry, employment of women appears to have increased significantly along with the decentralization of production into small and informal shops (Benton 1986; Ybarra 1982a, 1982b).

These European case studies contradict the view that the underground economy is primarily a consequence of immigration. Even in the United States, research has started to turn up evidence of participation of domestic workers in informal activities (Sassen-Koob and Grover 1985). Undoubtedly, immigrants provide *one* source of labor for the expansion of these activities, and they may be preferable to domestic workers because of their vulnerability. However, the underlying causes for the expansion of an informal economy in the advanced countries go well beyond the availability of a tractable foreign labor supply. An in-depth analysis of these causes is beyond the scope of this chapter, but we take a stab at outlining what appear to be the main forces at play after examining common structural features of informality in diverse settings.

The Structure of the Informal Economy

The informal economy encompasses such a diversity of situations and activities that it represents a heterogeneous universe, irreducible to any subset of specific rules of economic calculation. Nevertheless, there are three aspects, common to most such activities, that deserve special attention: (1) the systemic connection with the formal economy, (2) the special characteristics of labor employed in informal activities, and (3) government's attitude toward the nonregulated sector. We shall examine each of these elements in turn.

1. Research during the last ten years shows consistently that the informal sector is an integral component of total national economies, rather than a marginal appendix to them (Peattie 1981; Standing 1986; Benería, this volume). The specialized networks formed by unregulated enterprises free large firms from the constraints imposed upon them by social control and institutional norms. In fact, the economy in most countries tends to work in a two-tier system whose boundaries and interactions adopt a variable geometry according to the pace of social unrest and the political orientations of government. These two levels of the economy have little to do with the traditional distinction between "monopoly capital" and "competitive capital," since large corporations may engage also in sharp competition, and small businesses often operate within a captive market as extensions of large firms.

From an organizational perspective, this process amounts to the formation of decentralized networks of production and distribution which rapidly displace the more rigid hierarchies on which large corporations formerly relied (Piore and Sabel 1984). There are actually two intertwined processes at work: the decentralization of large corporations into semiautonomous units and the informalization of as many of these units as possible, so that to the benefits of flexibility are added the advantages of unregulated activities in a regulated environment.

2. Workers involved in the informal economy tend to have very specific characteristics that can be subsumed under the general heading of *downgraded labor* (Sassen-Koob 1984). Most workers who receive fewer benefits or less wages, or experience worse working conditions than those prevailing in the formal economy, do so because this is the prerequisite for their entry into the labor market. Their vulnerability is not randomly produced. It depends upon certain social characteristics that allow companies (or intermediaries) to enforce their demands. The most obvious instance is that involving immigrant workers, particularly the undocumented. But vulnerability also extends to all social situations that are marked by some kind of social stigma: ethnic minorities, women, and youth are common subjects of discrimination and, hence, potential candidates for working at home, part-time, and as temporary replacements (Fernández-Kelly 1983; Ybarra 1982a, this volume).

Yet, although these are the main sources for recruitment of informal workers, one must note that the boundaries of vulnerability are always historically specific. If a highly unionized steel-mills-based region becomes subject to high structural unemployment, experienced hard-hat proletarians might be ready to become undeclared repairmen or pirate cab drivers, if that is the only way to feed their families (Ansberry 1986). And in the opposite direction, Turkish workers in Germany can become the militant vanguard of the automobile workers union after a few years of experiencing their rights and acquiring a new sense of class solidarity (Castles and Kosack 1973). The informal economy evolves along the borders of social struggles, incorporating those too weak to defend themselves, rejecting those who become too conflictive, and propelling those with stamina and resources into surrogate entrepreneurship.

Although those in informal activities are frequently harassed, the informal sector as a whole tends to develop under the auspices of government tolerance. Governments tolerate or even stimulate informal economic activities as a way to resolve potential social conflicts or to promote political patronage. Such is the experience of most squatter settlements in Third World cities, which provide a cheap, easy "solution" to the housing crisis while predisposing squatters to political allegiance (Collier 1976; Castells 1980). But it is also the tacit policy of European governments that count on the informal sector to reduce the open rate of unemployment and to provide new incentives to battered national economies (Gerry 1984; Benton 1986; Offe 1985). Informalization is not a social process always developing outside the purview of the state; it is instead the expression of a new form of control characterized by the disenfranchisement of a large sector of the working class, often with the acquiescence of the state (see Standing, this volume). For the latter, the loss of formal control over these activities is compensated by the short-term potential for legitimation and renewed economic growth that they offer.

The Genesis of the Informal Economy

The analysis of the genesis of the process of informalization, as it has occurred in particular in the advanced countries, may provide some clarification of its functions and effects. To be sure, the precise causes of this process are specific to the societies in which it has taken place, and in-depth research is required in each particular context. Despite their great diversity, recent field studies sound a number of common themes that allow us to entertain a few general hypotheses.

A basic overarching idea is that the expansion of the informal economy is part of the process of economic restructuring aimed at superseding the structural crisis of the 1970s. Yet such a statement is both too limited and too general—too limited because some of the processes at work, particularly in the Third World and in countries like Italy, were in place before the 1970s; too general because it does not clarify precisely how this restructuring is taking place or identify the specific targets of the process.

The first specific cause, commonly mentioned in the literature, is the reaction by both firms and individual workers to the power of organized labor (Brusco 1982; Sabel 1982). In this view of things, unions appear as, simultaneously, an obstacle to capitalist accumulation and as a corporatist pressure group eager to defend its interests even at the expense of unorganized workers. Examples of labor aristocracies surrounded by an ocean of casual or unemployed workers abound in both the Third World and the advanced countries (Castells 1980; Sassen-Koob 1984). However, the main opposition to union power comes, as one can imagine, from business.

It is thus not surprising that the European country with the most developed informal economy is Italy, where the *autunno caldo* of 1969 brought an unprecedented level of social victories to the Italian labor unions. These achievements were followed by a serious downturn of capitalist profits, a situation that has been reversed only during the last ten years, after widespread unemployment and corporate austerity policies. Fiat, for instance, slowed down production in its own factories in order to increase subcontracting and multiple sourcing so as to achieve a significant comeback in its international competitiveness (Brusco 1982; Sabel 1982; Capecchi, this volume).

Undermining organized labor's control over the work process seems to be a common objective of informalization, although it is not its sole cause. Here, we note that many of the sectors which have undergone rapid informalization, such as restaurants and custodial and personal services, were previously dominated by small firms that were not highly unionized to begin with (Morales and Mines 1985; Stepick, this volume).

A second general cause of the new, unregulated dynamism is, precisely, the reaction against the state's regulation of the economy, both in terms of taxes and social legislation. Health and environmental controls imposed during the 1960s, social benefits achieved under the auspices of the welfare state, and the tax increases necessary to pay for them came under attack in the 1970s in the advanced countries in the context of a global recession. Ironically, the rise of the welfare state in the post–World War II period may have promoted informalization directly by stimulating companies' efforts to escape its reach, and indirectly by weakening the resistance of the working class to new forms of labor organization.

A third general cause, affecting labor-intensive industries in particular, is the impact of international competition on all countries. Because of the growing integration of national economies into the international system, there is a tendency toward the diffusion of low labor costs across countries and regions. Manufacturers of consumer goods, such as garments and footwear, who cannot compete with cheaper Third World imports must either close down their plants or move them underground (Waldinger 1985; Ybarra 1982b, this volume). This international competition affects not only producers in the advanced countries but those in the Third World as well, as they vie with each other to reduce labor costs in an endless downward spiral.

A fourth and related reason for the growth of the informal economy is the process of industrialization as it is taking place in many Third World countries, that is, under social and economic conditions that forbid much enforcement of standards previously set by the state. For example, if Mexico refused to let the U.S. runaway industries, or *maquiladoras,* in the border region circumvent the contracts obtained by the Mexican unions, these industries would simply move elsewhere, and the process of industrialization would stop (Hansen 1981; Fernández-Kelly 1983). Or, in another context, if China did not allow the special economic zones to function according to rules that do not apply to the Chinese economy as a whole, foreign companies would not locate there, and China would lose the chance of technology transfer which it so eagerly seeks (Wong 1982). In sum, the newly industrialized countries informalize themselves, vis-à-vis their competitors as well as vis-à-vis their own formal laws, so as to obtain a comparative advantage for their production relative to the more regulated areas of the world economy.

The final and important reason for the growth of an informal sector results from the effects of the economic crisis since the mid-1970s throughout the world. In many countries, millions of people have been subjected to harsh living conditions that have made them accept whatever ways out of their misery they could find. This is particularly the case in countries of the periphery, heavily affected by global recession and the austerity policies promoted by international financial institutions (Boyer and Mistral 1983; Schatan 1985; Walton 1985; U.N. Economic Commission for Latin America 1986). Under these conditions, formal employment has contracted significantly (Lagos and Tokman 1983).

This crisis will eventually end but, for the moment, people all over the world have mobilized to work and earn their living on the margins of rules and organizational arrangements that no longer fit their real condition and experience. And in their quest for survival, they have connected with a more flexible, ad hoc form of economic activity that, while reviving old methods of primitive exploitation, also provides more room for personal interaction. The small-scale and face-to-face features of these activities make living through the crisis a more manageable experience than waiting in line for relief from impersonal bureaucracies (Pahl 1984; Massey and Meegan 1982).

Effects of Informalization

The process we have described has significant economic and social effects at the global as well as the national level. The following are a few of the most important, presented in summary form.

First, this process greatly contributes to the formation of a decentralized model of economic organization. The large corporation, with its national vertical structure and the separation of its functions between staff and line, does not appear any more as the last stage of a necessary evolution toward rationalized industrial management. Networks of economic activities, networks of firms, and coordinated clusters of workers appear to comprise an emergent model of successful production and distribution. Although firms engaging in such networks are not, by any means, exclusively informal, there is a tendency for the informal economy to rely predominantly on networks, and their connection with the formal economy, through subcontracting, is also network-based. Linkages between different processes appear to be at the core of the new economy, so that we witness the reversal of the secular downward trend of small business as a proportion of overall economic activity (Williamson 1985; Piore and Sabel 1984; Granovetter 1984).

Related to the above, one cannot underestimate the potential for informal enterprises to proliferate in world markets through other small businesses that act as intermediaries. A good example is found in Hong Kong, where 75 percent of manufacturing exports are produced by local companies with less than fifty employees and marketed through fourteen thousand small import-export houses that connect to specific niches in world markets (Castells 1986). Thus, informal enterprise appears to lie at the core of the flexible production and decentralized networks that form the emerging model of industrial management.

The effects of the informal economy on productivity seem to be contradictory. On the one hand, the productivity of labor in the informal sector tends to be lower, because of the use of less advanced production technologies. Also, a substantial part of the informal sector is composed of service activities, particularly those connected with consumer services, in which productivity gains tend to be low. Thus, overall, the expansion of the informal sector tends to lower labor's productivity and to slow down the trend toward full automation and rationalization of the labor process (Ybarra, this volume). On the other hand, there is some evidence that the productivity of capital may be higher in the informal sector. The reason is the dramatic reduction of overhead costs vis-à-vis the bureaucratic structure of large-scale organizations, and the resultant concentration of most capital in directly productive investment (Waldinger 1985; Sanchis and Pico 1983; Benton 1986). Thus, the two trends could easily offset each other, or at least provide a complex pattern of combinations at variance with the conventional identification of informal activities with low productivity.

The best-known economic effect of the informalization process is to reduce the costs of labor substantially. As seen above, this reduction has been the main reason for the growth of such activities in many contexts. Yet, it must be emphasized that the main cost-saving feature of informality is less the absolute level of wages than the avoidance of the "indirect wage" formed by social benefits and other employee-related payments to the state. By lowering the cost of labor and reducing the state-imposed constraints on its free hiring and dismissal, the informal economy contributes directly to the profitability of capital. The latter may lead, in turn, to significant labor absorption, although mostly through channels that escape official record keeping and hence are not reflected in the employment statistics (Portes and Benton 1984).

As seen above, there is no clear-cut duality between a formal and an informal sector, but a series of complex interactions that establish distinct relationships between the economy and the state. Thus, we reject the notion of a "marginal society" linked to the informal economy as a distinct entity in both advanced and peripheral countries. Nevertheless, if the informal economy does not generate a distinct society, it does produce specific social effects of far-reaching significance.

The first such social effect is the undermining of the power of organized labor in all spheres: economic bargaining, social organization, and political influence. Undeclared, unprotected labor; small units of production; networks rather than socialized labor processes; homework rather than factories; unstable relations of production; multiple intermediaries between workers and capital; segmentation of labor along age, gender, and ethnic lines; dependence of the job upon the absence of legal control—all these are factors that, as noted above, are contributing to the de-collectivization of the labor process and to the reversal of the material conditions that historically allowed the emergence of the labor movement as an organized force.

In addition, the often defensive attitude of the labor movement in the areas of the formal economy still under its control contributes to an ideological split between employed, unionized workers and newcomers to the labor market, socialized outside or even against the influence of the trade unions (Murray 1983). Given the fundamental role played by organized labor in most capitalist societies, the acceleration of its crisis, brought about by a multiplicity of other political and economic factors, is perhaps the most significant of the foreseeable social consequences of the informal sector's growth.

A second related social effect concerns increasing heterogeneity of work situations and, thus, of social conditions. The industrial and service proletariat is fading away as the normative social condition of the labor force. Instead, heterogeneity is becoming the rule (Gorz 1982; Bano 1986; Berger and Piore 1980). Thus, the more the informal economy expands, the more the class structure of each society becomes blurred, with horizontal fluid networks of activities substituting for vertical stable relationships of production. To be sure, there are still exploiters and exploited, work authority relationships and submissive work; yet between the structural logic of production and appropriation of the product and the actual social organization of these processes, there are so many mediations that the experience of labor and the emergence of stable class positions do not correspond to each other any more. Thus, the woman sewing at home for a "friend of the family" who is a middleman selling to a commercial intermediary of a large department store, cannot be socially equated, nor does she equate herself, with a garment-factory worker.

The heterogeneity of working situations is reinforced, generally speaking, by the specific characteristics of the workers who tend to be involved in the informal economy: women, immigrant workers, ethnic minorities, and the young. It is in this sense that the process of informalization tends to reinforce some specific social groupings that differ markedly from those associated with stable class lines. Immigrant communities, for example, tend to be confined to specific markets, often combining residential and working functions in a segregated space; unskilled working women tend to develop a very distinct labor culture, different from that of the male-dominated trade unions; and the young often enter the informal labor market with a definite ideology of individualistic autonomy in relation to the institutions of their parents' generation (Capecchi, this volume).

The combination of an expanded informal economy and of segmented labor markets specified by gender, ethnicity, or age creates fundamental changes in the class structure. Again, this is not to say that the trend associated with informalization is toward a classless society and even less to imply that new collective social actors will not arise. Yet classes, old and new, may become defined more by their struggles than by their structure, and collective actors will appeal to their social projects and visions rather than to common position in the work process. The more the informal economy develops, the more economy and society become relatively autonomous spheres of social action.

Conclusion: The Moving Boundaries of Informality

Since the informal economy does not result from the intrinsic characteristics of activities, but from the social definition of state intervention, the boundaries of the informal economy will substantially vary in different contexts and historical circumstances. As seen above, however, the current process of worldwide economic restructuring, following the structural crisis of the 1970s and early 1980s, has promoted the expansion of informal activities and the realignment of the class structure of many societies. A final question is whether this trend will continue its growth in opposition to what has been considered a secular pattern of formal labor absorption by conventional theories of development. As outlined above, there are powerful forces sustaining this unexpected trend. However, these forces are not the whole story. On the technical side, there are a number of production and distribution processes that require long-term planned investment and predictability, so that they cannot be left to the hazards of ad-hoc organization and casual labor recruitment. More important, there are fundamental social obstacles to the generalization of informal relations. Powerful social groups, such as labor unions and official bureaucracies, will resist the encroachment of these practices into their spheres of influence and the consequent erosion of their privileges. In addition, new generations of workers are likely to mobilize to impose some form of social control on the wild economy into which they have been induced in recent years. Finally, the state itself may eventually have to react against the one-sided logic of unconstrained capital.

Thus, the moving boundaries of the informal economy will be determined by the dynamics of social struggles and political bargaining, which involve, but are not limited to, the changing conflict between capital and labor. The social challenge posed by these developments lies in the choice between the advantages of a new society based on the relationship between unrestrained capital and primary social networks and those of a society in which public institutions extend control over the logic of capital by incorporating into a new social contract workers and entrepreneurs operating outside the legal realm.

Although the outcome of this struggle is uncertain, what seems clear is that a return to the vertical, centralized, assembly-line model of industrial production is unlikely in the medium term. The structural crisis of the seventies persuaded corporations and state agencies alike that "business as usual" was no longer a viable option and that alternatives to the (until then) normative model of economic organization must be sought. Informalization is one such alternative; others include the transfer of plants to low-wage areas and experimental reorganization of production within plants to give workers greater autonomy. But the wholesale entry of new workers into the informal sector in cities of the Third World and the expansion of these practices throughout the advanced economies should persuade us that the process of decentralization is here to stay and that the question is whether it will continue uncontrolled or will be brought under some sort of regulation.

In an oft-quoted passage, Marx observed that history repeats itself, the second time as a parody of the first. There is irony indeed in the reenactment of putting-out, homework, and other informal practices, when compared with the multiple scholarly tracts that predicted their irreversible demise. In the real world, however, there is nothing ironic about the informal economy, for the livelihood of millions depends on its existence, and the future of many societies, on its form of evolution.

Notes

1. The material in this section is based on two earlier articles: A. Portes and L. Benton 1984 and A. Portes and S. Sassen-Koob 1987. The material is reprinted with permission of the respective journals.

2. Between 1900 and 1930, for example, the self-employed in the United States declined from 34 percent to 23 percent of the civilian labor force. See Lebergott 1964, tables A-3, A-7.

3. For a somewhat different estimation, which comes, however, to the same conclusion, see Lanzetta and Murillo, this volume.

4. An example is provided by Richard Edwards, who traces the evolution of the labor process in American industry from "simple control," characteristic of small firms at the turn of the century, to "bureaucratic control," characteristic of the mammoth

industrial plants of today. In Edwards's view (1979, 35), small competitive enterprises represent "a declining sector as the large corporations continually encroach on their markets."

     5. The origins and dynamics of the central Italian informal economy are described in depth by Capecchi, this volume.

References

Ansberry, C. 1986. "Survival Strategy: Underground Economy Keeps Mill Town Alive." *Wall Street Journal*, October 1, p. 1.

Bairoch, P. 1973. *Urban Unemployment in Developing Countries: The Nature of the Problem and Proposals for its Solution*. Geneva: International Labor Office.

Bano, R. 1986. *Notas sobre Organizaciones de Desocupados*. Santiago de Chile: FLACSO.

Benton, L. 1986. "The Role of the Informal Sector in Economic Development: Industrial Restructuring in Spain." Ph.D. dissertation, Department of Anthropology, The Johns Hopkins University.

Berger, S. and M. Piore, eds. 1980. *Dualism and Discontinuity in Industrial Societies*. Cambridge: Cambridge University Press.

Birbeck, C. 1979. "Garbage, Industry, and the 'Vultures' of Cali, Colombia." Pp. 161–83 in R. Bromley and C. Gerry (eds.), *Casual Work and Poverty in Third World Cities*. New York: John Wiley.

Boyer, R. and J. Mistral. 1983. *La Crise*. Paris: CEPREMAP.

Bromley, R. 1978. "Organization, Regulation, and Exploitation in the So-called 'Urban Informal Sector': The Street Traders of Cali, Colombia." *World Development* 6:1161–71.

Brusco, S. 1982. "The 'Emilian' Model: Productive Decentralization and Social Integration." *Cambridge Journal of Economics* 6: 167–84.

Castells, M. 1980. "Multinational Capital, National States, and Local Communities." I.U.R.D. Working Paper. University of California, Berkeley.

———. 1986. *The Sheik-Kip-Mei Syndrome*. Hong Kong: University of Hong Kong, Center for Urban Studies and Planning.

Castles, S. and G. Kosack. 1973. *Immigrant Workers and Class Structure*. Oxford: Oxford University Press.

Chaney, E. 1979. "The World Economy and Contemporary Migration." *International Migration Review* 13:204–12.

Collier, D. 1976. *Squatters and Oligarchs*. Baltimore: Johns Hopkins University Press.

Edwards, R. 1979. *Contested Terrain: The Transformation of the Workplace in the Twentieth Century*. New York: Basic Books.

Faría, V. 1984. "The Marginal Urban Sector at the Industrial Periphery: Research Note on the Brazilian Case." Pp. 111–38 in "The Urban Informal Sector: Recent Trends in Research and Theory." Conference Proceedings. Department of Sociology, The Johns Hopkins University, Baltimore. Mimeo.

Feige, E. L. 1979. "How Big is the Irregular Economy?" *Challenge* 22:5–13.

Ferman, L., L. Berndt, and E. Selo. 1978. *Analysis of the Irregular Economy: Cash-Flow in the Informal Sector*. Detroit: University of Michigan–Wayne State University Institute of Labor and Industrial Relations.

Fernández-Kelly, M. P. 1983. *For We Are Sold: Women and Industry in Mexico's Frontier*. Albany, N.Y.: State University of New York Press.

García, N. 1982. "Growing Labor Absorption with Persistent Underemployment." *CEPAL Review* 18:45–64.

Gerry, C. 1984. "How Important a Factor Will the 'Urban Informal Sector' Be in the UK Crisis Management Strategy?" Pp. 225–39 in "The Urban Informal Sector: Recent Trends in Research and Theory." Conference Proceedings. Department of Sociology, The Johns Hopkins University, Baltimore. Mimeo.

Gershuny, J. I. 1978. *After Industrial Society? The Emerging Self-Service Economy*. Atlantic Highlands, N.J.: Humanities Press.

Gorz, A. 1982. *Farewell to the Working Class*. London: Pluto Press.

Granovetter, M. 1984. "Small is Bountiful: Labor Markets and Establishment Size." *American Sociological Review* 49:323–34.

Green, S. 1983. "Silicon Valley's Women Workers." Pp. 273–331 in J. Nash and M. P. Fernández-Kelly (eds.), *Women, Men, and the International Division of Labor*. Albany: State University of New York Press.

Gutmann, P. M. 1979. "Statistical Illusions, Mistaken Policies." *Challenge* 22:14–17.

Hansen, N. 1981. *The Border Economy*. Austin: University of Texas Press.

Henry, S. 1978. *The Hidden Economy*. London: Martin Robertson.

Lagos, R. and V. Tokman. 1983. "Monetarismo Global, Empleo y Estratificación Social." *El Trimestre Económico* 50:1437–74.

Lebergott, S. 1964. *Manpower in Economic Growth: The American Record since 1800*. New York: McGraw-Hill.

Lewis, W. A. 1959. *The Theory of Economic Growth*. London: Allen and Unwin.

Lopez Castaño, H. 1984. "El Papel del Sector Informal: La Experiencia Colombiana." Pp. 139–59 in "The Urban Informal Sector: Recent Trends in Research and Theory." Conference Proceedings. Department of Sociology, The Johns Hopkins University, Baltimore. Mimeo.

Lozano, B. 1985. "High Technology, Cottage Industry." Ph.D. dissertation, Department of Sociology, University of California, Davis.

Massey, D. and R. Meegan. 1982. *The Anatomy of Job Loss*. London: Methuen.

Mingione, E. 1983. "Informalization, Restructuring, and the Survival Strategies of the Working Class." *International Journal of Urban and Regional Research* 7:311–39.

Morales, R. and R. Mines. 1985. "San Diego's Full-Service Restaurants: A View from the Back of the House." Report. Center for U.S.-Mexico Studies, University of California, San Diego.

Moser, C. 1978. "Informal Sector or Petty Commodity Production: Dualism or Dependence in Urban Development?" *World Development* 6:1041–64.

Murray, F. 1983. "The Decentralization of Production—The Decline of the Mass-Collective Worker?" *Capital and Class*, 74–99.

Offe, C. 1985. *Disorganized Capitalism: Contemporary Transformations of Work and Politics*. Cambridge, Mass.: MIT Press.

Pahl, R. E. 1984. *Divisions of Labour*. Oxford: Basil Blackwell.

Pahl, R. E. and J. H. Dennett. 1981. "Industry and Employment in the Isle of Sheppey." HWS Working Paper. University of Kent at Canterbury.

Peattie, L. R. 1981. "What Is to Be Done with the 'Informal Sector': A Case Study of

Shoe Manufacturers in Colombia." Department of City and Regional Planning, MIT. Typescript.

Perlman, J. 1976. *The Myth of Marginality.* Berkeley and Los Angeles: University of California Press.

Piore, M. J. and C. Sabel. 1984. *The Second Industrial Divide.* New York: Basic Books.

Portes, A. 1985. "Latin American Class Structures: Their Composition and Change During the Last Decades." *Latin American Research Review* 20:7–39.

Portes, A. and L. Benton. 1984. "Industrial Development and Labor Absorption: A Reinterpretation." *Population and Development Review* 10:589–611.

Portes, A., S. Blitzer, and J. Curtis. 1986. "The Urban Informal Sector in Uruguay: Its Internal Structure, Characteristics, and Effects." *World Development* 14:727–41.

Portes, A. and S. Sassen-Koob. 1987. "Making It Underground: Comparative Material on the Urban Informal Sector in Western Market Economies." *American Journal of Sociology* 93:30–61.

Prates, S. 1984. "El Trabajo 'Informal' o las Relaciones Contradictorias entre Reproducción y Estado." Pp. 519–87 in "The Urban Informal Sector: Recent Trends in Research and Theory." Conference Proceedings. Department of Sociology, The Johns Hopkins University, Baltimore. Mimeo.

PREALC. 1981. *Dinámica del Subempleo en América Latina.* Santiago de Chile: International Labor Office.

———. 1982. *Mercado de Trabajo en Cifras, 1950–1980.* Santiago de Chile: International Labor Office.

Renooy, P. H. 1984. *Twilight Economy: A Survey of the Informal Economy in the Netherlands.* Research Report. Faculty of Economic Sciences, University of Amsterdam.

Ruesga-Benito, S. 1984. "Economía Oculta y Mercado de Trabajo." *Información Comercial Española* 607:55–61.

Saba, A. 1980. *L'industria sommersa.* Padua: Marsilio.

Sabel, C. 1982. *The Division of Labor in Industry.* Cambridge: Cambridge University Press.

Sanchis, E. and J. Pico. 1983. "La Economía Sumergida: El Estado de la Cuestion en España." *Sociologia del Trabajo* 9:65–94.

Sassen-Koob, S. 1984. "Growth and Informalization at the Core: The Case of New York City." Pp. 492–518 in "The Urban Informal Sector: Recent Trends in Research and Theory." Conference Proceedings. Department of Sociology, The Johns Hopkins University, Baltimore. Mimeo.

Sassen-Koob, S. and S. Grover. 1985. "Unregistered Work in the New York Metropolitan Area." Working paper, Columbia University, Graduate School of Architecture and Planning, New York.

Schatan, J. 1985. "América Latina: Deuda Externa y Desarrollo." *Investigación Económica* 171:305–57.

Siegel, L. and J. Markoff. 1985. *The High Cost of High Tech: The Dark Side of the Chip.* New York: Harper and Row.

Spitznas, T. 1981. "Estimating the Size of the Underground Economy in New York City." *Regional Economic Digest* 1:2–3.

Standing, G. 1986. "Meshing Labour Flexibility with Security: An Answer to British Unemployment?" *International Labour Review* 125:87–106.

Statistical Abstracts of Latin America. 1978 J. W. Wilkie and P. Reich (eds.). Los Angeles: UCLA Latin American Center. Vol. 19, tables 2200 and 2201.

Statistical Department of Colombia. 1984. "National Household Survey No. 44, June 1984." In G. Murillo, *Perspective Macronalitica del Fenomeno de la Informalidad en Bogotá.* Report. Department of Political Science, University of the Andes.

Tanzi, V. 1980. "The Hidden Economy, a Cause of Increasing Concern." *FMI Bulletin* 9:34–37.

————. 1982. *The Underground Economy in the United States and Abroad.* Lexington, Mass.: D. C. Heath.

Tokman, V. 1982. "Unequal Development and the Absorption of Labor." *CEPAL Review* 17:121–33.

————. 1986. "The Informal Sector: Fifteen Years Later." Paper presented at conference, The Comparative Study of the Informal Sector, Harper's Ferry, West Virginia, October 2–6.

U.N. Economic Commission for Latin America (CEPAL). 1986. *Crisis Económica y Políticas de Ajuste, Estabilización y Crecimiento.* Document presented at the Twenty-first Session of CEPAL, Mexico, April.

Waldinger, R. 1985. "Immigration and Industrial Change in the New York City Apparel Industry." Pp. 323–49 in G. J. Borjas and M. Tienda (eds.), *Hispanics in the U.S. Economy.* New York: Academic Press.

Walton, J. 1985. "The IMF Riots." Paper delivered at the International Conference, Global Restructuring and Territorial Development, University of Hong Kong, September.

Williamson, O. E. 1985. *The Economic Institutions of Capitalism.* New York: Free Press.

Wong, K. Y. 1982. *Shenzhen Special Economic Zone: China's Experiment in Modernization.* Hong Kong: Hong Kong Geographical Association.

Ybarra, J. 1982a. "Economía Subterranea: Reflexiones sobre la Crisis Económica en España." *Economía Industrial* 218:33–46.

————. 1982b. "La Re-estructuración Espontanea de la Industria del Calzado Español." *Boletín de Estudios Económicos* 37:483–503.

2 Urban Labor Markets

2 Employment Structure, Life Cycle, and Life Chances: Formal and Informal Sectors in Guadalajara

Bryan R. Roberts

This chapter reports ongoing research into urban poverty, the informal sector, and labor markets in Guadalajara carried out in collaboration with a group of Mexican sociologists and anthropologists.[1] My aim is to examine the significance of the distinction between informal and formal sectors for the highly complex labor market of Guadalajara, created by the demands of firms of different sizes, levels of technology, and market position. By informal sector, I mean the set of economic activities often, but not exclusively, carried out in small firms or by the self-employed, which elude government requirements such as registration, tax and social security obligations, and health and safety rules. Informal sector activities are often illegal, but not necessarily clandestine since lack of coordination between state agencies, lax enforcement, and other types of official connivance, as Fernández-Kelly and García point out in this volume, can permit informally run enterprises to flourish openly.

In previous research in the provincial town of Huancayo, Peru, I used the notion of the informal sector to understand how an urban economy can absorb increasing numbers of migrants, despite the near absence of large-scale sources of employment in industry (Long and Roberts 1984, 140–68). In Huancayo, the absence of large firms and the intense competition for survival meant that most economic activities were carried out informally, in self-employment and in enterprises of less than ten employees in which workers were frequently relatives. Almost 50 percent of males were self-employed or family workers, and 76 percent of employed males worked in enterprises in which there were less than ten other workers (Long and Roberts 1984, 145).

The advantages of informality for generating employment were obvious: overhead costs were low when compared with the tax and social security obligations of formally registered firms; it was easy to become a small-scale entrepreneur, requiring no more than space in a house and a small amount of capital in tools, materials, or articles for sale; family relationships provided flexible access to labor, to credit, and to economic information. Informal economic activities flourished in Huancayo because they operated with a different social and political logic than that of formal economic activities. Hence my emphasis, in common with that of others, is on the importance of state regulations in creating the formal-informal distinction and on the importance of social relationships (Portes and Walton 1981, 67–106; Portes and Benton 1984).

Guadalajara offers an interesting comparison. The city has its "informal" side: Small-scale enterprises, particularly in the shoe and garment trades, are to be found in most neighborhoods, often in defiance of zoning ordinances and without formal registration. Outworking hierarchies, similar to those described by Benería for Mexico City, are common, and the visits by middlemen to homeworkers are a frequent sight in low-income neighborhoods (Arias and Roberts 1984). In a survey of manufacturing industry carried out in 1981 in Guadalajara and the state of Jalisco, it was found that 11 percent of firms subcontracted work, mainly to small shops. Subcontracting of this kind was more frequent among the largest firms, with 24 percent engaging in it, while the smaller firms were the most frequent users of homeworkers (DPD 1982, table 5.9.1).

In other respects, Guadalajara contrasts sharply with Huancayo. Guadalajara is a large city, with a population in 1980 of approximately 2.5 million, compared with Huancayo's 200,000. Guadalajara contains a substantial number of large-scale manufacturing and service establishments, including state and federal agencies and Latin America's largest shoe factory, Canada. Despite rapid growth in the city's population, averaging 6 percent per year between 1960 and 1970, the proportion of the self-employed and of unpaid family labor decreased in these years from 20.4 percent to 17 percent.[2] Unemployment rates in Guadalajara were low throughout the 1970s, and real wage rates were rising, albeit slowly. As Gregory (1986) has pointed out, for the Mexican economy in general, there is little evidence in these years of an oversupply of labor and consequent underemployment.

In Guadalajara, the significance of informal economic activities within the urban economy is markedly different from the Huancayo case. In Huancayo, labor markets were highly fragmented, but not segmented by educational, gender, or ethnic characteristics. In Guadalajara, informal economic activities are a less significant part of the urban economy. Moreover, I shall claim that it is the emerging segmentation of the labor market, within firms as well as between them, that best explains the life chances of Guadalajara's working population.[3] Large-scale employers play a dominant role in structuring labor markets through direct employment and through subcontracting. Their need for labor varies with the organization of the enterprise—its technology, its internal division of labor, and the work skills that it requires. Another factor affecting the demand for labor is the nature of the market that the enterprise supplies—whether it is stable, cyclical, or uncertain and whether it is monopsonistic or competitive.

These sources of variation in labor markets, both those internal to the firm and those external to it, have considerable power in explaining the characteristics of workers and their rates of pay. Cheapening the costs of production and attaining greater entrepreneurial flexibility through informalization is one strategy that firms adopt in Guadalajara, but the needs of both small and large firms are too diverse for this strategy to be uniformly adopted by any one sector. Also, informalization is not simply a strategy for lowering workers' wages and their control over production. Like the situation that Benton describes for Spain in this volume, there are different ways of organizing productive relations within small firms in Guadalajara. One pattern is based on low wages and a hierarchical organization of subcontracting in which workers have little control over production and little bargaining power. In other cases, however, craft skills are important to production, workers have more independence in setting the pace of work, and they move from firm to firm to better their pay.

I will use the formal-informal distinction to refer to the conditions of employment, but *not* to a relatively homogeneous economic sector of firms and their transactions (see Escobar 1986, 26–30). Employment, whether inside a firm or outside, as in the case of subcontracting, is informal when it is un-protected by government labor regulations and welfare provisions. Informal employment is carried out without work contracts or with purely temporary ones, and payment is often by piece rate rather than by a fixed wage. Informal employment can be found in the largest and most modern of firms, not just in small, back-street workshops. Informality is, from this perspective, a strategy adopted by economic actors, large and small, depending on market circum-stances and the strength and coherence of those interests opposed to infor-mality, such as government and trade unions.

To explore the diversity of labor markets and the incidence of infor-mality, we interviewed approximately eight hundred workers from firms of different sizes and different types of internal organization and market position.[4] In addition, we interviewed five hundred workers in construction and in various government dependencies.[5] The labor market survey was complemented by case studies of unregistered enterprises, by interviews with thirty-two workers in these enterprises, and by a neighborhood-based sample of one hundred low-income families from whom data were obtained on budgets, household work and life histories, and social networks.[6]

The Setting: The City in the National and International Economy

Guadalajara's labor market has been, and continues to be, structured by the city's particular role in the wider economy. Defining that role is an essential starting point in comparing Guadalajara's informal sector to that of other cities in Latin America or elsewhere. By the end of the nineteenth century, Guadala-jara had consolidated its position as the dominant regional center of the west and northwest of Mexico. Its merchants controlled trade in this region. The railroad helped to center both trade and production in the city, leading to the disappearance of village craft production and of industries in the smaller towns

(De la Pena 1984). Population concentrated in the city, abandoning the rural areas in the face of economic centralization and the modernization of agriculture that both preceded and followed agrarian reform. In 1930, Guadalajara was 4.2 times larger than the next four biggest urban areas in Jalisco combined; by 1950, the city was 6.2 times larger; and by 1970, it was 8.3 times larger (Walton 1978, 34–35).

The city's growth was driven by commercial capital. This capital was divided among a number of relatively large and medium-sized firms that subcontracted production of basic consumer goods (sandals and shoes, textiles, flour, oils, soaps, etc.) to many small and medium-sized firms (Arias 1982). With some exceptions, large-scale industry did not develop until the 1960s, nor did manufacturing industries other than those producing basic consumer goods. Urban land and property were mainly in the hands of the commercial class, many of whom had once had extensive landholdings in the region and had migrated to live permanently in the city (Arias and Roberts 1984). By the 1970s, Guadalajara's political and economic structure was dominated by small and medium-sized capital in commerce, industry, and land, resulting in significant contrasts between the style of local government and that of Mexico's other major provincial city, Monterrey, in which industrial capital had become consolidated early in the century (Walton 1977). The pattern of landownership gave a particular stamp to the housing market, which was notable for the absence of squatter settlements and the high proportion of rental accommodation, leading some commentators to see Guadalajara as an unusually "successful" and well-planned Latin American city.[7]

The salient features of Guadalajara's contemporary position in the wider economy derive from these historical trends. Today, the city remains an important regional commercial center, and the value and average size of its commercial establishments exceeds, for example, those of Monterrey. Supermarkets and large-scale shopping malls dominate commerce.

Guadalajara is also Mexico's third-largest center of industrial production, specializing in basic, nondurable consumer goods. In 1975, over 60 percent of Jalisco's industrial production, three-fourths of which was supplied by Guadalajara, was in such goods. Estimates based on the industrial census of that year indicate that 35 percent of industrial production was sold in Guadalajara or the state of Jalisco; 57 percent was sold nationally, a considerable part of which was composed of sales to the states surrounding Guadalajara; and 8 percent was sold abroad (DPD 1982, table 7.4). By 1980, Jalisco's industry was still heavily concentrated in basic goods production, in a more marked fashion than in either Mexico City or Monterrey (see table 2.1).

Guadalajara's specialization in basic industrial goods does not reflect a backward industrial economy. Using the same methodology designed by Garza (1985) to estimate the profitability of Mexico City industry, I found that the basic industrial goods sector in Guadalajara was the most profitable sector in

Table 2.1 Industrial Products by Sector, 1980

Sector	Jalisco (Guadalajara) (%)	Nuevo León (Monterrey) (%)	Mexico D.F. (Mexico City) (%)
Basic consumer goods[1]	56.8	27.3	32.8
Intermediate goods[2]	29.1	49.1	39.0
Capital and durable consumer goods[3]	14.1	23.6	29.0
Total	100.0	100.0	100.0

Source: INEGI, *Sistema de Cuentas Nacionales de México*, 1985, 182–83.

[1]Basic consumer goods are food, beverages, textiles, shoes, and tobacco.
[2]Intermediate goods are wood and paper products, oil products, chemicals, and steel.
[3]Capital and durable consumer goods are machinery, metal furnishings, transport equipment, cars, and household and office appliances.

the city and was more profitable than its counterpart in Mexico City.[8] This sector has become increasingly dominated by large-scale, capital-intensive firms that are often branches of national and multinational enterprises. Examples are Pepsi-Cola, Coca-Cola, and the large-scale breweries. Even the "local" footwear industry includes Latin America's largest shoe factory, Canada, with close to ten thousand employees in 1980.

The dominance of large-scale industrial and commercial firms has not displaced small and medium-sized enterprise. The reasons that Mexico City informants give for subcontracting and the advantages they see in the small firm apply even more strongly in Guadalajara because of the historical antecedents discussed above and the regional markets that the city supplies (Benería, this volume). The average number of employees in Guadalajara's 5,331 industrial establishments in 1970 was 13.6. This compares with an average of 16.7 for Mexico City's 29,436 establishments and of 28 for Nueva León's (Monterrey's) 4,420 establishments.

Most of Guadalajara's industrial production has either a seasonal demand, as in the case of beverages or certain foodstuffs, or is subject to changes of fashion, as in certain lines of shoes and garments. Bottlenecks of supply and marketing, due to poor communications, accentuate the fluctuations produced by demand factors. Under these conditions, it is convenient for firms to take on or lay off labor in tune with fluctuations of demand and to put out work to small workshops or even homeworkers.

A further reason for the compatibility of the large-scale, capital-intensive enterprise and the small one is that the latter provides and maintains an abundant supply of both skilled and unskilled labor for the former. This factor was cited as an important advantage by owners and managers of large firms when asked about their reasons for locating in Guadalajara. We found that 67 percent of workers presently employed in large-scale firms (over 100 employees) in the footwear, steel, and engineering sectors had begun their industrial careers working in firms of less than 20 employees (Escobar 1986, table 12).

The small-scale sector provides initial work experience and industrial training for new entrants in the urban labor force, whether migrants or natives of Guadalajara. The large firm "saves" the expense of such training: few of our sample of workers had received more than two weeks' training by their present employer. When workers are laid off by the large firm, they can seek work in the small-scale sector and are available for rehiring when demand picks up.

This economic structure has proved flexible in the face of market fluctuations and has enabled the city to show marked resilience in creating jobs, despite the current recession (Alba 1986, 135–41).[9] As shown in table 2.2, Guadalajara, in contrast with both Mexico City and Monterrey, substantially increased the numbers of formally registered workers between 1980 and 1985. Like the other two cities, Guadalajara registered a decline in enrollments between 1981 and 1982—the first year of the recession. Thereafter, enrollments increased rapidly in all branches of the economy.

In manufacturing industry, these trends have produced what appears to be a relatively polarized labor market, divided between employment in large- and small-scale firms. Estimates based on a 1981 survey of industrial firms registered with the state of Jalisco show high concentrations of workers in firms that employed less than twenty-five workers and in highly capitalized firms that employed more than five hundred (see table 2.3).[10]

This polarization in the size distribution of firms reflects Guadalajara's changing position within the wider economy. The U.S. enterprises that locate in Guadalajara are large-scale, pay the minimum wage, and enroll their employees in welfare programs. They require primary education but train workers on the job. There is some differentiation among them in the type of labor that they use. For example, the assembly plants recruit unmarried female labor, and the bottling plants, relatively unskilled male labor. This movement of capital into Guadalajara is creating the intermediate-type jobs in manufacturing which are becoming a less important proportion of the U.S. labor force.

The small-scale sector survives as a repository for (1) skilled, craft-based labor usually working on piece rate and (2) family workers and others who require flexible hours. The flows of labor within the regional labor market,

Table 2.2 Manufacturing Industry Registrations with Instituto Mexicanade Seguro Social (IMMS)

Metropolitan Region	Year				
	1981	1982	1983	1984	1985
Jalisco (Guadalajara)	164,613	155,722	159,356	173,591	175,751
Nuevo León (Monterrey)	206,624	184,638	178,837	190,731	192,974
Valle de México	940,405	827,606	784,817	827,899	847,072

Source: INEGI, *Anuario de Estadísticas Estatales*, 1985, cuadro, 3. 2.8.

Table 2.3 Employment in the Manufacturing Industry in Jalisco, 1981

Size of Firm (no. of workers)	Number of Firms	Number of Workers	Percentage of Work Force	Percentage of Firms
Small-scale sector				
5 or less	4,761	25,112	13.1	47.3
15 or less	2,628	16,514	8.6	26.1
25 or less	1,402	20,906	10.9	13.9
Medium-scale sector				
26–50	640	18,440	9.7	6.3
51–100	425	27,111	14.2	4.2
Large-scale sector				
101–500	117	15,106	7.9	1.2
500 or more	104	68,141	35.6	1.0
Total	10,047	191,330	100.0	100.0

Source: DPD, 1982, 3:12, table 9.12.

which includes California as well as the rural and urban areas of Jalisco, are influenced by these structures of urban job opportunities. The U.S. urban labor market for Mexican migrants is predominantly for unskilled service workers and tends to attract younger, unmarried, male migrants from rural areas. Fernández-Kelly and García point out in this volume that Mexicans have penetrated the U.S. labor market in a highly individuated and dispersed way. In contrast, migrants to Guadalajara tend to move as family groups. Guadalajara provides a cheap subsistence base and one that is attractive to families because job opportunities can be fitted to the changing needs of the life cycle and to the employment possibilities for different members of a household. Furthermore, prospective rural migrants with skills that are saleable in the Guadalajara labor market are likely to prefer it, initially at least, to trying their luck in the United States.[11] Those with craft skills or educational qualifications, such as primary schooling, have a greater relative advantage over those who do not in Guadalajara.

The variety of opportunities in the Guadalajara labor market, catering to different mixes of skills, educational qualifications, gender, and age characteristics, differentiates it from that described for Los Angeles and New York by Sassen-Koob (this volume; 1985). The polarization that is observable in the latter two cities is between low-paying and high-paying jobs. Polarization is based on the absence, in these cities, of jobs in the intermediate earnings classes, such as those in construction and manufacturing. Though Guadalajara has gained many of these latter types of jobs in recent years, partly through "displacement" of U.S. manufacturing operations, earnings in them, as we will see, are little or no higher than in the small workshop sector.[12]

Guadalajara's position in the national and international economy means that most jobs are low-wage jobs. Low wage rates are one of the city's principal attractions for foreign and national firms. What does differentiate jobs in Guadalajara is the degree of contractual security they offer, including welfare coverage. Informalization in Guadalajara is, I suggest, not primarily a strategy for lowering wages. Weak unions and an abundant supply of labor keep wages low in all sectors of the economy. However, market uncertainty and the large number of income opportunities in the city mean that it is useful for both employees and employers to have flexibility in allocating labor. Though this has consequences for the characteristics of those working informally—they are, for example, more likely to be female—it does not produce a sharp segmentation of labor markets according to such characteristics as gender, age, and migrant status.

The Informal Sector

In this section, I explore further the ways in which the informal-formal contrast affects the workings of Guadalajara's economy and the characteristics of those workers found in the different sectors of the urban economy. First, I will attempt to give two approximations of the size of the informal sector, one for the whole urban economy and one for the manufacturing sector.

My estimate of informal employment in Guadalajara is taken from the 1980 census categories of self-employed workers, family workers, and domestic servants. These categories are unlikely to have social security coverage, and their work is not subject to contract or protected by labor and welfare regulations. In 1980, 22.7 percent of Guadalajara's metropolitan population was employed informally (INEGI 1984, tomo 14, cuadro 9). This figure is an underestimate of informal employment, since many small firms in Guadalajara, and some large firms in manufacturing, commerce, and the services, employ people under the informal conditions noted above.

In manufacturing industry in that year, 14.1 percent of employment was self-employment or unremunerated family labor. This latter percentage is an increase over the 1970 figure of 11.4 percent.[13] A more accurate estimate of the extent of informal employment in manufacturing can be obtained from our labor market survey, which asked workers about social security coverage and type of contract. Approximately 39 percent of those in firms of under 25 people were not covered by social security and had, at best, a purely temporary contract. These conditions applied to 41 percent in firms of between 26 and 50 workers, 31.8 percent in firms of between 51 and 100 workers, 29.3 percent in firms of between 101 and 500 workers, and 19.9 percent in firms of over 500 workers.

If these workers are added to those who are self-employed or work in unregistered enterprises, then 96,500 people are working under informal employment conditions, or 42.1 percent of the state's manufacturing labor force.[14] Taking into account the fact that the metropolitan area of Guadalajara contains three-fourths of the state's manufacturing labor force and that small-scale enterprises, in which informal conditions of employment are concentrated, are disproportionately located outside the metropolitan area, I estimate that 40 percent of Guadalajara's manufacturing labor force is informally employed.[15]

Informal industrial employment in Guadalajara is basically a question of job conditions and status. The survey and the case studies that accompanied it give little support to the notion that it is exclusively found in particular types of economic enterprise (Escobar 1986, 189–91). Small workshops are more likely than large factories to employ their workers informally. Yet, a significant minority of small-scale enterprises are quite formal in these respects. Our survey found that 39 percent of workers in firms of twenty or less workers had the most secure contract of all and were covered by welfare provisions.

Informal employment is, moreover, a strategy that employers in different industrial sectors use to a dissimilar degree. In the food industry, which is subject to marked seasonal variations in demand, informal employment is common in the very large firms, in which 34 percent of workers reported being employed on temporary contracts, without welfare benefits. Twenty-eight percent of respondents in smaller food firms were similarly unprotected. In contrast, informal employment in the footwear industry is concentrated in the small firms; 48 percent of those working in firms of under fifty people have insecure contracts and limited access to welfare benefits. Of the seventy-two workers in large shoe factories (over 200 workers), only 16.7 percent had similar working conditions. The survey of Jalisco industry indicates a similar pattern: the food industry is the sector that reports the most workers on temporary contracts, followed by the drink industry; footwear and textiles have the fewest such workers (DPD 1982, table 9.2).

Construction and the construction materials industries have high levels of informal employment. Both of these sectors are subject to seasonal and cyclical variations in demand.[16] Most construction workers in our survey reported that they were on temporary contracts and were not covered by welfare benefits. In construction materials firms, 47 percent of workers were working informally, and in the largest firm (over 200 workers), twelve of the seventeen workers interviewed were on temporary contracts and, with the exception of four cases, were not covered by welfare benefits.

What are the characteristics of the workers who are informally employed? The informally employed tend to be younger than those employees with secure contracts and social security coverage. Over half (51 percent) of the informally employed in the survey were under twenty-five, as compared with 32 percent of those with secure contracts and social security. The oldest age groups in the survey (those over 35) were the most likely to be formally employed. González's (1986b) sample of poor households suggests, however, that as males get older they are likely to lose their jobs in manufacturing enterprises and become self-employed or take up casual jobs in workshops or the services.

Women are more likely to be found in informal employment than in formal employment and to be almost as numerous in the paid informal sector as males. The labor market survey showed that 54 percent of women were working under informal conditions of employment, as compared with 36 percent of males. Citywide, there is relatively little female employment in formally registered manufacturing enterprises, and that consists predominantly of young, unmarried women. In the industrial survey, 12.7 percent of Jalisco's industrial labor force was female, and this was concentrated in large firms in the textile, footwear, chemicals, and electronic industries (DPD 1982, table 9.1). In the large electronics firms, female employees outnumbered male employees. The Guadalajara-based firm of Burroughs, for example, has six hundred workers, 90 percent of whom are female.

Informal employment in Guadalajara appears to be as frequent among natives as among migrants (Escobar 1986, 182). The heterogeneous nature of informal employment opportunities, and the different channels of access to them, helps explain this finding. Natives have easiest access to the small, informally organized craft workshops, such as those in the shoe trade. The sectors in our sample in which migrants are most numerous are construction and the construction materials industries, where migrants make up to three-fourths of the labor force. These sectors have high levels of informal employment, as noted. Migrants are also informally employed in the large-scale firms in the food and drink industry. In addition, they predominate among the government workers in our sample, reflecting the rural patronage networks of state and municipal politicians.

The heterogeneous nature of informal employment means that its economic advantages and disadvantages vary. The absence of welfare coverage is a drawback, but, on the other hand, many informants cited the deductions made for welfare as a disadvantage of formal employment, particularly since the services they received were poor. Moreover, the income differences between formal and informal employment are not large. In some types of employment, workers could, in 1981, earn more money in informal than in formal employment. This was the case in the footwear industry, where a skilled worker on piece rate could earn more than his counterpart in a large factory. Workers cited the advantage of piecework as enabling them to set their own pace and to vary their income according to need. The large factories preferred to use shifts, paying the same rate for each shift rather than paying overtime.

In González's (1986a, 217) sample, male heads of household in informal employment earned, on average, a little more than those employed formally. These male heads included, however, owners of small workshops located in poor neighborhoods, whose earnings were substantially higher than those of informal workers. These cases illustrate a dimension of heterogeneity in informal employment similar to that reported for other cities, such as Montevideo: the differences in income and control over the work process that divide small-scale entrepreneurs and their employees (Portes, Blitzer, and Curtis 1986). These differences are often mitigated, however, by kinship and by craft skills.[17]

A regression analysis of the factors influencing wage levels in our labor market survey indicates that informal employment results in wages that are 16 percent lower than would be expected from informants' education, job position, and other relevant characteristics.[18] The average weekly earnings for informal workers interviewed in 1981 was 1,900 pesos compared with 2,384 pesos for those formally employed.[19] In the footwear industry, where the symbiosis of small and large firms is most marked, the difference is smaller, with informal employees earning an average of 2,241 pesos a week and those formally employed earning 2,551 pesos weekly. These earnings are substantially above the 1981 minimum daily salary for Guadalajara: 189.11 pesos daily, or 1,324 pesos a week (INEGI 1985, tomo 1, 171).

One interesting conclusion of our regression analysis is that construction workers are better paid than would be expected from their educational and other characteristics. This finding illustrates one of the central features of informal employment in Guadalajara: it provides reasonable income opportunities for people whose social circumstances debar them from better-paid jobs. The main handicap of construction workers is a low level of education, which is the single factor that best explains income differences among industrial workers. Large firms insist on educational credentials for both skilled and unskilled work. Stable, formal employment in a large firm usually brings with it union membership, and such membership also results in higher salaries.

The advantages are cumulative, producing a degree of polarization in the benefits received by Guadalajara's working class. This polarization is offset, as will be described, by the life and household cycles and by the fact that no firm in Guadalajara, whether small or large, pays wages that are sufficient for maintaining a worker and his or her family. Of Mexico's three major cities, Guadalajara pays the lowest wages and has the highest cost of living (Escobar 1986, 65–67). The U.S. multinationals in Guadalajara are no exception to this pattern.

The data in this section have indicated the importance of informal employment to Guadalajara's economy. Such employment is found throughout the city in both small and large firms. It enables large-scale employers to meet fluctuations in demand, while it substantially reduces the overhead of the small-scale enterprise. From the employer's perspective, the choice between offering formal or informal employment is a strategic one that depends on the economic climate and on the organization of the particular industrial sector.

Nineteen eighty-one was the last year before the Mexican recession, and Guadalajara's economy was still in relative boom. Firms, small or large, could sell all that they produced, and their strategies, and those of their workers, reflected this situation. Piecework was attractive in sectors such as the shoe industry, leading to a drift of workers out of the large enterprises and into the small-scale sector. The large firms could only attract workers through offering welfare benefits and stability of employment. In contrast, for many small-scale shoe workshops, the risks of operating outside of the law increased with the boom. Production levels were high and so were profits, but both made the small operations more visible to government inspectors and to union organizers. Several of our informants who owned small enterprises had to pay fines for noncompliance with the labor laws when workers complained to the tribunals after an accident or dismissal.[20]

Life and Household Cycles and the Formal-Informal Divide

In previous sections, I have concentrated on the implications for individuals of Guadalajara's urban economy. This is misleading since, in practice, the household is the relevant urban economic unit. In the case of Guadalajara, as in most Latin American cities, it would be difficult for either males or females to survive living on their own. Females' wages are so much below those paid to men that they do not meet the costs of renting accommodation and paying for food and other necessities. Even though males earn more, they depend on others, particularly women, for their economic survival and for the savings that pay for recreation and consumer items. Women's work at home drastically reduces food costs and makes possible the cheaper types of accommodation.

To argue that the household operates as an economic unit does not imply that a deliberate strategy is used in which the jobs and consumption of the different members are mutually agreed upon. Our female informants made clear, for example, that their husbands shared only part of their income and, in most cases, they did not know the full extent of the man's earnings. Children, particularly male children, who have paid employment reserve the greater part of their income for personal expenditures. Despite these practices, the Guadalajara household is an economic unit because membership permits patterns of economic activity that would not otherwise be possible.

At the most basic level, it is the pooling of household income that enables the poor to make out in a high-cost, low-wage city. Before the recession, this pooling enabled working-class households to accumulate a certain amount of material goods and helped create a sense of social mobility among even the poorest of families. In the present recession, pooling is the key to economic survival and is likely to intensify as members migrate more frequently to work in the United States.

The logic behind the differentiation of work roles within the household can be reconstructed from the previous analysis of the dynamics of the Guadalajara economy. Young married males have the best chance of obtaining and holding relatively well paid formal employment. In this stage of household development, the wife is unlikely to work outside the home. She will be busy raising young children and with the upkeep of the house. She is likely, however, to take in work to supplement the family income. Tasks such as sewing garments or cutting leather molds are fitted into the daily routine, with the help of the children as soon as they are old enough to undertake rudimentary tasks. This type of work is not well paid. Arias (1980) has pointed out that it is regarded as "pin money" both by the woman and by the husband. A woman's financial contribution to the household is welcomed and, at times, insisted upon, but it is regarded by males only as *ayuda* (help).

As the family grows, two changes occur.[21] The oldest children obtain paid work outside the household, at first usually in poorly paid informal employment. Male children become apprentices in small workshops, while females work as domestic servants or in informal commercial activities. The wife is now more likely to seek work outside the household, since economic pressures increase at this stage, with more mouths to feed, while some of the child-rearing tasks can be delegated to older children. The jobs that wives obtain are almost always in domestic service, going out to clean or cook in private homes.

At a later stage, or what González (1986a, 211–12) has called the consolidation stage, the wife is less likely to work outside the home. By this stage more children will have found paid work, and the older children—both males and females—are likely to be in reasonably well paid formal occupations. A change is now detectable in the occupations of the male heads. At this late stage in the household cycle, male heads are more likely to be working in informal employment and to be earning less. The final stage of the household cycle is its dispersion, as children marry and set up their own households and as one or the other of the parents dies. In the latter case, the survivor joins or is joined by one of the children's households.

This cycle produces a relatively flat curve in the income distribution of poor households in Guadalajara. Though incomes of male heads are lower in the late stages of the household cycle, this is compensated for by the earnings and contributions of more members of the household. In table 2.4, the data are

Table 2.4 Household Income (pesos per week)

Number of Contributors	Average Income of Male Head	Average Income of Female Head	Average Income of Children	Total Income	Number of Cases
1	3,252	129	38	3,420	26
2	3,032	647	1,158	4,837	32
3	1,689	211	1,795	3,696	17
4 or more	2,210	577	4,988	7,775	22

Source: Adapted from González 1986a, table 5.8.
Note: See note 22, this chapter.

arranged in terms of number of contributors: households with only one contributor are the "young" ones; those with more than two contributors are generally older.[22]

This household cycle sustains the pattern of job differentiation in Guadalajara described earlier. A great deal of informal employment, especially outworking and domestic service, consists of the labor of female heads of household who combine it with household work. The woman's household labor, with the assistance mainly of her daughters, makes it possible for other family members to subsist cheaply in the city. These members, at various stages of the life cycle, become suppliers of informal labor. Even the pittances that children receive when they first enter the labor market are a useful supplement to the subsistence with which they are provided at home. Older, male heads who have lost their formal employment can also make do on lower wages, despite the insecurity of informal employment, because of the contributions of other income earners in their household.

Until the recession of 1981–82, these arrangements enabled even poor families to get along in Guadalajara, despite the city's low wages and high costs. The flexibility and heterogeneity of the city's economic structure facilitated household-based survival, through combining within the same household different types of income opportunities. Most households have at least one member working in the formal sector, usually the male head, and thereby have some access to the social security system; but most households are also well integrated into informal employment, which offers opportunities to increase income in times of need. Under these conditions, economic necessity reinforces household ties, making the two-generation household, immediate kin, and neighborhood relationships important elements in surviving within the urban economy.

The diverse jobs held by household members also mean that Guadalajara's low-income population is not clearly differentiated along class lines, between, for example, an elite employed in large-scale enterprises, a semi-skilled proletariat, and a lumpen proletariat. A person's job position is unlikely to remain constant during his or her working life. A male will typically begin in informal, small-scale employment and move on to a formal occupation, but he will expect to end his working life as a self-employed worker. A female's paid employment is curtailed by marriage, child rearing, and household chores. This life cycle means that a worker's assessment of any job depends on what kind of work he or she has been doing before, what he or she can expect to get at that particular stage of his or her life, and what kind of job he or she expects to be getting next. Life history and life cycle, rather than class or formal and informal employment, are thus the differentiating factors within Guadalajara's low-income population.

Conclusions

In this chapter, I have simultaneously emphasized and sought to downplay the significance of the formal-informal sector distinction. This inconsistency is partly deliberate. Guadalajara's position within the wider national and international economy has increased the city's economic dualism. Large-scale, technologically advanced national and foreign firms dominate its economy. Their presence has accentuated the informal character of other enterprises by increasing the extent of union membership and social security coverage, thus creating a sharper distinction between those firms that operate formally and the rest. In some sectors, such as shoes and food products, competition with the large firms has led smaller ones to specialize in more labor-intensive branches of production in which significant savings can be made by informal operations.

Economic dualism is, however, only a tendency. In practice, most firms, large and small, operate both formally and informally depending on their product or service, the economic climate, and market demand. Informal employment opportunities are found throughout the economy. Even the largest, most "formal" multinationals will be a party to some informal arrangements.

The implications for the quality of urban life are contradictory. Household, kinship, and neighborhood ties are strengthened as these ties become essential supports for economic survival in the city. Yet the pressures on household and kinship relationships, and particularly on females, are heavy and, at times, destructive. Women are a valuable resource, but they are overworked and often treated brutally to keep them in line (Gonzalez 1986b). Males endure difficult working conditions, and they are irked by restrictions placed on spending by family responsibilities and a high cost of living. Alcoholism is a common refuge. They may abandon their families, but they usually end up returning. Neighbors are sources of solidarity to improve services and housing, but they are also divided by suspicion of each other's motives (since, ultimately, each household looks first to its own survival) and by personal and political conflicts.

Our research provides no reason to think that informal employment is declining in Guadalajara. The city's role in producing and commercializing basic goods for the regional and national market ensures that informal employment is to the advantage of both large- and small-scale firms. Though large enterprises may generate a greater proportion of the total product, they are likely to continue putting out work or hiring temporary workers to meet fluctuations in the structure of demand. The small-scale sector survives symbiotically in relation to the large, by specializing and, at times, creating certain economic niches. Indeed, the combination of formal and informal economic activities makes Guadalajara the Mexican city that is most likely to continue growing during the recession of the 1980s.

Notes

1. Those principally responsible for the Guadalajara research are Carlos Alba, Guillermo de la Peña, Agustín Escobar, Luisa Gabayet, and Mercedes González, all from the Colegio de Jalisco, Guadalajara, and the author.

2. These figures are taken from the censuses of 1960 and 1970 and refer to the municipalities of Guadalajara, Tlaquepaque, and Zapopán. The 1980 figures show an increase in the proportion of self-employed and unpaid family labor, to 18.5 percent. However, a more flexible criterion for employment was used for the 1980 census than for previous censuses, which probably resulted in an overestimation of self-employment and unpaid family labor.

3. My approach is similar to that of Gordon, Edwards, and Reich (1982, 1–13), who emphasize the importance of labor market segmentation—both within firms and between them—following historical changes in the pattern of economic organization in the United States.

4. We had access to the register of the state of Jalisco for industrial enterprises and drew a sample from enterprises of different sizes and different sectors of manufacturing. The sample concentrated on the important branches of industry in the city and included enterprises of different sizes, levels of technology, and industrial organization. The branches included were food, textiles, footwear, plastic and rubber products, construction materials, steel and engineering, electronic products, and photographic equipment.

5. Government workers included sanitation workers, skilled and unskilled workers in the water department, postmen, gardeners, and policemen. With the exception of some of the government employees, the sample does not include any white-collar workers, or workers in transport, commerce, and nongovernment services.

6. Agustín Escobar was responsible for organizing the survey of formal sector workers reported here, and for a subsequent study of one hundred informal sector workers. Mercedes González carried out the budget and life-history studies of approximately one hundred low-income families in 1982 and, with the help of Luisa Gabayet, carried out a follow-up study of the same families in 1985.

7. Walton (1978) drastically revised his earlier, more optimistic, view of Guadalajara, entitling his article "Creating the Divided City."

8. This estimate is based on the industrial census figures for value of production, value of the costs of production, and invested capital. Garza (1985, 380–82) takes account of the relative rotation of capital in estimating profitability.

9. A further factor in the resilience of the city's economy is that demand for the basic products and services in which Guadalajara specializes is less prone to be affected by recession.

10. This survey was carried out under the direction of Carlos Alba. My estimates take account of those firms that are registered but that did not respond to the questionnaire by increasing each size-class according to the proportion that did not reply. This is likely to produce a higher number than will be reported in the Industrial Census, but it should reflect more accurately the importance of the small-scale sector. Alba's classification is more subtle than appears in table 2.3. The strata of firms are divided not only by size, but by amount of annual sales.

11. This assertion is based on an analysis of those workers in our survey who had migrated to the United States. Those who had migrated to the United States before coming to Guadalajara had lower levels of education and were less likely to have craft skills than those who migrated from Guadalajara to the United States. Massey, Alarcón, and González's (1987) study of migrants from two rural communities in Michoacán and Jalisco suggests that U.S. migrants, while having levels of education superior to those of nonmigrants, had somewhat lower levels of education than those who migrated to Mexican cities.

12. We did not find the kinds of earnings differentials reported by Benería for Mexico City. One reason is the likelihood that Mexico City has a more differentiated earnings structure than Guadalajara, as befits its more central position in the national economy. Another reason is that, since our sample is based on formally registered enterprises, it excludes types of work, such as homework, which command very low pay.

13. The 1980 census uses a different definition of employment from that of 1970, and one that is likely to include more "informal" workers. Thus, these figures are not comparable, though the extent of the overestimation of self-employment or unpaid employment in the case of Jalisco is unlikely to be large enough to account for the increase in informal employment between 1970 and 1980.

14. The census reports 229,277 people in Jalisco engaged in manufacturing. I shall assume that the difference between the figure reported in table 2.3, which is based on registered enterprises, and the census figure is made up by people who are self-employed, who work as unremunerated family labor, or in unregistered enterprises.

15. The exceptions are the large paper mill in Atentique, employing over a thousand workers, some large mineral and cement-making enterprises, and a few synthetic fiber and pharmaceutical firms.

16. An important element in cyclical variations is the political one, associated with the *sexenio* pattern of government expenditure. Contracts for public works tend to be concentrated in the early years of a new administration.

17. This claim is based on Escobar's (1986) study of approximately one hundred workers in informally organized workshops. Escobar points out that the workers do enjoy a certain control over the work process based on craft skills, such as shoemaking. He shows how these skills give workers, both male and female, the power to bargain over wages.

18. David Forrest of the University of Salford, Great Britain, is analyzing the wage determinants of workers in the Guadalajara survey. These results are drawn from his preliminary analysis.

19. This sample size is 812. The remainder of the sample was interviewed in 1982 when inflation and changes in the minimum salary make it difficult to compare the wage data with those gathered in earlier interviews.

20. See Escobar's (1986, 131–65) detailed account of three small-scale enterprises. Inspectors and union officials can be bribed to avoid full enforcement of the law, and workers can cause a lot of legal trouble for the small-scale employer if the latter does not seek some official "protection."

21. This synoptic account of the household cycle is based on González's detailed analysis of ninety-nine poor households. See González 1986b.

22. The incomes of male heads in the top class number of contributors are high partly because of the presence of several successful informal entrepreneurs who have built their businesses over a period of years. While they are exceptional cases, they demonstrate the possibilities that informal employment offers to people in late stages of their occupational careers.

References

Alba, C. 1986. "La Industrialización en Jalisco: Evolución y Perspectivas." Pp. 89–146 in G. de la Peña and A. Escobar (eds.), *Cambio Regional, Mercado de Trabajo y Vida Obrera en Jalisco*. Guadalajara: El Colegio de Jalisco.

Arias, P. 1980. "El Proceso de Industrialización en Guadalajara, Jalisco: Siglo XX." *Relaciones* 1:9–47. El Colegio de Michoacán.

———. 1982. "Rutas Comerciales y Agentes Viajeros." *América Indígena* 42:171–253.

Arias, P. and B. R. Roberts. 1984. "The City in Permanent Transition: The Consequences of a National System of Industrial Specialization." Pp. 149–75 in J. Walton (ed.), *Capital and Labor in the Urbanized World*. Beverly Hills, Calif.: Sage Publications.

De la Peña, G. 1984. "Ideology and Practice in Southern Jalisco: Peasants, Rancheros, and Urban Entrepreneurs." Pp. 204–34 in R. T. Smith (ed.), *Kinship, Ideology, and Practice in Latin America*. Chapel Hill: University of North Carolina Press.

Departamento de Programación y Desarrollo (DPD). 1982. *La Situación Industrial de Jalisco*. Vols. 1–4. Guadalajara, Jalisco: Gobierno del Estado de Jalisco.

Escobar, A. 1986. *Con el Sudor de tu Frente*. Guadalajara: El Colegio de Jalisco.

Garza, G. 1985. *El Proceso de Industrialización en la Ciudad de Mexico*. Mexico, D.F.: El Colegio de Mexico.

González, M. 1986a. "Lo Público y lo Privado: El Grupo Doméstico Frente al Mercado de Trabajo Urbano." Pp. 191–234 in G. de la Peña and A. Escobar (eds.), *Cambio Regional*. Guadalajara: El Colegio de Jalisco.

———. 1986b. *Los Recursos de la Pobreza: Familias de Bajos Ingresos de Guadalajara*. Guadalajara: El Colegio de Jalisco.

Gordon, D. M., R. Edwards, and M. Reich. 1982. *Segmented Work, Divided Workers*. Cambridge: Cambridge University Press.

Gregory, P. 1986. *The Myth of Market Failure*. Baltimore: Johns Hopkins University Press.

Instituto Nacional de Estadística, Geografía e Informática (INEGI). 1984. *X Censo General de Población, 1980*. Tomo 14. Mexico, D.F.: Dirección General de Estadística.

———. 1985. *Estadísticas Históricas de México*. Tomo 1. Mexico, D.F.: Dirección General de Estadística.

Long, N. and B. R. Roberts. 1984. *Miners, Peasants, and Entrepreneurs*. Cambridge: Cambridge University Press.

Massey, D., R. Alarcón, and H. González. 1987. *Return to Aztlán*. Berkeley and Los Angeles: University of California Press.

Portes, A. and L. Benton. 1984. "Industrial Development and Labor Absorption: A Reinterpretation." *Population and Development Review* 10:589–611.

Portes, A., S. Blitzer, and J. Curtis. 1986. "The Urban Informal Sector in Uruguay: Its Internal Structure, Characteristics, and Effects." *World Development* 14:727–41.

Portes, A. and J. Walton. 1981. *Labor, Class, and the International System*. New York: Academic Press.

Sassen-Koob, S. 1985. "Capital Mobility and Labor Migration: Their Expression in Core Cities." Pp. 231–65 in M. Timberlake (ed.), *Urbanization in the World-Economy*. Orlando, Fla.: Academic Press.

Walton, J. 1977. *Elites and Economic Development*. Austin: ILAS/University of Texas Press.

————. 1978. "Guadalajara: Creating the Divided City." Pp. 25–50 in W. Cornelius and R. Kemper (eds.), *Latin American Urban Research*. Vol. 6. Beverly Hills, Calif.: Sage Publications.

3   New York City's Informal Economy

Saskia Sassen-Koob

A small but growing body of evidence points to the expansion of informal sectors in major cities of the United States over the last decade (Stepick 1984; Sassen-Koob 1981, 1984b; Sassen-Koob and Grover 1986). These studies focus on the production and sale of goods and services that are licit but are produced and sold outside the regulatory apparatus covering zoning, taxes, health and safety, minimum wage laws, and other types of standards. The evidence these studies are presenting runs counter to prevailing conceptions of the informal sector as well as of the nature of highly industrialized economies.

While criminal activities and underreporting of income are generally recognized as present in advanced industrialized economies, informal sectors are not. The literature on the informal sector has mostly focused on Third World countries and has, wittingly or not, assumed that as a social type such sectors are not to be expected in advanced industrialized countries (Feige 1979; Gutmann 1979; Spitznas 1981; Tanzi 1982). And the literature on industrialization has assumed that as development progresses, so will the standardization of production and generalization of the formal organization of work. Because the informal sector in the United States is perhaps most evident in immigrant communities, there has been a tendency to explain its expansion as a consequence of the large influx of Third World immigrants and their propensities to replicate survival strategies typical of home countries.

Not unrelated is the notion that the availability of a large supply of cheap immigrant workers facilitates the survival of backward sectors of the economy. Informalization contributes to lowering the costs of social reproduction and production. Both of these views posit or imply that if there is an informal sector in advanced industrialized countries, the sources are to be found in Third World immigration and in backward sectors of the economy. Explaining the expansion of informal arrangements as a Third World import or a remnant from an earlier phase of industrialization resolves the tension between this fact and prevailing conceptions of advanced industrialized economies (see Portes and Sassen-Koob 1987).

A central question for theory and policy is whether the formation and expansion of informal sectors in advanced industrialized countries is the result of conditions created by advanced capitalism. Rather than assume that Third World immigration is causing informalization, we need a critical examination of the role it may or may not play in this process. Immigrants, insofar as they tend to form communities, may be in a favorable position to seize the opportunities represented by informalization. But the opportunities are not necessarily created by immigrants. They may well be a structured outcome of current trends in the advanced industrialized economies.

This type of inquiry requires an analytic differentiation of immigration, informalization, and characteristics of the current phase of advanced industrialized economies. That should allow us to establish the differential impact of (1) immigration and (2) conditions in the economy at large on the formation and expansion of informal sectors.

An ongoing study, conducted with other investigators, of the informal sector in New York City seeks to contribute information on these various questions. The central hypothesis is that the current phase of advanced industrialization contains conditions that induce the growth of an informal economy in large cities. There are two distinct substantive components to the study. One is concerned with identifying conditions in the major growth sectors that may induce informalization (Sassen-Koob 1981, 1984a). The other attempts to identify characteristics of the informal sector itself. This chapter reports on the latter part of the study and its principal findings to date.

Economic Restructuring and Informalization

Changes in the sectoral composition of New York City's economy and in the organization of work generally over the last decade have brought about (1) an expansion of low-wage and of high-income jobs and (2) a proliferation of small units of production. Both trends contrast with what was typical in the post–World War II era, when growth was characterized by the vast expansion of a middle class and ever larger scales of production. The historical forms assumed by that expansion, notably capital intensity, standardization, and suburbanization, deterred the process of informalization. And so did the cultural forms accompanying the period of economic expansion, particularly as they shaped the structures of everyday life. A major inference that can be drawn from the post–World War II experience is that a large middle class contributes to patterns of consumption that promote standardization in production and hence, under certain conditions, are conducive to greater levels of unionization and other forms of worker empowerment. Empowerment is, in turn, conducive to middle-income jobs. The patterns of economic polarization evident today work, however, in the opposite direction, promoting small-scale enterprises and nonstandardized production.

Growing economic polarization has consequences for the organization of the labor process and for the structures of social reproduction. The evidence suggests that the increase in economic polarization and the emergence of new technical constraints have led to (1) a proliferation of small firms engaged in the production and retail of *both* highly priced and very cheap products for firms and for final consumers and (2) a spatial concentration of such small firms in major cities due to, first, the cities' critical mass of both high- and low-income residents and commuters and, second, the need for small firms to be close to suppliers and buyers. These growth trends contain inducements toward the informalization of a whole range of activities. One intervening process is the expansion of markets for both highly priced and extremely low cost goods and services (see Renooy 1984). An additional intervening process is the downgrading of labor conditions in manufacturing resulting partly from these changes in consumption but more generally from technical and politico-economic pressures.

The Study

The objectives of our ongoing research project include assessing the extent to which informal economic activities are growing in New York City and identifying the linkages between these informal activities and those in the formal economy. The research has involved a combination of secondary data analysis, ethnographic research in selected communities and workplaces, and interviews with informants, including local planning officials and community members, among others. We used data on occupational safety and health administration violators, along with those on overtime minimum wage legislation violators, to identify trends in informal production in New York City. On the basis of these data we targeted certain industries for in-depth study. Fieldwork was conducted in communities identified as having a large informal sector or as being places of concentration of immigrant populations.

In total, interviews with 55 informants, 30 homeworkers, and 30 shop owners were completed. Industries covered were (1) construction, (2) apparel, (3) footwear, (4) furniture, (5) retail activity, and (6) electronics. The research team conducted field visits in four of the five New York City boroughs. The main secondary sources for this research included comprehensive investigations conducted by the New York State Department of Labor (1982a, 1982b) and by the New Jersey Department of Labor (1982) to determine the number of unregistered commercial and manufacturing operations in these states. Besides these, there are several other completed studies (New York State Department of Taxation and Finance 1982; Leichter 1982; Assembly Committee on Oversight, Analysis, and Investigation 1982). Finally, there are two ongoing research projects focusing on the underground economy in general in the state of New York and the city of New York (City of New York 1986).

Informalization Trends in New York City

The following profile of the informal sector in the New York City area emerges from the analysis of these various sources:

1. In recent years, there has been a rapid proliferation of such operations (including industrial homework).
2. There is a wide range of industrial sectors in which such operations exist, including apparel, general construction contractors and operative buildings, heavy construction contractors, special trade contractors (particularly in masonry, stonework, and plastering), footwear, toys and sporting goods, and electronic components and accessories.
3. Informal operations were also found in lesser measure in other activities such as packaging notions, lampshade manufacturing, artificial flowers, jewelry, photo engraving, and manufacture of explosives. In all, most of the forty standard industrial classification (SIC) sectors examined were found to have unlicensed or unregistered work situations.
4. There is a strong tendency for such operations to be located in densely populated areas with very high shares of immigrants, mostly Hispanic. Chinese are also prominent, however, as are Koreans and certain European nationalities. Brighton Beach, an area with an almost exclusively Russian émigré population, was found to have an extremely diversified informal economy.
5. There is an emergent tendency for "traditional" sweatshop activity, notably in the apparel industry, to be forced out of areas undergoing residential or commercial gentrification. The space vacated by sweatshops is often occupied by new forms of informal enterprise catering to a high-income clientele. For example, high-quality wood cabinetmaking has replaced garment manufacture in Jackson Heights, and unregistered "sweater mills" have replaced cheap apparel production in Ridgewood.
6. There is evidence of a growing spatial dispersion of unlicensed and unregistered work to outlying areas. In the case of the apparel industry, for example, there has been a massive displacement out of the Chinatown area into northern Manhattan, Brooklyn, Queens, and New Jersey.

The following sections present a more detailed description of the construction, apparel, electronics, and furniture and fixtures industries. As the figures in table 3.1 indicate, there is a heavy incidence of small firms in these industries, which have a relatively disadvantaged position in the tax structure. While the unemployment tax rate is 3.13 percent for all manufacturing, it is around 4 percent for most of these industries. A similar disadvantage can be seen in the incidence of taxes as a percentage of total payroll; the average for all manufacturing was .7 percent compared with 1 or 1.2 percent for the industries examined. Small size and a relatively disadvantaged tax situation may well be factors contributing to the shift underground of many industries.

Construction

In 1982, there were over 10,700 registered construction firms in the New York City metropolitan area. As shown in table 3.1, most of these were special trade contractors (SIC 17). These firms employed a total of 120,339 workers and had

Table 3.1 Distribution of Firms by Sector and Size in New York SMSA, 1982

Sector	Employees				Total Number of Firms	Average Firm Size (no. of employees)	Total Number of Employees	Unemployment Tax Rate	Tax Rate as Percentage of Total Payroll
	1–9	10–49	50–249	250+					
General construction (SIC 15)	80.1	15.8	3.8	0.3	2,685	9.6	25,746	4.07	1.2
Special trade contractors (SIC 17)	77.9	18.6	3.2	0.4	7,602	11.2	84,820	4.01	1.1
All construction	78.1	18.2	3.3	0.4	10,710	11.2	120,339	—	—
Apparel (SIC 23)	40.4	45.8	13.2	0.6	5,290	27.6	145,773	3.81	1.2
Furniture and fixtures (SIC 25)	47.9	42.0	9.1	1.0	528	23.3	12,311	3.69	1.1
Electric and electronic equipment (SIC 36)	43.2	36.0	17.6	3.2	678	55.9	37,896	3.25	1.0
Toys and sporting goods (SIC 394)	41.0	42.3	13.5	3.2	156	39.2	6,110	3.92	1.2
All manufacturing	47.4	38.2	12.5	1.9	20,087	35.0	702,896	—	—
All industries	—	—	—	—	—	—	—	3.13	0.7

Sources: U.S. Bureau of the Census 1982; New York State Department of Labor 1982c.

an average of about 11 workers per firm; almost 80 percent of all firms employed from 1 to 9 workers. Major changes in the construction industry in this area are the growing polarization in the income structure for workers, with a loss of a wide range of middle-income construction jobs and the rapid growth of subcontracting. The number of Hispanics in the industry has increased significantly over the last decade, and much of the increase has been accounted for by subcontracting work (Balmori 1983). The share of unionized work in the industry has declined to 67 percent of all registered jobs.

The available evidence indicates that the incidence of informal work varies considerably according to sector. Most of the work in commercial and residential alterations and renovations, as well as small-store construction, is done without the required permits and is likely to be in violation of various codes. Based on a 1981 four-block survey in Manhattan done by the Department of Buildings, 90 percent of all interior work in that borough is done without a building permit. This finding has been confirmed by other surveys of citywide "illegal" work in construction. On the other hand, there is little informal employment in large public works projects. This was also the case, until recently, with sizable private sector projects, which tended to use union workers exclusively. Increasingly, however, such projects are resorting to subcontractors, including unlicensed operators, as revealed by a growing number of various violations registered by the Department of Buildings.

The Union of Construction Contractors estimates that 33 percent of the $4 billion private construction industry is now nonunion and that a rapidly growing share of the latter consists of unregistered work. Informal work is rising in new construction projects—particularly in foundation excavations and trenching—and mostly in outlying areas. In the words of one of our respondents, most of these are "fly-by-night operations," a term that has become increasingly common in the industry. Finally, there is an extremely high incidence of informal activities in highly specialized crafts work, particularly stonecutting, masonry, and plastering (SIC 174). These branches have experienced severe labor shortages and employ mostly skilled immigrants.

A recent accident at a major construction site in midtown Manhattan illustrates some of these trends. One of the operators in charge of a massive machine used in high-rise construction was found to be unlicensed. The accident and what it revealed led to a citywide inspection of major construction, that is, high-rise construction projects. The investigation revealed a widespread use of subcontractors for jobs that used to be done through direct hiring of unionized workers, as well as an unexpectedly high incidence of subcontractors without the requisite permits or in violation of one or more codes. It also found a growing presence of Hispanics among the subcontractors in an industry from which this ethnic group was excluded not long ago (see Gallo 1983).

Apparel

In 1982, there were about 5,300 registered firms in the apparel industry (SIC 23) in the New York metropolitan area. These firms employed a total of 145,773 workers. As shown in table 3.1, about 40 percent of all registered firms had between 1 and 9 workers, and approximately 45 percent had between 10 and 49 workers. A detailed occupational analysis of these employment figures for the area shows that over half of all the workers in registered firms were white-collar employees (Sassen-Koob with Benamou 1985). On the other hand, it is apparent that a majority of production workers are in unregistered work situations, notably sweatshops and industrial homework. Major changes in the apparel industry over the last decade include (1) a declining share of production work for large firms and their growing use of subcontractors; (2) a pronounced spatial dispersion of the production units, with growing numbers of firms moving into the outer boroughs, especially Queens and Brooklyn, and into the metropolitan area counties of New Jersey; and (3) a growing practice of subcontracting highly specialized and high-fashion work to industrial homeworkers, including women's gowns and fashionable knitwear (Sassen-Koob with Benamou 1985).

The available evidence indicates that the incidence of informal work has risen greatly since the early 1970s. According to the International Ladies Garment Workers Union there were fewer than 200 sweatshops in New York City in the early 1970s; by 1981 there were about 3,000, including growing numbers in areas of the city that had not contained any garment shops previously. Approximately 50,000 workers are employed in apparel sweatshops in New York City, to whom must be added some 10,000 homeworkers (New York State Department of Labor 1982a, 1982b). Separate studies (Leichter 1979, 1982; Abeles et al. 1983) tend to confirm these figures. If anything, these figures represent an underestimate because they disregard the spatial dispersion of informal production facilities into neighboring counties of New Jersey, as well as New York State localities adjacent to the city (Sassen-Koob with Benamou 1985; New Jersey Department of Labor 1982). The use of homeworkers in New Jersey has risen rapidly over the last few years, with production geared basically toward New York City firms.

The incidence of informal work varies according to branch. It is most prevalent in women's and children's wear and probably less common in men's wear. Branches in which sweatshops are growing rapidly include knitwear, furs, embroidery, and clothing for toys. In all of these, the use of homeworkers has also grown dramatically. Our interviews with homeworkers confirmed that hourly or piece-rate wages are extremely low. However, we also found a new trend toward an upgraded version of homework. One pattern was for some employers (typically free-lance or independent designers) to have immigrant workers come into their homes (usually large converted lofts in lower Manhattan) and work off-the-books. The other pattern involved middle-class women who did finishing work on very expensive clothing or highly specialized knitting requiring special machines purchased by the workers themselves. All the cases that we studied involved Chinese or Korean households in middle-class residential neighborhoods in the city.

The overall evidence from our study points to the existence of a very dynamic and growing high-price market in which production has been organized so as to incorporate sweatshops and homes (of workers and of designers) as key workplaces. Finally, a distinct pattern of ethnic ownership characterizes the informal sector in this industry. The new Latin American immigrants, especially Dominicans and Colombians, have replaced Puerto Ricans as the leading group of sweatshop owners among the Spanish-speaking population: the Chinese have increased their ownership of informal shops to a great extent over the last ten years; and the Koreans are emerging as the fastest-growing segment of small apparel entrepreneurs, setting up sweatshops and homework arrangements.

Electronics

There were 678 registered firms in the New York City metropolitan area in 1982 in electric and electronic equipment manufacturing (SIC 36). As shown in table 3.1, these firms employed a total of 37,896 workers, with an average employment of 55.9 workers. The characteristics and trends in electronics manufacturing, or even the broader category covered by SIC 36, have not received much study over the last decade in the New York City area. The available evidence points to considerable declines in the number of firms and in the levels of employment.

The main concern of our research project has been to identify general patterns, subcontracting arrangements, and the use of homeworkers in the electronics industry, narrowly defined. Thus the project has focused on a more specific set of branches than the overall SIC 36 group. Besides using secondary data, we have completed a survey of a random sample of one hundred electronics manufacturing firms in the New York City metropolitan area. Interviews with owners and managers of these firms lasted from one to two hours and focused on labor supply problems and arrangements.

On the basis of the evidence available at this time, it is possible to identify several significant patterns. First, the aggregate figures on decline of the general SIC category veiled the segmentation in this industry. The older branches, largely electrical, characterized by fairly large sized firms and unionized labor, are indeed declining. These branches have lost many firms and many jobs. But alongside this decline, we identified what could almost be described as a new subsector of the industry, namely, small firms that are mostly privately owned and employ almost no unionized labor. Such firms also rely heavily on subcontracting because of the greater efficiency, quality, and speed with which tasks can be accomplished. Among subcontractors, there were those described in our interviews as "garage fronts," "basement shops," and "neighbors." There was also mention of homework, but it frequently involved work taken home by technical personnel or owners. We did find, however, a few instances of illegal homework done by immigrant workers at very low wage rates. Further evidence of violations of various codes, provided by the New York State Department of Labor, New Jersey Department of Labor, and the Industrial Board of Appeals, confirms the existence of illegal homework in electronics in the New York City metropolitan area.

Second, several firms in our sample started as garage fronts or basement shops—operations located mostly in residential, middle-class neighborhoods. This locational pattern contrasts with that of the apparel industry in which most homework and sweatshops are located in low-income areas. Another contrast with the apparel industry is that homework in electronics tends to be carried out as "extra work" by otherwise formal employees of a firm. The finding that several firms in our sample started as garage fronts points, of course, to the possibility that shops involved in the subcontracting network may include quite a few that will eventually formalize.

In general, the pattern that emerges is one of many small concerns integrated into a dense network of subcontractors and contractors in which homework covers a rather broad range of tasks and in which the line between formal and informal tends to be less clearly drawn than in the apparel or construction industry. Finally, the role of informal work is less clearly linked to lowering wage costs than is typical of the apparel industry; it may represent a way of lowering costs of entry into the industry by allowing entrepreneurs to explore production and market conditions. It would seem, at this point, that this role of informal enterprise is linked to the predominance of small, independent-owned firms.

Furniture and Fixtures

There were 528 registered firms in this industry (SIC 25) in 1982 in the New York City metropolitan area. Almost half of all firms employed between 1 and 9 workers, and 42 percent from 10 to 49 workers (see table 3.1). Major changes in this industry over the last decade are a massive decline in larger, standardized enterprises, many of which left for the southern states, and an increase in firms making more highly crafted furniture and woodwork. A precise count is not possible because many of the latter firms are unregistered and located in residential areas.

The main sources of information on this sector are industry specialists and our own fieldwork. The emergence of informal enterprise in this sector is a rather recent event. Formal production accounted for almost all production in earlier decades, including both mass produced items and very highly priced customized work. The process of informalization during recent years seems linked to a rising demand for customized products associated with commercial and residential gentrification. Thus, while the industry lost 9 percent of its registered labor during the last five years, we found a number of new furniture-making shops that were created during that same period. Such shops are located mostly in areas of Queens (Ridgewood, Astoria, and Jackson Heights) and in Brooklyn (Sunset Park and Williamsburg).

Most of these shops employ skilled immigrants almost exclusively in the production of high-cost, crafted woodwork. With some exceptions, the shops we identified were meeting the demand for specialized woodwork from new higher-income residents and associated commercial gentrification taking place in these areas. Many of the furniture-making shops are located on second floors, since rents on main floors are becoming too expensive and the areas are zoned for residential and commercial uses.

We heard of the existence of low-cost furniture manufacturing shops catering to low-income communities and finally identified two of these in Manhattan basements. Both are informal operations, catering mostly to the local immigrant community, though increasingly nonimmigrants are going there to buy. These shops make very simple, basic furniture—tables, chairs, shelves, cabinets. A third pattern found in this industry was a clustering of small shops making unfinished goods for larger shops rather than for final consumers. It was not possible to establish how far informal enterprises went up the chain and where the formal sector took over.

Other Sectors

Other sectors on which information has been gathered include footwear, transportation, retail, and several types of services, notably auto repair and packaging.

The footwear industry has experienced massive losses in its registered work force; it lost 21 percent of its formal workers during the last five years alone. But information from industry specialists and various city agencies, and our own fieldwork, have made it evident that unregistered production both of standardized and highly crafted footwear (e.g., sandals and moccasins) has been increasing. The estimate is that 10 percent of all footwear production in New York at present is informal. Furthermore, subcontracting and use of home-workers have been increasing in unionized shops as well, according to the union that represents footwear workers (Amalgamated Clothing and Textile Workers Union [ACTWU]). The director of the union's shoe division, who has been actively involved in this industry for fifteen years, sees the expansion of unregistered work as a growing trend that began over the last five to ten years. There are many temporary manufacturing shops that operate for six to nine months and then close. There is also growing evidence of unregistered work in the manufacture of handbags and other leather goods. Data from the New York Department of Finance and Taxation show an increase in violations of various sorts of footwear manufacturing, confirming the trend observed in the field.

The most notable development of an informal sector in the transportation industry is the massive increase in the number of so-called gypsy cabs and unregistered vans operating in the city. There are now twice as many gypsy cabs as there are licensed taxi cabs. The evidence gathered by the commissioner of transportation cites 21,000 cars not licensed as cabs that are operating in this capacity. In addition, there is an as yet unidentified number of vans that function as an informal "mass transportation" system. Two major trends seem to be at work in this development. One is the proliferation of cabs and vans to service areas not well served by the formal transportation system. These are often low-income immigrant or minority neighborhoods. A second trend is the provision of services where the formal transportation system requires rides involving two and even three transfers, thereby making a single-fare one-ride informal van rather attractive to commuters.

In a variant of this trend, vans follow established public transporation routes and pick up people before or after the bus arrives. This alternative transportation system has provided employment and entrepreneurship opportunities for many immigrants. However, the common view that the main reason for the growth of this system is the presence of large numbers of undocumented immigrants is not warranted, because the available evidence shows that many native Americans are also involved in it.

There are also strong indications of the growth of informal operations in retail activity and in several industrial services. Records of the Department of Finance and Taxation show increases in violations and in the numbers of branches involved. Besides street vending and flea markets, which are frequently unlicensed, some high-priced shops dealing in jewelry and furs have established mechanisms for creating an informal market in order to avoid sales taxes. Auto-repair shops and various types of packaging are two industrial services that have expanded rapidly, mostly as informal operations or illegal homework. Hundreds of auto-repair "shops" can be seen on the streets of immigrant communities or in garages in more middle class residential neighborhoods. The evidence is too fragmentary on these sectors, however, to warrant generalization as to their origins and structure.

Spatial Organization

There are several discernible patterns in the spatial organization of the informal sector in New York. One is the concentration of informal activities in immigrant communities; some of these activities meet a demand that is internal to these communities, while others meet demand from the larger economy. A second pattern is the concentration of informal activities in areas undergoing rapid socioeconomic change, notably gentrification. A third is the concentration of informal activities in emergent manufacturing and industrial servicing areas. A more detailed description of each follows.

The first pattern reflects what are possibly two very different components of the informal sector. One is the use of immigrant workers and communities to lower costs of production in formal sector industries. The apparel industry is the clearest example. Certain elements of the construction industry, footwear industry, and industrial services also illustrate this pattern. Immigrant communities can be seen as collections of spatially concentrated resources that facilitate informal production or distribution of certain activities. These resources consist of cheap and flexible labor supplies, entrepreneurial initiative in the form of individuals willing to engage in the long hours and often low returns involved, and various informal credit arrangements that make possible small-scale capital formation.

The second component of the informal sector in immigrant communities is a type of neighborhood subeconomy. It consists of a variety of activities that meet the demand for goods and services inside the community, including the needs of immigrants residing in other neighborhoods that may lack commercial facilities. These goods and services may be of a kind not provided by the larger economy, or provided at too high a price, or provided in locations that entail a long and costly trip. Certain aspects of the informal transportation system are illustrative, notably gypsy cabs servicing low-income immigrant areas. Also illustrative are certain aspects of the construction industry, especially renovations and small-store alterations or construction.

Certain types of manufacturing, including apparel and footwear, and, at least in a few cases, furniture, are also carried out in the community in order to meet local demand. Such a local economic base may well represent a mechanism for maximizing the returns on whatever resources are available. In this manner, it may contribute to stabilizing low-income areas by providing jobs, entrepreneurial opportunities, and enough diversity to maximize the recirculation of money inside the community where the jobs are located and the goods and services are produced.

The second locational trend in the spatial organization of the informal sector is the concentration of informal activities in areas undergoing residential and commercial gentrification. The leading industrial sectors involved are construction and various forms of woodworking, including furniture making. Also involved in this process are various industries supplying the goods and services sold by the new commercial facilities associated with high-income gentrification—from clothing boutiques and gourmet food shops to sellers of customized household items. But unlike construction and furniture making, many of these activities are not necessarily located in the area undergoing gentrification. While immigrant workers were often found to provide the requisite labor, including highly skilled craftsmanship, the demand for the goods and services clearly stems from the larger economy.

The third locational pattern we can discern in the spatial organization of the informal sector is the concentration of manufacturing and industrial services in certain areas that emerge as a new type of manufacturing district or service market. For example, in one particular location (West Astoria), we found shops that make glasswork for buildings and vehicles, shops that refinish restaurant equipment, auto-repair shops, apparel shops, cabinet shops, and carpentry shops that make frames for furniture sent to other locations for finishing. All of these enterprises are operating in violation of various codes, and they are located in an area not zoned for manufacturing. This area has thus emerged as an informal manufacturing district. City government is well aware of its existence but, seemingly, has opted for disregarding the violations, probably because of the scarce supply of manufacturing space in Manhattan and the city's interest in retaining small businesses.

The concentration of manufacturing shops in this area has brought about a whole array of related service shops as well as contributed to the development of a zone where new industrial uses proliferate. For example, a major tile retailer in New York City warehouses tiles illegally in West Astoria. One implication of this example is that what may initially be a small cluster of manufacturing shops operating informally may develop into an industrial district with agglomeration economies that will draw an increasing number of large industrial users.

A variant of this pattern is illustrated by the case of Williamsburg in Brooklyn, an area that once was a thriving industrial zone near an active navy yard. After a long period of largely vacant industrial spaces, we are now seeing a proliferation of informal manufacturing shops that produce apparel, handbags, leather bags, knitted goods, and confectionery. These activities differ significantly from the original industrial uses in the area. We also noted seasonal-type subcontracting by brand-name cosmetics firms, which use the area to package Christmas and other special orders. This is becoming yet another small manufacturing zone meeting a citywide demand for certain kinds of goods and services.

Finally, we found significant clusters of auto-repair shops in several areas of the city, notably in Brooklyn, Queens, and Washington Heights in Manhattan. The number of shops and cars involved was large enough to point to a service being sold beyond the neighborhood. For example, one of these sites in Brooklyn handles one hundred cars per day on the average, clearly exceeding the demand for auto repairs that can be accounted for by the immediate neighborhood.

Conclusions

The evidence points to several distinctions in the process of informalization in New York City. These distinctions have implications for both theory and policy. First, we can identify informal activities that result from the demand for goods and services in the larger economy, either from final consumers or firms. Most of the informal work in the apparel, furniture, construction, and electronics industries is of this type. We can also identify informal activities that result from the demand of the communities where such activities are performed. Immigrant communities are a leading example, and probably account for most of this second type of demand (see Fernández-Kelly and García, this volume; Stepick, this volume).

Second, an examination of what engenders the demand for informal production and distribution indicates several sources. One of these is competitive pressures in certain industries, notably apparel, to reduce labor costs, given massive competition from lower-wage Third World countries (Safa 1981). Informal work in this instance represents an acute example of exploitation. Another source is a rapid increase in the volume of renovations, alterations, and small-scale new construction associated with the transformation of many areas of the city from low-income, dilapidated neighborhoods into higher-income commercial and residential areas. What in other American cities would have involved a massive program of new construction was mostly a process of rehabilitation of old structures in the case of New York. The volume of work, its small scale, its labor intensity and high skill content, and the short-term nature of each project were all conducive to a heavy incidence of informal work.

A third source is inadequate provision of services and goods by the formal sector. This inadequacy may consist of excessively high prices, inaccessible locations, or actual lack of supply. It seems that this condition affects mostly low-income individuals or areas. Its manifestations include the gypsy cabs serving areas not served by regular transportation, informal neighborhood child-care centers, low-cost furniture manufacturing shops, and a whole range of other activities providing personal services and goods. Finally, the existence of a diversified informal economy making use of a variety of labor supplies may lower entry costs for entrepreneurs and hence function as a factor inducing the further expansion of this sector. This last source can be construed as a supply-side factor.

Third, we can distinguish different types of informal enterprises. For some firms, access to cheap labor is the determining inducement for a New York City location. While access to the city's final or intermediate markets may also be significant, it is ultimately access to cheap labor, specifically, low-wage immigrant workers, which determines location because it allows these firms to compete with Third World factories. Certain segments of the apparel industry are illustrative. In contrast, many of the shops engaged in customized production or operating on subcontracts evince a whole host of locational dependencies on New York City. These firms are bound to the city (or to any large city in which they might be located) due to some or all of the following reasons: (1) demand is local and typically involves specific clients or customers; (2) vicinity to design and specialized services is necessary; (3) there is a short turnover time between completion of design and production; and (4) demand is predicated on the existence of a highly dynamic overall economic situation that generates a critical volume of spending capability.

Fourth, we can distinguish differences in the types of jobs found in the informal economy. Many of these are unskilled, with no training or advancement opportunities, and involving repetitive tasks. Another type of occupation, however, demands high skills. The growth of informalization in the construction and furniture industries, which increase the demand for the latter type, can thus be seen as bringing about a certain re-skilling of the labor force.

Fifth, we can identify various types of locations in the spatial organization of the informal sector. Immigrant communities are a key location for informal activities meeting both internal and external demand for goods and services. Gentrifying areas are a second important location type; these areas contain a large array of informal activities in renovation, alteration, small-scale new construction, and installations. A third type of location can be characterized as informal manufacturing and industrial service areas serving a city-wide market.

These distinctions, in addition to those that emerge in the more detailed descriptions, point to the need for a more differentiated policy approach than the one currently adopted by the city. New York's government has established a special unit charged with investigating and prosecuting tax evasion on regularly earned income or on the underground production and sale of licit goods. The definition and method of investigation of violations reduces this wide array of activities to the common denominator of tax evasion (City of New York 1986). While this approach is understandable insofar as most informal activity involves nonpayment of taxes, our research suggests that given high unemployment, the government's explicit policy of retaining small businesses, and the objective demands being met by informal producers, a policy that defines all of them only as tax evaders might prove destructive.

We need to distinguish those components of informality that are socially desirable from those that merely exploit powerless immigrants. In an urban economy that contains populations and areas with high levels of unemployment and poverty, the possibility of semiformal neighborhood subeconomies should be regarded with interest. These subeconomies, consisting of formal and informal activities, serve to stabilize low-income communities and generate internal resources that can be recirculated inside these areas.

Until now, neighborhood subeconomies have been a rather common development in immigrant communities, but rare in native minority neighborhoods. Overall socioeconomic conditions tend to be significantly better in the immigrant areas than in those occupied by native minorities. Thus it would seem that punishing informal entrepreneurs and workers in low-income communities may contribute to worsening their economic condition by promoting unemployment and the loss of self-initiated small business. The question for policymakers is whether what is now being defined as simple tax evasion can be redefined in a more constructive manner. Taking off from the notion of enterprise zones that currently grant tax concessions only to large, formal firms, one could design community zones that would enjoy similar benefits restricted to local entrepreneurs, individual contractors, and self-employed workers.

Yet another area that should be recognized as needing a more sophisticated policy approach is the growing array of small-scale manufacturing firms that are meeting a demand for customized products or for limited runs of a given product which are unlikely to be produced in large, standardized factories. Our evidence suggests that some of these small firms are informal because global development policies engender the assumption that modern manufacturing must be large-scale and standardized and, hence, that it does not fit into the economic base of so-called postindustrial cities. Whatever manufacturing does take place in such cities is thought to be interstitial and probably part of a declining and backward sector. Thus policies and tax structures come to reinforce the disadvantaged position of small urban manufacturing firms.

Yet there is a real and growing demand for a whole range of products whose producers benefit from the suppliers and markets in such large cities and typically can only survive there. These firms represent a growth sector and one of the few sources of manufacturing jobs in the city, frequently demanding specialized skills. It would seem that recognition of the vitality and contributions of this informal manufacturing sector might lead to policies that support its development, while at the same time seeking to reduce labor and health code violations.

Tax evasion, on the other hand, is probably the correct approach toward firms selling very high priced goods, especially furs and jewelry, which seek informal ways of marketing in order to avoid sales taxes. Sectors of the urban economy which are in a strong position should be distinguished from entities such as informal neighborhood enterprises that stabilize low-income communities. Finally, when pronounced forms of labor exploitation are the main aim of informalization, penalties should indeed by maximized.

Results from our study and other sources lead to the conclusion that the main forces at play in the informalization of various activities are to be found in characteristics of New York's economy. A corollary of this conclusion is that a good share of informal sector activities are not the result of immigrant survival strategies, but represent an outcome of structural patterns of economic transformation. Workers and firms respond to the opportunities created by these patterns. However, in order to respond, they need to be positioned in favorable ways. The association of immigrant communities within the informalization process is not necessary, but contingent. These communities frequently possess a "favored" structural location that enables them to seize the opportunities for entrepreneurship as well as the more and less desirable jobs being generated by the process. To the extent that these dynamics promote small business and reduce unemployment, they might well be encouraged rather than persecuted in immigrant as well as native low-income neighborhoods.

Notes

Research support was provided by the Graduate School of Architecture and Planning, Columbia University. I also thank the Revson Foundation for supporting research on the garment and electronics industries.

References

Abeles, Schwartz, Hackel, and Silverblatt, Inc. 1983. "The Chinatown Garment Industry Study." Report to ILGWU Locals 23–25 and the New York Sportswear Association.

Assembly Committee on Oversight, Analysis, and Investigation. 1982. "New York State's Underground Economy: Untaxed and Growing." Dennis Gorski, Chairman, June.

Balmori, D. 1983. *Hispanic Immigrants in the Construction Industry: New York City, 1960–1982*. Occasional Papers, no. 38. New York: Center for Latin American and Caribbean Studies.

City of New York. 1986. *Unearthing the Underground Economy*. New York: New York City Department of Finance.

Feige, E. L. 1979. "How Big is the Irregular Economy?" *Challenge* 22:5–13.

Gallo. 1983. "The Construction Industry in New York City: Immigrants and Black Entrepreneurs." Columbia University, Conservation of Human Resources, Research Program on Newcomers to NYC, January, New York.

Gutmann, P. M. 1979. "Statistical Illusions, Mistaken Policies." *Challenge* 22:14–17.

Leichter, F. S. 1979. "The Return of the Sweatshop: A Call for State Action." October.

———. 1982. "Sweatshops to Shakedowns: Organized Crime in New York's Garment Industry." Monthly Report. Office of the 29th District of the State of New York.

Lomnitz, L. 1978. "Mechanisms of Articulation between Shantytown Settlers and the Urban System." *Urban Anthropology* 7:185–205.

New Jersey Department of Labor. 1982. "Study of Industrial Homework." Report. Office of Wage and Hour Compliance, Division of Workplace Standards, Trenton, N.J.

New York State Department of Labor. 1982a. "Study of State-Federal Employment Standards for Industrial Homeworkers in New York City." Report. Division of Labor Standards, Albany.

———. 1982b. *Report to the Governor and the Legislature on the Garment Manufacturing Industry and Industrial Homework*. Albany: State of New York.

———. 1982c. "Statistics Relative to the New York State Unemployment Insurance Fund." Labor Research Report no. 3.

New York State Department of Taxation and Finance. 1982. *The Task Force on the Underground Economy: Preliminary Report.* Albany: State of New York.

Portes, A. and S. Sassen-Koob. 1987. "Making It Underground: Comparative Material on the Informal Sector in Western Market Economies." *American Journal of Sociology* 93: 30–61.

Renooy, P. H. 1984. "Twilight Economy: A Survey of the Informal Economy in the Netherlands." Research Report. Faculty of Economic Sciences, University of Amsterdam.

Safa, H. I. 1981. "Runaway Shops and Female Employment: The Search for Cheap Labor." *Signs* 7:418–33.

Sassen-Koob, S. 1981. *Exporting Capital and Importing Labor: Caribbean Migration to New York City.* Occasional Papers, no. 28. New York: Center for Latin American and Caribbean Studies, New York University.

———. 1984a. "The New Labor Demand in Global Cities." Pp. 139–71 in M. P. Smith (ed.), *Cities in Transformation: Capital, Class, and Urban Structure.* Beverly Hills, Calif.: Sage Publications.

———. 1984b. "Growth and Informalization at the Core: The Case of New York City." Pp. 492–518 in "The Urban Informal Sector: Recent Trends in Research and Theory." Conference Proceedings. Department of Sociology, The Johns Hopkins University, Baltimore. Mimeo.

Sassen-Koob, S. with C. Benamou. 1985. "Hispanic Women in the Garment and Electronics Industries in the New York Metropolitan Area." Research Progress Report presented to the Revson Foundation, New York City.

Sassen-Koob, S. and S. Grover. 1986. "Unregistered Work in the New York Metropolitan Area." Working Paper. Columbia University, Graduate School of Architecture and Planning.

Spitznas, T. 1981. "Estimating the Size of the Underground Economy in New York City." *The Regional Economic Digest* 1:1–3.

Stepick, A. 1984. "The Haitian Informal Sector in Miami." Pp. 384–434 in "The Urban Informal Sector: Recent Trends in Research and Theory." Conference Proceedings. Department of Sociology, The Johns Hopkins University, Baltimore. Mimeo.

Tanzi, V. 1982. *The Underground Economy in the United States and Abroad.* Lexington, Mass.: D. C. Heath.

4 Informal Sector versus Informalized Labor Relations in Uruguay

Juan Carlos Fortuna and Suzana Prates

Since the term *informal sector* was coined more than two decades ago, an abundant critical literature has been published on that subject. Nevertheless, a paradox persists: It seems unavoidable that we must resort to the notions of formality and informality in order to explain central processes in the socioeconomic dynamics of modern societies. At the same time, disagreements surround the theoretical status of the two concepts; their very definition is in question.

Often the gap between the use of terms of heuristic value and their theoretical legitimation increases over time. Since concepts have meaning only when considered as part of defined theoretical frameworks, the notions of formality and informality have become the epitome of a pretheoretical approach. In fact, "informal sector" has become a (pre) concept in search of a theory. This is neither good nor bad; it is merely the result of the advantages and difficulties that surround scientific endeavor.

Our purpose in this chapter is to examine a series of theoretical issues arising from empirical research on informality in Uruguay during 1984–85. There are several aspects derived from our investigation that we consider pertinent vis-à-vis the present theoretical debate.

First, interpretations of the informal sector which have captured the attention of academicians and planners since the seventies grew out of a dualistic approach. From the beginning, emphasis was not placed upon a structural understanding of chronic unemployment and poverty, the articulation between national and international levels, the styles of development adopted by individual countries, or the effects of the international division of labor.

Instead, the problems of underdevelopment were attributed to the existence of one single sector (not a whole system) which had to be transformed. Specific policies and stimuli were then outlined. The hopes of conservatives rested upon the old principle that "in order for everything to stay the same it is necessary that something changes." Thus, many believed that it was possible to correct anomalies by enacting policies and plans especially directed at the urban informal sector. But the stubborn persistence of the poverty-stricken, the unemployed, and the underemployed, as well as the continuation

---

Chapter 4 was translated by M. Patricia Fernández-Kelly.

of ecological and social marginality in Latin American countries, challenged this optimistic hypothesis and demolished the faith in "non-traumatic transitions."

Second, empirical evidence showed something else: informality was not enmeshed in poverty and marginality alone. The relative success and satisfactory earnings derived from informal activities in various forms of self-employment and small family enterprises surpassed, in some cases, the levels achieved by workers in the formal sector. Castells and Portes point out in this volume, with respect to both developed and developing countries, that there are informal relations that are not confined to the sphere of poverty and marginality. Our study confirms that finding and demonstrates that shifts from formality to informality are frequent. This phenomenon underscores the changing character of the relations of production as well as their complexity.

Therefore, in contrast with sectoral and dualistic approaches we maintain the need to conceptualize informality as a particular relationship in the organization of production. In other words, a central idea of our study is that informality is a feature of labor-capital relations. There is evidence that informality can be re-created under cyclical conditions of crisis and unemployment or under dynamic processes of economic growth. Informality can also emerge as a consequence of pressures from an immigrant labor supply (as shown by the essays on southern California and Mexico in this volume) or, as in the case of Uruguay, in conditions of an absolute loss of population due to emigration.

Third, in organizational terms and also in terms induced by technological transformations, we are now witnessing the rise of new modalities of informality (for example, in the Italian case discussed by Capecchi in this volume). Despite variations in origin and function, informal labor relations are distinguished primarily by a process of de-institutionalization of productive activities through a movement away from regulations issued by the state.

Production, Reproduction, and Domestic Units

The activities encompassed within the informal sector express a capitalist contradiction between the need to expand the mass of wage earners and the inability to provide secure employment to the labor force reproduced within the system. This is a fundamental opposition, although it varies in time and space in consonance with the degree of development of the productive forces and the social relations of production. In developing countries, where the social responsibility of reproducing the labor force is less than in developed nations, the tendency is toward the proletarianization of a decreasing proportion of the urban labor force. Large numbers of workers enter wage employment only intermittently and even then under agreements that ensure their exclusion from the provision of benefits and long-term employment security (Moser 1981).

Under these conditions, domestic units assume a key role as the only mechanism available for their own reproduction. The many activities performed by household members in popular sectors can be seen as a response to immediate survival needs that are historically defined and socially diverse. They are also a means to guarantee continuity and long-term subsistence. In the urban context of underdevelopment, household activities have ranged from the articulation of institutional resources to the generation of earnings, and they have assumed various forms: "backwards capitalist," precapitalist, "petty commodity production," or disguised wage labor (Portes 1983).

The horizontal interconnection of activities that are vertically articulated by capital and often highly stratified suggests a continuum of resource and income-generating strategies and not a simple dichotomy of the labor market. The midlevel categories *self-employed* and *protected wage workers* express a process of differentiation which does not necessarily entail a transition from petty commodity producers toward wage workers. On the contrary, all these forms can coexist, often involving the same individuals depending on the opportunities available for the generation of earnings vis-à-vis consumption needs.

The requirements of domestic units and the possibility, form, and level of their satisfaction depend on the ability to gain access to paid employment and on the composition of the labor force in terms of sex and age. They also depend on the prevailing system of values and intradomestic power distribution. All these factors have an impact on the relationships outlined above.

Uruguay in the Seventies: Economic and Sociopolitical Transformations

Between 1971 and 1973 Uruguay experienced the beginning of what has been the most dramatic rupture in its modern history, especially when seen in contrast with the styles of development and social life which preceded it. A new sociopolitical and economic model was implemented which included a highly coercive, bureaucratic-authoritarian state that backed the new monetarist orthodoxy. This model was much more than a short-term policy directed toward "monetary stabilization" or political control. Instead, a new image of society was proposed on the basis of a drastic redefinition of conditions for reproducing the labor force.

The political and economic policy devised had several consequences: (1) a reduction of real wages, which were 45 percent smaller in 1979 than in 1971; (2) a regressive distribution of earnings that shifted participation of the upper strata from 27.7 percent to 40.8 percent of total earnings between 1973 and 1979; (3) a negative growth of internal private consumption (Wonsewer and Notaro 1981); (4) the growth of sectoral unemployment, that is, jobs newly created did not expand at the rate of demand for employment but instead replaced disappearing jobs (PREALC 1977); (5) the reduction of government social expenditures, which made working-class families increasingly responsible for the reproduction of the labor force; and (6) the state's withdrawal from the provision of public housing.

Under these circumstances, domestic units modified the form and content of their relations with national society. The self-exploitation of family members became a typical phenomenon aimed at softening the impact of decreasing real wages. Between 1973 and 1979, 90 percent of the population in Montevideo maintained its level of family earnings due to the incorporation of more of its members into the labor force (Melgar 1981; Prates 1983; Laenz 1985). Women had a central part in this strategy; their contribution was vital even though their wages fluctuated between only 49.9 percent and 66 percent of male earnings (Melgar and Teja 1985).

The elimination of institutions capable of responding to the demands of working-class sectors, as well as the limitation of collective communication, further eroded the material, private, and social bases of reproduction of the labor force. Workers became increasingly dependent on the differential capacities of each domestic unit. This led to a redefinition of the foundations of social organization in a predominantly urban society that had enjoyed relative prosperity well into the sixties (Filgueira and Geneletti 1981).

Characteristics of Informality in the Low-Income Neighborhoods of Montevideo

Our analysis of informality is based on the premise that it is a qualitatively dynamic phenomenon and that it changes according to the level of development and the benefits achieved in the political arena by the working class. Thus, protection afforded to workers by the state at any given time marks a conjunctural moment subject to fluctuation.

For our purposes, we consider as "informal workers" those who participate in the labor force without access to benefits, who are employed in order to cover their future retirement but who do not have a claim to lay-off compensation or other privileges, or who are only partially covered. The findings reported below are based on a representative survey of popular areas of Montevideo conducted in 1983–84. Information was obtained on all members of seven hundred households drawn randomly.[1]

Thirty-five percent of workers in these households were involved in informal activities as a principal occupation. Forty-seven percent of these respondents were self-employed, while 36 percent were wage workers. However, it is also important to note that slightly over 10 percent were employers. With respect to the composition of the labor force, informality is more frequent among artisans and direct production workers (34%), those in personal services (27%), and vendors (26%). Female informality is most often found in the service sector (46%) and among sellers (23%). The educational profile of informal workers shows a high concentration at low levels of schooling. Nevertheless, it is significant that informally employed women have a higher level of instruction than men.

Informal workers also tend to be older. This is particularly apparent among women who are frequently involved in unremunerated family labor. In these situations, women tend to work steadily until they reach an advanced age. Overall, informal employment is strongly associated with a precarious economic situation. This is partially explained by the availability of other resources—transfer payments from government, consumption of services provided by the state, and the like—to formal workers and their families.

Forty-one percent of households with at least one employed member chaneled more than three-fourths of their total working time into informal activities. Approximately 18 percent of households used less than this amount, and the remaining 41 percent is formed by domestic units totally dedicated to formal activities. The families in the first group have the smallest per capita average incomes. The ones that combine various types of formal and informal activities have the highest average earnings. The homes whose subsistence depends the most on informal activities are also characterized by lower average levels of schooling, lower rates of male employment, higher rates of non-utilized labor capacity, and the smallest number of active labor hours per member of the household.

The strategy that combines protected and nonprotected activities thus emerges as the most efficient, on the basis of utilization of the available labor force and earning levels. However, this situation is only found among less than one-fifth of our households. The problems of households in which most labor time is spent informally are best understood in terms of structural difficulties caused by the presence of family members older than sixty-five, high levels of feminization of the available labor force, and low levels of education and skills.

Vertical Labor-Capital Integration and Informal Labor Relations

Survey results were supplemented by direct observation of the articulation of formal and informal activities in specific sectors of Montevideo. In this section, we summarize results of two of these studies involving the footwear and recycling industry, respectively.[2] The emergence of an informal putting-out system in footwear manufacturing corresponded to an expansive economic cycle between 1974 and 1981. During this period, footwear production had an important role in the implementation of a development model based on nontraditional exports. The collection and recycling of waste products in plastics and related industries acquired prominence, on the other hand, between 1982 and 1985 in the midst of a strong economic recession.[3]

Together, these two experiences highlight a theoretically significant point, namely, that the structuring and extension of informal activities is not limited to circumstances or periods characterized by low economic growth. Instead, they can also be found as part of expansive economic cycles and in sectors distinguished by high levels of development. Informality can even result from the rapid incorporation of technological innovation in some areas or specific operations (Landes 1981).

Overall, our findings are in agreement with research elsewhere demonstrating that home assembly is a modality of labor organization which can be re-created and expanded under the most diverse circumstances of contemporary capitalism. This is true for industrialized countries (Allen 1981; Goddard 1981; Fernández-Kelly and García, this volume) and for developing countries. In the latter, informality is often related to multinational investments (Peattie 1981; Roldán 1983; Benería and Roldán 1987), to the workings of national commercial capital (Schmukler 1977; Paiva Abreu 1986) or to the effect of state industrial capital investments (Alonso 1983; Lovesio 1986).

The Putting-out System in Footwear Manufacturing

Soon after the implementation of an export-oriented policy by the new military government in the early 1970s, the National Center of Technology and Industrial Productivity (NCTPI) reported that informal footwear production fluctuated between 12 percent and 50 percent of the national total, depending on the characteristics of particular firms. It is not farfetched to suppose that the higher levels of automation in existence since 1974 and the growing market demand from that year until 1980 may have contributed to an increase in that estimate. Historically, the combination of factory and homework tends to occur under conditions in which the labor process is susceptible to high levels of fragmentation and in those industries that are subjected to variations in demand due to factors like fashion and seasonality. In such cases, it is rational to maintain and even to expand the putting-out system, which "has survived in symbiotic relation with factories. Many manufacturers find it lucrative to install only the machinery which can respond to normal demands . . . relying upon a reserve of dispersed labor for additional production in times of prosperity" (Landes 1981).

The most decentralized operation in footwear manufacturing in Uruguay is stitching the uppers. The complexity of the labor process in this operation gives rise to the need to perform several distinct tasks and to have access to a diversified machinery and tool reserve. This explains certain relations that we have observed between capitalist firms and homeworkers which are, in turn, similar to those observed elsewhere in Latin America (see Peattie 1981). The data collected during our study show three large strata among homeworkers. Table 4.1 shows considerable social variation within the "informal factory," as well as different levels of legal coverage and a nonuniform cluster of labor

Table 4.1 The Uruguayan Footwear Industry

Level	Types
1 Shops employing wage labor	(a) Legal
	(b) Legal using clandestine labor
	(c) Underground
2 Shops employing unpaid family labor and, occasionally, wage workers	(a) Self-employment; no wage workers
	(b) Self-employment plus clandestine wage labor
3 Homeworkers	(a) Registered
	(b) Not registered

relations. Informal labor relations between firms and homeworkers are characterized by

1. piece-rate payments calculated on the basis of the supposed productive time spent by the worker but which do not include the restoration of his or her physical strength (nighttime, weekends, leaves of absence, etc.);
2. manipulation of noncontractual factors by the firms with the purpose of strengthening control over outworkers. Such practices include the loaning of machinery, the advance of inputs later discounted from payments, money advances, and other devices that re-create indebtedness;
3. concealment or total clandestinity of the contractual relation including absence of receipts or explicit protections against dismissals or layoffs; and
4. the requirement that outworkers "legalize" their situation by assuming social security expenses and recording fictitious figures on self-employment registration forms.

The skill of homeworkers and the piece-rate system by which they are compensated for their services leads to high levels of productivity.[4] Through observation and information provided by our informants we were able to assess the differential productivity of homework as compared with factory employment. Homeworkers, most of them women, consistently surpass factory operatives. Home stitchers produce a pair of uppers every nine minutes and thirty seconds on the average. The equivalent figure among factory operatives is sixteen minutes. Thus, the surplus time extracted through the use of homework is over six minutes per worker.

Of seven firms representative of level 1 (see table 4.1) in our study,[5] only one did not resort to the subcontracting of homeworkers. The other six used them in proportions that fluctuated between 10 percent and 50 percent of their total labor force. Three of these firms directed production exclusively to foreign markets, and the remaining ones dealt with both domestic and foreign buyers. All firms incorporated machinery of a higher technological sophistication between 1975 and 1978; the average age of their equipment was not more than ten years.

The discourse of the entrepreneurs or managers of these firms regarding their labor practices is worth noting. From statements made to us, it is clear that they are aware of the advantages of informal labor relations. Regarding payments to workers, an employer declared that "we pay small wages, otherwise we would have to increase the cost of shoes to consumers." Another noted that "we pay piece rates because we get 30 percent more productivity that way." Regarding social security coverage, a manager stated that "the advantage of homework is that we don't have to pay social benefits; this, of course, reduces our costs." Finally, employers are sensitive to the "preventive" advantages of homework in relation to workers' mobilization: "When workers toil on their own, they work harder and, besides, with fewer people, there are fewer problems in the factory and this is very important."

From the point of view of workers, there is also an appreciation of independence which validates homework as a legitimate option. This is even more evident among women who form the largest proportion of outworkers. The preference for home assembly may be explained by noting the contradictions confronted by women charged with the responsibilities of motherhood and family care. Their "option" depends on their responsibility regarding social reproduction and is often lived out as a highly conflictive choice. To be a mother among women in Uruguay includes the predestination to sacrifice, a concept that is not only accepted but also made a priority in deciding among labor alternatives.

For many women, factory work is a better situation than homework, but: "I can't think of myself alone because I have a family . . . once you assume a family responsibility you can't cast it aside just like that. When [children] grow up or when they get married you can go and do what you please with your life, but when they still depend on you, you have to be there [at home]." Among the women interviewed in our study, 90 percent were more than thirty years of age and 94.2 percent were married or lived in stable consentual unions. Forty-seven percent of these women worked for footwear export firms between 1974 and 1979. At the time of the study (1984–85), many were unemployed or irregularly employed in small shops. Clearly, this group offers a perfect cyclical labor reserve shifted from the precapitalist home sphere into remunerated production during expansive periods and ejected during recessive stages. The self-defining discourse of these women allows us to interpret more precisely their position within the labor process: they are subjected to patriarchal norms and are living a gender identity that includes subordination as a fact of life.

Therefore, it is not "marginality," understood as a cluster of poverty characteristics, which explains the conditions leading to the formation of this labor reserve. Instead, it is the relationship between patriarchy and capitalism that exposes these women to a double exploitation on the basis of gender and class. Unlike the backward phenomenon portrayed by many writings on the labor process in Latin America, the putting-out system emerges from this study as an important element of modern labor-capital relations re-created anew during periods of strong economic dynamism.

The Recycling Industry

The collection of recyclable waste has become not only the main, but also the only, source of income for a sizable sector of the Montevideo labor force. Most workers employed in these activities suffered a sustained process of impoverishment beginning in 1981 due to growing unemployment and the reduction of real wages. Another factor contributing to the growth of this phenomenon was the expansion of peripheral shantytowns known as *cantegriles,* which provided the physical setting for sorting out waste materials and other recycling tasks. The characteristics of space and structure in these shantytowns have thus led to a symbiosis between survival needs of the poor and the modest economic opportunities derived from garbage collection.

Cantegril dwellers collect a wide array of materials ranging from food remains to metallic parts, with paper and plastic as intermediate products. The specific materials gathered have varied depending on products being manufactured at different points in time. Thus, for example, plastic has replaced glass over the last few years as a preferred item in the manufacture of medical packaging, cleaning products, milk cartons, and the like. A graphic portrayal of the levels and activities that conform the chain of articulation in the recycling industry is presented in table 4.2.

Table 4.2 specifies three levels in this process. However, it is important to note that while level III (manufacturing) contains establishments of different sizes, level II (intermediary) includes, at most, midlevel establishments, judging by the number of workers employed in them. A factor explaining differences in size of establishment is the type of activity performed; commercialization of recyclables requires a smaller labor force than the man-

Table 4.2 The Garbage Recycling Industry in Montevideo

Level	Types
I Collection and sorting	(1) Foot collectors
	(2) Pushcart collectors
	(3) Horse cart collectors
II Intermediary	(1) Small deposit owners, washers
	(2) Stockers, buyers
	(3) Stockers, mills
III Manufacturing	(1) Small shops: recyclers and final goods producers
	(2) Mid-sized shops: recyclers and final goods producers
	(3) Large shops: final goods

ufacturing process. Similarly, the value of fixed capital is smaller in the former case.

Collecting

There are three key factors affecting the types of activities performed by waste collectors: the type and size of their domestic units, their labor tools, and their area of residence. There are also three basic work activities: gathering, classification, and packaging. Gathering is performed with simultaneous selection or preselection of usable materials. Collectors who have animal traction gather less selectively, while those who do not have horses or mules must gather in stages. For collectors without animal traction, nonmarketable waste or waste that cannot be used by the domestic unit for subsistence purposes (either through direct consumption or as animal feed) represents an additional burden that greatly limits the possibility of attaining a minimal daily income. Generally, these individuals cannot make more than one daily outing.

Collectors who have a horse and cart generally do two daily rounds: the head of the household makes the longest and most important round from the evening until dawn before municipal garbage collectors start their work. During the early evening, other household members (sons and daughters, spouses, etc.) may also go out as a strategy to increase family earnings. Such additional activities are made possible by the availability of surplus family labor without alternative possibilities for generating earnings in the labor market.

Classifying activities, particularly more subtle ones such as the separation of paper of different qualities, require additional domestic labor. Place of residence is also a factor shaping collection strategies. Those who live in more centrally located areas do not have access to spaces appropriate for selection; therefore, they are forced to classify waste in deserted lots found in their daily rounds. Peripheral *cantegril* dwellers, on the other hand, can avail themselves of the areas near their shacks in order to separate various types of waste.

Household members normally participate in classification. The more members a family has, the greater the refinement in separation of various waste materials. This, in turn, allows the collector to obtain more differentiated prices for his materials and, therefore, higher earnings. Materials that are not finely classified (for example, in the case of paper) are bought by *depositeros* (warehouse managers) wholesale as *papel sucio* (literally, "dirty paper"), or third-rate paper. This means that the collector can only charge, on the average, about 29 percent of the top price paid for items such as corrugated cardboard or 43 percent of the value of a kilogram of newspaper.

Some collectors who perform more refined classification add yet another step—the packaging or tying up of materials. Here again, family labor emerges as a central factor: "I try to separate items at the very moment I gather them but sometimes that's not possible. I bring bags, and in a deserted lot I do the selection mostly of paper . . . I throw out very dirty paper. My mother and I tie up paper and cardboard every day" (respondent, age 13).

Marketing

Depositeros form the lowest stratum in the chain of intermediaries processing recyclables. Generally, they do not specialize according to type of material. The only differentiation, found on the basis of detailed interviews, involves those wholesalers who specialize mainly in the purchase of metal. In this sense, there seems to be a difference between Montevideo and other cities, where buyers specialize in different types of a product (Birbeck 1978).

The effect of the degree of specialization on labor organization varies. Greater heterogeneity in the purchases requires larger storage spaces, more handling personnel, and tools for controlling the weight and quality of materials. The higher the specialization, the more frequent wholesale purchases become. This determines a pace of work with longer intervals of time between. Finally, there is another interesting aspect concerning the articulation of non-specialized deposits with other activities. Depositeros who buy rags, bottles, and plastics require an additional task prior to reselling: washing the materials. Washing can take place within the same storage area. However, depositeros frequently put out washing among women living in the cantegriles. According to qualified informants, a widespread practice of manufacturing enterprises is to subcontract, directly or indirectly, clandestine washers in the cantegriles. The chain of informal relations is thus extended again downward, through the hiring of highly dispersed labor of low skill and few alternatives in the job market.

Recycling in the Plastics Industry

Every recycled unit of waste requires special treatment in order to become usable raw material. The analysis of the steps necessary for recycling plastic, as well as the technological alternatives possible within them, provides a more precise description of the internal relations within this sector. The course followed by plastic from its collection to its marketing involves diverse routes. Part of the residues is bought by depositeros, another part is acquired by washers, and a third is bought directly by manufacturing firms of various sizes. This translates into four basic sequences, summarized in figure 4.1, within which there may be additional variants.

Washing is a necessary task in the chain of plastics recovery; for technical reasons, plastic cannot be used dirty. This task is performed by subcontracted personnel, by depositeros, or by manufacturers. From the point of view of large enterprises, it is more convenient to put out washing of plastic than to perform this task at the plant. Washing requires long hours of work. If this activity was integrated into regular factory operations, it would require

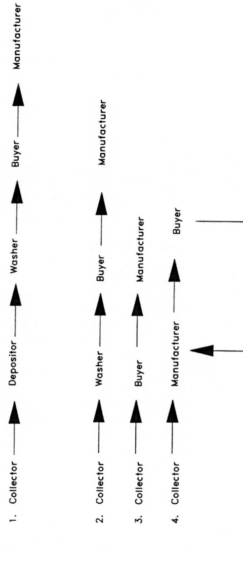

Figure 4.1. Sequential patterns in the recovery of plastic waste for recycling.

hiring a stable labor force. This course would increase administrative expenses as well as the provision of social security and other benefits to workers. Subcontracting eliminates these expenses. The owner of a small company told us that "the factory provides washers with the necessary items. Washers can be found in the cantegriles; washed materials return later to the factory where they are recycled."

The case of one of the largest Uruguayan enterprises in this sector provides an illustrative example. The company buys large quantities of fish-transporting containers for recycling. An informant reported that "recovery is very expensive because it requires lots of labor for washing . . . when this material is needed, we have to allocate many workers to washing in order to recycle." Thus, within the dynamics of this enterprise a space is created for subcontracting and for the emergence of small "independent" washing establishments. Such establishments operate on the basis of family and intermittent wage labor.

Washing and drying plastic by hand appears to be an activity that permits some small-scale entrepreneurship and modest capital accumulation. In two of the cases studied, subcontracted washing turned out to be the primary activity of a small producer and of a mechanized establishment. The machinery and capital for starting both enterprises came from severance pay from earlier formal employment. In one instance: "My brother was laid off and he started washing plastic in the back of his house; he used to buy plastic from the horse carts. Before that, he had worked for a plastic factory for twelve years." The two brothers used their severance pay to buy the necessary equipment for starting their business. The owner of the other small recovery firm started on her own in 1971 by using money received as indemnification after being fired. Originally, she only washed, but in 1980 she began to acquire machinery that allows for more elaborate forms of plastics recovery: the waste is washed, dried, classified, cut, crunched, and processed (pelletized) as new raw material.

The story of these small producers is repeated with little variation even among the larger enterprises (see table 4.3). From the smallest and most fragile establishments to the largest ones, all firms have some connection with the "informal sector." They also have relationships among themselves. This is the case, in particular, for the most modern firm in our study, which connects with other establishments in a downward-linked chain. Managers of this firm told us that "we buy waste and we pay other firms to recycle it. This way we save because the recycled materials come cheap." In the company's view, "It isn't profitable to allocate personnel to recycling; other establishments pay lower wages to workers so that it's cheaper to subcontract."

The stratification of firms thus gives way to a transfer of value from the lowest stratum up toward the larger firms. This shift is possible, among other reasons, because small establishments operate on the basis of family labor.

Table 4.3   Characteristics of Establishments in Plastics Recycling

Activity	Waste Material Providers	Clientele	Machinery	Average Total Employment
Washing	Horse and pushcart collectors Deposits	Buyers	(a) Washer-drier, cutters (b) Mill, struder, pelletizer	13
Small-scale buying	Deposits Horse and pushcart collectors Other Collectors	Manufacturers, resellers	Mill, struder, bus	8
Medium-scale buying	Deposits Scrap from factories	Small and midsized factories	Struder, mill, crusher, pelletizer, washer-drier	8
Small-scale manufacturing	Deposits	Wholesale sellers	Struder, mill, lathe, compressor, injectors	15
Large-scale manufacturing	Importers Horse and pushcart collectors Factories Deposits	Industries, government, wholesalers	High-tech equipment	300

Thirty-one percent of total personnel in the four smallest establishments in our study was formed by owners-partners and their families, whether remunerated or not. Further, 71 percent of nonfamily wage workers were women. Even when employed "formally," these women earn average hourly wages that are about 51 percent smaller than those received by men (Melgar and Teja 1985).

Small-business owners are acutely aware of limits to their growth: "I prefer being small and not grow too much and then collapse like it has happened to others." Another small producer said, "Our size is the right one . . . we shouldn't increase production, demand doesn't allow it, there is no margin." The decision "not to grow" reflects a conservative entrepreneurial approach that is related to an objective reality of size and possibilities in the Uruguayan market, particularly during the extended recession. The relation between these objective factors and their perceptions by small-business people makes it possible for large capitalist enterprises to increase profits by lowering costs of production through subcontracting.

Conclusions

Our findings indicate that the integration of labor and capital under informal labor relations conforms a structural dimension in the socioeconomic reality of contemporary Uruguay. Indeed, we should relinquish the notion that informality is exceptional or transitory in this context. Informalization of the labor market was not due to recession alone, nor did it derive from factors limited to the international economic order. The boom period of export manufactures which entailed high levels of benefit for entrepreneurs, the use of advanced technology, and the growth in the scale of production also fostered a process of informalization disguised as small independent entrepreneurship. In the same vein, this process led to de-skilling of the formal manufacturing labor force and its restructuring on the basis of sex and age.

The subsequent recession in Uruguay during the 1980s has been characterized by the mobilization of poverty-stricken urban strata seeking economic survival by whatever means are available. We do not adhere to mechanistic theories that argue that capitalism is "functionally" capable of reproducing the labor force required at every stage of its development. Nonetheless, we believe that there was deliberate intention in the creation of a fragmented labor force unable to guard its class identity, weakly organized, and with few possibilities for vindication.

This recomposition of the labor force has led to the consolidation of a large impoverished sector that is "functional" for the maintenance and expansion of groups of intermediaries and industrialists during a period in which the import of raw material became an obstacle to economic activity. The current crisis and the growth of urban poverty and unemployment in Uruguay do not augur well for the reduction of informal labor relations.

We must note, however, that the capacity for mobilization among the "new poor" in Uruguay is not entirely exhausted. This reserve of energy is created by hopes of a better life for this next generation. In the words of one respondent, "I would like to have a job that would allow me to have a family income . . . I would like to leave this neighborhood not so much for my own good—I can live anywhere—but for the good of my children who are still small. I would like to move them away from the cantegril. . . . But to achieve this, the government must change; the military must leave, although I don't think that we'll have elections soon" (garbage collector, age 49).

The understanding of how broader social processes impinge on personal problems is also evident in the testimony of a part-time construction worker whose son collects waste in order to improve family earnings: "It all depends on the new government, on who wins the elections; all can remain the same or it can get worse. Recently some candidates came to the cantegril inviting people to dinner. When they invited me I answered, 'Why didn't you invite me six months ago? I won't go because your dinner can turn out to be very expensive and I won't sell the country for a meal.' "

"Selling one's country" emerged as a collectively held concept. The ability of the "new poor" to resist class dislocation as well as the assault on citizenship conducted by the past military regime is one of the most valuable resources available for the consolidation of democracy.

The incorporation of those who have participated in the new social movements against the military in the transition to democracy constitutes perhaps the best assurance that informal labor relations will not be as perverse in the future as they have been in the past. Redistribution requires the consolidation of civil society as well as the participation of popular sectors in the political process. Only then will it be possible to put to rest the present false dichotomy between economic growth and equitable distribution.

Notes

The data on which this chapter is based were collected as part of a CIESU–Johns Hopkins University collaborative study of the urban informal sector in Uruguay, conducted with the support of the Tinker Foundation.

1. A detailed presentation of survey results is found in Portes, Blitzer, and Curtis 1986.

2. The following results are based on the CIESU-Hopkins study above. As part of this project, a representative survey of popular areas of Montevideo was conducted in 1983–84. Information was obtained on all adult members of seven hundred households drawn through a two-stage random sampling procedure with city blocks as primary sampling units.

3. Our study of the recycling industry included two additional subprojects: one centered on the processing of paper, and the second, on metals.

4. The personnel manager of a large exporting company described the advantages derived from the putting-out system in the following way: "An outworker can sew fifty pairs of uppers in the same time a factory employee can do thirty. Why? Because the former is in her own home, because she works on a piece rate, because the more she sews the larger the wage she gets. Factory workers don't care because no matter how many pairs they sew, they earn the same amount."

5. These are firms that had the largest daily output during the time of the study.

References

Allen, S. 1981. "Invisible Threads." *IDS Bulletin* 12.

Alonso, J. A. 1983. "The Domestic Clothing Workers in the Mexican Metropolis and Their Relation to Dependent Capitalism." Pp. 161–72 in J. Nash and M. P. Fernández-Kelly (eds.), *Women, Men, and the International Division of Labor.* Albany: State University of New York Press.

Benería, L. and M. Roldán. 1987. *The Crossroads of Class and Gender.* Chicago: University of Chicago Press.

Birbeck, C. 1978. "Self Employed Proletarians in an Informal Factory: The Case of Cali's Garbage Dump." *World Development* 6:1173–85.

Filgueira, C. and C. Geneletti. 1981. *Estratificación y Movilidad Ocupacional en América Latina*. Cuadernos de la CEPAL, no. 39. Santiago de Chile: United Nations.

Goddard, V. 1981. "The Leather Trade in the Bassi of Naples." *IDS Bulletin* 12.

Laenz, S. 1985. *Cambio Económico y Trabajo Femenino*. Serie Documentos Ocasionales, no. 5. Montevideo: GRECMU.

Landes, D. S. 1981. *The Unbound Prometheus: Technological Change and Industrial Development in Western Europe from 1750 to the Present*. Cambridge: Cambridge University Press.

Lovesio, B. 1986. "Las Penélopes Olvidadas: Artesanas o Asalariadas." In *Mujer y Trabajo en América Latina*. Montevideo: Editorial Banda Oriental.

Melgar, A. 1981. *Distribución del Ingreso en el Uruguay*. Cuadernos del CLAEH, no. 18. Montevideo: CLAEH.

Melgar, A. and A. Teja. 1985. *Participación de la Mujer en el Mercado de Trabajo e Ingresos Salariales Femeninos*. Serie Documentos Ocasionales, no. 5. Montevideo: GRECMU.

Moser, C. 1981. "Surviving in the Suburbios." *IDS Bulletin* 12.

Paiva Abreu, F. 1986. "Descentralización Productiva y Trabajo Femenino: Un Estudio de Caso en la Industria de la Confección en el Brasil." In *Mujer y Trabajo en América Latina*. Montevideo: Editorial Banda Oriental.

Peattie, L. 1981. "What Is to Be Done with the 'Informal Sector'? A Case Study of Shoe Manufacturers in Colombia." Working Paper. Massachusetts Institute of Technology, Department of City and Regional Planning, Cambridge. Mimeo.

Portes, A. 1983. "The Informal Sector: Definition, Controversy, and Relation to National Development." *Review* 7:151–74.

Portes, A., S. Blitzer, and J. Curtis. 1986. "The Urban Informal Sector in Uruguay: Its Internal Structure, Characteristics, and Effects." *World Development* 14:727–41.

Prates, A. 1983. "El Trabajo de la Mujer en una Epoca de Crisis (o Cuando se Pierde Ganando)." In *La Mujer en el Uruguay: Ayer y Hoy*. Montevideo: Editorial Banda Oriental.

PREALC. 1977. "La Búsqueda de Trabajo y los Mecanismos de Sobrevivencia de los Desocupados en el Gran Santiago." Document no. 117. Santiago de Chile.

Roldán, M. 1983. "Trabajo Industrial Domiciliario, Luchas por la Reproducción de la Familia Trabajadora y Subordinación Genérica." Working Paper. National University of México. Mimeo.

Schmukler, B. 1977. *Relaciones Actuales de Producción en Industrias Tradicionales Argentinas, Evolución de las Relaciones No-Capitalistas*. Estudios Sociales, no. 6. Buenos Aires: CEDES.

Wonsewer, I. and J. Notaro. 1981. "La Liberalización de los Precios y los Mercados y la Reducción y Reorientación de la Acción del Estado." Research Report. CEPAL IN/13. Santiago de Chile.

5 The Articulation of Formal and Informal Sectors in the Economy of Bogotá, Colombia

Mónica Lanzetta de Pardo and Gabriel Murillo Castaño, with Alvaro Triana Soto

Concerns over the growth of the informal sector have led to the study of diverse forms of noncapitalist production which emerge and reproduce as a response to adjustments in the process of accumulation both in central and peripheral countries. There is consensus that informalization is part of a strategy aimed at reducing the cost of capital reproduction under new historical conditions (Portes 1983).

The emergence and proliferation of informal relations are closely related to the prevalence of low wages (Ayala 1981). Even though wage labor is the principal form of employment in Colombian cities, insufficient levels of remuneration have led an increasing number of household members into independent income-earning activities. This survival strategy requires the pooling of informal income with earnings drawn from the formal sector. The process involves: "the articulation of non-capitalist and modern capitalist sectors, both at the level of the household and at the level of production of goods and services in the most backwards sectors. Goods and services thus produced are either consumed by workers themselves or integrated into modern production" (Rey de Marulanda and Ayala 1981).

Informal activities stemming from the survival needs of families are shaped by factors such as household composition, sex, age, kinship, life cycle, level of training, domestic power distribution and work ethic, among others. Therefore, a full understanding of informality must focus on the articulation of factors affecting productive activities and employment, on the one hand, and the reproduction of the labor force on the other.

The discussion below is based upon such a differentiation. Productive units were included within a *vertical perspective*. Our purpose, in that respect, was to understand how formal enterprises as well as small producers absorb informal labor in order to achieve higher levels of accumulation in the case of the former, and subsistence in the case of the latter. Households were observed from a *horizontal perspective* in order to assess the impact of reproductive processes of labor upon global economic behaviors.

Chapter 5 was translated by M. Patricia Fernández-Kelly.

The research upon which our findings are based aimed at studying informality from a microanalytic point of view as a complement to previous fieldwork conducted in urban and rural centers in Colombia (Kugler 1982; Murillo and Lanzetta 1984). Our findings were also compared with aggregate data provided by the National Department of Statistics (DANE).

Methodology

Six sectors of Bogotá's economy were selected for study: construction, public transportation, wholesale marketing, the garment industry, footwear, and auto repair. The first three activities were clustered together because of their importance in the creation of jobs and revenues. The study of a second group, formed by the remaining industries, permitted an in-depth probe into small productive units. In this chapter, we focus attention only on construction, transportation, the garment industry, and auto repair.

The vertical study of relations between formal and informal units was guided by the following hypotheses:

1. There is articulation and interdependence between the formal and informal sectors regarding type of activity, employment potential, and generation of revenues.
2. It is possible to determine the specific points of articulation between both types of activities.
3. Subcontracting is a widespread mechanism joining both sectors.
4. There is constant interoccupational and intraoccupational mobility in both sectors.

The horizontal study of survival strategies of poor households was guided, in turn, by these hypotheses:

1. A large proportion of household members in the lower economic strata participate in the labor market.
2. The global earnings of these families are derived mostly from participation in the informal sector.
3. The members of these households move intermittently from formal to informal employment.
4. Unremunerated subsistence activities are an important aspect of family survival strategies.
5. There is a close relationship between outside earnings and consumption patterns, which explains the character of qualitative and quantitative deficits in standards of living.

As part of the study, we conducted in-depth interviews of ten households in which the family head was employed in each of the six economic activities mentioned earlier. Each of these sixty case studies was elaborated on the basis of descriptive information regarding individual workers and their families and labor histories. For additional background, we conducted interviews with other relevant actors in each sector, including government officials, union leaders, suppliers of raw materials, and distributors and customers.

The Socioeconomic Context of Informality in Bogotá

According to the 1984 National Survey of Households conducted by DANE, one-third of the economically active population (EAP) of Bogotá is employed in occupations generally identified as informal—unremunerated family workers, domestic servants, and the self-employed. Government employees—whose occupations are defined as formal—represent 12 percent and employers, about 4 percent. Half of the EAP is formed by wage workers whose position in the economic structure is ambiguous. DANE defines informal work as a labor modality performed at least to some extent outside state regulations regarding employment. In contrast, formal sector employment is characterized by stable labor situations in which compensation is determined on the basis of legally approved shifts, overtime payments, and the provision of social security benefits for all workers. By definition, the formal sphere thus offers access to types of social security which are not available to informal workers.

Table 5.1 contains a summary of data regarding the extent of informality in Bogotá on the basis of more refined criteria based on social security coverage rather than specific occupational positions. As shown in the table, close to one-third of wage workers are unprotected by the social security system; comparable figures in the occupational category traditionally associated with the informal sector are about 90 percent. On the basis of these data, we estimate that the primary occupations of close to half (46%) of the urban EAP are informal. The estimate is conservative because it is based on workers who lack any social security protection and thus assigns to the formal sector those with even minimal coverage.

The analysis of aggregate information, not presented here, shows an average of 4.6 persons per household in Bogotá. This figure is consistent with other demographic trends indicating the reduction in the number of members per domestic unit as a consequence of accelerated urbanization since the 1940s. On the other hand, households with at least one informal worker are significantly larger than the average. As shown in table 5.2, over 55 percent of Bogotá's households had at least one informal worker in 1984, and close to 20 percent had two or more.

Table 5.3 presents the distribution by economic sector of the different categories of occupations in which informal workers concentrate. The majority of self-employed workers are in services (commerce, restaurants, hotels, etc.) but there are also sizable proportions in manufacturing and construction. Approximately 60 percent of unremunerated family workers are involved in commerce, restaurants, and hotels; street vending is known to be a widespread activity among members of this group. An additional 22 percent participates in

Table 5.1 Economically Active Population (EAP) in Bogotá, by Social Security Affiliation

| | Mostly Informal | | |
| | Unremunerated Family Worker (%) | Domestic Worker (%) | Self-employed Worker (%) |
Affiliation to Social Security			
Social security benefits	4.4	6.5	5.5
Optional medical insurance only	1.1	4.7	3.0
Unemployment compensation only	0.3	0.2	0.5
Not affiliated	93.6	87.2	87.8
No data available	0.6	1.4	3.1
Total	100.0	100.0	100.0
Percentage of EAP	3.0	5.5	25.4
	Mostly Formal		
	Laborer or Private Worker (%)	Government Employee (%)	Employer (%)
Social security benefits	58.2	82.0	19.2
Optional medical insurance only	2.3	5.4	9.4
Unemployment compensation only	1.5	8.3	1.3
Not affiliated	32.7	0.0	67.3
No data available	5.1	4.3	2.8
Total	100.0	100.0	100.0
Percentage of EAP	50.0	12.1	3.9

Source: DANE, *National Survey of Households,* September 1984.

manufacturing, a figure that reflects the significant dynamism acquired by small-scale industry employing family labor.

The data in table 5.4 indicate that about two-thirds of wage workers and of the self-employed are males and that their representation among unpaid family workers is only slightly lower. This last figure is probably due to the high

Table 5.2 Distribution of Informal Workers, by Household

Number of Informal Workers	Number of Households in Sample	Relative Frequency (%)
0	3,230	44.9
1	2,673	37.2
2 or more	1,288	17.9
Total	7,191	100.0

Source: DANE, *National Survey of Households,* September 1984.

Table 5.3 Distribution of Occupational Categories Including Informal Workers, by Economic Sector

Sector	Unremunerated Family Worker (%)	Domestic Worker (%)	Self-employed Worker (%)	Laborer or Private Worker (%)
Agriculture	1.4	0.0	1.2	1.2
Mining	0.0	0.0	0.0	0.5
Manufacturing	22.4	0.0	16.4	34.3
Electricity, gas, water	0.0	0.0	0.1	0.3
Construction	3.3	0.0	10.6	7.5
Commerce, restaurants, hotels	60.5	0.0	38.6	21.5
Transportation and communications	1.9	0.0	6.8	7.5
Financial establishments	1.1	0.0	6.3	11.8
Services	9.4	100.0	20.0	15.4
Total	100.0	100.0	100.0	100.0
Percentage of EAP	3.0	5.5	25.4	50.0

Source: DANE, *National Survey of Households,* September 1984.

number of male children in this category. On the other hand, domestic service is overwhelmingly a female occupation. This finding is consistent with the historical and contemporary trends found in other Latin American countries (see Benería, this volume).

Age is another factor affecting labor market insertion (see table 5.5). Participation in the informal sector is more prevalent among youths between fourteen and nineteen years old and among individuals older than fifty. These findings are comparable to those recorded in Guadalajara and in Montevideo (Roberts, this volume; Portes, Blitzer, and Curtis 1986; Fortuna and Prates, this volume). The very young and the aged do not form large percentages of the EAP, and they are thus overrepresented in the informal economy. The need to start earning money at an early age and to remain in the labor market for longer periods is associated with extreme levels of poverty and vulnerability because of lack of access to social security benefits. Informality is less frequent but still significant among those between the ages of twenty and forty.

Table 5.4 Distribution of Occupational Categories Including Informal Workers, by Sex

	Self-employed (%)	Domestic Worker (%)	Unremunerated Family Worker (%)	Laborer or Private Worker (%)
Men	68.1	3.7	62.2	63.96
Women	31.9	96.3	37.8	36.04
Total	100.0	100.0	100.0	100.0

Source: DANE, *National Survey of Households,* September 1984.

Table 5.5 Labor Market Insertion by Age

Age	Informal Workers[1] (%)	Formal Workers (%)
−14	1.6	0.1
15–19	12.4	5.3
20–29	30.7	41.0
30–39	22.9	29.5
40–49	15.9	15.4
50–59	10.7	6.9
60 or +	5.8	1.8
Total	100.0	100.0
Percentage of EAP	46.4	50.3

Source: DANE, *National Survey of Households,* March 1984.

[1]Includes unremunerated family workers; domestic workers; self-employed workers, except those in professional specialties; and workers in firms with 10 or fewer employees.

The data in table 5.6 also indicate that informality in Bogotá is more frequent among those with low levels of instruction. Over half of informally employed workers complete only elementary school; on the other hand, close to two-thirds of formal employees attained secondary schooling or higher. Note, however, that a sizable proportion of informal workers also attained advanced education. Hence, secondary or even university schooling is no guarantee of avoiding insertion into the informal labor market.

Recent migrants to Bogotá are overrepresented in the informal sector relative to natives. In table 5.7, the relevant data are percentaged across rows in order to show the composition of the EAP according to length of residence in the city. It is evident that informal employment declines monotonically with residence in Bogotá. Recent migrants tend to work in construction and industry if they are men, and in services if they are women. Formal employment tends to follow exactly the opposite trend, increasing with time in the city. Interestingly,

Table 5.6 Labor Market Insertion by Schooling Level

Schooling Level	Informal Workers[1] (%)	Formal Workers (%)
None	4.5	0.9
Elementary	47.7	25.5
High school	40.8	47.5
University	7.0	26.1
Total	100.0	100.0

Source: DANE, *National Survey of Households,* March 1984.

[1]See definition in table 5.5, note 1.

Table 5.7 Labor Market Insertion by Length of Residence in Bogotá

Years of Residence in Bogotá	Informal Workers[1] (%)	Formal Workers (%)	Employers (%)	Total (%)	As Percentage of EAP
Less than 1	70.3	27.3	2.4	100.0	2.4
1–2	56.2	42.9	0.9	100.0	4.3
3–5	47.2	51.6	1.2	100.0	6.7
More than 5	44.4	52.5	3.1	100.0	86.6

Source: DANE, *National Survey of Households,* March 1984.

[1]See definition in table 5.5, note 1.

the category of employers included in the last column of the table does not follow a similar trend, although employers are most numerous among natives and older migrants.

The data in table 5.8 provide evidence of the imperfect but strong correlation between informal employment and poverty. About a fourth of the working population earns less than the minimum wage; almost everyone in this situation is working informally. The association is close enough to identify earnings below the legal minimum as a criterion of informal labor, at least in the Colombian case. In contrast, formal workers monopolize the segment of the labor force which receives the equivalent of more than two minimum wages. However, about 20 percent of those in this segment are also employed informally. These results say that, while most poorly remunerated individuals are informal workers, not everyone participating in this sector is poor. The finding is also congruent with those in other Latin American cities (see Roberts, this volume; Portes, Blitzer, and Curtis 1986).

Census data are not available regarding the formal or informal origins of total earnings for low-income households. However, the existing information indicates a tendency for large families to be part of the informal sector. For example, 51 percent of households of four or less do not include informal workers. In contrast, 65 percent of households of six persons, and 75 percent of

Table 5.8 Labor Market Insertion by Earnings

Earnings	Informal Workers[1] (%)	Formal Workers (%)	Employers (%)	Total (%)	As Percentage of EAP
Less than minimum wage[2]	92.0	5.5	2.5	100.0	26.0
1–2 minimum wages	33.0	66.1	0.9	100.0	48.1
More than 2 minimum wages	22.9	70.3	6.8	100.0	25.9

Source: DANE, *National Survey of Households,* March 1984.

[1]See definition in table 5.5, note 1.
[2]Monthly minimum wage for urban workers in Colombia in 1984 was Colombian $10,865 (U.S. $54).

those of eight, contain at least one informal worker. An explanation for this trend is that large families contain more potential labor force participants and also require higher incomes, thus increasing the probability that one or more will be employed informally. However, an alternative explanation is that low-income individuals—many of whom are employed informally—tend to create or join income-pooling units for survival. Although the two explanations are not mutually exclusive, the latter probably comes closer to the actual dynamics of the process as indicated by our own field study, summarized next.

The basic finding to be drawn from census figures is the widespread character of informality, no matter how measured. As seen above, close to half of the working population of Bogotá is employed informally. In addition, 55 percent of all domestic units in the city include at least one informal worker. Finally, 35 percent of all heads of household are employed in this sector. Clearly, there is nothing tangential or marginal about informality, which is, instead, at the very core of the city's economy. Its significance for households and firms is explored in greater detail below.

Reproduction of the Labor Force: Case Studies

The domestic units in our sample had an average of 5.7 members, of whom 2.7 were workers. Reasons offered for this relatively high rate of labor market participation were the impossibility of economic survival on the basis of head-of-household earnings alone. Escalating costs of staple goods have led to a deterioration of standards of living among the poor. For many, the solution has been small businesses employing family labor. This explains why we found more workers per household than the average in those family units running small footwear and garment shops.

On the average, 80 percent of total earnings among the households studied originated in informal sources. For these households, improving standards of living generally meant sending additional members into the labor market. Another factor affecting household earnings is the life cycle. The family units studied whose members were involved in informal garment and transportation enterprises were generally mature in age. Heads of household were older than fifty, and children were old enough to contribute some income. This situation contrasts with households in which heads were informal construction and footwear shop workers and, in particular, with those whose heads worked in the city's wholesale market. Heads of households in the last category were much younger, averaging only thirty-five years of age. A possible explanation for this contrast may have to do with the physical effort, and thus the age, required by different types of informal work. Another explanation is the skill requirements for entry into the different sectors—lower in construction and market hauling, and higher in use and care of vehicles and garment production.

One of our research questions was the extent to which workers combine formal and informal activities in order to improve earnings. Our findings indicate that only 2.5 percent of all workers in the sample participate in both sectors. This is in agreement with the conclusions reached by other studies (see Fortuna and Prates, this volume). Factors such as the length of work shifts, characteristics of urban transportation, the limited availability of stable employment, and the difficult conditions under which household work must be done make it difficult for people to hold more than one job (Ayala 1981).

In addition, our study indicated that, by and large, households in the sample do not get much help from other families in the same kinship group. Only a few reciprocal exchanges between parents and offspring or relatives were found. However, the families in the survey declared that they sent remittances sporadically to relatives in other cities or towns. A larger study on family earnings in the four main Colombian cities found that 56 percent of homes lacking adequate income did not receive any reciprocal help (Ayala 1981). These findings contrast in significant ways with those reported elsewhere which emphasize the importance of reciprocal assistance networks among low-income families (Lomnitz 1977; Hardy 1985).

Unremunerated subsistence activities such as housecleaning, washing, ironing, sewing, grocery shopping, carrying water, and buying fuel take up large amounts of time, especially when public services are absent. Wives are generally responsible for these tasks, which grow in number as income shrinks. Children who work and contribute some income to the household are generally exempt from such work, although daughters tend to participate to some degree. Men perform subsistence work only when it is labeled "masculine," as in the case of home building.

Households studied spent approximately U.S. $73 a month for food on the average. Considering that the average number of persons per household is 5.7, the expediture per capita was only about $13, an amount entirely insufficient for an adequate diet. Qualitative and quantitative nutritional deficits are, therefore, another common characteristic of these low-income households. Women reported buying food in neighborhood stores, at popular fairs, and in supermarkets. Thus, they pay higher prices for staples than those who buy food in cooperatives or government-administered stores, to which they lack access because these stores are restricted to formal sector employees. Nevertheless, buying in neighborhoood stores can be advantageous at times, because these stores give credit and allow the purchase of basic items in small units.

Housing represents another serious problem. Most families interviewed do not own their homes. They pay rents averaging U.S. $43 a month. Because most families inhabit tenements where many other families live, they must share services. Crowding and unsanitary conditions are common features of life in the tenements. On the other hand, workers with the lowest earnings—

market haulers and low-skilled construction workers—tend to live in shan-tytowns in the urban periphery where services are not available. Shacks in these areas are built after illegal squatting or purchase of a lot from "pirate" ur-banizers. A positive side effect is that, not having to pay rent and service fees, shantytown dwellers are able to meet, albeit precariously, other basic needs.

Households in our sample did not lack all basic services. For example, government-managed companies provide water, electricity, and sewage to 80 percent of them. Thus, these households have at least some infrastructure allowing them a foothold into a modern life style. The remaining 20 percent lives in the peripheral shantytowns where regular urban infrastructure is weak or absent. These households must supply their own improvised services by illegally tapping nearby water sources and electricity lines. The inexistence of satisfactory garbage removal is one of the most important problems faced by the poor, wherever they live. On the other hand, public transportation, lighting, schools, and parks tend to be distributed along the same gradient described above, that is, satisfactory for those within the urbanized perimeter and insuffi-cient or absent for those in the periphery.

In synthesis, our field studies of informal workers' households support the hypotheses concerning the importance of informal earnings for the re-production of these units and the extensive participation of household members in this segment of the economy. In the absence of alternatives, entry of addi-tional members into the informal sector is about the only means available to improve household incomes. The study did not support expectations concern-ing widespread sharing of resources among low-income households, nor those positing simultaneous participation of workers in formal and informal ac-tivities. Finally, our data point to the importance and magnitude of unremune-rated subsistence activities, performed mostly by women, in the process of reproduction and offer insights into the spectrum of qualitative and quantitative deficits faced by members of this population.

The Articulation of Formal and Informal Sectors in Particular Economic Sectors

In this section, we present findings from the second part of the study, which focused on the vertical articulation of informal activities with firms in the regulated sector of the economy. Two phenomena observed in the course of field research will be discussed. The first links formal enterprises to informal labor and productive processes. Our focus here is on the construction and public transportation sectors. As will be discussed, formal units in each make use of informal labor to support high levels of capital accumulation. The second phenomenon is represented by the cases of garment manufacture and auto repair, in which small informal units are more autonomous and links with the formal sector are less direct.

Economic Processes Associated with Large Formal Enterprises

Construction

The construction industry encompasses an extensive spectrum of activities and social relations. Nonetheless, the study of the articulation between formal and informal sectors in this area was narrowed down to the limits imposed by public policy, which, since 1982, has emphasized the construction of popular housing.

The construction industry hires men exclusively. Their levels of schooling do not surpass six years on the average. Experience is the determinant of upward occupational mobility in this sector. As age advances, occupational advancement can occur as a result of more knowledge of particular skills. Young men are often employed as helpers and apprentices; older workers may become contractors and subcontractors after a long labor trajectory, a shift that leads to better earnings.

Our study led to the identification of a gradual transition from strictly formal and direct contracting schemes to indirect, informalized patterns of employment. We found three levels of direct subcontracting.

The first level includes contracts to specialized professionals; contractors are put on the firm's payroll for a specific period of time.

The second level is characterized by contracts with individuals whose level of technical knowledge and specialization derives from direct practical experience in construction. Payments are agreed upon by the parties on a case-by-case basis, and the exchange is treated as a professional service, not entailing legal labor responsibilities by the firm to the contractor. Such agreements include accident insurance policies limited only to fire damage in the construction area. Thus, workers hired according to this modality face numerous worksite risks.

On the third level, large numbers of workers are hired directly to perform the most difficult and hazardous construction activities. Written contracts are not part of these transactions. Instead, verbal agreements and personal relations based on kinship, or *compadrazgo,* serve as the basis for these labor exchanges. Contractors agree verbally on the type of work to be performed, the length of the shifts, and the amount of payments. Firms assume little additional responsibility for these workers; they may receive some protection against work-related accidents, but no extensive medical coverage either for themselves or their families. Workers are subjected to high rates of occupational instability given the short duration of contracts and the constant shift of tasks, particularly among helpers and apprentices. The latter often seek new jobs as a result of the harshness of tasks assigned to them.

Public Transportation

As in the case of construction, public transportation work in Bogotá is predominantly a male occupation. In this sector, most workers have some high-school instruction and a few have attained a university education. Older men in this sector tend to have lower educational levels, while those younger than thirty have generally completed secondary school. Workers who own vehicles have longer previous experience as wage laborers or have spent a long time as paid transport operators.

There were two kinds of transportation workers in the sample studied. First, there were those who received regular wages as part of a formal permanent contract. This allows them access to social benefits and privileges according to the labor code. They are remunerated on the basis of percentages of daily passengers transported and, in some cases, receive an additional bonus for a number of round trips completed. Second, owner-operators are exempt from many of the requirements imposed on wage workers. By choice, they do not affiliate with the social security system and avoid declaring total earnings to official authorities. These informal entrepreneurs protect themselves by purchasing limited accident insurance policies and by participating in mutual assistance and other cooperative exchanges.

In general, public transportation in Bogotá is characterized by the absence of regular working shifts; widely varying payments; overwork on nights, Sundays, and holidays; and irregular work contracts. Small owner-operators attempt to circumvent regulations in order to maximize use of their vehicles and profits; owners of large fleets also seek to bypass formal labor contracts, while their workers find ways to increase low wages through under-the-counter practices. Results of this hybrid and poorly regulated system are congestion, undependable service, and unsafe vehicles. These problems will continue to exist as long as informality prevails, under the veneer of official regulation, in this sector of the urban economy.

Small Semiautonomous Enterprises

Garment Manufacturing

The findings of our study in this sector are consistent with those reported for other cities, both in Latin America and in the United States (Sassen-Koob 1984; Roberts, this volume). Women predominate in garment assembly. Shop owners tend to be older men, and the majority are heads of households. Educational levels among workers are very low, with the vast majority having only elementary schooling. Women workers tend to be young, and their skills were mostly learned through informal apprenticeship in the shops and through instruction by kin and friends.

Small garment shops make widespread use of family labor. In those that hire outside workers, the typical form of payment is by piece rate, and no benefits are offered. Owners claim that piece-rate payments can be higher than in formal industries, thus compensating for the absence of other benefits. Highly skilled and reliable employees are customarily given annual bonuses amounting to one month of average payments. Depending on the size of shops, some tasks are shifted to the homes of workers. This situation leads to the familiar overlap between the spheres of production and reproduction among women working in this sector (see Ybarra, this volume).

Auto Repair

This is a predominantly male occupation. The occupational histories of workers show previous links to related activities such as transportation. Shop owners do not usually have comprehensive knowledge of all aspects of the business and must, therefore, rely on subcontractors. The prevailing educational level among owners is secondary school. Wage workers are generally younger than owners, and they tend to have fewer years of schooling. Some housewives participate in auto repair, particularly in upholstery work or in areas such as sales and accounting.

The types of subcontracting in auto repair which depend on the skill levels of workers involved include (1) verbal contracts with technicians who reach agreement with owners as to the value of their work. They generally keep between 50 percent and 70 percent of the proceeds while the remainder goes to the owner. The relationship does not involve fringe benefits or any other type of insurance for the contractor; (2) verbal agreements with unskilled temporal workers who perform specific tasks under the direction of skilled operatives and who are paid by piece rate. As in the first case, they do not receive any social security benefits; and (3) a mix of written and unwritten contracts with permanent unskilled workers who receive monthly or biweekly payments and some benefits but no social security.

Because auto repair shops are very small, they are unable to service large numbers of vehicles. Thus, they try to finish as many jobs as possible on a day-to-day basis. The type of repair agreed upon with customers depends on the availability of skilled personnel at any particular time. For the same reason, many repair shops illegally use part of the adjoining streets to do their job.

The general characteristics of many small-scale informal enterprises—represented in our study by garment manufacturing and auto repair shops—can be summarized as follows:

1. Informal enterprises tend to be located in middle- or low-income neighborhoods. They generally occupy rented quarters, and there is a high degree of overlap between place of residence and place of work, particularly in garment production.
2. The quality of goods and services is less than satisfactory, due to the need

to save as much as possible on the costs of inputs, including raw materials and technology.

3. When small businesses survive over long periods of time, they tend to diversify production as a result of the convergence of factors such as the accumulation of experience, the formation of relatively stable markets, and the acquisition of modern machinery.

4. Only a small number of small-business owners and managers can handle adequate objective indicators of costs of production. In addition, the majority does not keep accounting records.

5. Many informal enterprises cater exclusively to consumer needs of the low-income population. In the sectors studied, there was little evidence of production of intermediate goods under contract for larger firms. Sales were generally made directly by business owners.

6. Small businesses tend to hire both unskilled and skilled workers experienced in a particular task or process. Tasks and remunerations are agreed upon verbally; schedules for completion are generally vague. Employers see the main advantages of informal hiring as the avoidance of social security payments and the possibility of dismissing workers without incurring legal penalties.

Unlike garment production and auto repair, other sectors of informal enterprise—exemplified by the construction industry—tend to operate under contract for larger formal firms. There is, therefore, a plurality of modes of articulation between types of firms, modes of labor market insertion, and household economic strategies. In the absence of minimally paid employment in the regulated economy, individuals and households devise alternative options that include setting up small family businesses or working for others on a casual basis.

Labor hired informally benefits all employers, whether large or small, because it facilitates flexibility of production arrangements and thus makes possible market survival. To the extent that they are viable, informal enterprises also benefit households insofar as they permit survival of their members. When they produce directly for the market, such enterprises also contribute to the reproduction of other poor households by making available low-cost goods and services. In an economy of scarcity such as that of Bogotá, the dynamics of the informal sector thus furnish a central element for explaining both the survival of the formally unemployed and the continuing viability of capital accumulation in diverse sectors of the urban economy.

Conclusions

Our study did not uncover the extensive articulation of informal activities with large-scale formal enterprises reported elsewhere (see Benería, this volume; Fortuna and Prates, this volume). In part, this result may be due to the selection of economic sectors that with the exception of garments and construction, tend to involve production of informal goods and services directly for the market. Yet, even among garment producers, we found relatively weak linkages with larger formal firms. In contrast with those studies that have emphasized the significance of subcontracting, our results are interpretable as highlighting the significance of a second mode of articulation with the formal economy, namely, that in which informal activities play a central role in facilitating the reproduction of the urban working class by providing, simultaneously, access to (casual) income sources and to low-cost goods and services.

Our analysis of aggregate statistical data indicates how extensive this role is, both in the incidence of informal income earning among the majority of urban households in Bogotá and in the presence of informal workers in practically every sector of the urban economy. In terms of Capecchi's typology of informality (this volume), our results clearly indicate that Bogotá's case is one determined primarily by survival needs of working-class households and, only secondarily, by the interest of large-scale firms in decentralizing production to low-cost suppliers. Prospects for the development of a dynamic, technologically advanced small-scale sector on the basis of existing informal enterprise are remote, if not entirely absent. Our case thus represents another instance in which, "left to the market," informal units retain only a precarious space as reservoirs of low-wage labor and providers of low-quality consumer goods. In the absence of sustained outside support in the form of training programs, low-cost credit, and protected markets, it is most unlikely that Bogotá's informal sector will evolve out of its present condition.

References

Ayala, U. 1981. *El Empleo en las Grandes Ciudades*. Document no. 065. Bogotá: CEDE.

Departamento Administrativo Nacional de Estadística (DANE) September 1984, March 1984. *National Survey of Households*. Nos. 43, 44. Bogotá: DANE.

Hardy, C. 1985. "Estrategia Organizada de Subsistencia: Los Sectores Populares Frente a sus Necesidades en Chile." Document no. 41. Programa Economía del Trabajo, Academia de Humanismo Cristiano, Santiago de Chile.

Kugler, B. 1982. "Estudios, Programas y Políticas del Sector Informal Urbano en Colombia." Bogotá: International Labor Organization.

Lomnitz, L. A. 1977. *Networks and Marginality: Life in a Mexican Shantytown*. New York: Academic Press.

Murillo, G. and M. Lanzetta de Pardo. 1984. "Articulation of the Formal and Informal Sectors in Bogotá: An Empirical Study." Paper presented at seminar, The Urban Informal Economy, The Johns Hopkins University, Baltimore, June 8–10.

Portes, A. 1983. "The Informal Sector: Definition, Controversy, and Relation to National Development." *Review*.

Portes, A., S. Blitzer, and J. Curtis. 1986. "The Urban Informal Sector in Uruguay: Its Internal Structure, Characteristics, and Effects." *World Development* 14:727–41.

Rey de Marulanda, N. and U. Ayala. 1981. *Empleo y Pobreza*. Bogotá: CEDE, Universidad de los Andes.

Sassen-Koob, S. 1984. "The New Labor Demand in Global Cities." In M. P. Smith (ed.), *Cities in Transformation*. Beverly Hills, Calif.: Sage Publications.

6 Miami's Two Informal Sectors

Alex Stepick

This chapter examines informality in Miami,[1] Florida. It describes extensive informal activities that escape government regulation or violate labor laws (see Portes 1983; Portes and Sassen-Koob 1987), and that have expanded notably in the past twenty-five years. Perhaps Miami's largest informal activity is the importation and distribution of illegal drugs. Because of the clandestine and often violent character of this activity, however, research in this area is difficult, and this chapter does not focus on illegal drugs or the related area of money laundering. Instead, it examines Miami's two more distinct informal sectors, one closely linked with the broader economy and the other mostly isolated from it. The existence and growth of each informal sector is attributable to both immigration and racism. Cuban immigration contributed to the establishment of the informal sector linked to the broader economy, while Haitian immigration accounted for the creation of an isolated informal sector. Ethnic antagonism and the broader society's rejection of immigrants formed part of the foundation of each. I present below a description of the evolution of Miami's overall economy, followed by synopses of Cuban and Haitian immigration to the area. The bulk of the chapter consists of descriptions of informal activities, both those integrated within the broader economy and those isolated from it.[2]

Miami History

Typical of Sun Belt cities, Miami does not possess deep historical roots.[3] Miami was only a trading post when a partner of John D. Rockefeller, Henry M. Flagler, began developing its tourism potential in the 1890s. By the 1920s, the area had become a thriving center of tourism supplemented by a land boom in real estate and permanent migration, primarily from the northeastern United States. This population pattern continued through the 1930s in spite of the Great Depression. During World War II, the military found Miami's climate ideal for training purposes, and the area became dotted with airfields and inundated with young recruits. By 1940, the population of Miami and Dade County had grown to over a quarter of a million, but Miami was the least industrialized metropolitan area in the United States with only 3.3 percent of the labor force in factory jobs.

During the postwar era, Miami received sustained inmigration from the Northeast, touching off a building boom that made construction one of the local economy's largest sectors. A population increase of almost 85 percent between 1940 and 1950 initiated broader changes in the economy; trade, finance, service, and manufacturing all grew while tourism declined from about 35 percent of the area's product in 1940 to about 10 percent in 1979. Manufacturing in the immediate postwar period was primarily small-scale and focused on the local market. By the 1970s, new industries in plastics, electronic equipment, aircraft parts, and medical technology shifted the focus to national and international markets.

Miami has been characterized by some as the vortex of the Caribbean and even of the entire Latin American economy (Garreau 1981; Levine 1985). This role is rooted in the arrival of hundreds of thousands of Cubans, which began in the 1960s. It is reflected in the increasing importance in the local economy of transportation, import and export businesses, and diverse services, particularly international finance.

The transportation industry has grown significantly in the postwar era, but most especially during the past twenty years. Miami International Airport is the ninth busiest in the world in terms of passengers and the sixth largest in air cargo tonnage. In the United States, the Miami airport ranks second only to New York's Kennedy Airport in international passengers and cargo. About 160,000 workers, or one-fifth of the labor force in Miami, are directly or indirectly employed in airport and aviation activities. In addition, the Port of Miami provides a base for over eighty-five steamship companies and is the largest cruise-ship port in the world.

In the 1970s, Miami became a service-centered economy, focused especially on international finance. Multinational corporations began to locate their Latin American headquarters in Miami, and banks followed closely behind. Between 1970 and 1980, the most outstanding occupational change was the growth in executive and managerial occupations—from 9 percent to over 12 percent of the labor force. With this growth came also a 6 percent increase in clerical workers. Lumping the two categories together, there was a growth of about 10 percent in white-collar office jobs between 1970 and 1980. Finance, insurance, and real estate—the FIRE sector—also increased its participation in the labor force by about 2 percent in the same period. Finally, by 1982 Miami was the nation's second-largest international banking center (Mohl 1983, 76).

The area also has the largest free trade zone in the United States; export-import companies can store, process, manufacture, assemble, display, or re-export goods from abroad without paying tariffs. During the decline of Latin American economies which began in the mid-1970s, foreigners invested in Florida on an unprecedented scale. Most of the investment has been in Miami's real estate market, construction, manufacturing, retail and wholesale trade, transportation services, insurance, and banking. A substantial portion of the new capital is believed to come from illegal drug operations. From its earliest days as a tourist playground, Miami attracted gamblers, bookies, and gangsters. Today it also attracts drug dealers. Overall, Miami's economy has evolved from a strong reliance on tourism and retirement to a broader-based primarily service economy increasingly tied to Latin America. Manufacturing has never had much importance in the area, while construction has had continuing significance because of the constant population growth.

The Role of Immigration

A good portion of Miami's economic growth and particularly that which depends on relations with Latin America has been attributed to the immigration of Cubans into Miami (Jorge and Moncarz 1980). Immigration has played a central role in promoting local economic growth. This chapter attempts to demonstrate, however, that much of that growth has been underwritten by the expansion of an informal economy incorporating low-wage immigrant workers. This section briefly describes the two major immigrant flows—Cubans and Haitians—and their overall economic condition. The following section details the informal activities that have arisen as a result of the presence of these two groups.

 The original population growth of Miami was not due to large influxes of foreign immigration. It is fundamentally unlike the other U.S. cities described in this volume, the New York metropolitan area (Sassen-Koob) and the Los Angeles–San Diego area (Fernández-Kelly and García), both of which have long-standing dependencies on immigrant labor. Not until recently have immigrants played a central role in Miami's economy.

 In the early days, at the turn of the century, Bahamians provided the local unskilled labor. They outnumbered black Americans, who came to Miami primarily from northern Florida and Georgia. Significant immigration, however, did not begin until the early 1960s. Cuban refugees began arriving in large numbers in the 1960s following the failure of the Bay of Pigs invasion. The flow has been largely one-way. Once Cubans come to Miami, few return. The U.S. government encouraged and aided the flow by providing special immigration status and federal aid. While substantial numbers of Cubans settled in New York and New Jersey, Miami was the preferred destination of the vast majority, making Cubans the city's most visible ethnic group. Their numbers were considerably increased by the Mariel boatlift of 1980, which brought about 125,000 Cubans to the United States, the majority of whom also settled in Miami. By 1985, there were at least 750,000 Hispanics in the area, approximately 40 percent of the entire metropolitan population (Dade County Planning Department 1987).

 Cubans have been an extraordinarily successful immigrant group.[4] For every measure of family income, Cubans score higher than the U.S. Hispanic population and only slightly below the total U.S. population (Pérez 1986, 9). The bases for this success are multiple, but one of the Cuban community's outstanding characteristics is its peculiar form of economic adaptation, the enclave economy (see Wilson and Portes 1980; Portes 1981; Portes and Bach 1985, chap. 6; Houg and Portes 1980). Nearly 15 percent of Miami Cubans who came in the past decade are self-employed and over one-half of the most recent Mariel arrivals work in Cuban-owned firms.[5]

The Cuban community has a number of advantages in forming ethnic businesses. First, Cubans were welcomed warmly by the U.S. government and benefited from general public support. Even more important, many came from the middle and upper classes of Cuba, and their families owned, or they themselves had worked in, businesses before arriving in the United States.

Their timing was also fortunate. As a Sun Belt city, Miami expanded throughout the 1960s and 1970s. Because of the presence of both Cubans and relocated northerners, housing, condominium, and office construction boomed. The refugees arrived in Miami just as transportation links to Latin America were expanding. They self-consciously and effectively utilized their cultural background to grab a share of the rapidly expanding Latin business. In the early 1970s, Cubans first gained some influence in the world of local finance by becoming vice-presidents and chief loan officers of several banks. Within a few years, Cuban banks began to appear. Both steps eased the would-be entrepreneur's access to capital. These institutions were willing to assume ostensibly greater risks in loaning to Cubans, on the basis of their past business reputation in Cuba.

All of these factors combined to encourage exile entrepreneurship. Cuban enterprises have grown from just over nine hundred in 1967 to about twenty thousand presently. These Cuban businesses are concentrated in services (35%), retail (28%), manufacturing (11%), and construction (9%). Between 1969 and 1977, the number of manufacturing firms nearly doubled, and construction firms tripled. By the early 1970s, Cuban-owned construction companies were putting up at least 35 percent of all Dade County's new buildings (Portes and Bach 1985, 89; Díaz-Briquets 1984), and by the mid 1980s they were erecting more than half.

But only a minority of Cubans are entrepreneurs. Most are wage laborers. Cuban women, for example, have provided a large, low-wage labor force that helped maintain the garment industry in Miami while it declined in other parts of the United States. Indeed, the presence of a large, low-wage work force greatly contributed to the success of Cuban businesses (Peterson and Maidique 1986; Pérez 1986). As indicated in table 6.1, nearly one-third of the most recent Cuban arrivals work in informal enterprises and a similar percentage are employed in Cuban-owned formal enclave firms.[6]

The Haitian experience in Miami contrasts starkly with that of the Cubans.[7] Rather than being welcome, they have experienced rejection at every turn. The U.S. government has conducted a resolute and consistent policy of discouraging their arrival and encouraging their return to Haiti.[8] Although boat arrivals in south Florida total less than one-fifth the number of Haitians in New York, they have been the object of much publicity. The first Haitian boat arrived in Miami in 1963; the second did not come until 1973, and it was not until 1977 that Haitians began arriving regularly. Between 1977 and 1981, between 50,000 and 70,000 Haitians arrived by boat in Miami. Another 5,000 to 10,000 came by airplane, and a smaller number resettled in Miami after living in New York, Montreal, or some other northern city.

Those moving from the North are likely to have better occupational skills and to be easily absorbed into the local economy. The others, however, have had more difficulty. As shown in table 6.1, Haitian unemployment is nearly 60 percent, more than three times the figure for the Miami population.[9] Less than 1 percent report being self-employed and even fewer report working for other Haitians. Of the Haitian refugees in Miami who do manage to find work, almost half work for non-Haitians in dead-end secondary sector jobs, and another third work in informal enterprises. While a small Haitian business community has emerged, it compares poorly with the Cuban ethnic economy. Sales are low, the businesses employ few workers beyond the owners themselves, and the rate of failure is very high.

In sum, Miami has a short and unique history of incorporating immigrants. Unlike the immigrants to other U.S. cities described in this volume, Miami's immigrants have not encountered a well-developed industry with a historical reliance on low-wage, primarily immigrant labor. The local economy, therefore, was more likely to reject, rather than welcome, the new arrivals. Cubans have, nevertheless, achieved remarkable economic success, partially because of the creation of an enclave economy that incorporates about half of the Cuban labor force. Among the most recent Mariel arrivals, however, close to one-third are working informally. Haitians, on the other hand, remain mostly out of the labor market. Those few Haitians who have found employment are in the secondary sector or toil in minimally paid informal jobs.

Table 6.1 Cuban and Haitian Refugee Employment

Occupational Situation after Three Years	1973–74 Cuban Refugees (%)	Mariel 1980 Cuban Refugees (%)	1980 Haitian Refugees (%)
Unemployed	14.0	26.8	58.5
Males unemployed	14.0	25.8	38.8
Employed subsamples			
Self-employed	8.0	15.2	0.5
Working in co-ethnic firms	31.2	30.9	0.2
Working in secondary sector	—	24.9	47.7
Working in informal sector	—	31.4	33.4

Sources: Portes and Bach 1985; Portes and Stepick 1985, tables 2, 3.

Patterns of Informality

This section shifts attention to Miami's two distinct patterns of informalization. Cubans participate, as both owners and workers, in informal sector activities that are closely integrated with the broader economy, especially in the garment industry, restaurants, and construction. Haitians, on the other hand, participate minimally in informal enterprises linked to the outside; their main activities remain confined to their own ethnic community.

The Integrated Informal Sector

In Miami, the most common type of labor law violations, according to the U.S. Department of Labor, are the falsification of employee records to avoid paying overtime, homework in the garment industry, and the exploitation of child labor. The most common violators are found in the garment industry (described by Fernández-Kelly and García in this volume), construction, hotels, and restaurants. These industries employed a total of 16 percent of Miami's labor force in 1980, with construction having the highest proportion of the labor force, followed by restaurants, the garment industry, and hotels. As the data in table 6.2 indicates, the ethnic composition of the work force in all of these sectors has changed dramatically during the last twenty years.

Garment Industry

Behind tall fences and barren walls in the northwest section of Miami are many small garment firms, the epitome of Sun Belt industry. There are no smoke-stacks, no old grimy buildings—just low-lying concrete-block rectangles joined by acres and acres of pavement covered with thousands of automobiles. Inside the block buildings is the Sun Belt's most attractive economic asset: nonunion, low-wage labor. In Miami, nearly twenty-five thousand women, mainly Cuban, cut and sew the latest fashions in women's and children's clothes.

Table 6.2 Employment and Ethnicity

	1960[1]		1970			1980		
	Whites (%)	Blacks (%)	Whites (%)	Blacks (%)	Hispanics[2] (%)	Whites (%)	Blacks (%)	Hispanics[2] (%)
Garment industry	94.4	5.6	17.8	3.7	78.5	10.4	7.0	82.6
Construction	80.1	19.9	60.1	19.4	20.5	43.8	16.6	39.6
Hotels	83.8	16.2	77.5	14.1	18.4	37.3	22.9	39.8
Restaurants	90.7	9.3	61.7	12.9	25.4	60.5	9.3	30.2

Sources: U.S. Census, Florida, 1963, 1973, 1983.

[1]The 1960 U.S. Census did not distinguish Hispanics.
[2]Hispanics can be of any race.

Miami's garment industry has its roots in the 1940s' diversification of the local economy, but its biggest boost came in the late 1960s. Many New York (primarily Jewish) manufacturers relocated to Miami in the face of threatened unionization in the Northeast and waves of Cuban immigration to south Florida. Overall rates of employment in the garment sector have held steady in Miami for the past twenty years, in marked contrast with the deterioration of the industry in other regions of the United States. Miami's firms are almost all small, family-owned enterprises. Of the nearly 750 registered enterprises, only 20 percent have more than twenty workers, and the average number of employees is thirty.

While overall employment has been steady, ethnicity of workers has changed dramatically (see table 6.2). Twenty-five years ago, employees were nearly 95 percent native white;[10] and many, although by no means most, were unionized. Today, the garment workers are 85 percent Hispanic women, and far fewer shops are unionized. Miami manufacturers claim that they have had difficulty finding new workers to replace their aging and retiring female Cuban workers. The economic success of the Cuban community has allowed the second generation to forsake the low wages of the garment industry, while the virtual end of Cuban immigration has cut this labor source. Recent Central and South American immigrants provide a partial substitute, but their numbers are insufficient.

Haitians and black Americans could offer a potential solution, but manufacturers have been reluctant to hire them. In 1960, when the garment industry was starting, 5 percent of the workers were black. Twenty years later, the proportion had climbed only to 7 percent. In the early 1980s, Haitian women began to work in the garment industry, but after the falsely based AIDS scare (see Cooley 1983; Durand 1983; Laverdiere et al. 1983), Haitian employment plummeted. Currently, a typical factory of twenty to twenty-five workers is likely to have only one or two Haitians. Owners claim that Hispanic workers create a cultural closed shop, making others feel unwelcome. Haitian workers report that Hispanic supervisors favor Hispanic workers over Haitians. Regardless of the psychological and social motivations, the effect is racist exclusion. Blacks, both native and foreign, are not incorporated into the local garment industry in any significant numbers.

While the Cuban work force is retiring and owners refuse to replace them with blacks, Miami's garment industry has felt increasing competition from foreign imports and New York City's Chinatown garment district. The response has not been ethnic diversification of the factory labor force, but the informalization of work practices. Miami firms have divided themselves into three types: (1) completely above-ground legal firms with factories obeying all or most labor laws; (2) firms with factories that partially avoid labor laws; and (3) firms that specialize in putting out work.

The first category, the legal firms, have been the hardest hit by foreign competition and that from New York City's garment district. A number of large firms have closed shop in Miami; some went out of business and others resettled abroad. Union membership, which was concentrated in the largest firms, fell from five thousand in 1978 to only a thousand in 1986.

The other two types of firms are surviving and even thriving. In 1980, the U.S. Department of Labor, stating that Miami was swiftly becoming one of the sweatshop capitals of the nation, created a strike force that found labor violations in 132 firms. The violations represented $180 million in wages due to over five thousand workers (Risen 1981). A good portion of the violations consisted of homework, illegal in the garment industry, which was estimated to represent between 30 percent and 50 percent of local production. Many formally retired Cuban women still labor part-time in this manner. Their reasons for preferring homework to factory work are described by Fernández-Kelly and García in this volume. The U.S. Department of Labor claims that Miami homeworkers actually earn at least the minimum wage.[11] Nevertheless, homework in the garment industry is illegal, and it does eliminate social security protection even if workers receive relatively high wages.

In short, immigration is at the core of Miami's garment industry. The industry flourished on the basis of exile female Cuban labor. The decreased exile flows in recent years and the overall success of the Cuban community have greatly reduced the supply of "suitable" labor to garment factories. Racism prevents the incorporation into the industry of either Haitians or black Americans, groups that would seem logical substitutes. As a result, the industry has resorted to informal labor practices, particularly homework. In the process, the strength of unions has been severely eroded.

Construction

As in other Sun Belt cities, construction boomed in the postwar era in Miami. Between 1940 and 1960, Dade County's population increased by nearly 180 percent. During the following twenty years, the rate declined but remained a significant 30 percent per decade. Until the late 1960s, unions controlled 90 percent of all housing construction in Miami. But from the 1960s until the mid-1970s, local unions refused to accept Cuban workers. As Cuban immigrants began creating their own nonunion firms and competing for housing contracts, unionized construction workers focused on higher-paid jobs building condominiums in Miami Beach and office buildings in downtown Miami. Then, the 1973 recession, which severely depressed the construction industry, impelled many native white workers to abandon Dade County.

When the unions finally recognized their mistake, it was too late. The number of unionized workers declined from a high of ten thousand to three thousand in the late 1970s.[12] By the mid-1980s, Cuban firms controlled more than 50 percent of all Dade County construction and nearly 90 percent of new housing. Larger, domestic construction firms have virtually ceased operating in Dade County, except for building large high-rise office buildings downtown. The ethnic composition of the labor force (table 6.2), further reflects this transformation. The proportion of Hispanic construction workers doubled in the 1970s, from 20 percent to nearly 40 percent. Hispanics achieved this relative growth primarily at the expense of native whites, whose numbers declined from 60 percent to 44 percent.[13]

When Cubans started their own construction firms in the 1960s, they commonly relied on informal labor practices. At that time, small-scale entrepreneurs operated "out of the back of their trucks," accepting cash for payment and paying their workers, in turn, with cash. As the industry and the number of Cuban firms grew through the 1970s, work relationships became formalized. Larger enterprises, however, began subcontracting with smaller Cuban firms that employed at least a partially informal labor force. Most large firms at present pay by check, as do most of the larger subcontractors who also generally make all the appropriate deductions. Wages are assuredly lower, approximately by one-third, than the union wage scale, but they remain far above the minimum wage. The Cuban construction industry, in short, has become increasingly formalized but remains nonunion. It effectively undercut union wages with temporary violations of labor laws.

More recently, informal labor practices have reemerged in the wake of the 1980 Mariel influx. Smaller subcontractors began to hire these unemployed, impoverished new immigrants by offering lower wages, hovering near the minimum wage, paid in cash without any deductions. Since Mariel, many subcontractors no longer pay overtime, and they have adopted the practice of falsifying records to conceal the true number of hours worked. Hispanic firms, however, are by no means the sole culprits. The U.S. Department of Labor estimates that 40 percent of all violations of the labor code occur in non-Hispanic enterprises. In short, Hispanic firms exploiting newly arrived Cuban labor provided the impetus for the recent resurgence of informal practices, which the remaining domestic firms quickly followed.

Unlike the garment industry, the construction industry had been consolidated before the influx to incorporate Cuban immigrants. Also unlike the garment industry, established firms refused to incorporate Cuban workers. Ethnic prejudice in the construction industry assumed a different form, working against the employment chances of the earlier Cuban arrivals. But, because of the gradual emergence of construction firms as part of the Cuban enclave, Cuban construction workers obtained jobs in spite of the native unions' exclusionary policy. This process, however, did not benefit black workers. As in the garment industry, the proportion of blacks in the construction labor force did not grow between 1960 and 1980. While wages in construction are significantly above the minimum wage, immigration did produce an informalization process that drastically altered the character of the industry. As a result, unions collapsed, an increasing proportion of new construction is now awarded to new immigrants' firms, and much small-scale work is conducted without permits or observance of the labor laws.

Hotels and Restaurants

Tourism is a declining industry in Miami, but it remains important, especially in its informal segments. Many firms attempt to lower costs by violating labor laws, including paying less than the minimum wage, not paying for overtime, making illegal deductions (such as for equipment breakage), and not meeting health and safety standards.

Miami's hotels and restaurants fall into two basic categories: large-scale establishments that serve primarily the tourist trade and smaller ones that cater to the local population. The larger establishments are downtown, near the airport, and in Miami Beach. White Americans supplemented by black Americans and Bahamians traditionally provided these establishments' labor. Beginning with the Cuban influx in the 1960s, a significant shift took place in the labor supply. By 1970, blacks in the hotel industry had declined slightly, while Hispanics (mostly Cubans) constituted nearly 20 percent of the labor force (see table 6.2). By 1980, Hispanics had doubled their relative participation to nearly 40 percent; blacks had also surpassed their 1960 levels, capturing nearly 23 percent. The expansion of both groups' representation in the industry's labor force was thus at the expense of native whites. The evolution of labor trends in the restaurant industry is partially similar. Hispanics in 1980 constituted 30 percent of the labor force; blacks represented, however, slightly over 9 percent, which was the same percentage as in 1960.

Racism appears to have been less of an impediment to employment of more recent immigrants in the restaurant industry. Around 1980, Haitians started to enter these firms, especially in back-room positions as food preparers and dishwashers. Yet racism, or at least an anti-Haitian prejudice, still affects this area. Exploitation of Haitians in the restaurant industry was so extreme and pervasive that the U.S. Department of Labor organized a special local program to educate Haitian workers about their rights. Moreover, the incorporation of Haitians has been hampered by the fear created by their association, in the public mind, with transmission of tuberculosis and AIDS.[14]

The structure of informality in hotels and restaurants differs from that in garment manufacture and construction. Large hotels, which are most closely integrated into regional and even national circuits, are least likely to engage in informal practices. Neither hotels nor restaurants experienced a rapid process of informalization after the influx of Cuban immigrants, as was the case in the construction industry. Large restaurants are more likely than large hotels to engage in unregulated labor practices. Many concentrate their resources up front, in style and decor. The shadows and doors to the kitchen conceal the savings achieved by violating health and safety standards. They may also illegally deduct from workers' wages fees for uniforms or for equipment breakage. Again, however, these practices have not increased because of the influx of Cuban workers; rather, the historical weakness of organized labor in this industry meant that firms did not need the vulnerability of new immigrants to violate labor laws.

On the other hand, smaller firms, which are mainly restaurants, are far more likely to engage in these practices. They have also been most deeply affected by immigration. Small businesses are primarily ethnic ones. Miami is a highly segregated city with white Americans, black Americans, Cubans, and Haitians all living in separate neighborhoods. The largest and most well developed ethnic neighborhood is Little Havana, which is dotted with small restaurants in which the waiters, waitresses, busboys, and dishwashers may be Mariel Cubans or undocumented Central American workers who receive subminimum wages. Mariel Cubans have fulfilled, to a large extent, the function of a new wave of low-wage, exploitable immigrant labor. In 1985, our informants reported that they could be hired as dishwashers for $200 a week, while older immigrant workers would not settle for less than $300. Recent arrivals are also willing to accept cash and off-the-books payment with no deductions or benefits.

In sum, informality in the hotel and restaurant industries is concentrated in small, primarily ethnic restaurants. Those firms most integrated within the broader economy, especially hotels, are less likely to engage in these activities. The key issue is not links to the outside, however, but the strength of organized labor. The greater its strength and the associated pressure for higher wages, the greater the incentive to bypass constraints through informal labor practices. Racism also appears to be somewhat less important in hotels and restaurants, especially in the former, where blacks have significantly increased their share of employment during the past twenty-five years.

The Isolated Informal Sector

Garment manufacturing, construction, hotels, and restaurants constitute industries that are closely tied to the broader Miami economy and are characterized by widespread informalization. They do not constitute, however, the only informal economic activities in the city. Miami's Haitian community has constructed its own separate ethnic economy, one that is distinct from the larger one and is fueled primarily by immigrant survival strategies.

With the partial exception of hotels and restaurants, the economic activities discussed previously do not incorporate Haitians in any significant numbers. Rather, the modal form of labor market incorporation for recent Haitian refugees is no incorporation at all. Yet the Haitian unemployed seldom have access to the welfare system and hence must find some kind of remunerated work, generally in casual self-employment. Unlike incomes in recent descriptions of informal enterprises elsewhere (Portes and Sassen-Koob 1987), the earnings of the Haitian self-employed are low and generally below the poverty line (see table 6.3).[15] Most Haitian informal "entrepreneurs" drift back and forth between working for someone else in a low-paid job and their own activity. Generally, they do not leave wage labor voluntarily in favor of their own business. Instead, informal enterprise provides a supplement to, not a substitute for, wage labor. Haitian immigrants usually become full-time informal enterpreneurs when they have no choice, as when they lose or cannot obtain regular employment.

The most common of these petty businesses are dressmaking and tailoring, commerce, food preparation, child care, transportation, and the provision of semiskilled services in such areas as construction work, auto repair, and electronic repair. Those who make a living as dressmakers or tailors generally had that same profession in Haiti. They serve an almost exclusively Haitian market. As in other Third World countries, the sewing trades flourish in Haiti because of the relatively high expense of ready-made clothes and the low cost of labor. In Miami, they persist partially because of cultural tradition and a preference for tailor-made clothes, and because the cost of these informal dressmakers and tailors remains low. In Little Haiti, a custom-made woman's dress may be had for less than $15. Children's clothes go for less than $10. Correspondingly, dressmakers' and tailors' earnings are low. The highest yearly income reported was $9,130; most earn about $2,500, which they supplement by part-time, temporary work in the formal sector or through income sharing within the household (see table 6.3). While many of the women have worked in the garment industry, frequently cycling in and out of jobs, no Haitians have been found so far to engage in homework contracted out by a factory.

Even more common than sewing, at least for women, is petty commerce. In Haiti, it often seems as if every woman is a market vendor. In both

Table 6.3 Estimated Income among Self-employed Haitians (in 1985 dollars)

	Monthly[1]	Yearly[2]
Dressmaking and tailoring	65–200	2,500– 9,000
Construction	150–400	4,000–10,000
Auto repair	85–500	6,000–12,500
Transportation	40–100	4,000–12,500
Beauty and barber	30–500	6,000–12,500
Petty commerce	50–200	2,500– 6,000
Restaurants	200–600	4,000– 8,000

[1]Estimates of monthly income refer only to the particular informal sector activity.
[2]Estimates of yearly income refer to the individuals' total income including other employment or receipt of government benefits.

rural and urban areas, women frequently use small amounts of capital, sometimes $2 or less, to engage in small-scale commerce, sometimes walking miles to transport their few goods from producer to consumer for a profit of less than $1. In Little Haiti, the tradition continues. Women frequently use a small amount of capital, $15 to $50, to become petty merchants. Makeshift stands appear on corners and empty lots, a few during the week, many more on the weekends. Women also go door to door. The preferred form of petty commerce is the local flea market, where vendors may rent a stall for $20 per weekend or sublet part of a stall for $5 or $10.

Different women specialize in different goods. Some offer Haitian food products, such as yams and spiced pickled cabbage; others offer goods from Haiti such as toiletries and decorative ceramic goods; and still others sell ready-made clothes. Most goods, with the exception of products imported from Haiti, are purchased at retail price in downtown Miami, usually in stores run by Cubans. The clientele of the petty entrepreneurs is exclusively Haitian, and mostly Haitians of the same social class. The few well-off members of the community are more likely to shop in mainstream stores, and Haitian door-to-door vendors do not venture into middle-class neighborhoods.

Another common informal activity among women—food preparation—is invisible to non-Haitians but well known within the ethnic community. Women turn their home kitchens into restaurant kitchens and the backyard or perhaps the living room into a dining room. A high proportion of single men in Little Haiti either do not know how to cook or do not wish to do their own cooking. They rely almost exclusively upon restaurant food. The informal restaurants usually charge about $3 for a meal, about $1 to $2 less than the cheapest regular restaurants. Women who run these restaurants estimate they make about $500 a month on the average.

A final important female informal activity is child care. While walking the streets of Little Haiti, one frequently encounters houses spilling over with children. They are not, as some may presume, large overflowing families living in objectionably crowded conditions; rather, the children are likely to be in informal day care. The earnings of most working Haitians are too low to afford state-sanctioned commercial day care, and public facilities do not even approach community needs. Many women have stepped into the breach and offer low-cost day care. Most of their clients earn no more than the minimum wage. Many do day work in agriculture and average even less than the minimum wage. Day-care fees accordingly are at rock bottom, varying between $2 and $5 per day per child.

Men are less likely to engage in informal self-employment than women. Those who do are engaged in petty businesses in which they worked in Haiti and which are directed at the Haitian ethnic market. The most visible male activity is transportation. The cabs are usually older American cars, which individuals purchase used for between $500 and $1,500. They cruise primarily around the grocery stores that serve Little Haiti. On weekdays, there may be four or five drivers waiting patiently outside the stores' exits hoping to transport someone with groceries for $3 to $4. On weekends, the number of gypsy cabs waiting at grocery stores swells dramatically. The week-round drivers make about $100 a week; weekend ones earn about $40.

Vans and old school buses that transport people between cities and between Miami and the agricultural fields are another form of informal transportation. The vans are usually much newer and in better condition than the gypsy cabs, as they must be for the longer trips they make. They require an investment of at least a few thousand dollars, and some are brand new, costing over $10,000. The school buses require a smaller initial investment but have higher maintenance costs. The investment in these vehicles is well worth the cost because their owners have a captive market. There are no alternative forms of transportation easily accessible to the Haitians.

A few growers provide buses to the fields, but not all. There is commercial bus service between Miami and the agricultural communities in Florida, but it is very inconvenient. The vans are constantly in use. Trips to the agricultural fields bring only $4 to $5 per person, but the work is steady and the vans usually run full. The real money, however, is made on the weekends when the vans go between Miami and the agricultural towns such as Belle Glade, a ninety-minute drive away. For this trip, the vans can charge up to $25 per person. The van operators can easily earn $250 a week and $12,000 a year.

A slightly less visible but more common male activity is the provision of semiskilled services, in such areas as construction and auto and electronic repair. Individuals involved in these activities also had previous experience and training in these trades in Haiti before coming to the United States. Just like dressmakers and tailors, many worked in firms, usually at low wages. They begin by setting up a small business on the side while still working in a regular job. They usually devote full attention to their business only when they lose their regular employment. Some quit voluntarily, however, viewing their business as potentially more lucrative than wage labor.

Their clientele, as with other Haitian informal activities, is almost exclusively Haitian. Auto repair is linked to informal transportation and the need to keep vehicles running. Moreover, even informal transportation can be expensive in a dispersed Sun Belt city such as Miami. Many Haitians purchase automobiles, but those who work for a minimum wage and are frequently unemployed can only afford used cars of marginal quality, which require frequent repair. Haitian auto mechanics working on the street provide an affordable service. While prices are usually set by the task, the effective return for auto mechanics also hovers close to the minimum wage.

Some Haitians are becoming homeowners in Little Haiti. Frequently, they take advantage of the housing shortage by becoming landlords and illegally remodeling single-family homes into rooming houses or apartments.

The tasks of remodeling are undertaken by informal Haitian contractors who again earn close to the minimum.

In sum, Haitians have constructed a significant informal sector based upon casual self-employment. These activities are survival strategies and are neither inherently preferable to wage labor nor disguised work for firms in the broader economy. Instead, Haitian self-employment has produced an informal sector quite different from that associated with the Cuban enclave. It does not compete with individual workers or firms in the broader economy; it produces goods and services consumed exclusively within the Haitian community, although it also sells goods produced outside. And it generates incomes consistently close to the poverty threshold.

Conclusions

The first and most obvious conclusion from our survey of Miami's informal economy is that it is heterogeneous. It consists of two fundamentally different components. The first, integrated with the broader economy, concentrates in the garment, construction, hotel, and restaurant industries. For all of these, informal labor practices have been used to maintain low labor costs. Informalization in the garment industry reflects a deliberate and successful effort to increase competitiveness in the face of international competition and scarce labor supplies.

In the other three industries, international competition is irrelevant, but informalization of the construction industry did come at the expense of organized labor. Cuban construction firms utilizing informal labor practices, however, did not employ nonunion immigrant labor as a deliberate attempt to displace union workers. On the contrary, because of prejudice against foreigners the unions willfully ceded much of the industry to the immigrant entrepreneurs. Moreover, wages and working conditions did not fall below those mandated by law. The overall effect, nevertheless, was a rapid decrease in the power of the unions. In the hotel and restaurant industries, organized labor has never been very strong. Hence, immigrant labor and associated informal labor practices were not needed originally to lower firms' labor costs.

The creation of the Cuban enclave economy has added a peculiar dynamic to Miami's integrated informal sector, a co-ethnic alliance between capital and labor in which workers voluntarily submit to high levels of exploitation in return for assistance in subsequently establishing and maintaining their own businesses. While the relationship between capital and labor may be different in the enclave than it is in the remainder of the local economy, informal relations have a similar function—the maintenance of the low labor costs and the associated thwarting of organized labor.

Yet, the co-ethnic relationships in enclave enterprises also provide some impediments to the overall exploitation of labor. They appear, for example, to deter the incorporation of new sources of labor, like Haitian refugees, which may be even cheaper and more pliable. The Cuban enclave is not, however, the only sector reluctant to incorporate Haitian immigrants. The broader economy has evinced the same reluctance. The most striking characteristic of Haitian economic activities in Miami is thus their lack of ties with the broader economy. Because of Miami's relative lack of low-wage, unskilled manufacturing positions, the long-term decline in the tourism industry, and racism, Haitians remain a relatively marginal, redundant segment of the labor force.

In response to American society's rejection of their presence, Haitians have created their own informal sector that closely resembles the original descriptions of this phenomenon in Third World cities: casual self-employment isolated from the broader market and the use of informal enterprise primarily as a survival mechanism. Contemporary analyses of informal economies, such as those included in this volume, tend to emphasize their articulation with the formal sector. Yet, at this point, Haitian informal enterprise in Miami remains quite marginal. It is largely isolated from the broader market and little utilized by outside employers. Perhaps with more time, the longer-term interests of the broader economy in new sources of low-wage, pliant labor will overcome racial prejudices and thus transform the survival strategies of Haitians into backward capitalist informal relations. In the meantime, Miami remains characterized by a distinct, immigrant-dominated, and highly segmented informal economy.

Notes

Many people have helped contribute to this paper. They include the editors of this volume plus Robert Lamothe, Annette Williams, Marie Ade, Sophonie Milien, M. Patricia Fernández-Kelly, Max Castro, Oliver Kerr, Carlos Vélez-Ibáñez, Yves Colon, and Andy Banks. Carol Dutton Stepick's editorial comments are gratefully acknowledged. Research support was provided by the National Science Foundation, the Ford Foundation, Florida International University Foundation, School of Arts and Sciences at Florida International University, and the Haitian Task Force. I remain responsible for the final contents.

1. The word *Miami* can have a number of referents. Most narrowly, it means the City of Miami. It also can refer to the broader urban area encompassed by Dade County or the Miami SMSA. In some cases, it even loosely refers to all of south Florida, including Fort Lauderdale and the area farther north along Florida's east coast. In this chapter, I use *Miami* to refer to the contiguous urban area in Dade County.

2. A combination of methodologies has produced this chapter. I have been conducting participant-observation research among Haitians in Miami for six years. I live in Little Haiti and have worked with most Haitian community organizations in Miami. I also took part in a recently completed longitudinal study of the adaptation process of Cuban (Mariel) and Haitian refugees in the area. See Portes, Clark, and Manning 1985; Portes and Stepick 1985; Stepick and Portes 1986.

3. Literature on Miami is increasing rapidly. Banfield (1965) discusses Miami

as it was in the 1950s and early 1960s. Mohl, in a number of insightful articles, focuses on ethnic relations (1983, 1985a, 1986, in press). Warren, Stack, and Corbett (1986) and Stack and Warren (1986) discuss contemporary ethnic politics, while Porter and Dunn (1984) examine racial tensions as does the U.S. Commission on Civil Rights (1982). Most of my discussion, unless otherwise indicated, is drawn from Mohl's excellent 1983 article.

4. See Prohias and Casal 1973, 58–61; Stevenson 1973, 85–91; Díaz 1980, 51–52; Rogg and Cooney 1980; Jaffe, Cullen, and Boswell 1980; Borjas 1982. More generally, see MacCorkle 1984 and Mohl 1984 for bibliographies on exiled Cubans.

5. Portes, Clark, and Manning 1985. If one focuses just on males, over one-fifth are self-employed and nearly one-half work in Cuban enterprises (Portes and Bach 1985, 193–95).

6. Informal was defined as (1) workers paid in cash or without tax deductions; (2) domestic servants and kindred; (3) the itinerant self-employed, such as odd-jobbers and street vendors; and (4) wage workers whose hourly wages are below 80 percent of the legal minimum. See Portes and Stepick 1985, 500.

7. Haitian exiles are not primarily concentrated in Miami. When François "Papa Doc" Duvalier assumed power in 1958, people from all levels of Haitian society fled their homeland. Their primary destination was New York, although significant numbers are also in Paris, Montreal, Chicago, and Boston. Despite the size of the Haitian community in New York City and the fact that a substantial number appear to be in the country illegally, this immigration has received little public attention in the past. See especially Buchanan 1979, 1980, 1983; Laguerre 1984; Fouron 1984; and Glick 1975. For other concentrations see Dejean 1978; Woldemikael 1985. For reviews of the literature on Haitians in the United States, see Lawless 1986 and Mohl 1985b. See also Anderson 1975; Elwell et al. 1977; Keeley et al 1978; Pie 1975; Laguerre 1979, 1980.

8. See Miller 1984; Zucker 1983; Loescher and Scanlan 1984; Stepick 1982a, 1982b, for discussions of the U.S. government's actions toward Haitian boat people. See also Colbert 1980; Gollobin 1979; Jean-Barte 1983; Kurzban 1980, 1983; Powers 1976; Ryan 1982; Schey 1981; Walsh 1980; Wortham 1980. For overall reviews, see Stepick 1982a, 1987.

9. Based upon a random-sample survey, Stepick and Portes (1986) present an analysis of the condition of Haitians in Miami. Portes and Stepick (1987) provide an update of the situation of this group. In short, while conditions have improved, Haitians still remain worse off than either Cubans who arrived at the same time or other comparable immigrant groups.

10. Miami epitomizes the difficulties in making ethnic distinctions in the United States. The majority of Miami Cubans are of Spanish descent and many resent being contrasted with "whites." Conversely, many in Miami's dominant white population resent being identified by the residual category, non-hispanic white. Some also reject categorization as Anglo because of its ethnic specificity, which implicitly excludes Jews and numerous other European ethnic groups. Blacks of Caribbean descent also frequently object to being lumped together with American blacks.

11. Because wages are based upon piece rates, and garment homework is illegal, it is impossible to verify this claim.

12. Although by the mid-1980s, it had recovered to five thousand.

13. While the proportion of blacks dropped from 19.4 percent in 1970 to 16.6

percent in 1980, the absolute numbers of both blacks and whites increased as the total construction labor force grew during the 1970s from thirty-six thousand to almost fifty thousand (U.S. Census, Florida, 1973, 1983).

14. In 1979 and 1980, community health personnel indicated that a high proportion of arriving Haitian boat people had tuberculosis, a disease still endemic in Haiti. Some politicians called for health tests of all Haitians, particularly those working in restaurants. The crisis eventually subsided as it became obvious that tuberculosis was not rampant among Haitians in south Florida. When AIDS first became a national concern, the U.S. government's Centers for Disease Control (CDC) identified Haitians as one of the primary groups at risk. The Haitian community objected strongly, claiming that it was another example of the racism it faced in the United States and that the stigmatization would further impede Haitian efforts to adopt to U.S. society. After much debate, some study, and intense Haitian lobbying, the CDC removed Haitians from the official list of groups at risk.

15. The 1984 poverty threshold was $8,277 for a family of three.

References

Anderson, J. 1975. "The Haitians of New York." *New Yorker* 51:52–54, 58–60, 62–75.
Banfield, E. C. 1965. *Big City Politics*. New York: Random House.
Borjas, G. J. 1982. "The Earnings of Male Hispanic Immigrants in the United States." *Industrial and Labor Relations Review* 35:343–53.
Buchanan, S. 1979. "Haitian Women in New York City." *Migration Today* 7:19–25, 39.
———. 1980. *Scattered Seeds: The Meaning of Migration for Haitians in New York City*. Ph.D. dissertation, New York University.
———. 1983. "The Cultural Meaning of Social Class for Haitians in New York City." *Ethnic Groups* 5:7–30.
Colbert, L. 1980. "Haitian Aliens—a People in Limbo." *The Crisis* 8:235–38.
Cooley, M. 1983. "Haiti: The AIDS Stigma." *NACLA* 17:47–48.
Dade County Planning Department, Research Division. 1987. *Profile of the Hispanic Population*. Miami, Fla: Metro-Dade County Planning Department.
Dejean, P. 1978. *Les Haitiens au Québec*. Montreal: Presses de l'Université du Québec.
Díaz, G. M. 1980. *Evaluation and Identification of Policy Issues in the Cuban Community*. Miami: Cuban National Planning Council.
Díaz-Briquets, S. 1984. "Cuban-Owned Businesses in the United States." *Cuban Studies* 14:57–68.
Durand, G. 1983. "AIDS—the Fallacy of a Haitian Connection." *Bulletin de l'Association des Medecins Haitiens a l'Etranger* 19:17–20.
Elwell, P. J., C. B. Keeley, A. T. Fragomen, and S. M. Tomasi. 1977. "Haitian and Dominican Undocumented Aliens in New York City: A Preliminary Report." *Migration Today* 5:5–9.
Fouron, G. 1984. "Patterns of Adaptation of Haitian Immigrants of the 1970's in New York City." Ph.D. dissertation, Teachers College, Columbia University.
Garreau, J. 1981. *The Nine Nations of North America*. New York: Houghton Mifflin.
Glick, N. 1975. "The Formation of a Haitian Ethnic Group." Ph.D. dissertation, Columbia University.

Gollobin, I. 1979. "Haitian 'Boat People' and Equal Justice Under Law: Background and Perspective." *Migration Today* 7:40–41.

Haug, M. and A. Portes. 1980. "Immigrants' Social Assimilation: An Analysis of Individual and Structural Determinants." Paper. Duke University, August.

Jaffe, A. J., R. M. Cullen, and T. D. Boswell. 1980. *The Changing Demography of Spanish Americans*. New York: Academic Press.

Jean-Barte, R. 1983. "Afe Refijye yo Se Batay Pep Ayisyen an." *Sel* 54/55:27–31.

Jorge, A. and R. Moncarz. 1980. "The Cuban Entrepreneur and the Economic Development of the Miami SMSA." Manuscript. Department of Economics, Florida International University.

Keeley, C. B., P. J. Elwell, A. T. Fragomen, Jr., and S. M. Tomasi. 1978. *Profiles of Undocumented Aliens in New York City: Haitians and Dominicans*. Occasional Paper no. 5. Staten Island, New York: Center for Migration Studies.

Kurzban, I. 1980. "Haitian Refugees: A Flight from Persecution." *Rights* 25:13–15.

———. 1983. "Long and Perilous Journey: The Nelson Decision." *Human Rights* 25:41–44.

Laguerre, M. A. 1979. "The Haitian Niche in New York City." *Migration Today* 7:12–18.

———. 1980. "Haitians in the United States." Pp. 446–49 in S. Thernstrom (ed.), *Harvard Encyclopedia of American Ethnic Groups*. Cambridge: Harvard University Press.

———. 1984. *Haitians in the United States*. Ithaca: Cornell University Press.

Laverdiere, M. J. Tremblay, R. Lavallee, Y. Bonny, M. Lacombe, J. Boileau, J. Lachapelle, and C. Lamoureaux. 1983. "AIDS in Haitian Immigrants and in a Caucasian Woman Closely Associated with Haitians." *Canadian Medical Association Journal* 129:1209–12.

Lawless, R. 1986. "Haitian Migrants and Haitian-Americans: From Invisibility into the Spotlight." *Journal of Ethnic Studies* 14:29–70.

Levine, B. B. 1985. "The Capital of Latin America." *Wilson Quarterly*, Winter, 46–69.

Loescher, G. and J. Scanlan. 1984. "Human Rights, U.S. Foreign Policy, and Haitian Refugees." *Journal of Interamerican Studies and World Affairs* 26:313–56.

MacCorkle, L. 1984. *Cubans in the United States: A Bibliography for Research in the Social and Behavioral Sciences, 1960–1983*. Westport, Conn.: Greenwood Press.

Miller, J. C. 1984. *The Plight of Haitian Refugees*. New York: Praeger.

Mohl, R. 1983. "Miami: The Ethnic Cauldron." Pp. 58–99 in R. M. Bernard and B. R. Rice (eds.), *Sunbelt Cities: Politics and Growth Since World War II*. Austin: University of Texas Press.

———. 1984. "Cubans in Miami: A Preliminary Bibliography." *The Immigration History Newsletter* 16:1–10.

———. 1985a. "The Origins of Miami's Liberty City." *Florida Environmental and Urban Issues* 4:9–12.

———. 1985b. "The New Haitian Immigration: A Preliminary Bibliography." *The Immigration History Newsletter* 17:1–8.

———. 1986. "The Politics of Ethnicity in Contemporary Miami." *Migration World* 14:51–74.

Pérez, L. 1986. "Immigrant Economic Adjustment and Family Organization: The Cuban Success Story Reexamined." *International Migration Review* 20:4–20.

Peterson, M. F. and M. A. Maidique. 1986. *Success Patterns of the Leading Cuban-American Entrepreneurs*. WP 86-104, Research Report Series, Innovation and Entrepreneurship Institute, School of Business Administration, University of Miami.

Pie, R. 1975. "Kouman Yo Leve Ayisyin Nouyok." *Sel* 23/24:9–18.

Porter, B. and M. Dunn. 1984. *The Miami Riot of 1980: Crossing the Bounds*. Lexington, Mass.: Lexington Books.

Portes, A. 1981. "Modes of Structural Incorporation and Present Theories of Labor Immigration." Pp. 279–97 in M. M. Kritz, C. B. Keeley, and S. M. Tomasi (eds.), *Global Trends in Migration*. New York: Center for Migration Studies.

———. 1983. "The Informal Sector: Definition, Controversy, and Relation to National Development." *Review* 7:151–74.

Portes, A. and R. Bach. 1985. *Latin Journey: Cuban and Mexican Immigrants in the United States*. Berkeley and Los Angeles: University of California Press.

Portes, A., J. Clark, and R. Manning. 1985. "After Mariel: A Survey of the Resettlement Experiences of 1980 Cuban Refugees in Miami." *Cuban Studies* 15:37–59.

Portes, A. and S. Sassen-Koob. 1987. "Making It Underground: Comparative Materials on the Informal Sector in Western Market Economies." *American Journal of Sociology* 93:30–61.

Portes, A. and A. Stepick. 1985. "Unwelcome Immigrants: The Labor Market Experiences of 1980 (Mariel) Cuban and Haitian Refugees in South Florida." *American Sociological Review* 50:493–514.

———. 1987. *Haitian Refugees in South Florida, 1983–1986*. Dialogue no. 77, Occasional Papers Series, Latin American and Caribbean Center, Florida International University.

Powers, T. 1976. "The Scandal of U.S. Immigration: The Haitian Example." *Ms.* 48:62–66, 81–83.

Prohias, R. J. and L. Casal. 1973. "The Cuban Minority in the U.S.: Preliminary Report on Need Identification and Program Evaluation." Florida Atlantic University, Boca Raton, Fla. Mimeo.

Risen, J. 1981. "Sweatshops Pervasive in Miami." *Miami Herald*, May 18.

Rogg, E. M. and R. S. Cooney. 1980. *Adaptation and Adjustment of Cubans: West New York, New Jersey*. New York: Hispanic Research Center.

Ryan, M. C. P. 1982. "Political Asylum for the Haitians?" *Case Western Reserve Journal of International Law* 14:155–76.

Schey, P. A. 1981. "The Black Boat People Founder on the Shoals of U.S. Policy." *Migration Today* 9:7–10.

Stack, J. F. and C. L. Warren. 1986. "Ethnic Conflict and the Internationalization of Miami." In C. Alvarez (ed.), *Migration and Ethnicity: A Global Perspective*. In press.

Stepick, A. 1982a. "Haitians in Miami: An Assessment of their Background and Potential." In Dialogue no. 12, Occasional Papers Series, Latin American and Caribbean Center, Florida International University.

———. 1982b. "Haitian Boat People: A Study in the Conflicting Forces Shaping U.S. Refugee Policy." *Law and Contemporary Problems* 2:163–96.

———. 1987. *Haitian Refugees in the United States*. 2nd ed. London and New York: Minority Rights Group.

Stepick, A. and A. Portes. 1986. "Flight into Despair: A Profile of Recent Haitian Refugees in South Florida." *International Migration Review* 20:329–50.

Stevenson, J. M. 1973. "Cuban-Americans: New Urban Class." Ph.D. dissertation, Wayne State University.

U.S. Bureau of the Census. 1960 Census of Population. 1963. *Characteristics of the Population, Florida.* Washington, D.C.: U.S. Government Printing Office.

———. 1970 Census of Population. 1973. *General Social and Economic Characteristics, Florida.* Washington, D.C.: U.S. Government Printing Office.

———. 1980 Census of Population. 1983. *General Social and Economic Characteristics, Florida.* Washington, D.C.: U.S. Government Printing Office.

U.S. Commission on Civil Rights. 1982. *Confronting Racial Isolation in Miami.* Washington, D.C.: U.S. Government Printing Office.

Walsh, B. O. 1980. "The Boat People of South Florida." *America* 142:420–21.

Warren, C. L., J. F. Stack, J. G. Corbett. 1986. "Minority Mobilization in an International City: Rivalry and Conflict in Miami." *PS* 19:626–34.

Wilson, K. and A. Portes. 1980. "Immigrant Enclaves: An Analysis of the Labor Market Experiences of Cubans in Miami." *American Journal of Sociology* 86:295–319.

Woldemikael, T. M. 1985. "Opportunity Versus Constraint: Haitian Immigrants and Racial Ascription." *Migration Today* 13:7–12.

Wortham, J. 1980. "The Black Boat People." *Black Enterprise* 10:34–35.

Zucker, N. F. 1983. "The Haitians versus the United States: The Courts as Last Resort." *Annals of the American Academy of Political and Social Science* 467:151–62.

3   Black Money, Black Markets

7　Cocaine, Informality, and the Urban Economy in La Paz, Bolivia

José Blanes Jiménez

Over the last few years, Bolivia has experienced important changes as a result of the transition from a "tin economy" to an economy based on the production and export of cocaine. Throughout its history, Bolivia has been dependent upon the hazards of the international market, which, over time, have created a highly disarticulated society in which formal economic activities have been the exception rather than the rule and in which the state has been weak in its attempts to organize society and the economy. [1]

Economic informality has always been widespread in Bolivia. The formal sector has been, for the most part, small, fragile, dependent upon its relationship to the world market, and restricted to the small sphere of state-managed enterprises. The Bolivian government has been traditionally unable to control the private sector. The shift from the "tin connection" to the "drug connection" has brought about an expansion of informality in general, and especially of urban underground economic activities aimed at subsistence.

Drug traffic did not create the urban informal sector in Bolivia. However, it has rapidly penetrated previously existing underground activities, expanding and strengthening them. Thus, the triangle composed of drug traffic, clandestine economic transactions, and a vulnerable formal sector has become a distinctive feature throughout the country. In this triple relationship, urban informality increasingly depends upon the logic of clandestinity and less so on the dynamics of the formal sector. These circumstances have accentuated as a result of the recent economic crisis.

The purpose of this chapter is to document the links between the expansion of the cocaine-based economy and the growth of urban informality in the capital city of La Paz. The main focus is on the impact of this economic arrangement on family survival strategies as the tin economy collapses, leaving in its wake unprecedented rates of unemployment. First, the development of cocaine production and marketing are considered. Second, the characteristics and configuration of the urban informal sector are outlined. Finally, the role of the state is examined.

Chapter 7 was translated by M. Patricia Fernández-Kelly.

Cocaine Production and Marketing

The cocaine economy in Bolivia developed rapidly during the seventies due to external demand and the internal dislocation ensuing from it. Ironically, the country's comparative advantage in the production of coca leaves and in the manufacture and marketing of sulphates attracted capital investments denied to other sectors of the domestic economy. This competitive edge also effected the incorporation of peasant families into the international economy.

In Bolivia, the cultivation of coca (*Erythroxylon* Erythroxylaceae) is generally in the hands of families with plots of land averaging six hectares, of which two are dedicated to growing coca. There are larger fields but they are the exception (Blanes 1983). Growing coca has been the most advantageous and least difficult form of cultivation for settlers in the tropical zones of Chapare and Los Yungas since their arrival from the highlands and the valleys.[2] Originally, coca was grown to meet internal demand; the leaves are traditionally chewed and used for ritual purposes (Carter and Mamani 1986). However, production did not surpass an annual average of fifteen thousand metric tons, or less than 10 percent of total agricultural production (Flores-Blanes 1984).

By December 1981 (when the study on which this chapter is based was completed), approximately 15,000 families, or 80,000 people, were living in Chapare. These families were growing coca and selling it locally at prices so high that they provided excellent support for many peasants. A plot averaging twelve hectares, with two dedicated to coca, and not requiring more than family labor (Blanes 1983) yielded annual earnings that fluctuated between $15,000 and $20,000 in 1981 (Flores-Blanes 1984).

The differential advantage of coca production led to the reduction or elimination of other agricultural forms such as rice, banana, and citrus fruit cultivation. At present, an estimated 70,000 to 80,000 families are growing coca in Chapare. This represents a total population of about 400,000 people, that is, five times as many as were involved in coca production six years before.[3]

Attempts at controlling drug traffic toward the end of the 1970s made it difficult to sell basic ingredients to cocaine producers, who had to transport them by road to the region of Santa Cruz, seven hundred kilometers away from Chapare. In the face of this disruption, peasants intensified their own elaboration of raw paste, which had been manufactured earlier by agents outside the zone. As a result, knowledge of chemical procedures grew widely among peasants even though most of them are illiterate. Until 1983, the crystallization of cocaine powder had been done in Colombia, where loads of raw material arrived from hundreds of concealed landing fields in the intricate Bolivian jungle. At present, a large portion of crystallization is also being done in Bolivia. As a result of these changes, a transient population of merchants and *pisadores*[4] has grown. One of the latter can earn in two nights the equivalent of the monthly wages of a construction worker in the nearby city of Cochabamba.

Commercialization of cocaine attracted resources for financing operations not only in manufacturing but also in subsidiary activities. This situation offered opportunities for profit to small investors who lacked better options, particularly in recent times when economic crisis has prevailed.[5] Thus, the impact of the cocaine economy affected the labor market, leading resources and workers underground. Many activities involving a large number of people are indirectly related to cocaine production. However, their magnitude is difficult to appraise given their clandestine character. For example, "ant" merchants purchase raw materials in advance from relatives, friends, or acquaintances, often providing the necessary investment to cover coca production costs. The final phases involving the export of very large volumes of the crystallized or uncrystallized drug are in the hands of tightly knit groups that are guarded by sophisticated security systems.

Equally important as the physical infrastructure of the drug trade has been the development of a strategy for penetration of government agencies and the society at large. Complicity on the part of judges, police, and the armed forces has been necessary for the emergence of new drug empires. Without corruption, it would have been almost impossible to export more than 350 tons of cocaine and to import more than $100 million in contraband goods, as was done in 1985.

There are no reliable data regarding the production of coca and cocaine. Only estimates are available. Although these assessments offer vastly different pictures, they agree that there has been a rapid rate of growth in production. The figures in table 7.1 are from one of the most trustworthy

Table 7.1 Coca and Cocaine Production in Bolivia (in metric tons)

Year	Coca[1]	Cocaine[2]	Cocaine[3]
1980	20,000	68.67	58.86
1981	26,844	89.48	76.70
1982	37,992	126.41	108.55
1983	41,542	138.47	118.69
1984	86,400	288.00	246.86
1985	122,342	407.81	349.55

Source: Figures abstracted by the author from Doria Medina 1986, 67.

[1] Based on estimates from the Ministry of Peasant Affairs. Figures take into account a 20% subtraction of coca used for traditional chewing in Bolivia.
[2] Figures in this column assume that 300 kg of coca are needed to elaborate 1 kg of cocaine.
[3] Figures in this column assume that 350 kg of coca are needed to elaborate 1 kg of cocaine.

sources at present. As may be seen, the value derived from coca cultivation and cocaine production is extremely large. The rate of growth of these activities has greatly accelerated over the last few years, although there have been major conjunctural fluctuations. The figures in table 7.2 indicate that coca growers received between $370 million and close to $500 million for their goods in 1985. To these figures must be added another 20 percent derived from domestic coca sales for traditional chewing and ritual uses.

Cocaine's value grew at an accelerated rate during 1980–85. Table 7.3 contains estimates on the basis of two different hypotheses regarding the production of basic paste by volume of coca leaves. The differences in value depend on the type of leaf and on the chemical procedures used. Using primitive "laboratories" in their family kitchens, peasants generally obtain a highly impure paste and a lower yield per amount of raw coca.

The figures in table 7.3 indicate the rapid growth in the volume of cocaine production during the 1980s. This growth has transformed the Bolivian

Table 7.2 Value of Coca Production, by Year (in millions of dollars)

Year	$4,000 per Metric Ton ($)	$3,000 per Metric Ton ($)
1980	82.18	61.80
1981	107.38	80.53
1982	151.97	113.98
1983	166.17	124.63
1984	345.60	259.20
1985	489.37	367.03

Source: Figures abstracted by the author from Doria Medina 1986, 71.

Table 7.3 Value of Cocaine Production, by Year (in millions of dollars)

Year	$4,000 per Metric Ton ($)	$3,000 per Metric Ton ($)
1980	412.02	353.16
1981	536.88	460.20
1982	158.46	651.30
1983	830.82	712.14
1984	1,728.00	1,481.16
1985	2,446.86	2,097.30

Source: Figures abstracted by the author from Doria Medina 1986, 70.
Note: This information takes into consideration prices stipulated by the Drug Enforcement Administration.

formal sector into a near fiction. In 1980, only 11 percent of the economy was based on cocaine production; five years later, that figure had expanded to approximately 80 percent. Official figures do not provide an accurate portrayal of this trend because they record only the small portion of economic activity that is still legally sanctioned.

A formal economy as small as that of Bolivia cannot absorb the bulk of revenues generated by cocaine production and marketing, especially in view of the long-standing presence of free-floating capital outside state control and unable to find a profitable function in the private sector. This fluid capital has grown as a result of illegal cocaine traffic. Investments have been chaneled into activities such as contraband, black market currency deals, and the export of illegal revenues. All these activities have swelled, in turn, the informal economy. At the same time, earnings from cocaine production and the expansion of the informal economy in general have fed luxury markets fostering speculation and inflation. The latter reached almost 12,000 percent during 1985 (Núñez del Prado 1986).

Drug-related and other informal activities propelled a regressive income distribution, giving rise to social groups with high consumption power in the midst of recession. Patterns of consumption were distorted, particularly among the affluent, and new stratification schemes—containing middling groups as well as nouveaux riches—emerged. Legal productive activities came to be viewed with disdain, and labor markets became disarticulated. Illegality came to be the rule of economic activity.

Cocaine production and other illegal sectors further encouraged traditional patterns of tax and labor code evasion as well as the import of contraband and the flight of revenues. According to some economists, the size of illegal economic transactions is comparable to that of the official balance of trade. The laundering of illegal earnings has pushed up the price of durable commodities and even the price of nonperishable subsistence goods (Núñez del Prado 1986). The present structure of the Bolivian economy is summarized in table 7.4.

The Urban Informal Sector

Bolivian cities are inhabited mostly by a poor population of former peasants whose expectations regarding full citizenship and employment have been largely frustrated. The urban informal sector in Bolivia is closely linked to material survival. This is in contrast with findings of research elsewhere (see Roberts, this volume; Benería, this volume). In those case studies, productive industrial capital articulates with a wide series of informal activities. In the case of Bolivia, such connections are absent.

It is true that productive activities can be found within the urban informal sector. These range from crafts to services, sold as part of a traditional strategy for family subsistence. However, the liberalization of customs regula-

Table 7.4 Gross Domestic Production in
Market Values, by Sector, 1985 (in millions
of dollars)

Sector	Value
1. Coca and cocaine	2,447
2. Informal	
Commerce	400
Mining	100
Other production	150
Financial	50
Total	700
3. 1 + 2	3,147
4. Formal sector	3,055
5. (3÷4) × 100	103

Source: Doria Medina 1986, 172–73.

tions and the growth of contraband has eroded long-standing informal activities such as the manufacture of low-cost footwear and clothing. In this respect there is some resemblance to Roberts's (this volume) account of economic informalization in Guadalajara.

In Bolivian mining areas, informality expanded as a result of links to the formal economy, particularly to state-controlled firms. The families who extract and sell ore to COMIBOL (the state-managed mining corporation) bear striking similarities to the informal workers observed by Benería (this volume) in Mexico City. In both cases, informality is organized as a pyramid in which a large base of unskilled and semiskilled homeworkers are joined to formal firms through a chain of intermediaries.

In cities like La Paz, underground activities most intimately linked to the dynamics of capital are also related to the marketing of imported contraband. These activities encompass more than half of the informal sector in all larger urban centers. They have evolved in harmony with the growth in the purchasing of those benefiting from cocaine-related and other informal transactions.

According to the 1976 national census, and excluding domestic services, about 47 percent of the working urban population in Bolivia is part of the informal economy. This category includes both family enterprises and small semientrepreneurial establishments.[6] The most important group within the urban informal sector is that formed by self-employed workers, who represent approximately 66 percent of total informal employment (Casanovas and Escobar de Pabón 1984).

The private formal sector is extremely small, employing only 17 percent of the economically active urban population. In comparison, the public sector employs 26 percent. Thus, the urban economy is basically shaped by government-supported activity, on the one hand, and the small productive units in the informal sector, on the other. In 1983, 152,215 economic units were identified in the larger urban centers, but only 8,340 (5.5%) employed five or more workers. These larger units provided employment to 51.6 percent of the working population in large cities, or 414,606 individuals. In contrast, the informal sector contained 143,875 establishments (94% of the total), hiring 48.4 percent of this population (INE 1983).

Informal establishments are often no larger than booths or stands. All of them are highly dispersed, with the exception of certain commercial enterprises that are concentrated in specialized urban areas. Three different types of informal operations can be identified: those that have an actual establishment (65,235, or 45.3%) and employ 58 percent of those working informally, and those that rely on mobile or fixed stands. In 1983 there were 30,059 fixed stands, which provided 16.4 percent of informal jobs, and 48,581 mobile stands, which hired 25.6 percent of workers in the informal sector (see table 7.5). Almost 97 percent of the units are dedicated to commercial activities, while the remainder are involved in manufacturing, services, and nonspecified activities. Of 48,581 mobile units identified, 97.2 percent were involved in commerce (INE 1983).

The importance of the urban informal sector in the capital city of La Paz stems from the concentration of about half of the economically active population in that sector. An additional 5 percent are employed in domestic services. As the figures in table 7.6 indicate, the tendency during 1976–83 was toward relative parity between the formal and informal sectors in terms of the population employed in each. Within the informal economy, almost 96 percent of fixed and 96.6 percent of ambulatory stands were dedicated to commercial activities; this is a proportion similar to that found in other cities (INE 1983).

Informal commercial activities have attracted a growing number of people over the last few years. Levels of capitalization vary, but there is a common denominator—to survive and perhaps grow outside of state control. The small units comprising the informal sector are grouped in unions, but participation of those at the base is fragile. Instead, organized activity is dominated by powerful groups at the top. State control over this sector is almost nonexistent; most businesses are not even registered (Casanovas and Escobar de Pabón 1984). In contrast, union leaders have imposed strong hegemony and structure.

Small commercial activities employing most of those in the urban informal sector are highly heterogeneous. As observed by Donoso (1980), they are characterized by a stratification similar to that described by Benería for Mexico City. The pyramidal configurations found in both instances include a belt of prosperous merchants at the middle. In the case of La Paz, these individuals are directly or indirectly involved in contraband activities, marketing foreign goods through a myriad of small peddlers. Most of these are mobile, while others have fixed establishments in busy commercial zones or in neigh-

Table 7.5 The Urban Informal Sector by Type of Economic Unit: Principal Cities, 1983

Type of Unit	Number of Units	Percentage of Informal Units	Persons Employed	Percentage of Informal Employment
Establishments hiring up to 5 workers	65,235	45.3	117,159	58.0
Fixed stands	30,059	20.9	33,142	16.4
Mobile stands	48,581	33.8	51,657	25.6
Total informal sector	143,875	100.0	201,958	100.0

Source: INE 1983.

Table 7.6 Distribution of the Urban EAP in La Paz, 1976–1983

Sectors	1976[1] (%)	1980[2] (%)	1983[3] (%)
Formal			
State-related	21.0	24.0	20.0
Private	23.0	18.0	24.0
Total (formal)	44.0	42.0	44.0
Informal			
Small enterprises	18.0	17.0	19.0
Family-centered units	29.0	36.0	32.0
Total (informal)	47.0	53.0	51.0
Domestic service	9.0	5.0	5.0
Total	100.0	100.0	100.0

Source: Casanovas (1986, 155)

[1]National Census of Population and Housing 1976.
[2]Urban Survey on Migration and Employment 1980.
[3]Continuing Survey of Households 1983.

borhood markets (INE 1983; Blanes 1984). Depending on the type of product and the existing demand, the base of the pyramid contracts or expands. This form of peddling provides employment to many poor people willing to invest their meager savings. The top of the pyramid also contains fractions of informal capital invested in finance, particularly in loan sharking, and smuggling.

The commercial sector, constituted mostly by informal establishments, involves a large number of people. In 1980, there were 51,381 commercial establishments, restaurants, and hotels in La Paz.[7] There were 719,780 individuals living in the city in the same year. In other words, there was a business for every 14 persons. In addition, there were 27,606 stands for retail distribution selling mostly agricultural products, that is, a stand for every 26 urban dwellers (Blanes 1984).

During 1980–85, the commercialization of contraband also expanded in border areas. This was stimulated by the rise in relative prices of these goods and by stagnation in other sectors. Government policies aimed at encouraging free competition and opening up the economy to the exterior, as well as the pressure of free-floating capital, exacerbated the tendency toward informalization. However, the most powerful factor in the growth of contraband was the drug-traffic boom.

Cocaine and the Urban Informal Sector

What are the connections between the cocaine economy and the urban informal sector? The articulation of the two is rather complex. A first nexus can be found in the growth of revenues derived from cocaine production, which foster demand for consumer durables. A different link is formed by the very activity of smuggling, which acquires an independent dynamism given the volumes exchanged, the Bolivian industrial underdevelopment, and the weaknesses of state regulation. In sum, informal activities have promoted the insertion of revenues derived from cocaine production into the national economy.

Field research and direct observation in the zone of Chapare point to a differentiation of agents involved in the cocaine economy. All of these agents— coca producers and families manufacturing cocaine paste, buyers and intermediaries, those who process the drug in pure form, the exporters, and the corrupt state functionaries—move large sums of money. However, the behavior of each of these participants regarding the allocation of revenues derived from cocaine-related transactions varies. Some channel investments into the national economy; others export earnings.

A numerically important group in this respect is that of families involved in the growing, harvesting, and processing of coca. As part of our study, producers were probed in 1981 regarding the allocation of coca earnings. Most families spent those revenues on trucks and other types of transportation, domestic electrical appliances, land, homes, and education for their children. In addition, direct observation showed that conspicuous consumption of foreign-made commodities of all kinds was widespread in this group.

Another important cluster of agents involved in this process is formed by intermediaries and merchants. The social origin and economic composition of coca buyers and stockers differ from those found among coca producers in that the former are preponderantly urban and knowledgeable about the mechanisms for circulating cocaine. This group has been joined by middle-class elements deeply affected by the economic crisis. Such is the case of schoolteachers and other professionals. No research has been conducted among the members of this group. However, it is likely that their spending patterns are similar to those found among small producers, that is, closely linked to consumerism and social rites of passage.

An important difference, however, is that they are more familiar with informal and formal practices than peasants. Thus they often act as the agents of capital, introducing money into the finance system and feeding contraband as well as other illegal and legal activities. This group has substantial savings in banks, and its members form the most important market for real estate, automobiles, and other high-cost goods. In sum, this is a new social class that has used the drug and informal economies as channels for integration and upward social mobility. Alternative paths such as higher education, public employment, and professional careers had been exhausted by the end of the seventies.

Among cocaine exporters are those who prefer to move their profits to foreign banks, which are then used as direct connections to the international market. Doria Medina (1986, 72) notes that capital flight is a widespread phenomenon among the Bolivian bourgeoisie. He estimates that of the $2,446 million produced by cocaine in 1985, only $500 million remained in the country. However, it is also probable that a sizable portion of cocaine revenues is moved within the state-managed and private financial structures in Bolivia, since functionaries accept deposits or investments in dollars without inquiring about their origin.

Large but difficult-to-estimate amounts of money enter the Bolivian economy through corrupt officialdom. Among them are members of the police, the armed forces, the legislature, the judicial system, and the state agencies. Their illegal earnings move through the familiar paths described above. The only difference resides in their point of entry, at the level of official government. Some functionaries involved in this process have chosen to invest in Bolivia, particularly in the purchase of real estate and the import of contraband goods. In a manner similar to that of direct producers and intermediaries, officials have also greatly expanded demand for conspicuous consumption items, particularly foreign-made goods.

In Bolivia, where extreme poverty restricts large-scale industrial projects, where credit is costly, and where there is a tradition of speculation even within government, contraband trade has become a relatively safe and profitable activity. According to official sources, imports diminished over 1980–85. In fact, there was a shift of imports to contraband. Trading in smuggled goods yields profits that allow capital great velocity in circulation, making this type of investment more advantageous and less risky than industry. This trade also permits the expansion of capital, as shown by the increment in the number of business start-ups and shopping centers in neighborhoods specializing in the selling of contraband.

Smuggled commodities are of different kinds. It is necessary to differentiate among those preferred by high-income groups and those that are favored by the poor. The consumption of luxury automobiles and other very expensive products has grown over the last few years as a response to the formation of new social groups in which earnings are concentrated. This also explains the emergence of specialized grocery stores in La Paz where U.S.- and Brazilian-made foods are sold to the affluent.

There are other products sold to the poor in retail stands and small stores. It is at this level that the majority of ambulatory peddlers participate in the urban economy. They form a "reserve army of distribution" vis-à-vis large importers and wealthy intermediaries. In addition, there is demand for new products that are not manufactured in Bolivia. Goods of every kind and for every pocket can be found in the "Little Miami" of La Paz.

The preceding description suggests the articulation of several levels of economic activity: illegal transactions join the criminal and drug-related sectors in circuits that eventually feed into a small legitimate sphere. Ironically, this triple connection has ameliorated the impact of the economic crisis by expanding employment and the circulation of resources. In addition, the cocaine boom has contributed to the "dollarization" of the Bolivian economy, swelling the currency black market. This has reinforced the informal market for credit. Demand for dollars had diverse origins. However, all of them converge in the growing informalization of the financial sector.

Inflationary pressures during the period 1982–85 produced demand for large amounts of circulating currency. Coca production and basic paste started to be paid for in dollars. At the same time, peasant families saw dollars as a good means for protection of savings in the midst of galloping inflation (Núñez del Prado 1986). Dollars became common currency in Bolivia, allowing the state to save on the manufacture of paper money. The same process slowed down the excessive circulation of Bolivian pesos at a time when attempts were being made at containing inflation.[8] Obsolescence followed the emission of paper money: in 1982 the highest denomination was one hundred pesos; by 1985, it was ten million.

With such high levels of inflation, the circulation of dollars allowed the Bolivian economy to function. According to Doria Medina (1986, 59), 80 percent of the supply of dollars needed by the Bolivian economy between 1984 and 1985 came from drug-related activities. With the legalization of the currency black market in 1985, access to dollars became even easier. There are approximately 450 registered ambulatory currency traders, and a similar number of unregistered peddlers in the streets of La Paz. Together, they respond to the demand of small buyers, but many make contracts with commercial enterprises when the demand for dollars grows. Today any Bolivian bank can offer savings plans in dollars at an annual interest rate of 16 percent.

The State and Economic Informalization

The shift toward informality in Bolivia cannot be fully understood without giving attention to the role that the state has played over the last few years. The state's central participation in this process does not stem from its regulatory capability, as in the case of Uruguay (Fortuna and Prates, this volume), or from its ability to control the economy. Instead, it flows from state complicity and weakness. Government agencies and public officials were affected from the beginning by the rise of the cocaine economy. One of the main negative outcomes was escalating inflation, which demolished the formal sector, allowing the informal to emerge as a solution to many serious problems. In the same vein, drug-related transactions fanned by corruption have eroded the legitimacy of the state. Thus, the Bolivian informal economy is less linked to normal capitalist firms, as happens elsewhere, and more related to the wayward behavior of government agencies.

Drug trafficking was originally made possible by the paternalistic government of General Hugo Banzer during the 1970s. This period was followed by a stage of rapid accumulation during which the drug traffic became consolidated. Finally, a third phase was characterized by the further extension of the drug connection, as the tin economy collapsed. During this last period, the state has lost all power vis-à-vis drug traffickers while simultaneously becoming the main focus of economic, social, and political mobilization.

The shift begun during the seventies was marked by the dismantling of the welfare state instituted in 1952 and by the growing power of wealthy groups in the western part of the country dedicated to agriculture, industry, commerce, and the drug traffic. Contraband and other forms of informal economic activity were implicitly accepted by the state and even used as part of patron-client exchanges. The shift of investments from agriculture to drug-related production, as well as the allocation of large expanses of land to cocaine factories, made possible the emergence of a totally new economic configuration (Delpirou and Labrousse 1986, 132–33). Capital increases surpassing the capacity of the formal sector further encouraged the transition toward the cocaine economy.[9]

In the early 1980s, the state actually intervened to strengthen cocaine-related production and marketing. General García Meza's coup d'état was correctly portrayed as a drug-related move. Few governments have been as notoriously corrupt as the one headed by García Meza. During that period, the Ministry of the Interior became the main regulator of trade in coca. With that administration, the breakdown of state legitimacy accelerated. Moreover, during the same period, members of the armed forces became directly involved in the manufacture and export of cocaine at the same time that they smuggled precious stones out of the country. Under these circumstances, the press coined the term "narcocracy" to designate a situation in which public officials not only benefited from drug-related transactions but also constituted a new national power capable of articulating different levels of formal and informal economic activity.

At present, Bolivia is a state imprisoned by drug trafficking and its own weakness. On the one hand, cocaine-related capital has consolidated new social and political structures. On the other, the state has lost large revenues originally provided by its formal economic base. Finally, the external debt has further shown the inability of traditional structures to move the country forward. In spite of the relative autonomy of criminal capital, a central role is still being played by the state as it launders or legalizes revenues derived from cocaine production, tolerates the advance of the informal sector, and oversees the dismantling of formerly viable sectors such as government-managed mining.

What are the consequences of this new relationship between the Bolivian state and the economy? The state has forfeited its relationship with the popular sectors, as defined during the 1952 revolution. It now emerges as a class-specific mechanism rather than as an arbiter among the interests of various social groups. Within this new state there are clusters able to wield great power and more important, capable of directing the economy to their own advantage.

Under these conditions, the state is incapable of imposing discipline upon the vested interests of cocaine production. Furthermore, it cannot influence the links joining illegal activity to the international market. Government is now restricted by new banking and commercial interests and, particularly, by the international "narcocracy." In the absence of a viable economic base, it is witnessing its own demise as a sociopolitical actor.

At the same time, the drug connection represents a new form of dependence which deepens economic informalization and accelerates the disappearance of other socially significant organizations. Because informality has greatly expanded employment, it is becoming a mechanism for legitimizing drug-related activities. Thus, an economy known to be illegal and even criminal is becoming the principal source of income for large numbers of poverty-stricken Bolivian families.

Great ambiguity characterizes Bolivia at present. On the one hand, drug trafficking accounts for the largest percentage of criminal activities—including murder, corruption, and prostitution. On the other, the informal economy has expanded employment and the circulation of resources during times made difficult by the collapse of formal structures. Smuggling takes place in plain daylight because it is seen as an activity that generates employment. It is morally impossible to legitimize the cocaine economy. However, over the last three years, Bolivia has witnessed the destruction of its alternative bases for national development. The drug connection has simultaneously created a booming economy, at least for some sectors, and degraded social and political life to a point at which recovery and the adoption of a different national course are questionable.

Notes

1. The weakness of the Bolivian state is demonstrated by the following facts: Over the last twenty-five years there have been 323 registered political parties and more than twenty administrations. Between 1925 and 1983 there were 170 coups d'états. During 1985 alone there were more than six hundred strikes and seven major government crises (Calderón 1986, 127).
2. Chapare is a large territorial expanse containing both mountains and subtropical valleys in the Department of Cochabamba. *Yungas* are deep valleys extending from the high plateaus into the tropical portion of the Department of La Paz.
3. The total population in Bolivia in 1986 was six million.
4. *Pisadores* are young, generally unemployed individuals whose job is to step on bunches of coca leaf drenched in sulfuric acid and immersed in large pits covered with plastic.
5. Between 1980 and 1985, there was a steady drop of the gross internal product in Bolivia. In 1985, the decline in industrial production was 11.7 percent, and consumer prices reached an average annual growth rate of 11,749.6 percent.
6. The informal sector comprises the owners and workers in shops hiring fewer than five persons; self-employed workers; and, finally, unremunerated family helpers or apprentices.
7. This figure includes 11,025 fixed and 24,800 mobile stands as well as 15,556 small, medium-sized, and large establishments including restaurants and hotels.
8. At the end of 1986, dismissed miners demanded that severance payments be made in dollars. The Bolivian government had no objection.
9. Bolivia enjoyed a privileged status as an oil exporter at the time when the price of that product reached its peak. This situation coincided with rising tin prices in the international market. The government took advantage of the petrodollar supply and acquired a sizable debt amounting to more than $2,000 million. It is estimated that up to $8,000 million may have entered Bolivia during the 1970s as a result.

References

Blanes Jiménez, J. 1983. *De los Valles al Chapare: Estrategias Familiares en un Contexto de Cambios.* Cochabamba: Centro de Estudios de la Realidad Económica y Social (CERES).
———. 1984. *Bolivia: Agricultura Campesina y los Mercados de Alimentos.* Cochabamba: Centro de Estudios de la Realidad Económica y Social (CERES).
Calderón, F. 1986. "Nación, Movimientos Sociales y Democracia en Bolivia." Pp. 12–30 in CEPAL/UBA (eds.), *Escenarios Políticos y Sociales del Desarrollo Latinoamericano.* Buenos Aires: EUDEBA.
Carter, W. and M. Mamani. 1986. *Coca en Bolivia.* La Paz: Editorial Juventud.
Casanovas, R. 1986. "El Sector Informal Urbano en Bolivia: Apuntes para un Diagnóstico." Pp. 147–79 in CEDLA/FLACSO/ILDIS (eds.), *El Sector Informal en Bolivia.* La Paz: CEDLA/FLACSO/ILDIS.
Casanovas, R. and S. Escobar de Pabón. 1984. "Migración y Mercado de Trabajo en la Ciudad de la Paz: el Caso de los Trabajadores por Cuenta Propia." PISPAL-CERES, La Paz. Mimeo.

Delpirou, A. and A. Labrousse. 1986. *Coca Coke*. Paris: Editions La Decouverte.

Donoso, S. 1980. "Comercio, Acumulación y Reproducción." Tesis de Licenciatura, Universidad Mayor de San Andrés, La Paz.

Doria Medina, S. 1986. *La Economía Informal en Bolivia*. La Paz: Editorial Offset Bolivian Ltda.

Flores-Blanes. 1984. *Dónde va el Chaparé?* Cochabamba: Centro de Estudios de la Realidad Económica y Social (CERES).

Instituto Nacional de Estadística (INE). 1983. *Directorio Nacional de Establecimientos*. La Paz: Instituto Nacional de Estadística.

Núñez del Prado, A. 1986. "Bolivia: Inflación Democracia." Santiago de Chile. Mimeo.

8 Informal Personal Incomes and Outlays of the Soviet Urban Population

Gregory Grossman

The Soviet Informal Sector

Like any country of the world, and perhaps more than most, the Soviet Union contains an informal sector. But although this fact is now fairly common knowledge in the West—not to say in the East—and although the Soviet press and literature are replete with anecdotal and fragmentary information about it, no comprehensive or systematic estimates of the phenomenon are to be found in Soviet statistical sources, whether official or not. In fact, the sparse data on household budgets of nonpeasant families that are regularly printed in the official statistical yearbooks omit any explicit mention of informal income other than that from personal garden plots.[1]

The purposes of this chapter are to provide a brief description of the Soviet informal sector and to present some preliminary quantitative findings regarding the size and distribution of certain informal incomes and outlays by the Soviet urban population. The figures derive from a questionnaire survey in the United States among over one thousand families of recent emigrants from the U.S.S.R. that I conducted jointly with V. G. Treml of Duke University (this survey is briefly described below). The findings pertain solely to the urban population and relate essentially to the second half of the 1970s. The results have not as yet been normalized (reweighted) to better represent the parent urban population of the U.S.S.R.

The concept of an informal sector is very apt for the Soviet Union with its rigidly defined and sharply delimited formal socioeconomic structure, one that is characterized by socialist (mainly, state) ownership, central control, imperative planning, "command" management by a bureaucratic hierarchy, almost universal price fixing, widespread shortages, rationing of nearly all producer goods and some consumer goods, and the virtual absence of a market mechanism.

It is helpful to distinguish between the *informal ("second") economy*[2] in the sense of a set of certain production (value-creating) activities, albeit often illegal, and the set of *informal incomes* that derive partly from second-economy activities and partly from informal or illegal redistributive (not value-creating) transfers, such as embezzlement, misappropriation, misuse of state-owned production facilities, bribe taking, tip taking, and the like. Furthermore, we can also speak of *informal outlays* (expenditures), referring to goods and services whose purchase or other acquisition takes place outside formal channels. Informal outlay by a household typically generates informal income on someone's part. As the title of this chapter indicates, we are here concerned not with informal production (the second economy) but with the informal incomes and outlays of (urban) households[3] (as distinct from the informal transactions of socialist enterprises or organizations or other nonhousehold entities).

In the U.S.S.R. as in other Soviet-type economies, personal informal incomes and outlays are extremely widespread and to a large extent illegal (especially if sizable), and they assume diverse forms and stem from the greatest variety of second-economy activities or economic crimes. They are clearly rather important in the aggregate as well as in many individual cases. The data in table 8.1 come from our questionnaire survey and refer mostly to the second half of the 1970s. In each of the household groups listed (except for Leningrad pensioner households [line9]), 75 percent or more of households derived over 5 percent of total personal income from informal types of income. Perhaps more

Table 8.1 Percentage of all Households with Informal Incomes or Outlays Higher than the Indicated Proportion of Total Personal Income

Household Type and Location	Informal Incomes (I) and Outlays (O)	Proportion of Personal Income				
		0.05 (1)	0.25 (2)	0.50 (3)	0.75 (4)	N (households)
All households except those of pensioners only						
1. R.S.F.S.R. and Baltics	I	78.4	43.5	15.6	3.2	462
2.	O	94.8	57.8	15.6	3.7	462
3. Leningrad	I	75.7	43.2	14.9	3.2	222
4.	O	96.4	63.5	19.8	3.2	222
5. Belorussia, Moldavia, and the Ukraine	I	80.9	55.8	22.8	4.4	183
6.	O	96.7	70.5	31.1	7.7	183
7. Armenia (Armenians only)	I	97.2	85.7	62.5	29.5	176
8.	O	99.4	94.9	73.3	15.3	176
Households of pensioners only						
9. Leningrad	I	53.1	21.0	3.7	0.0	81
10.	O	93.8	67.9	22.2	9.9	81
11. Armenia (Armenians only)	I	100.0	93.3	80.0	26.7	15
12.	O	100.0	100.0	93.3	40.0	15

Source: Berkeley-Duke Questionnaire Survey, Project on the Second Economy, currently being conducted by G. Grossman and V. Treml.

Note: The first number of column (1) means that 78.4% of households that resided in the R.S.F.S.R. and in the Baltic republics, taken together, reported disaggregated data that, when aggregated, indicate that *over* 5% of each family's total personal income consisted of informal income. Thus, only 21.6% of these households derived 5% *or less* of total personal income from informal income. Data refer mostly to the second half of the 1970s. For definitions of categories see the section "The Survey," this chapter.

significantly, 40 percent or more of households in each group derived over one-fourth of total income, and 15 percent or more derived over one-half their total income, in this manner. For Armenian households in our sample, the respective percentages of households are much higher.

As for informal outlays, the proportions of households in each column are in nearly every instance even higher than in the case of informal income. At least 94 percent of households of each household type devoted over 5 percent of total personal income to informal outlay; at least 57 percent spent over one-fourth of total personal income in this way; and at least 15 percent spent over one-half. Again, for the Armenians the figures are much higher.

There is a pronounced spatial pattern to the Soviet informal sector. Broadly speaking, informal income tends to increase, both absolutely and relative to legitimate socialist income, as one moves from north to south (and particularly into Transcaucasia and central Asia), from east to west, and from major urban centers to smaller cities and to the countryside. Tables 8.1 and 8.3 (below) refer to only a few of these spatial components, yet they do illustrate these geographic gradients.

The Soviet informal sector, like that in any other country, is not so much the fringe of the formal economy as a complex intertwinement with it that is at once symbiotic and parasitic. Its economic activities and the related incomes and outlays often escape statistical notice (even when the activities are legal per se), for reasons that will become apparent presently. They are even more likely to escape systematic mention in official and semiofficial statistical publications. And yet, although Soviet informal activities, incomes, and out-lays arise spontaneously in pursuit of personal gain and are heavily illegal, they exist and operate—as do informal activities anywhere—within the bounds of certain traditions, customs, and ethical codes; according to certain laws of survival in a hostile official environment; and under the inevitable discipline of a free market.

Soviet informal incomes and outlays are traceable to many social causes, some of which are clearly systemic. The more important causes are as follows:

1. The ubiquitous presence of socialist (mostly, state) property, which is broadly regarded as "up for grabs" and is thus easily and widely stolen, embezzled, abused, and exploited for private gain—notwithstanding rigorous criminal and administrative provisions and a certain real risk of severe punishment. Indeed, the wholesale misappropriation of socialist property—often by the nominal custodians themselves—constitutes, as it were, the main physical base of a large pyramid of second-economy activity and informal private income.
2. Prohibition of all but a very narrow range of productive activity on private account.
3. Very heavy taxation of legal private income, which is therefore not

usually declared. Prohibition and taxation, as well as the need to obtain supplies in the black market, drive private activity underground.

4. Virtually universal price controls (hence, black markets), physical allocation and rationing of goods, and innumerable other kinds of official regulations. Violation of these controls and regulations is profitable and ipso facto criminalizing.

5. High taxes and monopoly profits derived by the state from some of its products, which invite sub rosa private competition.

6. The outright banning of a wide range of consumer articles and services, for example, those pertaining to Western youth culture, religion, some forms of minority nationalism, and pornography, among others. (Note, however, that prostitution as such is not illegal, on the premise that it cannot exist in a socialist society.)

7. The ineffectiveness and slowness of the formal production and distribution mechanism.

8. A chronic and generally growing excess of money in circulation, which, together with all of the above, helps stimulate private informal demand and, hence, illegal economic activity and the generation of private informal income.

9. The support, protection, and often deliberate promotion of illegal activity by corrupt authorities at various levels.

10. Finally, the important role of personal connections, a lattice of horizontal informal social networks and vertical patron-client links which activates and reinforces the just-mentioned factors. (I will have more to say in this chapter about the quantitative importance of such connections, as brought out in our sample survey.)

It follows that informal income assumes a great variety of guises. In an economy of repressed inflation, widespread shortages, prohibitions, and controls, some of it is "gatekeeper's" take—the economic rent within the grasp of any individual who physically or administratively controls access to scarce, socialist-owned goods or services and officially bestowed permissions and benefits. Some of it, on the other hand, is the earnings of honest-to-goodness labor, but often legally prohibited or overtaxed (and on which tax is evaded) and, hence, criminalized by the system. Some of the informal income is entrepreneurial or trading profit, brokerage fees, or professional fees, likewise magnified by shortages, criminal risk, and tax evasion. Some is plain theft from the state or cheating of the public, as previously noted. And a great many moderate incomes, and a large proportion of the very largest, are the fruit of widespread corruption by officialdom of nearly every stripe, rank, sector, and region.

Income and Outlay Types in the Soviet Economy

On the whole, the second economy and informal incomes and outlays in the household sector seem to be rather highly monetized, which would seem to attest to a high degree of development, institutionalization, and effectiveness.[4] The means of payment in informal personal transactions is primarily currency, not only for greater security, as in other systems, but also because checks are seldom used by individuals in any case. In the frequent event of relatively small labor services or favors, bargains are often struck and payments are made in what is in effect the second currency of the Soviet Union—vodka (Treml 1985a, 1985b).

While illicit payments are often given in kind (i.e., large tips or smaller bribes), barter seems to be only moderately employed between individuals (though widely used by socialist enterprises in informal transactions between themselves). On the other hand, exchange of favors in the form of access to goods or services is not only common practice but a salient feature of the Soviet informal economy, embedded as it is in the elaborate interweaving of horizontal informal social networks and vertical patron-client relations. The favors are chiefly at the expense of third parties, primarily the state, though indirectly also at the expense of third-party individuals whose own access to goods or services may be impaired in this manner.

Hence, access to favor-dispensing opportunities—and, of course, to networks and patrons—is a most important private asset in the very personal Soviet economy. So is access to opportunities for misappropriating and misusing state property more directly. Large sums are paid for both kinds of opportunities, in lump sums and as periodic bribes. Jobs are bought and sold to this end, as are the jobs of those who sell the jobs, and so on up the line. Needless to say, all of this is illegal.[5]

The Soviet informal sector is not the preserve solely of the unemployed, the poor, and the weak. In any case, though not unknown, official unemployment is low thanks to both macroeconomic and microeconomic conditions that lead Soviet employers and the economy as a whole to overemploy labor. Moreover, joblessness is virtually a criminal offense ("parasitism," "living off unearned income") for an able-bodied person of working age who lacks a proper excuse, such as being a student. Individuals devoting most of their time and effort to the second economy often take low-paying official jobs that require little work, or even buy phony official jobs, in order to pass occasional police checks. Accordingly, official employment statistics are poor indicators of the extent of aggregate labor commitment to the informal economy, or of its change over time.

Though unemployment is rare in the U.S.S.R., wages and salaries at the lower end of the official scale and nearly all pensions are by themselves barely enough for even a modest material existence, especially with dependents in the family.[6] Hence, those with low official incomes tend to seek out opportunities to obtain informal income of one kind or another. Added to this is the need to accumulate substantial savings for side payments in the event of costly emergencies (medical, legal), to bribe a child's way into a university, to purchase durable goods and private housing, to handle the large expenses necessitated by traditional rites of passage (weddings, funerals), and to buy a lucrative job. When the hunger for material comforts and the vogue to emulate life in the West are also added, it becomes clear that the quest for informal income is widespread and reaches into all economic strata. Demand for informal income and the supply of informal goods and services inevitably reinforce one another. At any rate, one is often reassured that "everybody does it anyway." In sum, to be really rich (apart from official perquisites), or even only comfortable, one has to rely heavily on informally—mostly illegally—obtained income and wealth.

We define the total personal income of a household (TPIH) as the sum of all household income on current account during the given period, whether earned or received as transfer, whether formal or informal, whether in money or in kind, after taxes withheld at the place of work. "Current account" denotes the exclusion of capital transactions, such as loan receipts or inheritance receipts. The legitimate socialist income of a household (LSIH) is income that is legitimately received from the formal sector, including transfer payments from the state but excluding receipts of self-employed persons working on a contractual basis with socialist entities.[7] Informal household income (AOIH) may also originate in the socialist sector (e.g., the just-mentioned contractual receipts, or theft of state property) as well as in the household sector (wages, profits, bribes, tips, cheating proceeds in retail trade). LSIH + AOIH = TPIH. The same income categories recomputed per capita are designated by the same symbols minus the H—LSI, AOI, TPI (see Appendix).

Total informal outlay—total private payments and consumption per household (TPCPH) or per capita (TPCP)—includes purchases from and payments to private persons, in-kind private receipts of goods and services, and self-produced food—all on current account only. It also includes services "purchased" by means of bribes or tips, in cash or in kind. Additional details of measurement are given in the Appendix.

The Survey

The émigré survey of household budgets is the empirical pillar of our project on the second economy of the U.S.S.R. Before launching it, we conducted several dozen nonquestionnaire (open-ended) interviews with well-informed Soviet emigrants (former defense lawyers, prosecutors, judges, underground businessmen, police officials, journalists, etc.) to help us design the questionnaire and the sample. We were also encouraged and inspired by the early signs of success of a similar survey among Soviet emigrants in Israel.[8]

The units of observation of our survey are three: the household (usually, family) for most variables; the individual income earner within the household for personal income; and every adult in the household, regardless of past

Table 8.2 Distribution of Soviet Emigrant Sample by Republic and Family Type

	Total Households	Full, Working Families (F-W)	Pensioner Families	Families of Single Woman and Child(ren)	Single Women	Single Men	Total Persons
Northern Republics	(729)[1]	(525)	(83)	(43)	(28)	(50)	(1,947)
1. R.S.F.S.R.	448[1]	246[2]	82	42	28	50	1,060
a. Leningrad	303	103	81	42	28	49	622
b. Other Cities	145	143	1	—	—	1	438
2. Ukraine	119	119	—	—	—	—	361
3. Belorussia	37	36	1	—	—	—	110
4. Moldavia	28	28	—	—	—	—	89
5. Latvia	44[2]	44	—	—	—	—	131
6. Lithuania	53	52	—	1	—	—	196
Southern Republics	(332)	(316)	(15)	(0)	(0)	(1)	(1,076)
7. Georgia	46	46	—	—	—	—	167
8. Azerbaidzhan	38	38	—	—	—	—	130
9. Armenia	211	195	15	—	—	1	658
a. Armenian	191	175	15	—	—	1	591
b. Non-Armenian	20	20	—	—	—	—	67
10. Uzbekistan	37[3]	37	—	—	—	—	121
Total Households	1,061	841	98	43	28	51	
Total Persons	3,023	2,657	198	89	28	51	3,023

[1]Includes 1 household from northern Kazakhstan.
[2]Includes 2 households from Estonia.
[3]Includes 4 households from southern Kazakhstan.

income earning, for "perceptions" of side incomes by the public at large. As with the Israeli survey, our sample is limited to the urban population (chiefly because of a paucity of emigrants from rural areas); but unlike that survey, ours contains an ethnic southern component, namely, Armenians. Almost all questionnaire interviews took place in the United States; interviewers were also Soviet emigrants.

Recent Soviet emigrants in the United States are, of course, not representative of the "parent" Soviet urban population in a number of important socioeconomic respects. By nationality, they are predominantly, though far from exclusively, Jewish and Armenian, and they are well-educated and from white-collar backgrounds. Accordingly, we made a determined effort to give additional representation to other nationalities, to blue-collar income earners, to less-educated families, to residents of cities other than the largest ones (except Leningrad, as explained below), and to those from the southern republics.

The sample covers 1,061 households containing 3,023 individuals, of whom 2,299 were adults (16 years of age and over) at the time to which the data refer. A matrix of household types against geographic locations is presented in table 8.2. Of the adults, 52.8 percent are Jewish, 22.0 percent are Armenian, and 18.1 percent are Russian, Ukranian, or Belorussian. Nationality is as recorded in the person's internal Soviet passport. Despite our effort to balance the sample, it is a relatively highly educated one. Of the adults, 38.5 percent had gone beyond the secondary level and 33.8 percent had completed higher education.

Two geographic locations, Armenia and Leningrad, constitute special case studies within our survey; the two together account for half the households in the total sample. The subsample from Armenia accounts for 19.9 percent of households and 21.8 percent of persons. Of these persons, 89.9 percent are ethnic Armenians, which is very close to the actual proportion in the republic's total population, as reported by the 1979 census (89.7%). Since ethnic Armenians are the only titular nationality from a southern republic in our sample, this group also stands as proxy for Transcaucasia—a region that plays an important and distinctive role in the Soviet second economy.

The other special case, Leningrad, accounts for 28.5 percent of the sample households. Here, in addition to the full working families that are our exclusive object for all other localities, we collected subsamples of other types of household, namely, single working males, single working females with children, single working females without children, and pensioner families.

The survey employed the snowball technique of collecting interviews, constrained in the just-mentioned ways, rather than random sampling. To hold down the risk of sample inbreeding in the course of questionnaire collection, we interviewed in a number of American cities using many interviewers (except in the case of Armenians, who were all interviewed in the Los Angeles area, where they are concentrated). The questionnaire consists of two parts. The first deals with individual perceptions of the size of informal incomes as supplements to the official earnings of thirty-six occupations, professions, and jobs listed by us in the questionnaire. Altogether, 2,076 persons answered this part.

The remaining and larger part of the questionnaire pertains mainly to the composition and demographics of the household and to its expenditure, income, and wealth in the "last normal year" (LNY) in the U.S.S.R. LNY is defined as the last calendar year in which the household's material circumstances were not yet significantly affected by the prospect of emigration; it is not necessarily a typical year in the family's experience.

In regard to expenditures, the questionnaire asks for considerable detail about payments to private individuals for goods and services purchased and for repairs performed, tips and bribes given, rentals paid, and so forth. These data allow us to estimate, albeit approximately, the dependence of the urban population on private sources of supply. At a further remove, the expenditure data should help throw light on the aggregate hidden incomes of private producers and traders who sell to the urban sector, including those outside the direct purview of our survey.[9]

Still in regard to household expenditures, the questionnaire dwells on a number of special problems, such as privately owned housing and related matters; private automobile ownership and outlay on repairs, gasoline, and the like; and alcohol purchase, consumption, and use, including illegal home distillation and the use of vodka as a means of payment and as an incentive. It also inquires into methods of circumventing goods shortages that were practiced by our respondents (such as exploiting personal connections, paying under the counter, traveling some distance to obtain goods, and using "closed distributors").

Our sample is probably unrepresentative in another respect: both tails of the sample's personal income distribution are probably shortened in comparison with those in the Soviet urban population. At the low end we have very few families with a formal income of less than fifty rubles per capita per month, the poverty line below which a Soviet family became, in 1974, eligible for supplemental child support.[10] At the upper tail of the distribution, the recent emigration omits, for reasons of both ethnic affiliation and political position, the not inconsiderable element of tribute-collecting and bribe-taking party functionaries and higher officials, government administrators, and police officers, as well as the stereotypical cash-heavy underground businessman from the south.

Survey Findings and Commentary

An explanation of terms and abbreviations used in our analysis is presented in the Appendix. The main results are summarized in this section. While, as already mentioned, Soviet official statistics on (nonpeasant) consumer budgets indicate almost no income other than legitimate socialist (formal) income, our survey finds a fundamentally different picture, one that is fully in tune with the virtually unlimited anecdotal information in the Soviet literature and other sources.[11]

Our results show a considerable amount of informal income (AOI) based on a large volume of second-economy and other informal activity— legal, gray, and black. In turn, informal income provides the means for a comparable amount of informal (private) spending. These are, of course, not mere statistical statements; they also betoken significant economic and social realities and have profound implications for policy. Surely, the first two years of Mr. Gorbachev's leadership have amply confirmed such an appraisal.

The figures in table 8.1 have indicated the widespread nature of involvement of our sample households in the informal sector, on both the income and the outlay sides. The involvement on the outlay side is more widespread than on the income side, but quite considerable on the latter as well. Moreover, there is a strong differentiation by geographic region, both informal income and informal outlays rising steeply from north to south. Tables 8.3 and 8.4 present the mean values for the basic income and outlay aggregates by geographic group. They also introduce a distinction between two household types, namely, full, working (F-W) households and pensioner households.

A word about the geographic classification in these two tables. Here "North" is divided into three subregions. One combines the three European republics of Belorussia, Moldavia, and the Ukraine (BMU, collectively) which, on the whole, show a considerably greater presence of the informal sector than does the rest of the north. The Russian Soviet Federated Socialist Republic (R.S.F.S.R.) and the Baltics are divided into two additional subregions: Leningrad, which is roughly representative of the capitals of these four republics (i.e., Moscow, Riga, Vilnius, and Tallin), and all the other cities of the north, that is, all cities other than the just-named five. An important distinction between the five major cities and the other cities is that the former tend to be much better supplied officially with goods and services than the latter. Other cities are thus forced to rely more on informally supplied goods and services, and, incidentally, may also be better situated with regard to privately marketed or self-produced food.

In table 8.3, the values of formal income per capita by geographic location (line 3) are very close to what can be inferred from 1977 official Soviet statistics. Since official data on socialist income is generally regarded as reasonably reliable, it seems likely that—at least in this regard—we are dealing with a fairly representative sample of the Soviet urban population. The new findings are those on line 1 and lines 5–12. For the north they show (line 7) that informal income adds on the average to formal income some 38–41 percent in the R.S.F.S.R. and Baltics (Leningrad and other cities), and some 67 percent in

Table 8.3 Soviet Emigrant Subsamples: Mean Values of Demographic, Income, and Outlay Variables per Capita

	Full, Working Households (F-W)				Pensioner Households	
	North					
	R.S.F.S.R. and Baltics					
	Belorussia, Moldavia, and the Ukraine	Other Cities	Leningrad	Armenians from Armenia (AA)	Leningrad	Armenians from Armenia (AA)
	(1)	(2)	(3)	(4)	(5)	(6)
1. N (persons)	558	382	294	560	164	30
2. Total personal income (TPI), rubles per year	2,174	1,540	1,943	3,220	1,241	2,839
3. Formal income (LSI), rubles per year	1,300	1,089	1,405	1,155	1,046	963
4. LSI as percentage of TPI	59.8	70.8	72.3	35.9	84.3	33.9
5. Informal income (AOI), rubles per year	874	450	538	2,065	195	1,876
6. AOI as percentage of TPI	40.2	29.2	27.7	64.1	15.7	66.1
7. TPI ÷ LSI	1.67	1.41	1.38	2.79	1.19	2.95
8. Informal Outlay (TPCP), ruble per year	880	442	674	1,988	497	2,023
9. TPCP as percentage of TPI	40.5	28.7	34.7	61.7	40.1	71.3
10. Of which: private food purchase, rubles per year	328	167	149	617	161	648
11. As percentage of TPI	15.1	10.8	10.9	5.2	13.0	22.8
12. As percentage of TPCP	37.3	37.8	22.1	31.0	32.4	32.0
13. Persons per household	3.05	3.18	2.85	3.20	2.03	2.00
14. Age, years	37.5	38.3	39.1	40.9	63.9	61.7
15. Education, years	11.2	11.05	13.0	9.80	12.4	5.65
16. Blue-collar, percentage	34.3	35.5	15.7	44.5	—	—

Source: See table 8.1.
Note: See the section ''The Survey,'' this chapter.

Table 8.4 Soviet Emigrant Subsamples: Mean Values of *Blat* and Gain Therefrom, per Capita

	Full, Working Households (F-W)				Pensioner Households	
	North					
		R.S.F.S.R. and Baltics				
	Belorussia, Moldavia, and the Ukraine	Other Cities	Leningrad	Armenians from Armenia (AA)	Leningrad	Armenians from Armenia (AA)
	(1)	(2)	(3)	(4)	(5)	(6)
1. N (persons)	558	382	294	560	164	30
2. Total personal income (TPI), rubles per year	2,174	1,540	1,943	3,220	1,241	2,839
3. *Blat* purchases, official value, rubles per year	193	161	170	118	151	261
4. *Blat* purchases as percentage of TPI	8.9	10.5	8.8	3.7	12.2	9.2
5. Additional payment with *blat* purchases, rubles per year	23.6	13.1	15.1	12.2	12.9	23.6
6. Line 5 ÷ line 3 × 100	12.2	8.1	8.8	10.4	8.5	9.0
7. Gain from *blat* purchases, perceived, rubles per year	98.3	58.0	65.0	89.6	42.5	304
8. Line 7 as percentage of TPI	4.5	3.8	3.3	2.8	3.4	10.7
9. Line 7 ÷ line 5	4.16	4.46	4.32	7.32	3.29	12.9

Source: See table 8.1.

Note: See the section "The Survey," this chapter.

BMU. These figures are for full, working families, on a per capita basis. On the other hand, northern pensioner households, in our case all from Leningrad, add 19 percent by way of informal income to their formal income. It may be noted that their mean formal income—1,046 rubles per capita per year—is rather high for pensions alone; in point of fact, many worked part-time at official jobs, which can be done without loss of pension income.

Turning to the south, our data confirm the enormously greater importance there of the informal sector. Indeed, our F-W Armenian households (column 4) averaged a per capita total income 66 percent higher than, and a per capita informal income almost four times as high as, those of our Leningrad households—despite an 18 percent lower formal income, considerably larger families (line 9), and less education. In these Armenian households, informal income constitutes as much as 64.1 percent of the total, and multiplies their formal income by a factor of 2.79. Their advantage over the northerners is fully reflected in their annual savings and gross assets, the incidence of ownership of dwellings (house or apartment), and private automobiles (data not included in these tables).

An interesting case are our Armenian pensioners, though unfortunately we had access only to a very small subsample. Bearing this in mind, we found that they are almost as well off per capita as the full, working Armenian families and strikingly better off than their pensioner-household counterparts in Leningrad. Thus, their mean total income is 2.3 times as large as that of the Leningrad pensioners, and their mean informal income is 9.6 times as large, per capita, while their assets are 3.8 times as large. Clearly, the household sector in Armenia—and probably in all of Transcaucasia—has a quantitatively and qualitatively very different economic profile from that of the north. This result casts serious doubt on the official data, which would have the populations of the south, Armenia included, enjoy a considerably lower material standard of life than the rest of the country.

Table 8.3, line 8, also shows for each geographic group the mean value of the households' total private consumption and payments—in other words, informal outlay—per capita (TPCP). For a country in which private transactions are formally held to a minimum, and are often criminally prosecutable, TPCP turns out on the average to take as much as 30 percent to 40 percent of total personal income in the north and over 60 percent among Armenians in Armenia (line 9). In relation to formal income alone, the corresponding ratios are of course much higher, namely, between one-half and two-thirds for the north in the vicinity of 200 percent for Armenians. In other words, sample Armenians spent around twice as much informally as they earned formally, which is of course quite possible given their very high informal incomes.

For nearly every geographic group, the most important single component of informal outlay is privately purchased food, which tends to account for between 30 percent and 40 percent of all informal outlay in table 8.3, except in the case of households in Leningrad, where the figure is 22 percent. The low figure for Leningrad (F-W) is not surprising, since the city is presumably relatively well supplied with "official" food. Somewhat of a mystery is the high outlay on private food by Leningrad pensioner households. After all, with their low involvement in the formal economy, pensioners ought to have the time to queue for the cheaper food in official stores. Or are they, by virtue of age and experience, particularly sensitive to the quality of their nourishment?

Incidentally, the outlay on private food revealed by our data is several times as high as that suggested by official Soviet statistics for sales in private peasant (*kolkhoz*) markets, thus tending to confirm what has been long suspected, namely, the very dubious quality of Soviet data on food sales in kolkhoz markets (see Treml 1985a; Shenfield 1986). Also interesting is the correlation between per capita value of private purchases and payment (TPCP) and per capita informal income (AOI). Thus, in rubles per year:

	AOI	TPCP
Belorussia, Moldavia, the Ukraine	874	880
R.S.F.S.R. and Baltics, other cities	450	442
Leningrad, F-W	538	674
Armenians, F-W	2,065	1,998
Leningrad, pensioner households	195	497
Armenians, pensioner households	1,876	2,023

Apparently, in the U.S.S.R. one goes after private income in order to spend it on private (nonsocialist) purchases and payments, or, alternatively, one tends to spend the "discretionary" informal income on private goods and services.[12]

In table 8.4, of some interest are the figures expressing the importance of connections (*blat*) in the household's budget. The total of goods purchased with the help of blat, valued at the official prices paid to the socialist store or outlet, averages between 9 percent and 12 percent of total income in the case of the northern groups and Armenian pensioners, but stands at only 3.7 percent in the case of Armenian F-W families. One wonders whether a very highly developed black market, as in Armenia, tends to crowd out the use of blat as a means of obtaining the desired goods. Yet, when blat is used in Armenia, it turns out to be, in the respondents' own estimation, relatively more profitable than in the north (line 9), expressed in terms of perceived gain from blat as a ratio of additional payments to secure such purchases.

Conclusions

The brief and bare figures just presented suggest a significant, energetic, and well nigh ubiquitous informal sector—mostly illegal at that—which shapes the lives of the majority of the Soviet population. True, our data still remain to be normalized and cannot be held to be fully representative of the parent urban population. But unless something is very wrong with these data, we can advance with some confidence several preliminary conclusions.[13]

As mentioned, our data pertain overwhelmingly to the second half of the seventies and have been "indexed" to 1977. The period is noteworthy. It corresponds to the later years of Brezhnev's rule and leads up to the eve of the sharp turn for the worse in the "first economy" (and a sharp turn for the better for the second) which occurred in 1979–80. The term *laissez-faire* is hardly apposite to anything in the U.S.S.R., but it is perhaps least inapposite with reference to the second economy in Brezhnev's time, when a combination of halfhearted law enforcement and ballooning corruption did wonders for the supply side of the underground, at the same time as monetary expansion inflated demand.

Needless to say, the Soviet second economy and corruption did not begin with Brezhnev; they began with the October Revolution, with roots reaching deep into the Russian past. But they spread, grew, and flourished under his rule. In regard to personal income and wealth the results included, insofar as we can discern, the rise of a class of Brezhnevian nouveaux riches—the big underground operators and their graft-taking official patrons—as well as a more moderate but numerous "middle class" of significant beneficiaries from the second economy, and so on down to the Brezhnevian "nouveaux pauvres"—those who could not or would not partake of expanding opportunities for informal and illicit gain and had to face rising prices and buyers' competition from the more affluent.[14]

The bad years from 1979 on presented even greater opportunities for informal and illegal activities. Shortages spread and worsened in all branches of the economy, open (kolkhoz market) and black free-market prices accelerated their upward march, and printing presses rolled faster to fill private pockets with ever more currency. Materialism and acquisitiveness intensified, if eyewitnesses can be believed. Our survey data do not capture these later years; but, though ignorant of the actual dimensions, we can be fairly sure of the trend in the early eighties.

Mr. Gorbachev's rise to supreme power in March 1985 launched a new era, at once heavily affected by the growth and spread of informality and illegality during the previous decades and mobilized to "reconstruct"—in large measure, even to sanitize—the society by the twin policies of severe crackdown on illegal economic activity ("nonlabor income") and an appreciable effort to legalize and co-opt the second economy into society's legitimate mainstream. But this is a separate story; the outcome of these policies remains to be seen.

Appendix: Explanation of Terms and Abbreviations

Household (family) Types

Full, working (F-W) households. Those households in which both members of the central couple are present, and at least one is working in the official sector. Pensioner households consist of pensioners only; in our sample, there are almost always two pensioners per household. There are pensioners also within some F-W households.

Locational Categories

North. Those portions of the U.S.S.R. that lie north of the Caucasus range and of central Asia.

Armenians from Armenia (AA). Our overall sample also contains twenty families of non-Armenians who lived in Armenia in the given year (LNY, see below). The latter group has a very different economic profile from AA; hence, they are included in the SRNAA category.

SRNAA. Emigrants from southern republics who are not AA. These are all ethnic "northerners" who lived in one or another southern republic in the given year. For numbers from individual republics see table 8.2.

Time Period

LNY. Last normal year, that is, the last calendar year of the household's residence in the U.S.S.R. which was not affected by the decision to emigrate. Except in the case of a few questions, each respondent was asked to answer and provide data with reference to his or her household's own LNY. For the sample as a whole, LNYs range from 1970 through 1981, but 98 percent of them fall between 1974 and 1980, and 85 percent between 1976 and 1979, inclusive. Both mean and median values of LNY are 1977.

Indexing. To adjust for the steady growth in the official ruble value of a man-year during the period, not to speak of the growth in consumer prices of most kinds and in most markets, all ruble values on both the income and the expenditure side were brought to the 1977 level by means of the index of the average monthly gross wage/salary for the U.S.S.R. as a whole (examples: 1970 = 77.5; 1974 = 90.0; 1977 = 100; 1979 = 105.8; 1981 = 112.5).

Income Categories

All categories relate only to *personal* income on *current* account, including both factor earnings and transfers of all kinds, legal and illegal (including theft). In-kind income, primarily from private gardens and orchards (which are in principle legal) and from theft (not so), is evaluated by the respondents themselves. In-kind income appears simultaneously as in-kind expenditure in our accounts. Noncash benefits from what the Soviets call the "social consumption fund"—in-kind benefits distributed by the state, such as educational or medical services and subsidies to prices of consumer goods and services—are not included as income. Also not included are (1) imputed rent of owner-occupied dwellings and of other real estate and major consumer durables and (2) implicit income from "connections."

TPI. Total personal income per capita (i.e., per member of a household) as specified in the preceding paragraph. TPI = LSI + AOI.

LSI. Legitimate socialist income per capita, that is, that part of TPI that is formally (officially, legally) obtained from the socialist sector, mainly the state. It includes legally sanctioned nonlabor income such as interest on savings in the savings bank, official transfer payments (e.g., old-age pensions), as well as labor earnings. But the source of income must be the socialist sector; even legally obtained income from another household is not included under LSI.

AOI. All other income per capita, defined as TPI minus LSI. As such it includes (1) illicit income from the socialist sector; (2) any earnings or income from the household sector, in money or in kind, legal or illegal; (3) earnings from home-grown food; and (4) income from abroad. For any large value of AOI, (1) and (2) are likely to be much more important than (3) and (4).

Age, Education, and Blue-Collar Percentage

Age and education refer only to husbands and wives in LNY. Blue-collar percentage is the percentage of blue-collar workers (*rabochie*) in the sum of blue-collar and white-collar workers, taking account only of husbands and wives who were employed during LNY.

Consumption and Payments

Food purchases, private. Purchases from (1) private sellers in organized peasants' markets (kolkhoz markets), (2) individual sellers outside of organized markets, and (3) private persons while at a summer house in the countryside. The small fraction of purchases at peasant markets bought from socialist entities rather than private persons is not deducted here. This overstatement may be offset by the significant phenomenon of crypto-private sales of foodstuffs—that is, sales purportedly on socialist account but in fact on private account, which our respondents would not have been able to identify and report as private foodstuffs.

Nonfood goods, private. All goods other than food purchased from private persons (other than automobiles and real estate), whether at flea markets or elsewhere. A certain, probably substantial, part of these purchases may refer to secondhand goods. For nonfood goods, as for food, crypto-private sales may cause appreciable understatement of estimates of private pur-chases by respondents.

Medical payments, private. Fees, tips, bribes, and the like paid in money to various kinds of medical and health-care personnel, a common practice in the U.S.S.R. and other Communist countries. Much of it is illegal or at least tax-evaded by the recipient, especially in the case of the larger payments. Not included are purchases of medicines and other medical goods on the black market.

Other services and tips, private. A catch-all category that includes in addition to "everyday services" (to use the Soviet term) such items as rent paid for a *dacha* and transport to same.

Gifts. In the questionnaire this category is defined as "the total value of those goods in short supply (of any type) which your family received as gifts during [the given year] from grateful clients, customers, students, patients, etc." In other words, these are essentially fees, tips, bribes, and so forth, in kind, as evaluated by the respondent. In this context, gifts are regarded as part of consumption, a type of barter purchase of goods from the household sector in exchange for one's services rather than one's cash. As income, their value is included in AOI.

Bribes. So named in the questionnaire, bribes can be for any purpose.

Extra payments. See below.

Connections (*blat*). The Russian word *blat* stems from traditional criminal argot and denotes, in both its substantive and the adjectival form (*blatnoi*), anything of a criminal character. In everyday Soviet usage it has also acquired the diluted meaning of "pull," "connection," and the like. Other words convey the same meaning; we have chosen blat over its synonyms for its brevity. Though blat can be invoked for any purpose, in our tables the term refers only to the method of effecting purchases. We asked our respondents to estimate the total value of purchases (by household, in LNY) in official stores at official prices in which blat played a role, with or without additional payment "under the counter." Blat is only one "irregular" method of obtaining goods from official outlets. Other methods are (1) with under-the-counter payment without the benefit of connections; (2) by purchasing a more favorable place in a waiting line or queue; (3) by means of a "tied sale," that is, buying a nondesired item as a condition of buying the desired item; (4) buying the desired goods at some distance from one's town (here defined as at least 100 km away); and (5) buying in so-called closed distributors, stores to which access is limited to persons with certain employers or positions, but whose goods are not infrequently obtainable for a bribe.

Extra payments in conjunction with [irregular purchases]. The sum of the bribes and under-the-counter payments and of the value of the nondesired goods bought in "tied sales."

Gain from *blat* purchases, perceived. The respondent's own estimate of the benefit obtained by the household, per capita, by being able to use connections and thus forgo or reduce extra outlays on bribes, under-the-counter payments, and other surcharges.

Notes

The research underlying this chapter has been generously supported by the Ford Foundation, the National Council for Soviet and East European Research, Wharton Econometric Forecasting Associates, and also by several units of the University of California, Berkeley. This support is gratefully and cheerfully acknowledged. Thanks also go for wise counsel to V. G. Treml and Michael Alexeev; for able research assistance to Anna Meyendorff, Tina Perry, and David J. Sedik; and for computer skills to Davida J. Weinberg.

1. TsSU SSSR, *Narodnoe khoziaistvo SSSR v 1985 g.* (1986, 417–18) prints on the basis of a sample survey the (mean) household incomes and expenditures of (1) a family of a (combined) blue- or white-collar worker and (2) the family of a blue-collar worker in industry.

2. The working definition of the "second economy" that I have generally used with reference to Soviet-type economies is the set of "productive" activities which meet at least one of the two following tests: (1) they are directly on private account, whether conducted legally or illegally, and (2) they are to a significant extent in knowing contravention of the law. I have described and discussed the second economy in a number of publications; see especially Grossman 1977, 1979.

3. In the relevant literature, personal informal incomes (outlays) are often also called "private" incomes (outlays). Note that the consumption or investment use of self-produced goods and services (insofar as they are considered in this chapter) generates at once both informal income and informal outlay for the given household and for the household sector as a whole.

4. Contrast this with the fact that many of the official perquisites of status and success are *not* in money but, rather, in privileged access to superior goods and services.

5. For a vivid and extensive description of an economy of favors exchange in present-day Poland, see Wedel 1986.

6. On poverty in the U.S.S.R., see especially Matthews 1985, 1986.

7. Such contractual arrangements can be legal and, when so, cover a wide range of activities and, compared with employment, are often of considerable advantage to the individual in terms of earnings and otherwise. Also widespread and often even more lucrative are illegal (or "semilegal") contractual arrangements, individual or collective, especially common in construction (*shabashniki*).

8. For preliminary findings on informal incomes and expenditures based on this survey, see Ofer and Vinokur 1980. For a number of technical and other reasons, they find lower relative informal incomes and informal outlays than does our survey. See also the descriptive article by O'Hearn (1980).

9. In this connection, a serious problem of estimation is created by incomes from crypto-private production, that is, private activity that hides behind the facade of a socialist enterprise. Such incomes are numerous and can be quite large individually but are not likely to be reported by our respondents as payments to private persons. The reason is that the products of crypto-private production are often indistinguishable, physically or by price, from identical products sold on the state's account and, in fact,

are sold side by side with them. While this helps protect the private operation against discovery by authorities, it also fools the customer into thinking that he is buying "socialist" and not private goods. Unless we find a convincing way to estimate crypto-private sales, the corresponding hidden income, the extent of the second economy, and the true size of the Soviet GNP may all be significantly understated.

10. In terms of formal (legitimate) income, which is presumably close to the income definition for the child-supplement program, 101 families in our sample, or 9.5 percent, were making fifty rubles or less per person per month. However, in terms of total personal income, inclusive of informal income, only four out of the 1,061 families in the sample were making fifty rubles or less per person per month.

11. Other studies that report similar findings include Ofer and Vinokur 1980, Matthews 1986, and Millar and Donhowe 1986.

12. The substantial disparity for Leningrad pensioners may be related to their high preference for private food and possibly low spending on "official" goods.

13. A cautionary word: aggregate personal income is not the gross national product. To go quantitatively from the former to the latter is no simple matter, and it is especially complicated for a macro- and micro-disequilibrated economy such as that of the Soviet Union. Thus, no estimates of the share of the second economy in the Soviet GNP are implied herein.

14. On the social character of the Brezhnev years see Millar 1985; on the post-1979 inflation and its effects see Grossman 1986.

References

Grossman, G. 1977. "The 'Second Economy' of the USSR." *Problems of Communism* 26:25–40.
———. 1979. "Notes on the Illegal Private Economy and Corruption." Pp. 834–55 in U.S. Congress, Joint Economic Committee, *The Soviet Economy in a Time of Change.* Washington, D.C.: U.S. Government Printing Office.
———. 1986. "Inflationary, Political, and Social Implications of the Current Economic Slowdown." Pp. 172–97 in H. H. Höhmann et al. (eds.), *Economics and Politics in the USSR: Problems of Interdependence.* Boulder, Colo.: Westview Press.
Matthews, M. 1985. "Poverty in the Soviet Union." *Wilson Quarterly,* pp. 75–84.
———. 1986. *Poverty and Patterns of Deprivation in the Soviet Union.* Berkeley-Duke Occasional Papers on the Second Economy in the USSR, no. 6, June.
Millar, J. R. 1985. "The Little Deal: Brezhnev's Contribution to Acquisitive Socialism." *Slavic Review* 44:694–706.
Millar, J. R. and P. Donhowe. 1986. "The Soviet Union's Rich and Poor." *San Francisco Chronicle,* February 19. Based on an émigré questionnaire survey.
Ofer, G. and A. Vinokur. 1980. "The Private Sector in Urban USSR." The Rand Corporation, Report R-2359-NA, Santa Monica, Calif.
O'Hearn, D. 1980. "The Consumer Second Economy: Size and Effects." *Soviet Studies* 32:218–34.
Shenfield, S. 1986. "How Reliable are Soviet Statistics on the Kolkhoz Markets?" *Journal of Official Statistics* 2:181–91. An earlier and longer version appears as Discussion Papers, G1, Centre for Russian and East European Studies, University of Birmingham (U.K.), November 1984.

Treml, V. G. 1985a. *Purchases of Food from Private Sources in Soviet Urban Areas.* Berkeley-Duke Occasional Papers on the Second Economy in the USSR, no. 3, September.

————. 1985b. *Alcohol Underground in the USSR*. Berkeley-Duke Occasional Papers on the Second Economy in the USSR, no. 5, December.

Wedel, J. 1986. *The Private Poland.* New York: Facts on File.

4 Industrial Restructuring and the Informal Sector

9   Subcontracting and Employment Dynamics in Mexico City

Lourdes Benería

Early in 1981 I participated, with Martha Roldán, in a research project on industrial homework in Mexico City. Our objectives were to analyze this type of economic activity as it takes place within the context of a Third World country today and to investigate the extent and nature of women's participation in it. Since garment work had been the subject of previous research (e.g., Alonso 1979, 1983; Connolly 1982), our interest was in focusing on nongarment activities, about which very little was known. We conducted extensive interviews in different sectors, ranging from plastics to toys and electronics. We included, for comparative purposes, a group of garment workers that represented 11.4 percent of the total.

Soon after initiating the interviews, we became intrigued with the question of who provided homework. The jobbers with whom the women had direct contact were mostly middlemen working on behalf of firms, and often the women received their work directly from a workshop or even a factory. Our questions were obvious: Where was homework ultimately coming from? Was it the last step in a more complex process of subcontracting and, if so, what firms were involved in it? What factors determined the tendency to send production outside of the firm? How prevalent was this tendency in Mexico City? What employment dynamics did subcontracting generate? What was the relationship of homework to the wider economy, and what was the articulation between activities classified as part of the formal and informal sectors?

With a per capita gross national product of $2,240 for 1982 (in dollars of that year), Mexico is ranked by the World Bank as an upper-middle-income country. Mexico's economy grew rapidly during the 1960s and early 1970s. This was particularly true for the manufacturing sector; while the average growth of the gross domestic product was 7.6 percent for 1960–70 and 6.5 percent for 1970–80, the corresponding rate of growth for manufacturing was 10.1 percent and 7.1 percent, respectively. As a result, industrial production grew from 26 percent of the country's total output in 1950 to 40 percent in 1980 (Cordera and Tello 1981). However, industrial production slowed during 1975–78, and strong inflationary pressures accelerated and continued during the vigorous recovery initiated in 1979. These inflationary pressures, together with the sluggish growth of some key industrial sectors, were at the root of the difficulties that surfaced in the early 1980s.

Mexico's uneven development has taken place within the context of a high degree of inequality in the distribution of resources and income. For example, in 1977, the lowest 20 percent of households received 2.9 percent of total household income, with the highest 10 percent receiving over 40 percent (World Bank 1983, table 21). Migration from rural to urban areas has made more obvious the lack of absorption of a large segment of the labor force, a phenomenon that is reflected in the growing importance of the informal sector. This is particularly the case for Mexico City, which represents the largest industrial concentration in the country and which has experienced one of the highest rates of population growth in the world (García, Muñoz, and Oliveira 1979).

Foreign capital has played and continues to play a fundamental role in Mexico's industrialization. Multinational firms produce more than one-third of the country's industrial output. This proportion has been as high as 40 percent for the capital goods sector, over 60 percent for consumer durables, and 50 percent for manufactured exports (Cordera and Tello 1981; Jenkins 1984). Multinational firms are among the most dynamic sources of industrial growth and technology transfers, even though they contribute heavily to the country's external deficit (Mercado 1980; Soria 1980). As will be described below, they also constitute a fundamental source of subcontracting.

Our study was done at a time of transition in the Mexican economy—from the period of recovery in 1979–81 to the crisis that surfaced with the devaluation of the peso and the freezing of dollar accounts in the summer of 1982. By then, the accumulation of foreign debt, with the debt service representing 29.5 percent of the country's exports, had become a problem of intense national and international concern. Policies to reduce imports affected key inputs of capital equipment and other industrial commodities. Signs of the economic downturn were noticeable at the time fieldwork took place in the summer of 1982, in contrast with the previous year, when firms still reported optimistic signs in the economy. For example, some of the subcontracting arrangements were the result of the need to replace imports with domestic production resulting from import-reduction policies. On the other hand, subcontracting orders connected with some consumer goods were reported not to flow as regularly as before. There were, therefore, contradictory economic forces at work regarding the directions and effects of subcontracting.

In order to discover the process by which production reached homeworkers, I interviewed representatives of sixty-seven firms of different sizes and industries during the summer of 1981 and 1982. Whenever possible, interviews were accompanied with a visit to the site of production; for some firms, visits were repeated during the two consecutive years. The list of firms visited derived from their direct or indirect connection with the women homeworkers interviewed. The jobber or firm distributing homework was the first level of subcontracting visited, and this interview provided the information necessary for subsequent visits to firms at other levels. There were, however, some exceptions to this sequence; when small firms were reluctant or unwilling to provide the information necessary to visit their (normally much larger) subcontractors, the contact with the larger firms had to be made from the top down. All subcontracting chains could not be completed, since some firms refused to grant an interview or to provide the information necessary.[1] This problem was particularly noticeable at levels in which production was on the borderline of illegality, but it was also encountered among large multinational firms. In addition, not all types of homework were linked to subcontracting chains; a small number of cases involved only the producer-distributor and the homeworkers.

The analysis in this chapter is based mostly on the information collected during these interviews and tours of production sites but also on data collected from the homeworkers. The chapter presents, first, an analysis of the mechanics of subcontracting. The sample of firms available illustrates the connections between different productive establishments that range from homework units to small workshops, middle-sized factories, and large national and multinational firms. Second, the chapter analyzes the reasons behind subcontracting and refers briefly to the tendency for employment of women to increase among the firms studied. Finally, some questions are raised regarding the role of small firms in making production more flexible and fostering development.

Subcontracting Links

The literature on industrial subcontracting has distinguished between two types of business arrangements: one in which production is contracted out but raw materials are not provided and another in which raw materials and other inputs are provided (Watanabe 1983). The first system might be called *horizontal subcontracting*, and involves orders of goods regularly produced and sold by a firm to a variety of clients. The second arrangement, *vertical subcontracting*, amounts to producing orders specific to the firm that subcontracts out. In Mexico, vertical subcontracting is normally referred to as "maquila," or "domestic maquila" in the case of homework. It generally consists of processing work or production carried out for another firm under very specific contract arrangements, including exact specifications regarding design and other product characteristics. It affects mostly labor-intensive tasks resulting from the ability to fragment the production process in such a way that different parts can be carried out by different firms. In the case of Mexico City, maquila work does not usually occur in export-processing activities. As will be argued below, it is mainly oriented toward production for the domestic market and is therefore quite different from the export-oriented subcontracting predominant in areas such as the U.S.-Mexican border (Fernández-Kelly 1983).

Vertical subcontracting was found to predominate in the sample of firms studied. In most cases, this type of subcontracting can be equated with a putting-out system that, as Murray (1983, 81) has defined it for the case of Italy, is "the transfer of work formally done within a firm to another firm, an artisan workshop or to domestic outworkers." The relatively small proportion of large and medium-sized firms in the sample (see table 9.1) is due to the pyramid-like structure of subcontracting in which one large firm deals with a large group of subcontractors, even for the same type of product. Most subcontractors produce exclusively for other firms. Yet there are cases—particularly among medium-sized units—in which they also produce final goods for the market. (For example, some small toy manufacturers produce their own toys and also do subcontracted work for larger firms.) Thus, although 40.3 percent of the firms in the sample sold directly to the market—that is, they represent the final level of production—25.4 percent among them also produced intermediate goods for other firms. Overall, 75 percent of the firms in the sample were engaged in some form of subcontracted production of intermediate goods.

Among the industries listed in table 9.1, the garment and textile industries represent the type of industry whose traditional subcontracting either to workshops or to homework units has already been documented (Alonso 1979, 1983). Of the others, although maquila work may be new and involve new products, none of the cases included the type of subcontracting related to high-tech production for export which is typical of the U.S.-Mexican border industries. In all but two cases, production was oriented toward the domestic market and, of these two cases, the proportion that was exported was very small.

The importance of non-Mexican capital in generating these linkages is quite clear: although only eleven firms (16.4%) were multinationals, over 69 percent of the remaining firms were working under subcontracts with multinational capital. Table 9.2 contains three typical subcontracting chains of four, three, and two levels that range from multinational capital to homework. In

Table 9.1 Number of Firms by Industry and Size

Industry	Number of Workers in Firm						
	19 or less	20–99	100–299	300–999	1000+	Total	Percentage
Electrical and electronics	3	2	2	3	—	10	14.9
Consumer durables	1	—	1	3	5	10	14.9
Cosmetics	1	2	—	2	1	6	8.9
Plastics	6	9	2	0	—	17	25.4
Metal	2	3	—	3	—	8	11.9
Garment and textile	5	1	—	—	1	7	10.5
Other[1]	5	3	—	—	1	9	13.4
Total	23	20	5	11	8	67	
Percentage of total	34.3	29.8	7.5	16.4	12.0		100.0

[1]Glass, toys, food, and decoration of glass and plastic containers.

Table 9.2 Subcontracting Chains

	Chain A		Chain B		Chain C	
	No. of Workers	Description	No. of Workers	Description	No. of Workers	Description
Level 1	3,000	Electrical appliances	2,500	Cosmetics	2,500	Electrical outlets
Level 2	350	Radio and TV antennas and microphones	50	Plastic injection	20	Parts for level 1
Level 3	6	Electronic coils and assembling	Fluctuating number	Homework: plastic polishing	n.h.[1]	
Level 4	Fluctuating number	Homework: tasks as in level 3			n.h.[1]	

[1] No homework in this chain.

chain A, production is subcontracted from a large multinational to increasingly smaller firms. The last level is homework, in this case distributed from a workshop operating illegally in the basement of the owner's home. The multinational firm at the top draws from a list of three hundred regular and fifteen hundred occasional subcontractors and sends out 70 percent of its production.[2]

The firm at level 2 represents Mexican capital. It employs 350 workers and subcontracts out 5 percent of its production—mostly to units such as that at level 3, a sweatshop that operates illegally in the basement of the owner's residence and employs six young workers (15–17 years of age) and a fluctuating number of homeworkers. Employment at the last two levels is occasional and follows the patterns of work associated with the informal sector (see Castells and Portes, this volume). Workers at level 3 were paid a minimum wage without fringe benefits, and homeworkers received an average wage equivalent to one-third of the minimum, according to our estimates (see Benería and Roldán 1987).

In chain B, the cosmetics firm at the top is also a multinational, which contracts out the production of plastic containers to firms at level 2. The specific firm referred to at that level employs an average of fifty workers but shows wide fluctuation in employment according to the number of orders coming in. Such fluctuation is due not only to variations in economic activity in the subcontracting industries (cosmetics and pharmaceutical) but also to a high degree of competition among subcontractors to attract orders from the larger firms.

Chain C is one of the few in which homework has been eliminated. At the time of fieldwork, the small unit of twenty workers (all women) operating at level 2 was managed by the only woman encountered in that position. The enterprise was an underground workshop whose employees assembled electrical components on the patio of the woman's house. Although some homework had been distributed to women in the past, the woman reported that her home operation allowed her a greater degree of control over production.

Watanabe (1983) has argued that subcontracting in Mexico tends to be limited to two or a maximum of three levels involving mostly large and middle-sized firms, with a low degree of involvement on the part of small units. As a result, he argues, Mexican subcontracting, in contrast with the Japanese version, does not take the form of a pyramid with a small number of large firms at the top and a large number of medium- and small-sized firms at the bottom; instead, the Mexican structure narrows down in the second and third levels like a diamond cut. However, his sample of forty-six firms concentrated mainly on metal engineering subcontracting from the automobile industry. It also included some producers of electronic and electrical appliances, as in our study. Our observations differ from his in that we found three and four levels of subcontracting to be common. This disparity is probably due not only to the different industries studied but also to the cases in our sample, in which production was either underground or at the borderline of illegality; this added one or two levels to subcontracting chains. For example, in table 9.2, levels 3 and 4 in chain A, level 3 in chain B, and level 2 in chain C represent the type of units not present in Watanabe's study. As a result, the structure of subcontracting in our sample resembles much more that of a pyramid—with a larger number of units as firm size decreases and with only some narrowing at the level of medium-sized firms in the 100–299 worker category.

This finding does not, of course, imply that the structure and extent of Mexican subcontracting resemble those in the Japanese system of heavy reliance on numerous and highly productive small firms. It does imply, however, that subcontracting in Mexico involves spheres of production not previously documented, and that an incipient subcontracting system is at work which performs similar functions to those attributed to the Japanese model. Although data on the extent of subcontracting are lacking, this practice seems to be widespread in industrial centers such as Mexico City.

What emerges from these mechanisms of subcontracting is a continuum of firms in a highly integrated system of production segmented out at different levels. From an economic perspective, the clearest discontinuity in this process is that between legal and illegal, or regulated and unregulated, activities for the reasons that will be given below. The articulation between these activities in our sample follows three basic patterns. It can be a *direct articulation* involving a regular firm that sends production out to illegal operations without the use of intermediaries. This pattern can be found among small firms that have direct contact with illegal workshops or with homeworkers, as illustrated in the connections between levels 2 and 3 in both chains A and B. Large firms rarely exhibit this pattern. An exception in our sample was the case of a large textile factory with twelve hundred workers that was giving piecework to prisoners and to nuns in charge of an orphanage. Another exception is the case of chain C, in which a large firm is directly linked with a home-based workshop.

The second pattern might be called *mediated articulation* and takes place through a jobber. In this case, the mediator's function consists merely of establishing the connection between the legal and illegal operations. No production takes place at the jobber's level, although in many cases he or she performs an indirect supervisory role in the activities that are subcontracted or performs other functions, such as the distribution, transportation, and gathering of materials and goods produced.

Finally, a *mixed articulation* takes place when the connection between legal and illegal production is centered at a point at which a small firm combines legal and underground operations. An illustration is a workshop that produces plastic parts for different firms: the storefront is a formal operation, that is, it pays taxes and minimum wages and fulfills other legal requirements, while at the back of the building a varying number of women do plastic polishing at wages below the minimum and without fringe benefits. The workshop also sends work to homeworkers in the neighborhood depending upon the amount of work available.

Reasons for Subcontracting and Firm Hierarchies

Why do firms send production out and under what circumstances? What are the factors affecting this process? Clearly the answer to these questions, as the studies in this volume show, depend on a variety of factors that range from industrial relations to technological conditions, state legislation, and market competition. More concretely, for each country, industry, and firm, subcontracting will ultimately depend on the specific factors that affect profitability. In the case of Mexico, and although our study is of a pioneer character and much more needs to be known about subcontracting processes, our data allow us to make some generalizations regarding these questions.

Among the reasons given by firms for subcontracting, the most prevalent was the lowering of labor costs—mentioned as the first reason in 79 percent of the cases. Considerable savings can result from wage disparities existing between different subcontracting levels. As can be seen in table 9.3, the ratio of average monthly wages (not including fringe benefits) paid to manual workers in the top firm and to homeworkers in chain A was estimated to be 6.76 to 1. Chains B and C further illustrate these disparities; wage ratios between top and bottom levels of production are 6 to 19 and 3.67 to 1, respectively. The largest drop in wages takes place at points at which production goes underground, and particularly when the labor force is female. This is clearly the case with homework, which, in our sample, was entirely done by women who received on the average less than a third of the minimum wage; it was also true for the other levels of subcontracting, found to be progressively more feminized at lower

Table 9.3 Average Monthly Wages for Manual Workers
by Subcontracting Level, 1981 (1981 Mexican pesos)

	Chain A	Chain B	Chain C
Level 1	12,000	11,000	11,000
Level 2	8,500	5,880	3,000
Level 3	5,880	1,776 (homework)	—
Level 4	1,776 (homework)	—	—
Wage ratio	6.76 : 1	6.19 : 1	3.67 : 1

Note: U.S. $1.00 = 83 pesos in 1981.

positions in the subcontracting pyramid (see Benería and Roldán 1987, chaps. 3, 4).

It can be argued that productivity is lower at lower levels of sub-contracting and that therefore wage ratios reflect productivity ratios. Unfortunately, there are no available data that allow us to compare productivity and wages in a systematic way. However, given the labor-intensive character of subcontracting, there is no reason to believe that significant disparities in productivity exist for identical jobs performed at different subcontracting levels, particularly for the more unskilled tasks. Even if some disparities do exist, the mere fact that firms resort to subcontracting indicates that wage differentials more than compensate for productivity differences. To the extent that wages more than compensate for lower productivity, labor costs are reduced and the rate of exploitation is higher.

From this perspective, subcontracting is clearly a shift of production in search of cheap labor. Following Braverman (1974), one can argue that this process of decentralization responds to the Babbage principle, namely, that labor costs are reduced through changes in the division of labor. This is made possible by the fragmentation of tasks in such a way that those subcontracted out are associated with lower skill and lower wages. Although Braverman focuses on the division of labor within the capitalist firm, this approach can be applied to an analysis of the division of labor among firms—as in the case of subcontracting.

The literature on the new international division of labor has made use of a Braverman framework to understand processes of fragmentation and relocation on a world scale (Brighton Labor Process Group 1977; Fröbel, Heinrichs, and Kreye 1980). To be sure, emphasis on the Babbage principle does not exclude the possibility that firms can lower production costs by other means, particularly through technological change.[3] Whether firms resort to subcontracting or to the introduction of new technologies will depend on the relative price of labor and capital investment and on the ongoing dialectic between capital and labor. But it seems clear that subcontracting responds to a cheap labor strategy of lowering costs. This strategy takes advantage of the existing fragmentation in the labor market in which the most clear-cut division is that between the legal and the underground economy—with the corresponding sharp drop in wages, the disappearance of fringe benefits, and the deterioration of working conditions.

At the same time, this strategy can explain the tendency found in our study for the employment of women to increase among the firms studied. As shown in table 9.4, over 40 percent of the firms reported an increase in the proportion of women employed during the three preceding years or under current plans at the time of fieldwork. The trend was found particularly among firms whose work force was already 30 percent or more female. Given the higher proportion of women found among middle-sized and small firms, this finding implies that feminization of these firms was linked to a cheap labor strategy and can be explained by the possibility of hiring women at lower wages.[4]

In this sense, our study adds to other evidence showing the tendency toward a growing employment of women in many Third World industrialization processes. However, the literature on this subject has concentrated on the effects of the globalization of production on the employment of women in export-related industries (Fröbel, Heinrichs, and Kreye 1980; Elson and Pearson 1981). A high concentration of women workers has been documented for the more traditional "women's industries," such as the garment and textile industries, as well as for the newer industries, such as electronics and toys, often geared toward the international market (Safa 1981; Nash and Fernández-Kelly 1983). The literature has also emphasized the location of these export-oriented industries in free-trade zones and in areas, such as the U.S.-Mexican border, with a heavy concentration of foreign investment. Our study shows that this tendency can also be found in an industrial center such as Mexico City and

Table 9.4 Female Employment

Percentage of Women in the Firm's Work Force	Number of Firms	Number of Workers Employed	Percentage of Firms Reporting an Increase in the Proportion of Women Employed[1]
10 or less	12	2,892	23.5
10–29	9	2,154	33.3
30–49	12	4,639	42.8
50 or more	26	4,085	51.8
Total	59	13,770	40.6

Note: For firms that registered an increase in the proportion of women employed between the summer of 1981 and that of 1982, I have used figures for 1982.

[1]During the three preceding years or under current plans.

among firms whose production is predominantly oriented toward the domestic market. In both cases the increase in women's employment corresponds to the search for lower wages, among other factors.

In addition to lowering labor costs, other reasons were given for sending production out. The answers provided by firms can be summarized as follows:

1. Production of parts is highly specialized and can be obtained at lower costs by firms that concentrate on a few products. This is particularly the case when the number of parts required by the subcontracting firm is relatively small and does not justify the investment required by internal production. In other words, the objective in this case is the lowering of fixed costs.

2. When production is cyclical or unstable, subcontracting offers the possibility of transferring the risk and avoiding the problems associated with fluctuations of production, such as layoffs and costs associated with a temporary increase in production. For example, a small subcontractor working for large companies in the cosmetics industry listed thirty to sixty workers as the oscillating number of employees working according to the availability of contracts. Only the supervisory and clerical personnel had permanent contracts.[5] Similarly, the toy and garment industries offer numerous examples of this type of subcontracting.

3. In the case of a family business or a medium-sized firm controlled by an owner-manager, a factor mentioned was the avoidance of growth as a way of keeping control of the enterprise. As one manager put it, "Further growth would require a more sophisticated system of accounting, a large bureaucracy, and the loss of control on my part." Faced with a trade-off between a high degree of direct control and further expansion, this type of entrepreneur seems to be opting for the first alternative. This allows the permanence of firms in what Garofoli (1978) has called the "peripheral" area of the economy consisting of small, specialized units of production—different from the "central" area of large firms and the "marginal" area of informal and relatively "underdeveloped" productive units.

4. A related factor is the avoidance of labor conflicts and, in particular, of unionization among small, growing firms. When firms exceed twenty workers, unionization is required by Mexican law. The most explicit case along these lines was that of a family business subdivided into five different legal entities under the ownership of different family members, all of them with fewer than twenty workers.

Other factors mentioned as influencing decisions about subcontracting out were transportation costs, the ease with which tasks can be separated from the overall production process, and requirements of quality control. The extent to which subcontracting takes place can therefore vary substantially according to the weight of these factors, even for the same firm. For example, in 1981 a large multinational producing household appliances was subcontracting out an average of 80 percent of its production in Brazil and 60 percent in Mexico.[6]

The overall picture emerging from a close observation of subcontracting links is that of a hierarchy of firms with a pyramid shape, that is, with a small number at the top and an increasingly larger number as subcontracting flows from the larger to the smaller firms. Although segmented by subcontracting levels, the pyramid is formed by interconnected units that form part of the same productive process. In addition to wage disparities, the different levels in this hierarchy can be distinguished by other factors, such as working conditions, access to financial and other resources, levels of technology, and work stability. Working conditions—evaluated in terms of factors such as working space, light, services available for workers within the firm, safety measures, and temperature level—deteriorate at lower levels of the pyramid. In the same way, although the restrictions against firing workers in Mexico are quite severe, many firms make frequent use of the possibility, granted by law, of hiring workers for a period of twenty-eight days; for many workers, this practice results in intermittent or occasional employment. Here, too, we found a gender distinction, since the proportion of women in this type of intermittent work is very high.

This hierarchy also has other dimensions, such as the dependency of medium- and small-sized firms on large enterprises and of Mexican on multinational capital to obtain production contracts. As mentioned earlier, the great bulk of subcontracting in our sample ultimately depends on multinational firms. The exceptions are found mainly in the garment, food, textile, and some of the metals industries. A close look at these links reveals a window on the form of dependent development of the newly industrialized countries in the Third World, which Mexico typifies (Evans 1979; MacEwan 1985). As an engineer from a firm of fifty workers which produced mainly auto parts put it, "We need the multinationals to generate work and employment."

Large firms tend to enjoy monopsony power, and there is intense competition among small subcontractors to obtain work from the larger firms. The result is often resentment on the part of the smaller enterprises of what one manager called "the princely tendencies of the large firms that can impose their own terms." Yet theoretical models dealing with the division of labor within firms, including Braverman's, tend to emphasize internal hierarchies only, without taking into consideration the macrodimensions that transcend each firm.

Finally, subcontracting also implies that a given firm at the top of the pyramid has a number of options, beyond altering the internal structure of the firm, for reordering the division of labor and the location of production; that is, subcontracting expands the mechanisms by which the firm's demand for labor can be met and increases the range of choices regarding the conditions under which labor is hired. This amounts to the firm's access to a more flexible labor supply. Various chapters in this volume show that this paramount factor can be observed in other countries under different conditions.

In sum, our study provides further evidence for the argument that the division between the formal and informal sector cannot be viewed as that between two separate sectors. Instead, we find in industrial subcontracting a high level of integration among firms connected to the same production process, although differentiated by subcontracting levels that function as segments of a fragmented labor market. Subcontracting can be viewed as a shift of production to lower-cost segments. The clearest boundaries between these segments are those between legal and illegal areas. This is because illegality—and its corresponding sharp decrease in wages and other costs which results from the absence of regulation—represents a clear shift in the conditions under which production takes place. In this sense, a definition of informality that emphasizes legal regulation or the lack of it can establish clear conceptual boundaries between the formal and informal sectors without creating the problems associated with definitions that are related, for example, to size of production, marginality, nature of production, and forms of management.[7]

Subcontracting, the Small Business Sector, and Gender Asymmetry: Concluding Comments

Although it is difficult to generalize from a sample of sixty-seven firms, industrial subcontracting seemed to be on the increase in Mexico City at the time when fieldwork took place; while almost half of the firms reported an increasing tendency to send production out, none of them reported a general tendency for maquila work to decrease (despite temporary decreases in demand). However, more research needs to be done in order to assert the extent of geographic dispersion of production in Mexico as well as the degree of subcontracting that involves small artisan firms (see Roberts, this volume). To be sure, the current economic crisis is likely to have a significant impact on the restructuring of these processes.

Subcontracting permits the shifting of employment toward the more informal, or underground, segments of the economic system, thereby providing a way to escape state regulations on production and market transactions, union contracts, taxes, and fringe benefits. Subcontracting provides for a great deal of flexibility in expanding and contracting productive capacity in the small-business sector. For these reasons, and given the high proportion of active labor in the informal sector in Third World countries, it is often suggested that this flexibility may be very important in building an infrastructure of small firms that would provide a basis for growth. This would be the case particularly if productivity levels among these firms were comparable to those of larger units. The positive aspects of this sector are that it stimulates the development of small business, which is more adaptable to the economic conditions prevalent in the Third World, and creates the basis for fostering and channeling entrepreneurial skills and developing productive forces in general.[8]

There are, in fact, different versions of this optimistic view. Some see the informal sector as a way of facilitating the functioning of a free market and optimizing the results of a free-enterprise economy in the face of excessive state regulation. Others see it as a way of fostering initiative and technological change in the Third World, with the purpose of delinking local economies from their dependency on the industrialized world.[9]

There are limits, however, to such optimistic views. At least for the small businesses associated with subcontracting, the development of a small-business sector is highly dependent on the large firms in which it originates; it will be self-sustaining only to the extent that the general development of the country is so. In addition, small firms' permanence in the market is constantly threatened by the competition of large firms and the tendency toward economic concentration. The obstacles faced by small, informal operations are numerous and include lack of access to credit, poor marketing information, and low access to new technological developments. Turning this situation around would require much more than a free-market mechanism, given that it is precisely the market that has created the conditions found in the informal sector.

From labor's perspective, decentralized production under the circumstances described by our study implies a recomposition of the industrial working class (or a *new* composition) to include more marginal workers and, especially, more women. This process takes place in such a way that it intensifies labor's weaknesses rather than its strengths, a situation fostered by low wages, poor working conditions, and a low degree of job stability. The invisibility to which workers are subject makes them politically, if not economically, marginal. In fact, this sector is built precisely on labor's general vulnerability. This is particularly the case for women, heavily represented at the lower echelons of subcontracting and typified by the low earnings and precarious working conditions prevalent in domestic maquila.

Notes

Different versions of the chapter were presented at the Forty-fifth Congress of Latinoamericanists, Bogotá, Colombia, July 1985, and at the conference, The Comparative Study of the Informal Sector, Harper's Ferry, West Virginia, October 1986. I want to thank Alejandro Portes and Lauren Benton for their useful comments on the version of this chapter presented at the conference. The research on which this chapter is based was financed by the Ford Foundation and the Social Science Research Council.

1. In one case of a large textile firm, the questionnaire was withdrawn after completion on the grounds that some of the information provided had to be double-checked. As expected, it was never recovered.

2. It should be noted that this is not the case for all industries. Watanabe (1983) has reported, for example, that the automobile industry tends to rely on a very small number of subcontractors.

3. Jenkins (1984) has criticized the use of the Babbage principle to explain the new international division of labor on the grounds that it neglects the role of technical change in increasing labor productivity. My point here is that the emphasis on cheap labor does not exclude the possibility that capital uses other strategies to lower costs of production.

4. This does not mean that women's wages are the only reason for the increase in the proportion of women employed; for a more detailed discussion, see Benería and Roldán 1987, chap. 3.

5. This situation gives firms a great degree of flexibility while minimizing labor problems. Murray (1983) gives an example of an Italian firm that shifted from putting out 10 percent of its production in 1969 to 46 percent in 1972. When production fell rapidly in 1974–75, the reduction in work sent out resulted in a loss of 550 jobs while internal employment remained stable. This flexibility is also emphasized repeatedly in other chapters in this volume; see especially those by Ybarra and Benton on the Spanish case.

6. This information was obtained through personal communication with an economist who had worked in both branches.

7. See Castells and Portes in this volume and Portes and Sassen-Koob 1987 for a discussion of different definitions.

8. As Doeringer (1984, 122) has put it, small businesses have a "wide range of generic strengths" such as "the ability to expand productive capacity almost at will; the flexibility of production that comes out of the small business sector; the ability to operate on various kinds of short-term credits, informal credit systems; the ability to get raw materials and second-hand parts . . . on very short notice."

9. The first view typifies the position often taken by the United States government and international agencies such as the World Bank and the International Monetary Fund (and popularized by writings such as Mario Vargas Llosa's "In Defense of the Black Market," *New York Times Magazine,* March 1, 1987). The second is illustrated by the ongoing discussion in African development circles among writers such as Samir Amin and Azzam Mahjoub.

References

Alonso, J. A. 1979. "The Domestic Seamstresses of Netzahualcoyotl: A Case Study of Feminine Overexploitation in a Marginal Urban Area." Ph.D. dissertation, Department of Sociology, New York University, February.
———. 1983. "The Domestic Clothing Workers in the Mexican Metropolis and Their Relations to Dependent Capitalism." Pp. 161–172 in J. Nash and P. Fernández-Kelly (eds.), *Women, Men, and the International Division of Labor.* Albany, N.Y.: State University of New York Press.
Benería, L. and M. I. Roldán. 1987. *The Crossroads of Class and Gender: Homework, Subcontracting, and Household Dynamics in Mexico City.* Chicago: University of Chicago Press.

Braverman, H. 1974. *Labor and Monopoly Capital*. New York: Monthly Review Press.
Brighton Labor Process Group. 1977. "The Capitalist Labor Process." *Capital and Class*, 3–26.
Connolly, P. 1982. "Crítica del 'Sector Informal' como Concepto Aplicado con Referencia a la Estructura Ocupacional de la Ciudad de México." Paper presented at symposium, Informal and Peripheral Economies in Sociological Theory, Tenth World Congress of Sociology, Mexico City.
Cordera, R. and C. Tello. 1981. *México: La Disputa por la Nación: Perspectiva y Opciones del Desarrollo*. México: Siglo Veintiuno Editores.
Doeringer, P. B. 1984. "Gender, Skill, and the Dynamics of Women's Employment: Comment." Conference, Gender in the Work Place, The Brookings Institution, November.
Elson, D. and R. Pearson. 1981. "The Subordination of Women and the Internationalization of Factory Production." Pp. 144–66 in K. Young, C. Wolkowitz, and R. McCullagh (eds.), *Of Marriage and the Market*. London: CSE Books.
Evans, P. 1979. *Dependent Development: The Alliance of Multinational State and Local Capital in Brazil*. Princeton: Princeton University Press.
Fernández-Kelly, M. P. 1983. "Mexican Border Industrialization, Female Labor Force Participation, and Migration." Pp. 205–23 in J. Nash and P. Fernández-Kelly (eds.), *Women, Men, and the International Division of Labor*, Albany, N.Y.: State University of New York Press.
Fröbel, F., J. Heinrichs, and O. Kreye. 1980. *The New International Division of Labor*. Cambridge: Cambridge University Press.
García, B., H. Muñoz, and O. de Oliveira. 1979. *Migración, Família y Fuerza de Trabajo de la Ciudad de México*, Cuadernos del CES, no. 26. México City: Centro de Estudios Sociológicos, El Colegio de México.
Garofoli, G. 1978. *Ristrutturazione Industriale e Territorio*. Milano: Franco Angeli Editore.
Jenkins, R. 1984. "Divisions over the International Division of Labor." *Capital and Class* 22 (Spring): 28–57.
MacEwan, A. 1985. "The Current Crisis in Latin America." *Monthly Review* 36 (February): 1–18.
Mercado, A. 1980. "La Transferencia de Tecnología Dentro y Fuera de Empresas Transnacionales en la Industria de Fibras Poliester: Las Experiencias Internacional y Mexicana." *Iztapalapa* 1:181–93.
Murray, F. 1983. "The Decentralization of Production—the Decline of the Mass-Collective Worker?" *Capital and Class* 19 (Spring): 74–99.
Nash, J. and M. P. Fernández-Kelly, eds. 1983. *Women, Men, and the International Division of Labor*, Albany, N.Y.: State University of New York Press.
Portes, A. and S. Sassen-Koob. 1987. "The Informal Sector: Comparative Material from Latin America, the United States, and Western Europe." *American Journal of Sociology*, July.
Safa, H. I. 1981. "Runaway Shops and Female Employment: The Search for Cheap Labor." *Signs* 7 (Winter): 418–33.
Soria, V. M. 1980. "Estructura y Comportamiento de la Industria Farmacéutica en México. El Papel de las Empresas Transnacionales." *Iztapalapa* 1 (January–June): 111–41.

Watanabe, S., ed. 1983. *Technology, Marketing, and Industrialization: Linkages between Large and Small Enterprises*. New Delhi: Macmillan.

The World Bank. 1983. *World Development Report*. New York: Oxford University Press.

10 The Informal Economy and the Development of Flexible Specialization In Emilia-Romagna

Vittorio Capecchi

In the recent European and American debates over how best to study the economy of a given region or country (summarized in Capecchi and Pesce 1983), two research methods emerged as particularly significant in determining the theoretical and empirical limits of traditional economic analysis.

A first line of inquiry has followed the analyses of economic historians such as Polanyi and Braudel who focus attention on the informal monetary economy and on the nonmonetary economy, attempting in this way to reconstruct how families organize themselves along the lines of gender and generational differences so as to arrange their labor time and consumption. These studies have demonstrated the impossibility of speaking about employment solely in the official economy (i.e., that which appears in the official statistics) without also taking into consideration informally paid labor and employment in the nonmonetary economy, namely, family and domestic labor and labor dedicated to the auto-production of goods and services. Thus both the official economic statistics and some of the better-known economic theories—such as those regarding price and market formation—are placed in doubt; simultaneously, the importance of carrying out an employment analysis that takes gender and generational differences into account has been emphasized.

The second research approach[1] has considered the ways in which industrial development has taken place, singling out a number of different courses by which the passage from agriculture to industry has been effected. Thus it can be verified that in Europe, as well as in the United States, multiple models of industrialization have coexisted; there has not been a single model of development based on the large enterprise. The increasing attention given to the various ways in which small enterprises may be organized reflects the importance of the model of flexible industrialization, typical of certain regions of both Europe and the United States. This second research approach has again indicated the limits of the official economy, which often takes the large enterprise as its only point of reference and considers the distinction between large and small enterprises as merely one of scale.

In the pages that follow, the interface of these two diverse research

---

Chapter 10 was translated by C. Frisch and A. Portes.

perspectives is examined by considering an Italian region—Emilia-Romagna—that represents the ideal case of a region in which a flexible, specialized industrial development has occurred; this development influenced, in turn, the subsequent expansion of the tertiary sector.

In this region (see tables 10.1 and 10.2), three principal phases of development may be distinguished for this century. The first period, 1901–51, is characterized by the prevalence of agricultural activities. In 1901, 64.6 percent of the officially employed population was employed in agriculture, and in 1951 this percentage was still quite high at 51.8 percent. The migratory balance was negative in these fifty years—by 265,000 people—indicating a situation of widespread poverty. The second period, 1951–71, is characterized by the development of flexible specialized industrialization based on small metallurgical, mechanical, and textile enterprises. The migratory balance was almost zero (the major migrations in Italy were taking place from southern to northern regions). The period 1971–81 is characterized by the expansion of the service sector and by technological change, which brought the new information and electronic technologies into the region. The migratory balance here becomes positive (an indication of the attainment of a higher standard of living).

An important point is that each phase of economic development is distinguished by a particular political culture. In the period 1901–51, "socialism in the countryside" spread throughout Emilia-Romagna, oscillating between corporate reformism and anarcho-syndicalism. The Fascist government attempted to stir up controversy between sharecroppers and day laborers and between skilled workers and the unemployed. In this region, however, one of the strongest armed anti-Fascist resistance movements took root and, at the end of World War II, led to the widespread presence of the Communist party. The Emilian Communist party carried forward a policy of support for small entrepreneurs drawn from peasant and working-class families; the significant presence of the party in both regional and local government very much typified Emilia-Romagna at this time.

Table 10.1 Distribution of Employed Workers in Emilia-Romagna

	1901 (%)	1951 (%)	1971 (%)	1981 (%)
Agriculture	64.6	51.8	20.0	13.4
Industry	19.9	25.2	42.6	38.1
Other activities	15.5	23.0	37.4	48.5
Total	100.0	100.0	100.0	100.0

	1901–51	1951–71	1971–81
Difference between emigrants and immigrants (absolute values)	−265,000	+1,000	+137,000

Source: ISTAT, General Census of the Italian population, various years.

Table 10.2 Distribution of Employed Workers in Mechanical Firms in Emilia-Romagna, by Firm Size

Firm Size	1927 (%)	1937 (%)	1951 (%)	1961 (%)	1971[1] (%)	1981[1] (%)
<10	52.1	28.6	36.9	37.4	18.2	22.1
11–100	23.3	16.3	23.1	32.6	38.7	40.2
101–500	16.8	20.6	21.4	19.7	25.0	23.0
501>	7.7	34.4	18.6	10.3	17.1	14.7
Total	100.0	100.0	100.0	100.0	100.0	100.0

Source: ISTAT, General Census of the Italian population, various years.
[1]Repair industries excluded.

Capecchi and Pesce (1983) have analyzed how the positive interface of the official and the informal economies in the region encouraged the political left to wage a struggle against inequality, while also making use of the diversity among individuals in outlooks, personal capabilities, and the like. For each of the above three phases of socioeconomic development, I will attempt to specify the role played by the informal economy (both monetary and nonmonetary) as it has interlinked with the official one.[2] My analysis excludes criminal activities (prostitution, drugs, etc.) in order to concentrate on "tolerated" informal enterprises.[3]

Five Questions and Two Hypotheses on the Informal Economy

Issues concerning the informal economy may be reduced to five main questions. The first question concerns the presence of informality in a given region (or in a given period): Is informality more prevalent in the labor market (work may not be paid for, may be paid for informally, or may be paid for in the officially prescribed manner) or in the market for goods and services (which may be had without payment, paid for informally, or paid for in the officially prescribed manner)? The labor market does not coincide with the market for goods and services, and within either or both there may be a nonmonetary economy (in which there are no payments or compensation), an informal monetary economy (in which there are payments and compensation, but they take place outside of official channels), or an official monetary economy.

Table 10.3 indicates the various situations to which the combination of these dimensions may give rise. Cells 1, 5, and 9 indicate "pure" types of nonmonetary, informal monetary, and official economies, respectively.

Cells 4 and 7 represent instances in which goods and services are not directly paid for by families; they are furnished by public institutions that allocate them to their clientele according to legally prescribed rules, or they are provided by private institutions that may also distribute them in an informal

Table 10.3 Informality in Two Markets

Labor Market	Market for Goods and Services		
	Nonmonetary	Informal Monetary	Official
Nonmonetary	(1) Unpaid labor to produce goods and services for direct consumption or barter	(2) Unpaid labor to produce goods and services sold in the informal market	(3) Unpaid labor to produce goods and services sold in the official market
Informal Monetary	(4) Informally paid labor to produce goods and services for direct consumption	(5) Informally paid labor to produce goods and services sold in the informal market	(6) Informally paid labor to produce goods and services sold in the official market
Official	(7) Officially paid labor to produce goods and services for direct consumption	(8) Officially paid labor to produce goods and services sold in the informal market	(9) Officially paid labor to produce goods and services sold in the official market

manner. Cells 2 and 3 represent, instead, situations in which labor is not compensated, but the products of this labor are sold on the informal or the official market in order to finance, for example, associations or political parties.

Cells 8 and 6 outline two very pervasive situations: that in which labor is compensated in the official manner, but the product is sold informally (for example, the case of Emilian firms that currently produce "clones" of American personal computers which are then sold in informal markets); and that in which the product or service is sold in the official market, but the labor is compensated informally.

The second question is, What role does the informal economy play with respect to the resources that a family has at its disposal? In a given area (and time period), a *subsistence* informal economy may prevail—an economy in which informally paid labor is in fact the only employment opportunity that enables the various family members to survive. There may be instead an *integrative* informal economy, in the sense that the products and services sold informally are combined with official incomes earned by other family members. Finally, there may be an informal economy of *growth*, when the activities carried out informally provide a path for individual or familial mobility.

The third question—What are the relationships among the various actors present in the informal economy?—involves relationships of two possible types: (1) the individual sells the goods or services he has produced directly on the market or (2) he or she is informally compensated by an employer who then makes provisions to sell the products of that labor.

In both cases one may distinguish between a relation of *exploitation* and a relation of *complicity*. An exploitative relation exists when the stronger actor uses his greater leverage to take advantage of the weaker one (for example, the seller of goods and services might impose very high prices on the buyer in a shortage situation; similarly, an employer could impose very low salaries on his informally paid employees during periods of widespread unemployment). On the other hand, a relation of complicity (between buyer and seller or between employee and employer) exists when both parties find it convenient to conduct transactions informally.

Exploitation and *complicity* are never found in pure form, since conditions of exploitation are often tolerated through a sort of collusion with employers that puts less emphasis on the current situation than on future opportunities. For example, a homeworker might accept a difficult and poorly paid job because, by means of this job, she hopes to obtain a skill level that will enable her to have her own small firm in the future.

The fourth question is, What opportunities for entering the informal economy (either through the labor market or through the market for goods and services) are open to different categories of social actors? Here I will consider four major social groups: (1) individuals under the age of fourteen who, if they work in the informal economy, have probably dropped out of school; (2) young persons who study and work part-time in the informal economy; (3) adult men and women whose only employment is informal or who hold a second job in the informal economy; and (4) older persons who, once they have retired, continue to work informally.

The fifth question concerns the role of women, namely, What relationship exists between their family and domestic labor and the welfare state strategies put into effect by the local government? This relationship changes over time and very much influences the interface of informal and official activities.

Answers to these five questions will provide, in turn, an empirical assessment of the two hypotheses most commonly put forward in relation to regions such as Emilia-Romagna: The first, advanced by some of the most prestigious European newspapers such as the *Times, Le monde,* and *El país,* explains the diffusion of small enterprises as a consequence of the policy of "deregulation." This hypothesis holds that an Emilian or Italian economic "miracle" could have taken place only by allowing certain "illegalities" — such as having small firms pay few taxes or allowing them to pay their employees a low wage. The second hypothesis is that the informal economy expands when the official one enters a crisis period. In other words, informalization is a "response" to difficulties in the regulated economy.

The Period 1900–1950: The Informal Economy in an Agricultural Region

According to the census of 1901, 65 percent of the work force in Emilia-Romagna was employed in agriculture. All the social indicators converge to paint the picture of a poor region where the supply of labor outstripped the demand and in which the only solution for many individuals was to emigrate.

This precarious economic situation was accompanied by widespread illiteracy. At least part of the dominant class considered this situation convenient. For example, at the end of the nineteenth century, the Agrarian Society of Bologna took a public stand against the diffusion of education in the countryside. The 1901 census shows that out of every one hundred people surveyed who were employed in agriculture, 40 percent were farm laborers (paid on a daily basis or else with a fixed salary), 35 percent were sharecroppers, 18 percent owned the land they cultivated, and 7 percent were tenant farmers.

There is thus a significant difference between an agricultural region like Emilia-Romagna and other agricultural regions, particularly those in southern Italy. In fact, in Emilia-Romagna 60 percent of the laborers were associated with small agricultural enterprises, while in regions where large holdings were more prevalent, the majority of the laborers were simple farm workers without a contract. To understand the interface of official and informal activities it is necessary to note how employment was divided among the male and female members of these farm families, taking into consideration the fact that many of the women who worked in agriculture were officially classified as "housewives."

Families in which husband or wife worked as an agricultural laborer were generally very poor, and the descriptions recorded during the first half of the century shed light on their daily struggles. Both husbands and wives were available for any type of employment (in the fields, in the rice paddies, in public works, etc.), and in order to find work they often moved far away from home. Their informal activities (those not officially surveyed) were thus of a *subsistence* nature; in the majority of cases the reason why these activities were not surveyed is that they were of a temporary or short-term nature. The poverty of these families did not allow them to acquire machines for homework, and the women who worked at home in nonagricultural activities were engaged in poorly remunerated crafts and handiworks (hand spinning, basket weaving, and the like).

The situation of sharecroppers' families was different. Although they were also relatively poor, the sharecropping agreement allowed them to organize a family business based on an allotment of land. Whereas in the laborer family the work was wholly dependent on the market, each person working where he or she succeeded in finding employment, in the sharecropper family there was a much more precise organization of male and female roles and a greater possibility of conducting economic activities with a view toward one's own entrepreneurial project (cultivating the land in a given manner, raising certain types of livestock, among others).

The sharecropper family was in fact multinuclear, with the father ("the administrator") and the mother ("the administratrix") at the top. Moreover, there was a rigid hierarchy of duties, in the sense that the father was responsible for the activities of the business and gave orders to his male off-spring, while the mother had power over her daughters and daughters-in-law (sons who married brought their wives to live at home; daughters who married had no rights in the business and took with them only a dowry).

The mother administered a fund made of the proceeds from small sales. These informal activities were of the *integrative* type. In fact, womens' labor was principally oriented toward the family business, and even those officially classified as "housewives" worked long hours in the fields, especially during harvest time. However, the economic limitations of sharecropping impeded the development of protoindustrial activities (such as mechanical weaving). Hence, in the winter months the women spun, wove, and sewed predominantly for family consumption or for sale to nearby neighbors (an informal market).

Another relevant activity of these families was tied to the sharecropper's need to keep two sets of books, so as to give the landlord somewhat less than what was owed to him. In this manner, a number of informal management practices were developed, called by the historian Carlo Poni (1982) "malicious techniques" (*tecniche di malizia*).

Finally, there were those who owned the land they cultivated. In this case, the family businesses were richer and there was greater freedom to make decisions and to take initiatives. It was these families of small cultivators who initiated informal protoindustrial activities of some importance. Some were able to acquire power looms, and the women started cottage industries that became successful enough to promote an informal economy of *growth*.

Thus, the Emilian countryside during this period was not exclusively dependent on agriculture. Rural protoindustrial activities found points of correspondence in the small urban centers of the region. For example, in Carpi (a small town in the province of Modena), the production of straw hats expanded so greatly that by the turn of the century, Carpi's hat "industry" had branches in London, New York, Paris, Manila, and Tien-tsin.

On the other hand, in the larger Emilian cities, there was a deeply rooted industrial and artisan culture that distinguished the development of this region from that of others, such as southern Italy. Bologna, for example, was already "the city of silk" in the 1500s and had developed a complex industrial organization by making use of hydraulic power (many of the city's streets were actually canals employed to turn flour and silk mills). Moreover, thanks to the efforts of some intellectuals, some community technical schools had been established by the early 1900s and were teaching mechanical science to artisans and skilled laborers in the region. The Aldini-Valeriani Technical Institute in Bologna had been founded in 1878, and the Alberghetti Institute in Imola, in 1881. The Corni Institute in Modena was established in 1921. These schools were administered by individuals dedicated to the diffusion of the new technologies, brought into Italy from the more technologically advanced nations such as England. These three schools were open to men only, but there were also technical schools for women in the clothing and textile industries.

By the turn of the century, a mechanical and textile culture began to spread and to produce results. In 1924, the ACMA (Anonima Costruzione Macchine Automatiche) company, which made machines for boxing and packaging, was formed in Bologna. Little by little, mechanical factories specializing in the production of limited-run machines for the various needs of their clients sprang up in the region, particularly in the areas around Bologna, Modena, and Reggio Emilia. Flexible specialized industrial development had started.

It is important to consider all the cultural and political characteristics of the region during this period. In the 1909 elections, 40 percent of the voters chose the Socialist candidates, and then in 1913, when universal male suffrage was introduced, four provinces of Emilia (Bologna, Ferrara, Reggio Emilia, and Parma) became Socialist. Socialism in the agricultural areas of Emilia meant the formation of leagues and cooperatives and the spread of a "reformist" tendency that was to become (together with anarchist-unionist components) one of the deepest roots of the Communist party in Emilia.

Fascism gave new strength to the traditional conservative alliance of the agricultural landowners and promoted conflict between sharecroppers and agricultural workers (in the same way fascism promoted the conflict between skilled and unskilled workers). Political opposition to fascism contributed to unifying these agricultural and working-class social groups, so that by the end of World War II Emilia-Romagna became a "red" region (in 1948 51.2% of the voters opted for the Communist and the Socialist parties, while that percentage in Italy as a whole was 31.0).

Returning to the questions and hypotheses presented above, the informal economy in Emilia-Romagna in the period 1900–50 may be characterized as follows: As regards informality in the labor market and in the market for goods and services (table 10.3), there was a high incidence of production for direct consumption (cell 1); however, there was also some agricultural production for sale in informal markets, as well as the sale of goods produced by hand or machine labor (according to the family's financial condition) in the official or informal markets. The imbalance between the supply and demand for labor during this period also meant that women were paid almost always informally for work in the fields and rice paddies. Referring again to table 10.3, cells representing other than the "pure" economy types were almost entirely absent, since the more complex interfaces of the official and informal economies had no place in a situation of widespread poverty.

In families of male and female agricultural laborers, informal activities were clearly of a *subsistence* nature; in sharecropping families, they were mostly *integrative;* and only among families of small cultivators can one find the skilled protoindustrial activities characteristic of an informal economy of *growth*.

The relations of *exploitation* and *complicity* between employers and laborers in agriculture were, as discussed, mostly exploitative. The incidence of complicity was rare, except in the few cases of homework in the textile sector among the richer families.

The center of the entire informal economy was the adult woman officially classified as "housewife." However, there were also males and females under the age of fourteen working in the fields or operating a family business who were not officially recognized as "employed." Furthermore, there were many older persons who continued to work although they were officially "retired."

As regards the interface of the womens' family and domestic labor and the presence of the welfare state, the most common situation during this period was the almost complete absence of help from outside the family and a very significant connection between domestic labor and productive activities. Women who worked in the fields (or in the factories) had to bear the entire burden of domestic labor, but this latter task was subordinated to their productive roles. In general, offspring were numerous, although there was also a high infant mortality rate. Overall, the principal family objectives were survival and production for direct consumption or for sale in the market. Thus, for the majority of these women, domestic labor did not have the centrality that it had, say, for women who were classified as "housewives" in English working-class families in the first half of the century and who lived in large part on the salary of their husband.

With regard to the first hypothesis about the relation between lack of government regulation and the growth of small enterprises, the analysis of this earlier period demonstrates that, in contrast with other agricultural regions such as those of southern Italy, there were specific factors in the Emilian countryside (forms of small agricultural entrepreneurship and protoindustrial activities) and in the cities (industrial and artisan traditions and the presence of the technical schools) that set the region apart and helped explain its subsequent industrial development.

As for the hypothesis that the informal economy depends on a crisis in the official economy, it was verified that the poorer the families were, the poorer their informal activities (pure subsistence); an expansion of these activities required a better economic position. Hence, the extent and complexity of the informal economy grew *in tandem* with the wealth of producer households rather than with their destitution.

The Period 1950–1970: The Informal Economy and Flexible Specialized Industrial Development

The period 1950–70 is the time in which the distinctive aspects of industrial development based on flexible specialization spread throughout Emilia-Romagna: the proportion of the work force employed in agriculture fell from 52 percent to 20 percent; the number of laborers employed in industry rose from 23 percent to 43 percent, and within this group the percentage of workers in the metallurgical and mechanical industries increased even more rapidly. The lead sectors of this industrialization were metallurgical, mechanical, garment, and textile industries, based on networks of small and medium-sized enterprises specializing in the production of capital goods (limited-production-run machines for industry and agriculture) and consumer goods (clothing and fabrics) according to the needs of the client.

Table 10.2 indicates that the number of businesses in the region with more than five hundred employees was very small. However, the important point is that small and medium-sized industrial enterprises in the area constituted a self-sufficient system not dependent on contracts from larger firms.

At the end of World War II, men between the ages of twenty and thirty were confronted with a series of obstacles and opportunities that pointed them in the direction of autonomous entrepreneurship (see fig. 10.1). In the immediate postwar period, Emilia-Romagna was the region with the highest percentage of voters for the parties of the Left (especially the Communist party), while the national government was instead of the center-Right (Christian Democrat). This government did not support Emilia-Romagna,[4] and the few large munitions plants that could have been converted into mass production metallurgical and mechanical factories were actually closed down.[5]

The national government was interested in promoting the large mass production factories in northern Italy, which led many unskilled laborers from the south to emigrate there during this period. In Emilia-Romagna, on the other hand, the regional government and the local governments (of the Left) helped spur the development of small industrial enterprise directly from the working class. Their aid (in the form of credit, equipment, social services to families, etc.) accounted for the fact that, while provinces of the south were experiencing a sizable labor emigration to the north, the population figure for Emilia-Romagna remained stable (there being neither sizable emigration nor immigration).

A sustained economic expansion followed. Emilian exports increased from 6 percent to 8.4 percent of total Italian exports in the period 1963–76, with a noteworthy qualitative change in the nature of the exported goods. Whereas at the beginning of the 1950s agricultural goods were the primary regional exports, by the beginning of the 1960s the bulk was composed of mechanical goods (limited-production-run machines) plus textiles and clothing.

An explanation for this economic success cannot be given merely in terms of the type of industrialization chosen or on the basis of the protoindustrial traditions that I have mentioned above. The clash with the national government (Christian Democratic) on the part of a (Communist) region leads, as a matter of fact, to the formation of a "community" culture (analogous to what happens in ethnic or religious communities), in which local administrators, artisans, and workers are "united" as against a common enemy.

The shift in social status of agricultural and working-class families to that of small-entrepreneur families, as described by Barbagli, Capecchi, and Cobalti (1987), was facilitated by this "red" culture in three ways: (1) local administrators[6] easily found ways to help workers toward artisan and small industrial enterprises as they were "all communists," and since the administrators had continual formal and informal contacts with workers and artisans, decisions were made taking into consideration their real needs; (2) when the national government shut down the big munitions factories, the skilled workers often had only one way out, which was to start their own entrepreneurial activity, and the "community" helped those workers; and (3) the result of the 1984 elections brought major disillusionment to the Socialist and Communist militants, and so they channeled "revenge" energies into work. The search for self-realization and the desire for social mobility were the expression of important energies first stirred up during the period of resistance against fascism.

The "red" culture and the type of industrialization facilitated the realization of social mobility and determined the relations between the formal and informal economy.

It is important to understand how the informal economy interfaced with the official economy within the metallurgical, the mechanical, and the garment and textile industries. As regards the mechanical industry, a typical example is the production of packaging and boxing machines in Bologna. As noted, the first factories to produce this type of specialized machinery were built between 1920 and 1950. In the period 1950–70, the industry passed from two or three factories to a conglomeration of around three hundred small plants, of which about forty (ranging in number of employees from 50 to between 400 and 500) produced finished products, and the rest (employing generally 20 to 50 workers) made components or performed specialized labor in relation to these products.

The establishment of these new small and medium-sized factories was a direct result of three mechanisms. The first was a mechanism that may be defined as *imitation/complementarity:* technicians from the older factories such as ACMA left to start up new concerns that did not enter into direct competition with the parent firm. If the older factory made machines for the packaging of foodstuffs, for example, the second factory might produce machines to package cigarettes; the third, machines to package medicines; and the fourth, bottling equipment.

The second mechanism involved the machines that, at the beginning,

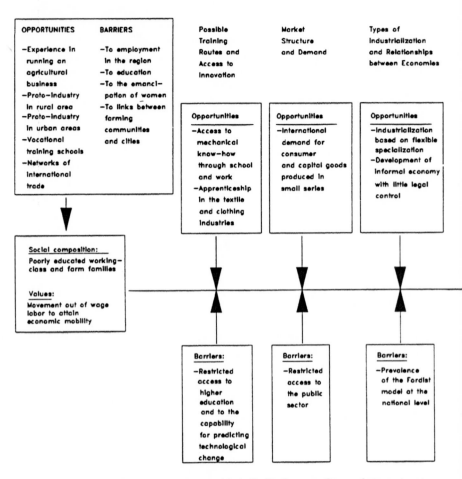

Figure 10.1. Transition to small entrepreneurship in Emilia-Romagna for men between twenty and thirty years of age in 1950.

were produced in their entirety by a single firm (the first Bolognese factories encompassed foundries). The production of these machines was subdivided into parts, resulting in a diffusion of entrepreneurship by means of *decentralization.* A whole series of manufacturing operations were contracted out to ever-smaller-sized businesses so that the core firms remained small to medium-sized, with an average of between two hundred and three hundred employees.

The third mechanism was *specialization,* in the sense that many small enterprises concentrated on performing certain manufacturing operations or on producing certain parts of a machine. This specialization allowed such firms a much greater autonomy, since they worked for a number of businesses within the same sector.

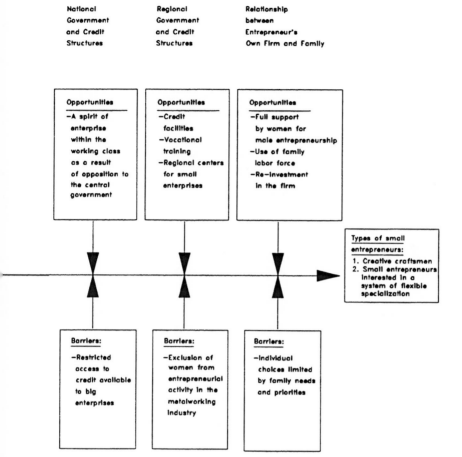

National Government and Credit Structures	Regional Government and Credit Structures	Relationship between Entrepreneur's Own Firm and Family
Opportunities —A spirit of enterprise within the working class as a result of opposition to the central government	**Opportunities** —Credit facilities —Vocational training —Regional centers for small enterprises	**Opportunities** —Full support by women for male entrepreneurship —Use of family labor force —Re-investment in the firm
Barriers: —Restricted access to credit available to big enterprises	**Barriers:** —Exclusion of women from entrepreneurial activity in the metalworking industry	**Barriers:** —Individual choices limited by family needs and priorities

Types of small entrepreneurs:
1. Creative craftsmen
2. Small entrepreneurs interested in a system of flexible specialization

Thus, a subsystem of enterprises gradually evolved in which there was no leading firm. The factory that produced the final good did not necessarily constitute the center of the subsystem because its role was often only that of assembling various parts produced by other firms, and some of these parts were so vital that their producers could set their own prices.

This subsystem of small enterprises was therefore a networked conglomeration, very different from the large-factory–small-enterprise relationship common elsewhere (see Benería, this volume). A large Fordist-style factory may in fact decentralize its manufacturing operations or the production of component parts to smaller firms, but the relationship remains one of dependence for the small enterprise. In a flexible specialized subsystem there are, on the contrary, many relatively autonomous small enterprises, including those that manufacture the finished product and those that produce parts or perform special operations (see fig. 10.2).

The characteristics that distinguish this specialized industrial system from the Fordist model are as follows:

1. The production of machines such as those already mentioned (automatic boxing and packaging equipment) is carried out by numerous small enterprises; the above example includes about three hundred firms with a total of between ten thousand and fifteen thousand employees.
2. The firms are localized in a delimited geographic area; every province in Emilia-Romagna has specialized areas for certain types of products.
3. The product is generally a consumer good or a limited-run capital good that is made on order for certain clients. It is therefore characterized by *flexible* production.
4. There is in force a logic of *complementarity* rather than competition among the concerns that produce certain types of machines. This logic facilitates agreements concerning the acquisition of raw materials, the organization of sales and foreign marketing networks, and so forth.
5. Worker skills (predominantly male in the mechanical industries) are much higher than those found in a large Fordist-style factory, for two reasons: first, a system of small, complementary factories facilitates the diffusion of skills and their acquisition in the workplace; and, second, in a small factory that produces components or limited-run goods, the acquisition of multiple skills is necessary, and so employees learn the different phases of the production process.
6. This system promotes entrepreneurial mobility. After acquiring different production skills, an employee may decide, for example, to establish his own business for the production of the particular component or the performance of the specialized process that, on the basis of current conditions, seems most remunerative to him.

The small firms of the metallurgical and mechanical sectors are not informal since they are registered in accordance with the law, and the agreements among the enterprises are visible and public. In this setting, informal activities encompass, above all, the labor of wives. The wife who continues to work for her husband provides direct assistance to his business; this officially unrecognized assistance often includes keeping the books of the firm. Thus there is a direct informal presence of women in small metal-craft firms, even when only the man is listed as employed.

On the other hand, the presence of women is much more explicit and visible in the textile and garment sectors that developed in the agricultural areas where there had been protoindustrial experiences in the preceding period. In this case, women were present both in the technical area (use of machines) and on the design side of the industry (designing clothes, choosing colors and patterns, etc.).

As several studies have shown, this process usually begins with the woman's working with machines at home to produce knitted goods or clothes, while her husband continues to work in the factory. Then, when the home production becomes fairly stable, the wife officially establishes a craft-work business and the husband leaves the factory where he was employed in order to work alongside her. This phase of homework thus constitutes an informal economy of *growth*. Moreover, there is often a relation of *complicity* with the contractors who employ female homeworkers; the contractors do not pay for social benefits, while the homeworker is also afforded a savings since she does not have to pay taxes (and she is socially covered as the spouse of a formal worker).

At this point, it is useful to examine how the questions and hypotheses above relate to the activities during this period.

The production of goods for auto-consumption continued in the countryside, since the fall in the number of farm workers did not signify an exodus from the agricultural areas, where middle-aged parents often remained with sons and daughters who worked in the industry. Informal agricultural production thus came to have an *integrative* rather than an exclusively subsistence character. There were also substantial increases in informal (homework) production for the market—especially in textiles and clothing—and in the informal assistance provided by women to the small mechanical firms.

As regards the combinations presented in table 10.3, almost all of them were present in this phase. The parties of the Left, in particular the Communist party, in fact utilized much unpaid voluntary labor to produce goods and services (as for the famous Festival de L'Unita) so as to earn a profit for the organization (cells 2 and 3). Even more important were the interventions of public institutions that provided social services such as day-care centers at little or no cost (cell 7), as well as those of the charitable organizations (generally Catholic) that also offered free services, financing them with public funding and paying their employees informally (cell 4). There was thus a diffusion of all the different forms that the informal economy may assume.

Economic progress translated itself into a reduction of informal *subsistence* activities. Those of the *integrative* type carried out by women (who added to their husbands' income by homework), by younger people (for example, the informal part-time labor of students), and by the older generation (labor performed by retirees) were, however, very numerous. Finally, an informal economy of *growth* also acquired a strong presence, above all in the garment and textile sectors.

Part of the informal economy remained typically *exploitative* (in the less skilled forms of homework, for example). However, another part was carried out under relationships of *complicity* having, as its joint objective, the evasion of taxes and social contributions (the common enemy being the national tax collection system).

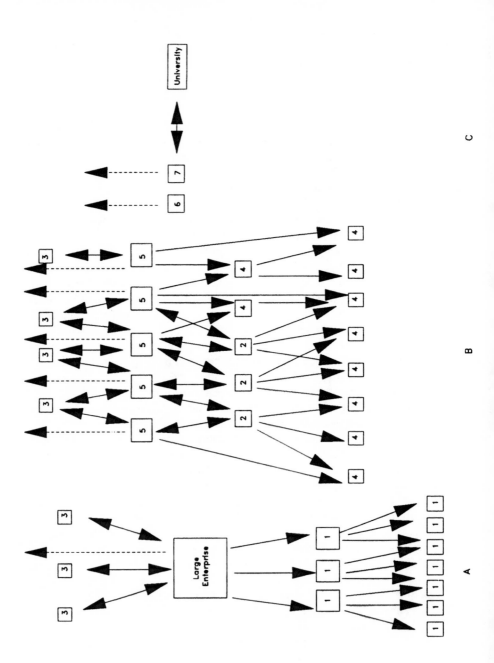

————————▶ = product output

◀━━━━━━━▶ = interaction

━━━━━━━━▶ = orders

1 Small enterprise with limited autonomy of decision within a traditional Ford–style system

2 Small enterprise dedicated to specialized production, which interacts with a large enterprise to produce the final product

3 Small consulting enterprise that interacts with large enterprise with regard to entrepreneurial decisions ("advanced tertiary")

4 Small enterprise with limited autonomy of decision within the system based on flexible specialization

5 Medium or small enterprise producing the final product in the system of flexible specialization

6 Small traditional craft enterprise

7 Small enterprise that produces prototypes in connection with university structures or research centers

Figure 10.2. Systems of industrialization: *A.* the Fordist system; *B.* flexible specialization before new technologies; *C.* special cases.

Adult women continued to be at the center of the informal economy because of their role in homework. Almost as important were the older men and women in the countryside who produced informally for direct consumption. Child labor decreased due to the law mandating compulsory education for children until the age of fourteen. However, there were increases in informal student employment and in moonlighting among public sector workers (municipal employees, teachers, nurses, etc.). Thus there was an overall increase in the diversity of social actors who intervened in the informal economy.

As regards the relation between women's domestic labor and the welfare state, there was a comprehensive increase in the care of young children. There was also a sharp increase in the obligatory relations with public institutions, as compared with life in the countryside in the first half of the century; for example, children had to be taken to school, and various bureaucratic matters had to be handled. Hence daily life was less harsh, and the burden of sons and daughters began to diminish (the progressive reduction in the birth rate continued). Increasing attention was thus given to domestic matters that had been pushed into the background in the earlier period due to the exigencies of material survival. Even women of the working class, for example, questioned themselves as to the care of their children. Wholly unchanged with respect to the past, however, was the estrangement of husbands from this domestic sphere.

Public services in the region also changed significantly. One of the major initiatives of the parties of the Left in Emilia-Romagna was the creation of day-care centers and the simultaneous propagation of the image of a woman who enters the official labor market and can permit herself to work continually without having to take time off for the birth of a child. As a concrete example of the difference between Emilia-Romagna and other regions, 12 percent of children aged three and under were enrolled in day-care centers in Bologna at a time when, in Naples, the population in the same age group enrolled in day-care centers was only three out of every thousand (.3%).

The relation between the development of small enterprises and the process of deregulation differs according to whether we are dealing with the metallurgical and mechanical sectors or with the textile and garment sectors, in which there was a large increase of small enterprises originating in homework. The important point that the analysis highlights, however, is that the principal causes of the rise of small flexible industry had little to do with a sudden increase in official tolerance for informal activities, even in the textile and garment sectors. Instead, it is necessary to consider both the presence of the technical schools at the outset of the twentieth century and the craft-work and protoindustrial traditions in the cities and in the countryside.

The analysis of regional development during this period also refutes the hypothesis that the informal economy flourishes when the official economy is in crisis. It is precisely the expansion of the latter, following a particular model of industrial development, that enlarges the possibilities for the informal economy. In the preceding phase (1900–50), the informal economy (except for forms of subsistence) was less widespread; in this period (1950–70) there was instead both a resurgence and diffusion of all types of informality.

The Period 1970–1987: The Informal Economy, the New Technologies, and the Expansion of the Tertiary Sector

In this last phase, the principal changes in the productive apparatus have included the diffusion of new information and electronic technologies and a more general expansion of the service sector. This growth has been visible not only because of the increase in tertiary employment but also because of the proliferation of new small enterprises—those that sprang to offer services to businesses (the so-called advanced tertiary composed of research and development firms, etc.) and those that were established to provide personal and household services.

An important change took place in the relations between large firms and the subsystem of small enterprises based on flexible specialization, as can be seen in figure 10.2. The new electronic and computer technologies have made it possible for large firms to be more flexible in their production (at the same time the organization of labor has changed: small firms producing goods and services for large enterprises have a higher degree of autonomy). Within a few of these small areas of production in Emilia (i.e., those producing motorcycles and tile machines) in which the organization of labor was not improved, Japanese firms have been able to beat local production. Nevertheless, on the whole, industrial production in Emilia (like that of the packaging and boxing machines mentioned above) have been able to withstand Japanese competition by changing strategies of vocational training[7] and using public and private service centers (the small consulting enterprises mentioned in fig. 10.2). And now the new trend is toward small enterprises that produce prototypes in connection with university research centers (type 7 in fig. 10.2).

In a parallel fashion, three significant changes have occurred in the social structure: First, there has been a sizable decrease in the birthrate with a corresponding increase in the percentage of older people; women have had fewer children and hence entered the official economy, bringing about a drastic reduction in the number of "housewives." Second, there has been a generalized increase in education, with females surpassing males in high school and university attendance. Third, one effect of the economic development in the region has been that the rate of unemployment among the males and females has become one of the lowest in Italy (in 1985 the unemployment rates of the male and female labor force were, respectively, 4.6% and 13.4% in Emilia-Romagna, while in Italy rates were, respectively, 7.0% and 17.3%). There has been an increase, on the other hand, in job expectations and the search for higher-level

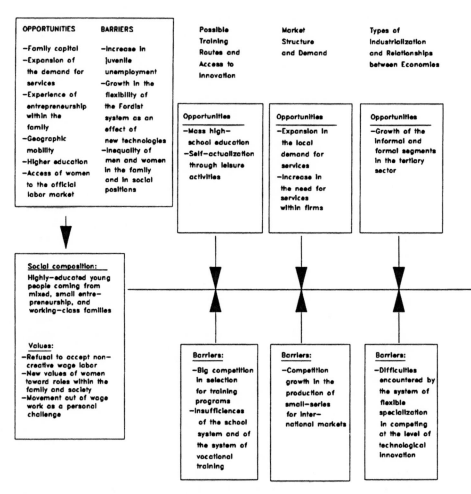

| OPPORTUNITIES | BARRIERS | Possible Training Routes and Access to Innovation | Market Structure and Demand | Types of Industrialization and Relationships between Economies |

OPPORTUNITIES
- Family capital
- Expansion of the demand for services
- Experience of entrepreneurship within the family
- Geographic mobility
- Higher education
- Access of women to the official labor market

BARRIERS
- Increase in juvenile unemployment
- Growth in the flexibility of the Fordist system as an effect of new technologies
- Inequality of men and women in the family and in social positions

Opportunities
- Mass high-school education
- Self-actualization through leisure activities

Opportunities
- Expansion in the local demand for services
- Increase in the need for services within firms

Opportunities
- Growth of the informal and formal segments in the tertiary sector

Social composition:
Highly-educated young people coming from mixed, small entrepreneurship, and working-class families

Values:
- Refusal to accept non-creative wage labor
- New values of women toward roles within the family and society
- Movement out of wage work as a personal challenge

Barriers:
- Big competition in selection for training programs
- Insufficiencies of the school system and of the system of vocational training

Barriers:
- Competition growth in the production of small-series for international markets

Barriers:
- Difficulties encountered by the system of flexible specialization in competing at the level of technological innovation

Figure 10.3. Transition to small entrepreneurship in Emilia-Romagna for people between twenty and thirty years of age in 1980.

work on the part of the younger generation (see fig. 10.3).

The interface of the new type of economic development and the informal economy has assumed diverse characteristics and has evolved in different directions. Industry in Emilia-Romagna retained its characteristics of flexible specialization; however, it now has to compete in the production of limited-run specialized goods with larger enterprises made competitive by the new electronic and information technologies.

The development of personal computers resulted in the establishment of small firms able to produce perfect imitations of the best-known American

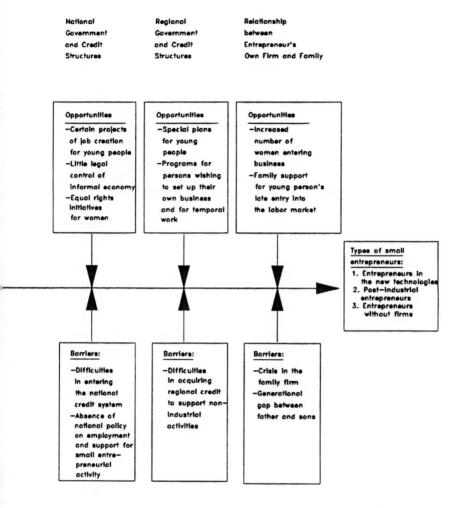

National Government and Credit Structures	Regional Government and Credit Structures	Relationship between Entrepreneur's Own Firm and Family

Opportunities
- Certain projects of job creation for young people
- Little legal control of informal economy
- Equal rights initiatives for women

Opportunities
- Special plans for young people
- Programs for persons wishing to set up their own business and for temporal work

Opportunities
- Increased number of women entering business
- Family support for young person's late entry into the labor market

Types of small entrepreneurs:
1. Entrepreneurs in the new technologies
2. Post-industrial entrepreneurs
3. Entrepreneurs without firms

Barriers:
- Difficulties in entering the national credit system
- Absence of national policy on employment and support for small entrepreneurial activity

Barriers:
- Difficulties in acquiring regional credit to support non-industrial activities

Barriers:
- Crisis in the family firm
- Generational gap between father and sons

computers and to sell them for a third of their price on the informal market. In agriculture, the production for direct consumption decreased as compared with the previous period, but a policy of the local governments encouraged the cultivation of urban gardens. In consequence, this auto-consumption activity has spread among older persons.

In any case, the sector in which the informal economy has expanded most vigorously has been the tertiary. A first area of growth was summer tourism along the Adriatic coast. The boom in mass tourism resulted in much informal employment at seaside resorts, involving both younger and older individuals. Next, in industrial consulting firms and personal and household services—businesses of the "advanced" tertiary—informal relations have been mostly between the head of the consulting firm and the young people who begin their careers performing the less-skilled programming work. In this case, informal hiring of these employees allows the consulting firm to pay them less and simultaneously enables the young workers to avoid paying taxes. Hence, there is a situation of *complicity* deriving from the fact that these employees plan to start their own firms once they have become more proficient and have acquired a better grasp of the business cycle.

Generalized economic well-being has also led to a rising demand for personalized services (nursing care, the care of older and handicapped individuals, instruction in physical exercise and nutrition, etc.). Thus a network has been created comprising small concerns or individuals (students, adults who perform this kind of activity as a second job, retired persons, etc.) who seek to offer their services through a *direct* (informal) monetary relationship with the consumer.

A study by Capecchi and Pesce (1986) of young people in a suburban neighborhood in Bologna has demonstrated that there is a positive correlation between part-time informal employment, expanded education, and plans to start one's own business. There is a kind of *entrepreneurship without enterprises,* since these new generations often conceive small entrepreneurial projects without being able to implement them. For this group, informally paid activities represent a first approach toward a possible future move into self-employment, which utilizes not only educational resources but also skills acquired during so-called free-time (knowing how to play a sport, how to play an instrument, how to dance, etc.).

What is striking about these new, small entrepreneurial ventures is that even they follow the model of flexible specialization: the enterprise seeks to offer services that take into account the client's specific requirements, whether this client is a business or a single individual. The following are the features that characterize the informal economy in the region in this most recent phase of industrial development.

The presence of informal labor markets has certainly increased, due to the expansion of the tertiary sector; however, informal markets for goods and services have also increased. There are now informal markets both for goods and services dependent on the new technologies (personal computers and programming) and for personal and household services, offered directly to the consumer.

Instances of a *subsistence* informal economy are rare, but the cycle is beginning again for immigrants in the region (especially those from North Africa) who are employed in the most unskilled jobs (the men in heavy and dangerous work, the women as housemaids). A rise in immigration is currently foreseeable, and this trend may encourage the reemergence of a subsistence informal economy.

The *integrative* informal economy is even more widespread owing to the existence and expansion of the area of personal and household services. Next, there is also an informal economy of *growth* in the advanced tertiary (one begins to work informally in order to learn a profession), as well as in the formation of small businesses and entrepreneurial activities in the personal and household services sector.

Exploitative relations are widespread, and not only in regard to immigrant workers. In fact, there are many temporary, unskilled (and often dangerous) jobs that present characteristics of exploitation and that are taken for brief periods by young people. Youngsters accept these jobs because they consider such occupations temporary and because they are often carried out by small groups of friends. However, there are also many situations of an informal economy of *complicity* in the advanced tertiary, as well as in the rest of the service sector, because the temporary nature of employment may be in accordance with the individual worker's own projects.

Despite some changes, the social actors present in the informal economy include all those described for the prior phase. The presence of adult women in informal activities has diminished because a larger number now take jobs in the official economy. There is, however, a growing incidence of younger people working informally, although they are listed in the official statistics as "searching for work"; the presence of students and older individuals among the informally employed is very high, as is the incidence of moonlighters, mostly males.

As regards domestic labor, Emilia-Romagna is today the Italian region with the lowest birthrate, and, as a consequence of this change, young women have begun to raise the question of whether domestic labor should be considered an exclusively "feminine" occupation. The majority of young women enter the official labor market, and there are diverse demands made of the welfare state. There is a close relation between women who are consumers of welfare state services and those employed in the distribution of the same services.

Services change because local governments seek to avoid directly administering them, preferring instead to pay small private cooperatives (often run by young people) to perform these tasks. There is thus a public and private interface that depends on an interface of informal and official activities within the domestic sphere; women are continually involved in these various roles.

The proposition about a causal relation between the diffusion of small enterprise and prior deregulation of the economy does not hold, even for the new approaches to small entrepreneurship in the tertiary sector. The diffusion of the small services enterprise has other origins: the increase in education among the younger generations, the spread of the new technologies, and the growing demand for personal and household services.

The hypothesis of an informal economy that expands when the official economy enters a crisis period is once again refuted. What our research indicates is that there is a supportive relationship between the official and informal economies: the growth of one tends to accompany the development of the other, so that both are simultaneously "poorer" or "richer." The better off families are (in terms of economic, social, and cultural capital), the greater their possibilities of access to the informal economy; while among the poorer families, access is limited to mostly subsistence activities. Thus a tendency toward a segmented society in which there exists an ever greater discrepancy between poor areas and families and increasingly wealthy areas and families is supported.

Estimates of the Informal Economy

It is possible to give an idea of the number of persons involved in the informal economy by stratifying the population according to gender, age, and employment situation. Estimates are available for the mid-1970s for both Emilia-Romagna and Italy as a whole, and a number of comparisons are also possible. Results are presented in table 10.4, which gives estimates for Italy compiled by L. Frey (1979a, 1979b), ISFOL-CENSIS (1979), and B. S. Frey and Weck (1982). For Emilia-Romagna, I have utilized estimates made by L. Frey (1975), Bergonzini (1973, 1979), and Capecchi (1983).

In the mid-1970s 13,700,000 men and 5,300,000 women were officially employed in Italy, 66 percent and 24 percent, respectively, of the population aged fourteen or over. Males involved in the informal economy numbered about 2,400,000, and women totaled 2,600,000. Women thus constituted an absolute majority of the informally employed, and informality was far more prevalent within the female labor force. The ratio of the informal to the officially employed was only 18 percent for males, but reached half (49%) of the female labor force. Further, most adult women who worked informally in the mid-1970s did not hold a job in the official economy; most male informal workers, on the other hand, also had an officially sanctioned job.

At this point a comparison of the national estimates with those compiled for Emilia-Romagna is in order. The individuals officially occupied in this region in the mid-1970s totaled 1,070,000 men and 540,000 women. In terms of percentages, more women were officially employed in Emilia-Romagna than in Italy, but the point to emphasize is that there was also a higher percentage of women employed in informal activities (14% of the female population over the age of 14 as against the national average of 12%). Again in relative terms, there were also more men both officially and informally employed in Emilia-Romagna than in Italy. These figures again verify the thesis that the richer a region is in

Table 10.4 Estimates of Employment in the Informal Economy in Italy and in Emilia-Romagna, Mid-1970s

	Italy		Emilia-Romagna	
	Men	Women	Men	Women
Informal employment of persons aged 10–15	300,000	143,000	10,000	5,000
Informal employment of persons aged 14–29	510,000	890,000	40,000	60,000
Informal employment of persons aged 30–50	200,000	600,000	30,000	90,000
Adult men and women (30–50) holding second jobs	916,000	241,000	70,000	20,000
Informal employment of persons aged 50 and over	500,000	750,000	40,000	50,000
Total	2,426,000	2,624,000	190,000	225,000
Percentage of the population over 14 employed in the official economy	66	24	70	34
Percentage of the population over 14 employed in the informal economy	18	12	13	14
Workers in the informal economy as a percentage of those employed in the official economy	18	49	18	38
Percentage estimate of the contribution of the informal economy to the gross national product	10.5		12	

Sources: L. Frey 1975, 1979a, 1979b; Bergonzini 1973, 1979; ISFOL-CENSIS 1979; B. S. Frey and Weck 1982; Capecchi 1983.

its official economy, the greater the possibilities of finding additional work in informal activities.

In Emilia-Romagna, there are proportionately fewer individuals under the age of fourteen employed informally, since violations of the compulsory education laws are almost nonexistent (in contrast with southern Italy where such violations are common). On the other hand, informal employment among all other social categories is higher in Emilia-Romagna than in Italy. According to B. S. Frey and Weck (1982), the informal economy contributes 10.5 percent of the Italian GNP. Assuming that this estimate is reliable, it can be hypothesized that this percentage is higher for Emilia-Romagna, precisely because there is in this region an informal economy that is at once more broadly based (i.e., one in which more people participate) and more technologically advanced.

Conclusions

This study of an Italian region characterized by the relatively recent development of flexible industrialization and by the even more recent expansion of the tertiary sector highlights the advantages of a method of analysis based on systematic comparison between regions—within and across nation-states. In Italy, at least, analyses conducted exclusively at the national level represent an average of widely divergent regional situations. It is therefore important to supplement such studies with analyses that focus on the particular socioeconomic history of individual regions.

This method of analysis pays particular attention to the characterization of each region according to its type of industrialization and to the form in which the passage from agriculture to industry took place (see Benton, this volume). Also to be considered is how the expansion of the tertiary sector was effected. The analysis must begin at the level of family structure, keeping in mind, however, both the political and social organization of the regional labor market.

Informality cannot be studied separately from the official economy. There is, in fact, *a single economy* in which informal and official activities intersect, and in which women and men, generations, and different social groups participate in various ways. To take all of these aspects into consideration is not a simple task, but an in-depth understanding of the informal economy can only result from an analysis at this level of complexity.

Notes

1. For a further discussion of this point see, in addition to Capecchi and Pesce 1983, Sabel and Zeitlin 1985; Piore and Sabel 1984; Becattini 1979, 1987.

2. For a historical analysis of Emilia-Romagna see Capecchi 1982; Barbagli, Capecchi, and Cobalti 1987. Other studies on the interface of the official and informal economies in Emilia-Romagna are those by Brusco 1982; Fua and Zacchia 1983; Capecchi 1983.

3. When discovered by the authorities, "legally tolerated" informal activities are subject only to economic sanctions for the failure to pay taxes and social contributions. These sanctions are, in fact, rarely imposed. It is also important to keep in mind that, in the official Italian economy, the rate of tax evasion is very high, which means that a more rigorous system of tax collection would have as its priorities areas other than small informal enterprises.

4. Melossi's essay (1977) points out that 25 percent of the aid provided by the Marshall Plan for the acquisition of industrial plants was given to the Piedmont region and 28 percent, to the Lombardy region, where the big firms of the north are located, while Emilia-Romagna received only 0.7 percent.

5. It must be kept in mind, for instance, that during World War II the Reggiane factory in Reggio Emilia was employing 12,000 workers, while in 1952 only 700 were employed; the Ducati factory in Bologna went down from 6,000–7,000 workers during the war to only 1,300 in 1954; the Calzoni factory in Bologna went from 1,600 to 130; the Cogne factory in Imola, from 2,400 to 600. The subsequent shutdown of these factories linked to the national government also meant loss of work for the artisan firms that had contracts with them.

6. For a recent analysis of the studies on leading classes during the last hundred years see Baldissara 1987.

7. For an analysis of present issues concerning vocational training see Capecchi 1987.

References

Baldissara, L. 1987. "Le Classi Dirigenti Emiliane fra Politica e Poteri Locali 1860/1960: Percorsi de Lettura." *Italia Contemporanea* 167:65–84.

Barbagli, M., V. Capecchi, and A. Cobalti. 1987. *La Mobilita Sociale in Italia*. Bologna: Il Mulino.

Becattini, G. 1979. "Dal Settore Industriale al Distretto Industriale: Alcune Considerazioni Sull'unita di Indagine." *Rivista di Economia e Politica Industriale* 1:7–21.

———. 1987. *Mercato e Forze Locali: Il Distretto Industriale*. Bologna: Il Mulino.

Bergonzini, L. 1973. "Casalinghe o Lavoranti a Domicilio?" *Inchiesta* 10:50–54.

———. 1979. "Occupazione Occulta e Risultati di una Ricerca sul Secondo Lavoro a Bologna." *Inchiesta* 37:10–18.

Brusco, S. 1982. "The 'Emilian' Model: Productive Decentralization and Social Integration." *Cambridge Journal of Economics* 6:167–84.

Capecchi, V. 1982. "Classe Operaia e Cultura Borghese." Pp. 159–292 in AA.VV. (ed.), *Famiglia Operaia, Mutamenti Culturali, 150 Ore*. Bologna: Il Mulino.

———. 1983. "La Economia Sumergida in Italia." *Sociologia del Trabajo* 9:35–64.

———. 1987. "Formation Professionnelle et Petite Entreprise: Le Developpement Industrial a Specialisation Flexible en Emilie-Romagne." *Formation Emploi* 19:3–18.

Capecchi, V. and A. Pesce. 1983. "Se la Diversita e un Valore." *Inchiesta* 59–60:1–37.

———. 1986. *Vivere lo Spazio e il Tempo*. Bologna: Comune di Bologna.

Frey, B. S. and H. Weck. 1982. *The Hidden Economy as an Unobserved Variable*. University of Zurich. Mimeo.

Frey, L. 1975. *Il Potenziale di Lavoro in Italia: Offerta e Domanda di Lavoro Nelle Aree dell'Emilia Romagna*. Documenti ISVET 50/1.

———. 1979a. "Il Lavoro Minorile in Italia." *Tendenze dell'Occupazione* 4:1–8.

———. 1979b. "Dal Lavoro Nero Alla Misurazione del Lavoro Sommerso." *Notiziario CERES dell'Economia del Lavoro* 10:1–4.

Fua, G. and C. Zacchia, eds. 1983. *Industrializzazione Senza Fratture*. Bologna: Il Mulino.

ISFOL CENSIS. 1979. *Primo Rapporto Sulla Mano d'Opera*. Roma.

Melossi, D. 1977. "Lotta di Classe nel Piano del Lavoro." Pp. 11–129 in AA.VV. (eds.), *Restaurazione Capitalistica e Piano del Lavoro*. Roma: Editrice Sindacale Italiana.

Piore, M. J. and C. Sabel. 1984. *The Second Industrial Divide*. New York: Basic Books.

Poni, C. 1982. *Fossi e Cavedagne Benedicon le Campagne*. Bologna: Il Mulino.

Sabel, C. and J. Zeitlin. 1985. "Historical Alternatives to Mass Production: Politics, Markets, and Technology in Nineteenth Century Industrialization." *Past and Present* 108:133–75.

11 Informalization in the Valencian Economy: A Model for Underdevelopment

Josep-Antoni Ybarra

I denounce all those
Who are indifferent to the other half . . .
For we want our daily bread,
Alder flower and perennial tenderness
  dropping like beads,
For we ask that the will of the earth
  be fulfilled,
The earth who gives its harvest to all.
—Federico García Lorca, *The Poet in New York*

The presence of informal activities in the Spanish economy and particularly in the Valencian region is not a new development. Many firms and much current formal employment grew out of diffuse industrialization processes that started as informal. However, the importance of the informal sector at present derives from its erosion of painstakingly created social, productive, and institutional relationships.

The relevance of the phenomenon is larger than raw quantitative figures might suggest because it fosters qualitative changes affecting the future of society. Three aspects are particularly relevant: The first is the growth of a system of economic and social relations which places constant pressure upon the official and formal sectors, accelerating their shift from legality to illegality. Thus, the informal sector self-generates on the basis of the collapsing legal economy.

Second, the process involves a degradation of existing social and productive relations. Finally, informalization generally occurs in old, traditional economic sectors in which the process is used as a mechanism for survival. This slows down the emergence of alternative growth models and the modernization of the production plant.

The purpose of this chapter is to document the interrelationships

Chapter 11 was translated by M. Patricia Fernández-Kelly.

among these three aspects on the basis of recent empirical research in the Valencian region of Spain and, in particular, in the province of Alicante.

Methodology and Research Location

Research on the informalization process requires different methodologies suited to the specific models of development, types of social organization, and the like in the relevant country or region (Peattie 1980). In the case of Spain, informality adopts numerous forms, for it is observable in large and small companies, in capital-intensive and labor-intensive industries, and in sectors directed toward the domestic market as well as in export-oriented industries (Sanchis 1984; Celada, López, and Parra 1985; García de Blas and Ruesga 1985; Benton, this volume). Given the heterogeneity of the phenomenon, a plural strategy that combined quantitative and qualitative methods was adopted for this study (Gaudin and Schiray 1984).

Operationally, informality was defined as a system of economic and social relations characterized by three features:

1. The production or exchange of goods and services conducted at the margins of official and administrative regulations.
2. The remuneration of such activities either in kind or in currency.
3. The regularity of these activities; in other words, they do not take place as isolated events.

The selection of the province of Alicante as a research site was determined by existing legal-territorial definitions. However, the character of informalization in the area led well beyond the original narrow boundaries of the province and into the entire southern Valencian region. The focus of the study was on industrial activities that give economic identity to the region, both locally and as part of the whole Spanish economy (see table 11.1). Three sectors were found to be most significant in this respect: footwear, textiles, and toy manufacturing. Southern Valencia is the area of Spain in which footwear and toy production are concentrated, and it ranks third as a textile center. Results of the quantitative surveys for this study are comparable to those obtained with similar methodologies elsewhere in Spain. This allows for extensive comparisons and generalizable findings (Casals and Vidal 1982; Miguélez 1982; Sanchis 1984).

Selection of the research site and the specific industries to be studied was followed by an in-depth probe of the functional and productive characteristics of each type of manufacture. A two-fold approach was followed: first, the research focused on formal enterprises that appeared to rely, partially or totally, on informal production; second, we considered the strictly informal labor process and the workers involved in it.

Interviews were conducted between the end of 1984 and the beginning

Table 11.1 Sectoral Participation in Industrial Production in the Province of Alicante and in Spain, 1983

Regional and Nationwide Production		
Sector	Alicante (%)	Spain (%)
Construction and public works	14.3	13.3
Water, gas, electricity, and mining	2.8	14.5
Food	10.9	15.4
Footwear and textiles	40.8	8.8
Wood, cork, and paper	4.8	6.6
Chemicals, ceramics, and cement	19.2	16.1
Metals	7.2	25.3
Total[1]	100.0	100.0
	(733)	(21,414)
Alicante's Participation in the National Product		
	Firms (%)	Employment (%)	Exports (%)
Footwear	51.6	49.7	63.7
Textiles	8.0	5.2	4.8
Toys	31.2	48.8	41.4

Sources: Bank of Bilbao, *Renta Nacional de España y su Distribución Provincial,* 1983; National Institute of Statistics, *Censo Industrial de España,* 1978.

[1]Figures in parentheses are thousands of millions of pesetas.

of 1985 on the basis of a sample formed by 154 companies that provide over 20 percent of recorded employment in the area. Information about the actual daily, weekly, and monthly activities of each company was collected from employers. In these interviews, questions were asked about wages, hiring practices, productivity, and technology. The focus of the second part of the study was on the most common type of informal employment in all three sectors, namely, homework performed by women (Sanchis 1984). Two hundred and forty-six interviews were conducted with these informal workers with the purpose of learning more about their social and family relations and about the impact of homework on the internal dynamics of their households.

Magnitude of the Informal Economy

Studies of informality are often based on the analysis of aggregate demographic and production data. This approach can lead to distorted conclusions for several reasons. First, it is difficult to pinpoint what really belongs to each sector. In the case of production, for example, researchers are likely to find only final goods that have undergone transformations in moving through a sequence of formal and informal phases linked in an integrated process. Second, it is also difficult to carry out a quantitative appraisal of the number of workers involved in concealed production (see Kritz and Ramos 1976; Souza and Tokman 1976; Portes and Benton 1984; Anker 1984). There is considerable versatility among workers, who can easily shift from fully regulated to clandestine activities. Just as it is often not possible to separate formal from informal products, it is equally difficult to distinguish formal and informal workers. Thus, any quantitative assessment must be seen as a tentative approximation (García de Blas and Ruesga 1985).

The research summarized in this chapter took stock of the preceding considerations in evaluating the characteristics and volume of informal activities in southern Valencia. Thus, it allowed for convergent approximations from the point of view of production, employment capacity, and population. As shown in table 11.2 however, informality, no matter how measured, is a widespread phenomenon in the three industries selected. The vast majority of companies in each of these sectors depend, at least to some extent, on concealed labor and engage in informal activities at some point in their productive processes. The value of informal production surpasses, in every case, 33 percent of the total. In the case of textiles, however, up to 43 percent of total production is informal.

From the point of view of workers, informal activities are as important or more important than legal employment. This is mainly due to the presence of clandestine female labor that, in every case, surpasses women's formal employment (see table 11.2). Thus, female workers emerge as the largest category of informal employees in Valencia. Most of this work takes place at home, according to the typical constraints of an underground economy in which even minimal legal requirements are not followed. Shifts are, however, as regular as those in the factories; payments, on the other hand, are by piece rate, and hourly wages are lower than those received in formal employment (see table 11.3).

The extension of this phenomenon, as well as the widespread involvement of women in informal activities, is also demonstrated through the analysis

Table 11.2 Informality in Three Industrial Sectors of Alicante, 1985

	Footwear (%)	Textiles (%)	Toys (%)
Informal production ÷ total production	33.0	43.0	37.0
Firms using informal production ÷ total firms	91.0	86.5	94.5
Informal employment ÷ formal employment	54.8	38.7	45.4
Men	9.9	6.3	16.2
Women	251.5	463.8	124.7
Informal employment ÷ EAP in sector	22.3	20.7	38.7
Men	9.9	6.3	16.2
Women	62.2	63.4	115.1

Table 11.3 Characteristics of Women Homeworkers in Alicante

	Percentage of Women
Items paid for by employers	
Vacations	21.9
Electricity used in production	2.8
Rental expenses	2.4
Sick leave	3.4
Materials and components	8.9
Months per year allocated to homework	
6 or less	6.6
6–10	22.6
10 or more	70.8
Daily hours	
5 or less	8.9
5–8	51.6
8 or more	39.5
Expected remuneration if same work was performed in factories	
Higher	84.8
Same	13.9
Smaller	1.3

Note: $N = 246$.

of employment figures as compared with the economically active population in the area (see table 11.2). The noteworthy finding is that the rate of economic activity obtained if informal work is taken into account is much higher than official data indicate. Especially for women, official figures would have to be multiplied by 4.5 in order to achieve consistency between actual and official participation rates in the labor force. This gives way to a curious situation in toy manufacture in which the actual size of female employment cannot be explained even by assuming the participation of the total economically active female population in the sectoral labor force. This result suggests that informal labor is such a commonplace reality that it has created its own social environment in which these practices are accepted as an employment alternative by all workers—whether employed formally or not.

Causes of Informalization

What is the explanation for the expansion of the informal economy in Valencia? There is no single answer to this question. However, there has been a tendency to attribute the existence of these economic activities to the presence of conjunctural anomalies in a particular area of the economic system (Vázquez and Trigo 1982; Sauvy 1984). The underground economy is portrayed then as an inevitable but temporary phenomenon caused by the absence of realistic government policies. This argument has been used as a justification for the bypassing of legal regulations.

Other less ideological and more plausible causal interpretations center on the creation of a parallel socioeconomic system that satisfies more effectively the needs of households and individuals. In this case, the emphasis is not on conjunctural justifications but on structural conditions. According to this view, dissatisfaction and confrontation with official legislation produces a reaction on the part of individuals or families who see their objectives frustrated by the state. As a response, they generate an alternative economic sphere that gives them access to what they perceive as legitimate claims (Miguélez 1984). Writings adhering to this position are many (Capecchi and Pesce 1984); the justifications that they provide are based on personal (Illich 1980), political (Negri 1979), technological (Piore and Sabel 1985), and educational considerations (Capecchi 1983, this volume).

In the case of the sectors studied in Valencia, the motives that industries have for moving underground are generally economic—maintaining a short-term competitive edge, for example (Sanchis 1982; Gómez Perezagua 1982). In each of the three sectors studied, informality allows employers to fulfill a triple objective: first, to reduce direct and indirect costs of production; second, to gain access to a flexible labor pool; and third, to differentiate production.

The functional model adopted by companies can be labeled *spontaneous restructuring*. This strategy consists of intensifying traditional modalities of production on the basis of informal labor in order to reduce costs. Reliance on informal manufacturing has been due, to a large extent, to the pressure exercised by newly industrializing countries able to produce cheap export goods. However, the necessary restructuring has not been conducted by modernizing machinery or by improving the quality of manufacturing skills and finished products. Instead, the trend has been toward maintaining traditional manufacturing schemes while intensifying the use of cheap unskilled and semiskilled labor. Employers frequently argue that the rigidity of legislation imposed by the state is responsible for the rise of the underground economy. However, it can be argued that it is the growing *rigidity of the productive model* which is responsible for its lack of international competitiveness.

Spontaneity in the restructuring of production does not negate the existence of forethought, internal order, and individual company planning (Delorozoy 1981; Ovejero 1985). As pointed out above, informality provides benefits that ultimately make any other short-term alternative less attractive. As shown in table 11.4, employers of firms in which production has been completely decentralized into informal arrangements report significantly higher net earnings than those that retain formal factory production.

Steps taken by companies as they move toward decentralization in-

Table 11.4 Net Earnings as a Percentage of Total Revenues among Firms in Alicante

Sector	Formal Firms (%)	Partly Informal Establishments (%)	Informal Establishments (%)	Total (%)
Footwear	23.3	25.6	38.4	27.1
Textiles	28.0	30.7	40.1	31.3
Toys	28.0	42.8	47.4	40.7

volve a division of labor and integration of formal and informal phases of production. In all instances, the legal establishment takes responsibility for the following tasks:

1. Initial stages of production, that is, the purchase and stocking of raw materials as well as links with suppliers
2. Coordination of intermediate phases in the productive process, whether legal or illegal
3. Finishing stages in the process, or quality control, packaging, and marketing

Intermediate stages in the production process tend to be fully decentralized through subcontracting to illegal or partially legal operations.

Fully illegal operations are characterized, in turn, by

1. specialization in intermediate productive tasks,
2. intensive and low-skill labor processes,
3. high levels of female participation,
4. relative absence of technology as compared with that in modern formal industries,
5. homework, and
6. disaggregation of manufacturing, with each unit taking responsibility for no more than two productive stages.

There is another form of partially legal establishment characterized by

1. similar specialization in intermediate productive tasks,
2. capital-intensive operations and relatively advanced technology, and
3. higher levels of skill in comparison with those in informal enterprises.

Coexisting with fully and partially informal establishments, there is yet another modality that occurs *inside* legal plants and not on the basis of subcontracting. It consists of using productive tools and processes without abiding by legal labor rules. Practices range from hiring workers without a contract, to the absence of overtime compensation, to the use of plants and buildings in off-hours without government knowledge or control.

In Valencia, the abundance of potentially employable labor allows for the maintenance and expansion of informal practices. In addition, informal employment does not require particular skills due to the low technological input of labor-intensive production. In general, minimal training and some previous knowledge of a specific task are enough. The latter can be acquired directly, as a result of earlier employment in the formal sector, or indirectly through kin and friends (Bernabé 1977).

In this study, informal employment emerged clearly as a response to need and the absence of better alternatives in the labor market. However, the earnings derived from informal work cannot be considered by any means secondary or residual. The image of underground labor as an advantageous choice entailing independence, personal fulfillment, creativity, and the allocation of leisure time (Illich 1980; De Grazia 1983) is far removed from the reality faced by people in this region. As shown in table 11.5, the main reason given by 85 percent of homeworkers surveyed for their involvement in clandestine activities was that their earnings are vital—not supplementary—to the subsis-

Table 11.5 Reasons for Female Homework and Effect on Household Incomes in Alicante

	Percentage of Women
Main motive for working	
Family is dependent on her income	16.5
Spouse/father laid off	7.4
Head of household's income is insufficient	46.7
Insecure labor situation	14.5
Personal expenses, autonomy, leisure, etc.	14.9
Clandestine homework earnings as percentage of comparable factory work[1]	
Footwear	32.0
Textiles	43.0
Toys	50.0
Homework as a percentage of total household income[2]	
Footwear	30.0
Textiles	35.0
Toys	36.0
Main reason for working at home	
Lack of regular employment	55.9
Unemployment	7.4
Domestic responsibilities	30.9
"Women shouldn't work outside the home"	5.8
Education of homeworkers	
Can't read or write	1.9
Fewer than 6 years of schooling	28.3
6 years of schooling	59.9
High school education	3.3
Professional or graduate education	6.5

Note: $N = 246$.

[1] Actual working hours of homeworkers were compared with wages paid in the formal sector to similarly qualified employees.

[2] Figures are average incomes of families in which the head of household is employed in the formal sector and in which women perform informal activities.

tence of their families. Twenty-four percent of the women surveyed reported being the only source of income for their households. Earnings derived from homework represent 30 percent or more, on the average, of total family income.

Individuals generally choose to work at home because of the absence of other options (Janjic 1981). Married women, who represent the prototype of illegal home workers, cannot find regular employment easily because companies prefer to hire them informally, thus reducing production costs and avoiding legal obligations. As seen in table 11.5, payments to informal workers are always a fraction of those received by legal factory employees. Agreements are established verbally, and payments are on the basis of piece rates. Further, employers can also shift direct costs of production (for example, electricity bills and amortization charges on machinery) to informal workers.

The absence of labor alternatives for these women is reinforced by their own perception that homework allows them to attend to family responsibilities (see Fortuna and Prates, this volume; Benería, this volume). Almost 31 percent of women interviewed reported that the need to fulfill family responsibilities was the main reason for choosing homework. Finally, as also shown in table 11.5, educational attainment also limits women's access to better employment alternatives; most have minimal schooling, and less than 10 percent have some education beyond grammar school.

As can be seen from all the above, factors explaining the presence of the underground economy are manifold, and it is necessary to take the perspective of each of the different actors involved in order to gain a full understanding of the process. In Valencia's economy, a key causal variable in the informalization process is the ease with which it is possible to continue operating within a productive model characterized by low-skilled cheap labor. This brings considerable benefits to employers and yields necessary earnings to a labor force with few employment alternatives.

Conclusion: Consequences of Informality

Implicit in the description of the causes of informalization in Valencia are its likely consequences. Clandestinity fosters a climate of general crisis in the formal sector (as reflected in figures on plant closings, bankruptcies, reductions in social security payments, layoffs, etc.) which actually has little to do with real economic conditions as reflected in volume of production and value of exports. In this manner, the "crisis" is used as blackmail, as a weapon of employers to demand exemptions from the legislation protecting workers. The argument is always the same: the need to maintain "competitiveness" vis-à-vis Third World producers and local firms that have gone completely underground.

Informalization creates and strengthens its own rules: labor conditions erode and wages shrink; entrepreneurial efforts center on strategies to conceal clandestine activities more and better. This reduces or eliminates incentives for technological progress, innovation, and investment. At the level of the household, personal relations are strained by the need to intensify informal productive tasks in order to increase earnings. The process affects housewives in particular. To this must be added the personal and collective damages derived from homework as well as the physical and psychological risks faced by workers. Seventy-two percent of working women interviewed during our study reported physical and psychological ailments related to the type of work that they performed. The household becomes a workshop where workers must handle, without necessary safeguards, flammable and toxic substances, to say nothing of the poor sanitary conditions under which they must work (Vilanova and Vicedo 1984).

An important element of modern development theory is to show how technological innovation and dissemination foster objective conditions for progress and the flow of vital resources (see among others Hirschman 1973, 50; Richardson 1977, 95). Those who have transposed part of this theoretical scheme to the process of informalization have portrayed small-scale and personal inventiveness as a positive outcome in some cases (Piore and Sabel 1985; Veltz 1986). It has also been suggested that informal entrepreneurship can have a modernizing influence (Gill 1984; Ebel 1985; Cavestro 1984). However, the preceding analysis shows how the process can lead to the opposite outcome, namely, the replacement of modern methods of production by others believed to have disappeared long ago. In this manner, obsolete tools and equipment destined for the scrap heap are resurrected, and the use of new technologies is simultaneously postponed. In sum, shifting production underground has destroyed incentives in such a way that at present both employers and workers in Valencia cannot see options for survival other than further informalization. Under these conditions, how can they even contemplate alternative and viable models for progress and development?

References

Anker, R. 1984. "Actividad de la Mano de Obra Femenina en los Países en Desarrollo: Examen Crítico de las Definiciones y los Métodos de Compilación de Datos." *Revista Internacional de Trabajo* 1:95–111.
Bernabé, J. M. 1977. "Factores de Localización y Crisis de la Industria Valenciana del Calzado." Bolsín Oficial de Comercio, *Panorama Bursátil* 6:71–87.
Capecchi, V. 1983. "Economía Sumergida, Trayectorias Masculinas y Femeninas, Organización del Tiempo." Pp. 47–92 in *Descentralización de la Producción, Economía Informal y Territorio en la Crisis Económica*. Madrid: Excma. Diputación, Area de Urbanismo y Ordenación Territorial.
Capecchi, V. and A. Pesce. 1984. "Si la Diversidad es un Valor." *Debats* 10:29–49.
Casals, M. and J. M. Vidal. 1982. "L'economía de Sabadell: Estructura, Diagnostic i Perspectives." Ajuntament de Sabadell. Mimeo.

Cavestro, W. 1984. "Automatisation, Organisation du Travail, et Qualification dans les PME." *Sociologie du Travail* 4:434–46.

Celada, F., F. López, and T. Parra. 1985. *Efectos Espaciales de los Procesos de Reorganización del Sistema Productivo en Madrid*. Madrid: Comunidad Autónoma de Madrid.

De Grazia, R. 1983. *Le Travail Clandestin*. Geneve: BIT.

Delorozoy, R. 1981. "Le Travail Clandestin." *Droit Social* 7–8:580–96.

Ebel, K. H. 1985. "Consecuencias Sociales y Laborales de los Sistemas de Fabricación Flexible." *Revista Internacional de Trabajo* 2:175–89.

García de Blas, A. and B. Ruesga. 1985. *Mercado de Trabajo y Economía Oculta en Andalucía*. Sevilla: Instituto de Desarrollo Regional, Universidad de Sevilla.

Gaudin, J. and M. Schiray. 1984. "L'economie Cachés en France: Etat du Débat et Bilan des Travaux." *Revue Economique* 4:691–731.

Gill, C. 1984. "Nouvelle Technologie, Dequalification, et Strategies de l'Entreprise." *Sociologie du Travail* 4:558–63.

Gómez Perezagua, R. 1982. "Estructura Empresarial y Economía Oculta." *Información Comercial Española* 587:109–17.

Hirschman, A. O. 1973. *La Estrategia del Desarrollo Económico*. Mexico, D.F.: Fondo de Cultura Económica.

Illich, I. 1980. *Le Travail Fantôme*. Paris: Seuil.

Janjic, M. 1981. "Diversificar el Trabajo de las Mujeres: Condición Indispensable Para una Auténtica Igualdad de Oportunidades." *Revista Internacional de Trabajo* 2:163–79.

Kritz, E. and J. Ramos. 1976. "Medición del Subempleo Urbano." *Revista Internacional de Trabajo* 1:127–40.

Miguélez, F. 1982. "Economía Sumergida y Tranformaciones Socio-Laborales." *Boletín de Estudios Económicos* 117:439–60.

———. 1984. "Economía Sumergida y Transformaciones de las Relaciones Laborales." *ICE Semanal* 1928:862–68.

Negri, T. 1979. "La Fabrica Deforme." *Rivista Maggazino*, pp. 2–5.

Ovejero, F. 1985. "La Economía de los Otros Trabajadores." *Mientras Tanto* 23:87–95.

Peattie, L. R. 1980. "Anthropological Perspectives on the Concepts of Dualism, the Informal Sector, and Marginality in Developing Urban Economies." *International Regional Science Review* 1:1–31.

Piore, M. and C. Sabel. 1985. "Le Paradigme de la Production de Masse et ses Alternatives, le Cas des Etats-Unis et de l'Italie." Pp. 1–20 in *Conventions Economiques*. Paris: PUF.

Portes, A. and L. Benton. 1984. "Industrial Development and Labor Absorption: A Reinterpretation." *Population and Development Review* 4:590–611.

Richardson, H. W. 1977. *Teoría del Crecimiento Regional*. Madrid: Pirámide.

Sanchis, E. 1982. "Economía Subterránea y Descentralización Productiva en la Industria Manufacturera." *Boletín de Estudios Económicos* 117:461–81.

———. 1984. *El Trabajo a Domicilio en el País Valenciano*. Madrid: Instituto de la Mujer, Ministerio de Cultura.

Sauvy, A. 1984. *Le Travail Noir et L'economie de Demain*. Paris: Calmann-Lévy.

Souza, P. and V. Tokman. 1976. "El Sector Informal Urbano en América Latina." *Revista Internacional del Trabajo* 3:385–97.

Vázquez, C. and J. Trigo. 1982. "Las Vías de Transformación de la Economía Formal en Irregular." *Información Comercial Española* 587:81–89.

Veltz, P. 1986. "Informalisation des Industries Manufacturieres et Intellectualisation de la Production." *Sociologie du Travail* 1:5–22.

Vilanova, E. and J. Vicedo. 1984. *Neuropatías de la Industria del Calzado.* Alicante: Facultad de Medicina, Universidad de Alicante.

12 Industrial Subcontracting and the Informal Sector: The Politics of Restructuring in the Madrid Electronics Industry

Lauren A. Benton

Industrial subcontracting often operates as a mechanism for siphoning cheap, unprotected labor into modern production processes. By replacing employees with outworkers, firms lower their wage costs and enhance their ability to adjust cheaply and quickly to shifts in demand. As Benería, Fernández-Kelly and García, Ybarra, and others show in this volume, subcontracting often results in substandard working conditions, low pay, and unstable employment for industrial outworkers.

But industrial subcontracting is not always of this type. In contrast with the largely negative characterization of the role of industrial outwork in developing countries and among immigrant communities, an alternative view has emerged from writings on productive decentralization in some sectors of advanced economies. The spectrum of firms engaged in outwork has been shown to include specialty subcontractors who supply their own technology, contribute to product design, and exercise independent control over how production is organized (see Holmes 1986). Productive decentralization may even open opportunities for skilled workers to take a more active role in reorganizing production and devising new technologies (Piore and Sabel 1984). Such expanded scope for control over the production process by outworkers has been linked directly to increased dynamism in some industries and to their improved capacity to adjust to changing conditions in world markets.[1]

The two contrasting views of industrial outwork are not as contradictory as they may appear. Similar causes—mainly employers' attempts to cut costs and increase flexibility—may lead to quite different roles for industrial outwork and thus to different patterns of industrial change. The outcome of productive decentralization and informalization varies according to three overlapping sets of factors: the timing of such trends in relation to world economic shifts, the placement of a given country in the world economy, and the nature of internal political alliances.

This chapter analyzes the impact of such factors on the process of industrial restructuring in the Madrid electronics industry. Given Spain's position in the world economy, the economic crisis of the 1970s led to rapid informalization and decentralization in Spanish industry after the middle of that decade. The nature of political alliances, I will argue, diminished the potential for a positive outcome of these trends, in particular by limiting the ability of industrial outworkers to overcome debilitating dependence on more established producers. While some of the conditions opposed to dynamic restructuring are specific to Spain, and even to Madrid, others may be true for semiperipheral countries in general, which face conflicting pressures to maintain strong, centralized states and to provide flexible, locally administered support for informal industry.

Industrial Restructuring in the Semiperiphery

Spain belongs to a middle group of nations, sometimes referred to as newly industrializing countries, which emerged in the 1960s with a striking record of growth of industrial output and exports. Although for some of these nations industrialization is not "new," the recent period of growth has certainly outpaced earlier phases of development and has involved substantial growth of both labor-intensive exports and more capital-intensive industries (see OECD 1979; Edwards 1979; Balassa 1981; Turner and McMullen 1982). The recent pattern of growth has often been described as a shift from import-substituting to export-oriented industrialization.

In the wake of the economic crisis of the 1970s, several problems have emerged which endanger continued export-led growth. First, these "semiperipheral" countries' success in markets in the advanced economies is continually threatened by competition from other, lower-cost producers elsewhere in the developing world.[2] Particularly in less differentiated, lower quality ends of any given market, countries with lower labor costs may rapidly replace more experienced suppliers. Second, in increasing their exports to OECD markets, semiperipheral nations have become more vulnerable to fluctuations in demand for consumer goods in the advanced economies. This danger is compounded by a third problem, namely, the threat that the advanced economies may expand protectionist measures specifically designed to limit imports from the semiperiphery. Such a strategy is particularly likely to be adopted during periods of slow growth in the advanced economies, when exporting countries are most vulnerable.

Countries in the semiperiphery must act either to hold down production costs or to move aggressively into other, higher quality or more variable markets for manufactures. Attempts to pursue the former strategy may encounter significant opposition; official wage rates have in fact tended to rise faster in the semiperiphery than in either more or less advanced countries. Where efforts to hold down official wage rates fail, however, employers' tactics for increasing the use of unregulated labor are likely to be more effective. As employers decentralize production and incorporate more casual labor, both directly and indirectly, into the production process, wage costs go down, and the threat of encountering effective opposition from organized labor diminishes. This function of informal labor explains in part the "dualist" structure of industry in many rapidly industrializing countries (see Portes and Benton 1984; Castells and Portes, this volume).

The question remains whether restructuring along these lines will also be capable of promoting international competitiveness based on flexible production of higher-quality or more specialized goods. In other words, does informalization represent only a short-term reaction or also a long-term solution to the new challenges to export-led growth? Previous research suggests the need to examine several aspects of this process closely to arrive at an answer: the conditions of work in newly created subcontracting firms, their relationship with other producers, and the nature of support they receive from the state together affect their potential for introducing innovative changes in industry (see especially Sabel 1982). Before turning to a specific analysis of such political factors and their influence in the Madrid electronics industry, it is necessary first to review the broader economic and political context of industrial restructuring in Spain.

The Rise of the Informal Sector in Spain

The situation of Spain summarizes, in many respects, that of all the semiperipheral countries. No longer able to compete with low-cost producers and severely affected by the crisis, Spain needs to have its industry secure a more competitive position in upscale markets and more technologically advanced industries. In some sectors, the state has forced noncompetitive firms to shut down and has cut back state support to all but the most promising ventures; in other areas, industrial restructuring has been taking place spontaneously, albeit with the quiet complicity of the state, through the expansion of the informal sector.

Evaluating the impact of this recent phase of industrial restructuring in Spain requires understanding its place in the historical evolution of state-worker relations. Throughout most of the Franco regime, the Spanish economy was highly "formal." A paternalistic labor code favored stable jobs for industrial workers, while the very low wages that were made possible by the repression of organized labor reduced the incentives for employers to seek unprotected labor. The situation began to change somewhat in the late 1960s, as worker protests escalated and wages began to rise sharply. The government responded with further repression, but also with expanded benefits to workers designed to stall their opposition. The burden of paying for additional benefits continued to fall mostly on employers, who began increasingly to use irregular hiring practices in order both to avoid these costs and to protect themselves against potential future unrest.

The events of the mid-1970s intensified pressures on employers to adopt such a strategy. In 1975, the same year that Franco's death set the stage for an uncertain political transition, the Spanish economy entered a severe crisis. Capital investment plunged and the GDP grew by only 1.1 percent, compared with an average yearly growth rate of 6.4 percent during the preceding seven years. Following massive strikes in 1975 and 1976, labor unions were legalized and wages surged upward. Although the political situation was stabilized with the signing of the first social and economic accords in 1977, the economy did not experience the same modest recovery that occurred in the rest of Europe, and it was ill-prepared for the jolt of a second petroleum crisis in 1979.

Successive governments contributed to pressures for firms to reduce employment by adopting anti-inflationary policies to stabilize the economy. In the absence of significant growth in productivity, inflation was needed to offset the steady rise in wages. Massive plant closures and layoffs ensued. Between 1975 and 1983, the number of salaried jobs declined by 12.2 percent, the largest drop in the European OECD; the number of industrial salaried jobs decreased in the same period by 19.5 percent. Unemployment increased from 5 percent in 1976 to nearly 22 percent in 1984.

While these figures indicate the gravity of the crisis Spain experienced, there is mounting evidence that they tell only one side of the story. As unemployment has gone up, the informal sector has also swelled enormously. Some estimates suggest that the informal sector may account for as much as a fifth of the Spanish GDP and from 15 percent to 50 percent of production in selected industries.[3] A 1985 government survey designed specifically to measure the labor force in the informal sector shows that one out of five persons employed in some remunerative activity is not properly registered for social security or not making payments (see table 12.1).[4] Over 30 percent of these are in full-time jobs. For certain categories of workers, the proportion employed in the informal sector is much higher. For example, 30 percent of self-employed workers and 36 percent of women in the labor force are casual workers; of all informal sector workers, 38 percent are under the age of twenty-five, compared with only 12 percent in the formal sector.

According to the national survey, casual labor is most common in agriculture, in which 30.9 percent of the work force is "off the books." The proportion of informal labor is next highest in the service sector (22.7%) and in construction, where 18.7 percent of work is unregulated. The proportion of informal sector workers in industry is hardly negligible, however, at 15.7 percent. Indeed, there is considerable evidence that many industrial jobs have been shifted to the informal sector through a reorganization of production within the formal sector. For example, many self-employed industrial workers are former employees of formal sector firms or casually employed outworkers. In the 1985 survey, 46.4 percent of informal, self-employed workers are re-

Table 12.1 Informal Sector Workers as a Percentage of the Work Force and by Professional Category

	Professional Category		
Sector of employment	Salaried Workers	Self-Employed Workers	Total Employment[1]
Informal sector[2]	18.9	30.4	21.9
Formal sector	81.1	69.6	78.1
Total employment[1]	100.0	100.0	100.0

Source: Survey on Conditions of Life and Work in Spain, Ministry of Economy and Finance, 1986.

[1] Workers who were employed during the previous week for a minimum of 13 hours per week on average over the three-month period preceding the survey data and who are required by law to make social security payments in connection with their work (excludes family labor, paid and unpaid).

[2] Includes workers in five categories distributed as follows: employed but not registered with social security (65.7%); employed and registered but not making payments (15.2%); employed for a salary but registered as self-employed (8.8%); self-employed and registered as salaried (5.1%); and employed and receiving unemployment compensation (5.2%).

corded as previously salaried workers. This finding echoes a 1983 study of homeworkers which revealed that 17 percent had taken up homework because they had lost outside jobs, while nearly half of those engaged in industrial tasks at home were working for firms (Benton 1986).

Not surprisingly, the highest rates of informality are found in labor-intensive industries. According to the 1985 study, the informal sector accounts for a small proportion of the work force in industries characterized by large firm size and high capital intensity—only 5.3 percent, for example, in metalwork. In contrast, light manufacturing industries and those with small firm size are highly informal; 42.9 percent of workers in the garment industry and 32 percent in the shoe industry are casually employed. A handful of studies of restructuring in such industries has shown that in the wake of the economic crisis of the mid-1970s, the production process rapidly became fragmented and many phases of production were shifted underground. Established firms have frequently closed their doors precisely in order to restructure production in this way (Miguélez-Lobo 1982; Ybarra 1982; Casals and Vidal 1985).

As Ybarra shows for the case of the Spanish shoe industry in this volume, the effects of informalization on employment conditions in such industries appear to be quite negative. The trend is also probably detrimental to the long-term adjustment strategies in the industries. Employers' ability to cut costs through subcontracting to informal firms and hiring casual workers considerably reduces their incentives to upgrade technological capacity or experiment with other innovative changes. At the same time, quality remains limited by the reliance on relatively capital-poor workshops that produce to specifications without participating in the design process itself. The strict subordination of the new, small firms to more established producers is thus itself an obstacle to the needed shift to production for higher-fashion, higher-priced markets (see also Sanchis 1984; Benton 1986).

The question remains whether it is reasonable to conclude from these cases that informalization necessarily has negative implications for industrial restructuring in Spain and in the semiperiphery in general. Clearly, some of the above conclusions are specific to the cases described. Most of the research done in Spain has examined informalization in labor-intensive industries; several studies have focused specifically on homeworkers, whose particular working conditions make it extremely difficult for them to alter their strict subordination to the interests of established firms. To broaden this view, I focus here on changes taking place in a high-technology Spanish industry and in small enterprises also newly generated by a process of productive decentralization.

Decentralization in the Madrid Electronics Industry

The little research that has been done on informalization outside traditional industries has shown that the phenomenon is indeed widespread. For example, a recent study of small firms on the outskirts of Madrid showed that a large proportion of the firms consists of new microenterprises generated by decentralization in metalworking, woodworking, printing, chemicals, and electronics. Although the study does not reveal to what degree the small firms use unregulated labor, it does show that many of them are precariously placed in industrial "squatter" areas (Celada, López Groh, and Parra 1985). Important questions only partially answered by this and other studies are how relations of production within the new firms are structured and whether the new microenterprises are prospering and altering their relations with other producers.

The Madrid electronics industry offers an interesting case study of the effects of decentralization. Growth in this industry is of critical importance to Spain, since it would signify both an improved technological base for Spanish industry and the potential for increased import substitution and exports in electronics. Madrid is the center of production in this industry; it has been estimated that 70 percent of all electronics production is concentrated in Madrid, including as much as 90 percent of production in professional electronics. The industry is both a leading employer in the area and the prime focus of the regional government's development plans for the next decade (Estevan 1984).

Since 1979 the industry has undergone a process of restructuring similar to the one described in more labor-intensive industries. Few established electronics producers have purposely closed their firms in order to move production underground. But the large firms have been forced to make substantial cutbacks in employment, and scores of small- and medium-sized firms have been started by professionals and skilled workers from the industry. The new firms have almost invariably adopted a novel structure. Maintaining control over the design of products, as well as their final testing and installation, the new, smaller producers have decentralized most other phases of production. A panoply of small subcontractors has formed to respond to the surge in demand generated by this trend. Of the forty-five small- and medium-sized electronics producers studied by Antonio Estevan for the Madrid regional government in 1984, over half had been founded after 1978; most were firms with between ten and fifty workers and were headed by engineers or other professionals who had left larger enterprises to start their own businesses.

Very little was known about the subcontractors supplying these new producers—whether they were also new enterprises, whether they were successful or highly dependent on a few clients, and how their workers were faring compared with workers in larger firms. In 1985, I conducted semistructured interviews with owner-entrepreneurs in twenty-five subcontracting firms on the outskirts of Madrid to attempt to answer such questions.[5] The firms represented five different areas of production and were grouped as follows: metalwork (7), painting and silkscreening (6), assembly of subcomponents (5), printed circuits (4), and transformers (3). Differences in production techniques did not obscure the many similarities of the subcontractors. Only one firm was founded before 1970 and nearly two-thirds were started after 1978, mainly to fulfill the demand for outwork from the newly formed small- and medium-sized electronics producers. The firms are small; only three of them have more than twenty-five workers. They are scattered on the periphery of Madrid, some in areas that are not zoned for industrial use.

Most of the enterprises were started by skilled workers, many of whom voluntarily left other jobs to start their own businesses. Although all the firms are legal entities in which some or all workers are "on the books," the use of unregulated labor was the rule rather than the exception in the early stages of the firms' development. Before leaving other jobs, skilled workers often began accepting work on a casual basis in order to save the capital necessary to become fully independent. A number of others started outwork under rudimentary conditions, producing in their own homes or in small, ill-equipped workshops, or even paying to use machinery in other factories. Particularly during this early stage, worker-entrepreneurs commonly relied on family labor, which had the double advantage of being less expensive (sometimes unpaid) and also highly flexible. In addition, the workers themselves usually continued for many months before establishing their firms legally or being *dado de alta* (enrolled in social security) as self-employed workers.

The process by which firms were formed has affected the way the labor process within them is now organized. Many firms preserve characteristics of the initial, informal stage. Contract regulations about overtime and vacation pay, for example, are often replaced with informal agreements between workers and owners that allow for greater flexibility in work schedules. In some firms, owners also admit to hiring extra workers on an unofficial, temporary basis during busy periods. The use of this type of casual labor is of course greater in firms that face more volatile demand and rely more heavily on unskilled labor, such as those specializing in the assembly of subcomponents or the production of transformers.

Several firms continue to use family labor, particularly for low-skilled jobs. In other cases, although the firms themselves are well established, only a portion of the work force is on the books; an example is a small factory that produces printed circuits for about fifteen regular clients, including some of the largest electronics producers in Spain, but that does not provide social security benefits for five out of its seven workers.

Although the subcontractors do use various forms of unregulated labor to cut costs, the ability to produce cheaply is only one factor—often not the most important factor—enabling them to attract clients. The subcontractors believe that their clients place greater emphasis on high standards of quality and precision in production. The claim is confirmed by the clients themselves (Estevan 1984), and it is reinforced by the finding that those subcontractors that have been able to establish a reputation for quality have no difficulties finding work. Entrepreneurs questioned about their marketing strategies often say that they have none; clients "just hear about [them] and show up on their own."

Once they have established a reputation for high-quality work and reliability, some small firms can afford to choose among prospective clients. While beginning firms hope to work for large companies in order to garner prestige, the more successful subcontractors often prefer smaller clients. This finding suggests that the small scale of enterprises neither poses an obstacle to success nor represents merely a transitional phase of growth. In fact, the structure of small firms is more appropriate to meet the demand for diversified, short series now being generated by the new small- and medium-sized electronics producers. Owners also value the potential for contributing to the design of specifications through close contact with clients. A partner in a small and highly successful metalworking firm makes this point.

> For me, it's a thousand times better to work for a small firm. With the big ones, you're not supposed to make any changes. For example, a while ago we had an order from S____ to make some boxes for cables. The man who was working on them here realized that in the design the hole for the cables was misplaced. So he moved it. When they found out, you can't imagine how upset they were. We had to change [the boxes] all over again—that is, make them *wrong*. [In the future] I want to be able to talk with the man who gives me work and explain to him how it has to be done and then show him.

The more intimate atmosphere surrounding production appears to have some significant advantages for the small firms. In particular, the small setting makes it easier for workers to help each other with difficult tasks and give each other advice on how to adjust to different jobs. Greater attention can be given to individual talents and preferences of workers for particular jobs, and this in and of itself helps boost productivity and improve quality. A few firms have taken advantage of the smaller setting to reorganize production along unorthodox lines. For example, a particularly successful metalworking firm has workers completing entire jobs on their own, by rotating at different posts, rather than specializing in only one part of production. This firm is a classic example of an enterprise in which high-quality production of short series is facilitated by giving greater scope to skilled workers to exercise control over production.

These findings may suggest that the Madrid electronics industry has emerged from the process of restructuring with a flexible, specialized structure that will enable it to move ahead in national as well as international markets. Certain benefits have already accrued to the industry from the willingness and ability of the new, small firms to produce high-quality goods in a flexible way. Nevertheless, obstacles remain to progress in this direction. The political context of production, in particular, places limits on the firms' capacity both to restructure production internally and to establish cooperative ties with other producers.

The Limits to Effective Restructuring

Multiple subcontracting is fairly common in the Madrid electronics industry, and smaller workshops with no direct access to clients often remain heavily dependent on a few larger subcontractors. The latter act as middlemen, earning a premium for coordinating production in smaller shops in addition to performing some tasks themselves. This system gives rise to striking cases of very small workshops that indirectly supply components to very large electronics producers at low cost. For example, one tiny family firm silkscreens components for several of the largest multinational computer producers in Spain; the orders are channeled through two and sometimes three larger subcontractors. In the dependent sub-subcontracting firms, entrepreneurs may be forced to continue to pressure workers to accept longer hours and unregulated conditions.

The figures in table 12.2 show that roughly half of the twenty-five subcontracting firms are still struggling for a secure footing as small specialty producers. This is particularly true of the newest firms; nine of the twenty-five subcontractors are poorly endowed workshops that were founded after 1978. Various factors limit the ability of these smaller, newer workshops to attract clients directly. An important obstacle is the difficulty they encounter in obtaining credit to make capital improvements. Clients usually visit firms to examine their productive capacity and equipment before agreeing to give them work, yet firms find it difficult to get credit until they can demonstrate that they have established solid ties with a range of clients. This catch-22 can usually be avoided only by owners' offering their personal assets as collateral, a risk that

Table 12.2 Economic Health of Subcontracting Firms by Year Founded

Year Founded	Economic Health[1]			Total
	Poor–Fair	Good	Excellent	
Before 1969			1	1
1969–1973		1	1	2
1974–1978	3	2	1	6
1979–1985	9	4	3	16
Total	12	7	6	25

[1]Firms were reluctant to provide precise information about assets and profits. Relative economic health was determined by averaging the rankings for performance in five areas: gross yearly sales; number of full-time, paid employees; amount and quality of machinery; type and tenure of physical plant; and number of regular clients.

many worker-entrepreneurs with limited resources are hesitant to take.

A second important obstacle to growth faced by many of the small subcontracting firms derives from problems of internal organization. As former employees, most worker-entrepreneurs have no formal training and little direct experience in running a business. But the very structure of production in the small firms makes learning business skills more difficult. Precisely because the owners of many small firms are skilled workers, they have difficulty freeing more of their time to attend to marketing, product development, and administrative tasks. Some of the small entrepreneurs have tried to cope with this problem by relying on family members or other trusted individuals to supervise production in their absence. Owners without this option work under considerable strain. The owner of a painting workshop, for example, was forced to scale down production by half because he could not effectively supervise two shifts.

An active campaign by the government to improve credit for small firms, provide training for new entrepreneurs, and engender cooperation among small enterprises would presumably go a long way toward solving some of the above problems. But even if the state enthusiastically embraced these objectives—the Spanish government has in fact implemented various programs to these ends—the decentralized structure of industry itself poses obstacles to effective state-led reforms. On the one hand, the smallest subcontractors are the least likely to seek state assistance. Worker-entrepreneurs often cannot spare the time to seek such support, and firms that employ casual labor are, in any case, hesitant to invite scrutiny by state officials. On the other hand, the state bureaucracy is quite limited in its capacity to reach small, and especially informal, producers. As one government official put it, the fragmentation of industry leaves program administrators without "valid interlocutors" within industry who could distribute information about state benefits.

At the same time, the state is understandably reluctant to implement across-the-board assistance to small firms that may operate partially or entirely in the informal sector. To do so would be to recognize the right of employers to bypass state controls and taxes. It is not surprising to find, then, that government assistance in the electronics industry has been limited to programs to assist mainly large producers, based on the assumption that the benefits of this aid will eventually "trickle down" to smaller firms.[6]

The constraints imposed by politics can be clearly seen in the limited impact the cooperativist movement has had in the industry. Despite the significant potential benefits of forming cooperatives, few of the subcontracting firms have formalized loose associations among skilled workers. Only three of the twenty-five firms studied are cooperatives, and one of these is an example of what union leaders refer to as a "false cooperative," that is, one that was formed by workers to save their jobs when a privately held firm was closing. Some worker-entrepreneurs show great reluctance to share responsibility or ownership with other workers with whom they have no family ties. In a few cases, cooperative formats were tried and later abandoned.

The reluctance of workers to form cooperatives is significant in light of evidence that sharing risks and burdens among skilled workers can go a long way toward solving the problems of credit and internal management. For example, by pooling their resources, members of one metalworking cooperative were able to obtain credit to purchase a numerical control machine, a move that immediately brought them more business. The problem of control over production has also been solved in many cases by sharing production and administrative tasks among several skilled workers. In some cases workers start out rotating positions of responsibility before determining which of them are most suited to, and happiest with, particular managerial tasks. If such duties are distributed widely, all worker-entrepreneurs may still maintain a hand in the production process. The effect is to remove the need for supervision over workers altogether.

Given the advantages, why have cooperative formats been adopted in so few cases? The reasons appear to be rooted in both past and present political experience. First, it is of great importance that the labor movement that emerged with such force in the late-1960s and mid-1970s drew its strength mainly from workers' interest in narrow economic issues on the one hand, and the broad political goal of reinstating democracy on the other. The movement was not focused on challenging employers' prerogatives in the workplace, and it was thus an unlikely source of inspiration for a cooperativist movement. Indeed, after democracy was established and substantial wage hikes had been won, active membership in the new labor unions waned rapidly.

Deunionization was no doubt accelerated by the increasing fragmentation of industry that accompanied informalization after 1979. In Madrid, the effect of the labor movement on workers' attitudes toward collectivization was particularly limited because of the nature of protests before and during the transition. Conflicts centered in the large industrial firms concentrated in the southern industrial zones of the city. Many of the interviewed workers and entrepreneurs in small firms had observed the protests from a distance; many younger workers—about a third of the labor force in small subcontracting firms is made up of workers under the age of thirty—were not even in the work force at the time of the last great wave of strikes.

A second reason the cooperative movement has not been stronger is that it has received minimal institutional support. Worker-entrepreneurs find burdensome the restrictions imposed on cooperatives' use of nonmembers' labor; many are also aware of the red tape entailed in obtaining credit, including government-sponsored loans to cooperatives. Most important, local initiatives to assist cooperatives are hampered by the limited autonomy in industrial policy that exists within the still-centralized Spanish system. In contrast with successful local efforts to help industrial cooperatives in the "red belt" of central Italy, local initiatives in Spain have suffered from the dearth of funding and lack of control over tax incentives and zoning (see Capecchi, this volume). For example, efforts by the Communist-led Madrid municipality of Arganda del Rey to aid industrial cooperatives were paralyzed by a lack of support from the underfinanced regional government.

Finally, I should note that a broader type of cooperativism—the formation of collective associations among various producers—has also been marginally effective. In the various subfields represented by subcontractors, small producers have met to try to regulate competition and prevent price wars. While these efforts have been useful, many of the entrepreneurs express a need for a more formal association of auxiliary producers. The potential role of such an organization would be to circulate information about government assistance and credit programs, to represent the interests of the auxiliary firms before government agencies, and even to help firms by sponsoring cooperative commercial ventures. But progress toward the formation of an organization capable of such initiatives has been hindered by the same factors that have prevented the emergence of a strong cooperative movement.[7]

The problems faced by the new, small firms cannot thus be resolved completely independently of the state or without the cooperation of powerful political actors, including local officials and industry representatives of both business and labor. In other words, productive decentralization cannot *in and of itself* constitute an effective development strategy. The new microenterprises in the Madrid electronics industry have faced exceptionally favorable circumstances: expanding demand, a limited pool of highly skilled labor, and technological factors facilitating the decentralization of skilled tasks and capital-intensive phases of production.

They continue to face, however, formidable difficulties. Neither the small size of firms nor their ability to operate beyond the purview of the state ensures their ability to reduce their dependence on larger, more established enterprises. Both the political attitudes of workers and entrepreneurs, and the political alliances that exist among workers, employers, and the state outside the arena of production determine the scope that exists for the informal sector to develop into more than a source of cheap labor.

Conclusions

Informalization in labor-intensive industries in Spain and productive decentralization in the Madrid electronics industry reveal two very different patterns of industrial change. Both patterns result from responses to wage increases and to strong pressures to introduce greater flexibility into the productive structure. To differing degrees, the strategy of productive decentralization adopted in both cases succeeds in achieving these results. But the industrial structures that result are strikingly different, both in their effects on the opportunities available to new small firms and in the incentives generated for change in established firms.

In the electronics industry, the emerging industrial structure approximates a system of multiple layers of interconnected but independent industrial producers which elsewhere has given rise to the term "flexible specialization" (Sabel 1982). In this system, small subcontractors generated through productive decentralization are able to reduce their dependence on a single firm or a small group of clients. More important, their ability to attract clients depends more on the quality or newness of the goods they produce than on the lower prices they can offer because of lower wage costs. In fact, the pressure to maintain low wage costs should decrease as the firms become more specialized and are no longer directly competing with each other. The structure approximates Capecchi's diagram of a system of flexible specialization (see Capecchi, this volume), in which the lines connecting firms trace an intricate web linking even very small firms with a widely varied array of other enterprises.

In other industries studied in Spain, in contrast, productive decentralization has not generated significant new opportunities for new, small producers. These firms have remained, for the most part, highly dependent on larger producers for design specifications and orders. In some cases they are set up by established producers who then control the small firms through the ownership of credit and machinery. A somewhat simplified diagram of the Spanish shoe industry, for example, would resemble a downward-pointing branch, with homeworkers and small firms each connected to and dependent on a single larger enterprise or intermediary (see Ybarra, this volume). As an outcome of productive decentralization, such a structure also augments the flexibility of industry, but it does so in a very different way. Flexibility in this case comes from the improved ability of firms to respond to shifts in the market by altering the cost, size, and makeup of the labor force without incurring the costs of adjustment.

The contrast between the two systems is highlighted when we imagine the consequences of a rapid drop in demand such as the one experienced by exporters of manufactured goods in the 1970s. In a fragmented, but not specialized, industrial system, producers at the top of the pyramid would respond to a reduction in orders by cutting back on the work given out to subcontractors. Since the principal motivation for putting out work to other producers is to lower costs, not to improve quality or style, this step would not necessarily force firms to alter the nature or style of their products. The main change brought about by such a strategy would be massive unemployment of workers in the subcontracting firms.

A system in which these small producers have begun to specialize and have access to markets independent of a few clients is in a better position to meet dramatic shifts in demand by reorienting production toward different and healthier segments of the market. These movements do not always have to be toward higher-priced and higher-quality ends of the market for finished goods. Part of the process of innovation is the design of new products that are low in price. In other words, new producers begin to anticipate, instead of respond to, the needs of established firms and to create rather than follow trends in the demand for finished goods (see Piore and Sabel 1984).

The contrast between the two scenarios parallels a contrast between different ways of organizing productive relations within the firms. On the one hand, there is a curious similarity between relations of production that reproduce the hierarchy of the established factory and relations of production based on some family and social networks. Workers with limited authority within either system also have limited autonomy in altering the system of production or marketing styles. Firms that rely on family labor or patron-client relations are highly flexible, but this is mainly because they can easily maintain low wages, change the size of the labor force, and alter the intensity of work. On the other hand, in the context of rapidly changing demand and production techniques in industry, cooperative systems of production based on sharing and rotating various tasks seem to offer greater possibilities for optimizing the use of workers' organizational and technical skills. The nature of relations of production *within* informal industry thus help determine the possibilities for the emergence of innovative strategies in the wake of informalization.

This view is consistent with claims that productive decentralization and informalization sometimes give rise to innovative enterprises. But my findings also suggest that internal reorganization is not a sufficient condition for recasting relationships among industrial firms. A spontaneous movement by workers to experiment in small firms with new types of organization must be answered by institutional support. This missing element in the Madrid electronics industry has left many small new firms doubting their capacity to emulate the success of other experimental enterprises. The case study supports more general speculation about the obstacles to the emergence of "flexible specialization" in the semiperiphery. Although the changing nature of global markets and the problems of maintaining export-oriented industrialization urge a shift in this direction, common political features of semiperipheral countries may hinder such a movement. Highly centralized, strong states are, for many reasons, poorly positioned to act to recast the relationship between formal and informal industry.[8] Where authoritarian controls or centralized political bargaining overshadows local or sectoral alliance building, industrial outworkers will be left to strive on their own for a more stable and constructive role in industrial growth.

The transformation of the informal sector into a catalyst for the creation of flexible, specialized, and highly competitive industry thus clearly depends on the convergence of a remarkably varied set of social and political conditions. It is unlikely that these will be reproduced with frequency in the developing world, even in the most advanced developing countries. Categorical prescriptions for turning informal sector growth into a boon for industry must be regarded with caution, if not skepticism. The view of the informal sector as uniformly backward and exploitative must also be replaced with a more sophisticated understanding of the sector's role in a complex and open process of industrial restructuring.

Notes

I would like to thank the Social Science Research Council, the Fulbright Foundation, and the Wenner-Gren Foundation for Anthropological Research for their support of my research on the informal sector in Spain. I also wish to thank Antonio Estevan for sharing his data on the electronics industry with me, and Manuel Castells, Alejandro Portes, and Charles Sabel for helpful comments on the research and results.
1. The argument summarized here is based mainly on analyses of the Italian case. See Saba 1981; Sabel 1982; Brusco 1982; Capecchi, this volume. A general statement of the argument can be found in Piore and Sabel 1984.

2. On the criteria used to define the semiperiphery and the reasons for including Spain, see Arrighi 1985.

3. For estimates of the size of the informal sector in Spain, see Ruesga 1984 and Lafuente 1980. For discussion of its scope and significance in particular Spanish industries, see Gómez Perezagua 1982; Vázquez and Trigo 1982; Benton 1986; Ybarra 1982, this volume.

4. The survey was carried out under the direction of the Ministry of Economy and Finance in November 1985, and I participated in the team that designed the questionnaire. The survey was national in scope and was administered to respondents aged fourteen and older. The sample size (63,120) was intended to approximate that used in the government's quarterly employment surveys.

5. The firms were selected from 160 subcontractors named by producers in Estevan's study for the Madrid regional government (Estevan 1984). The sample could not be representative, but an attempt was made to include firms of varying size, reputation, and location based on the information provided in that study. Whenever possible, observation of work on the shop floor and conversations with workers were used to complement and corroborate statements by worker-entrepreneurs.

6. In addition to special low-interest loans available for developing technology, several types of assistance have been offered to the electronics industry. One is connected with the Industrial Reconversion program, the results of which were disappointing in electronics, mainly because the program benefited only large firms in one subsector of the industry. The burden of promoting growth in the industry was shifted to the Plan Electrónica e Informática Nacional (PEIN), which encompassed broader measures designed to affect the industry as a whole. It is still too soon to evaluate the latter set of measures (see De Oyarzábal 1984; Estevan 1984). Finally, using funds from the reconversion program, the regional government is creating a high-technology industrial park on the outskirts of Madrid, centered around a new ATT computer-chip plant. Critics have pointed out that this objective has involved mainly tax incentives and other types of assistance to ATT rather than to smaller Spanish firms.

7. Linz (1981) discusses the reasons for the general weakness of business organizations during and after the transition to democracy.

8. On the relation between recent trends in the international economy and the rise of strong states in semipheripheral countries, see Evans 1985.

References

Arrighi, G., ed. 1985. *Semiperipheral Development: The Politics of Southern Europe in the Twentieth Century.* Beverly Hills, Calif.: Sage Publications.

Balassa, B. 1981. *The Newly Industrializing Countries in the World Economy.* New York: Pergamon Press.

Benton, L. 1986. "The Role of the Informal Sector in Economic Development: Industrial Restructuring in Spain." Ph.D. dissertation, Department of Anthropology, The Johns Hopkins University.

Brusco, S. 1982. "The Emilian Model: Productive Decentralization and Social Integration." *Cambridge Journal of Economics* 6:167–84.

Casals Couturier, M. and J. M. Vidal Villa. 1985. "La Economía Subterránea en Sabadell." *Papeles de Economía Española* 22:395–402.

Celada, F., F. López Groh, and T. Parra. 1985. *Efectos Espaciales de los Procesos de Reorganización del Sistema Productivo en Madrid.* Madrid: Comunidad de Madrid.

De Oyarzábel, M. 1984. "Políticas de Promoción Industrial: El Plan Electrónico e Informático Nacional." *Economistas* 11:82–84.

Edwards, A. 1979. *The New Industrial Countries and their Impact on Western Manufacturing.* London: The Economist Intelligence Unit, Ltd.

Estevan, A. 1984. *Relaciones Interindustriales entre un Grupo de PYMES Tecnológicamente Cualificadas en la Comunidad de Madrid.* Madrid: Comunidad de Madrid.

Evans, P. 1985. "Transnational Linkages and the State." Pp. 192–226 in T. Skocpol et al. (eds.), *Bringing the State Back In.* Cambridge: Cambridge University Press.

Gómez Perezagua, R. 1982. "Estructura Empresarial y Economía Oculta." *Información Comercial Española* 587:109–17.

Holmes, J. 1986. "The Organization and Locational Structure of Production Subcontracting." Pp. 80–106 in A. Scott and M. Storper (eds.), *Production, Work, Territory.* Boston: Allen and Unwin.

Lafuente Félez, A. 1980. "Una Medición de la Economía Oculta en España." *Boletín de Estudios Económicos de Deuste* 857:103–7.

Linz, J. 1981. "A Century of Politics and Interests in Spain." Pp. 365–415 in S. Berger (ed.), *Organizing Interests in Western Europe: Pluralism, Corporatism, and the Transformation of Politics.* Cambridge: Cambridge University Press.

Miguélez-Lobo, F. 1982. "Economía Sumergida y Transformaciones Socio-Laborales." *Boletín de Estudios Económicos* 117:439–60.

OECD. 1979. *The Impact of the Newly Industrializing Countries on Production and Trade in Manufactures.* Paris: OECD.

Piore, M. J. and C. F. Sabel. 1984. *The Second Industrial Divide.* New York: Basic Books.

Portes, A. and L. Benton. 1984. "Industrial Development and Labor Absorption: A Reinterpretation." *Population and Development Review* 10:589–611.

Ruesga Benito, S. 1984. "Economía Oculta y Mercado de Trabajo." *Información Comercial Española* 607:55–61.

Saba, A. 1981. *La Industria Subterránea: Un Nuevo Modelo de Desarrollo.* Valencia: Institut Alfons el Magnánim.

Sabel, C. F. 1982. *Work and Politics.* Cambridge: Cambridge University Press.

Sanchis, E. 1984. *El Trabajo a Domicilio en el País Valenciano.* Madrid: Ministerio de Cultura, Instituto de la Mujer.

Turner, L. and N. McMullen, eds. 1982. *The Newly Industrializing Countries: Trade and Adjustment.* London: Allen and Unwin.

Vázquez, A., C. and J. Trigo Portela. 1982. "Las Vías de Transformación de la Economía Formal en Irregular." *Información Comercial Española* 587:81–89.

Ybarra, J-A. 1982. "La Reestructuración de la Industria del Calzado Español: Aspectos Laborales y Territoriales." *Boletín de Estudios Económicos* 117:483–503.

5 The Informal Sector and the State

13 Informalization at the Core: Hispanic Women, Homework, and the Advanced Capitalist State

M. Patricia Fernández-Kelly and Anna M. García

In the waning years of the twentieth century, there is renewed interest in an apparent contradiction: the expansion of underground economies in advanced industrial regions like the United States and Western Europe. The proliferation of sweatshops, unlicensed industrial operations, and homework seem antithetical to the very definition of societies in which business conglomerates share plaudits with advanced technology. Nevertheless, a growing body of quantitative and qualitative evidence points to economic informalization as a distinctive and ongoing process at the core of the modern world system (Leichter 1982; Tanzi 1982).

Our purpose in this essay is to provide preliminary documentation of some of the mechanisms that are leading to the growth of the underground economy in two different urban settings: Los Angeles and Miami. Both locations possess flourishing businesses in the midst of enviable climates, both contain some of the fastest growing Hispanic populations in the United States, and both are characterized by the coexistence of large industries and small manufacturing operations that escape government legislation. Our focus is on the garment industry, which links old and new patterns of production in surprising ways.

Two lines of thought guide our analysis. First, we consider the extent to which the advanced capitalist state, through the actions of local and federal agencies, is contributing to the expansion of the underground economy. Although there is continuing research on the characteristics and functions of informal manufacturing in central and peripheral countries, the specific role of the state has been insufficiently examined. In previous studies the state merely appears as a source of legislation, and the informal economy, as a series of activities outside the existing body of law. Our purpose is to increase the understanding of actual practices carried out by state representatives as part and parcel of the process of informalization.

In both southern California and southern Florida we have found a complex series of events linking informal assembly shops, subcontractors, homeworkers, and government agencies. Our initial research reveals that informal economic exchanges are often made possible by ambiguous legislation, exemptions to the Labor Code, conflicting interpretations of the law by state and federal agencies, and a differential ability to enforce labor and wage legislation. Beyond economic considerations, these state-related variables are decisive in creating a climate suitable for the expansion of the informal sector (Gershuny 1979).

Second, we provide a schematic comparison of Miami and Los Angeles illustrating the proposition that informal economies are characterized by a considerable degree of internal variation. The examination of household structures to which informal workers and entrepreneurs belong, leads to a better understanding of this differentiation. It is within the household that the constraints of class and gender mesh, resulting in dissimilar modes of adaptation to the surrounding economic system and in contrasting patterns of labor market insertion. Homework involving Hispanic women, particularly immigrants and refugees, is widespread in Los Angeles and Miami. On the surface, the two cases appear to have similar outcomes resulting from identical economic processes. However, we will propose that in Miami the existence of an ethnic enclave formed by Cuban entrepreneurs, most of them political exiles, enabled women from the same families and community to use homework as a strategy for improving earnings and for reconciling cultural and economic demands.

In contrast, in Los Angeles, Mexican immigrants have not formed an economic enclave. Instead, most workers have entered the labor force in a highly atomized manner and are, thus, at the mercy of market forces entirely beyond their control. Dependency on the broad wage economy, in addition to a working-class background, common undocumented immigrant status, and certain household characteristics, has accentuated the vulnerability of Mexican women. For many, homework and even the purchase of small garment shops are measures of last resort, strategies to stay a step above destitution. Before examining these cases in detail, we offer a sketch of current knowledge of the informal economy.

Economic Informalization: The State of Current Research

The title of this chapter is meant to stress the idea that the informal, or underground, economy is not a fixed entity but rather a fluid process involving particular interactions between investors, workers, and state agencies (Peattie 1980; Sassen-Koob 1985). There is an ongoing controversy surrounding the salient features, functions, and methods for the evaluation of underground economies in central and peripheral countries. However, for our purposes, it will suffice to underscore four points:

First, the view that informalization is a marginal phenomenon caused by the survival needs of the poor is being replaced by a complex understanding of the informal sector as an integral part of advanced capitalist economies.

Poverty-stricken populations are likely to engage in imaginative strategies for maintaining minimal levels of subsistence. Such activities often appear to the casual observer as superfluous economic exchanges. However, systematic research reveals a multiplicity of apparent and concealed links between modern industries and unregulated operations in services and manufacturing. In this respect, subcontracting is a growing phenomenon joining the formal and informal sectors in both central and peripheral countries.

Subcontracting involves several complementary advantages from the point of view of producers. From a strictly economic perspective, the reliance on subcontracting offers the possibility of lowering the costs of production, particularly but not exclusively through a reduction of the wage bill. Moreover, in both economic and political terms, subcontracting allows manufacturers and service providers to diversify risks among several contractors vying for a share of production. This is especially evident in highly competitive industries in which the costs of unionized labor can threaten the very survival of firms.

Second, in the same vein, informalization in central economies cannot be considered as an aberration resulting from the survival of preindustrial patterns of production. The resurgence of the underground economy in large U.S. cities during the seventies and eighties strongly suggests that informalization is a recurring phenomenon tied in to the changing political and economic relationship between capital and labor. The internationalization of capital investments and the rapid increase of foreign imports have also prompted the restructuring of domestic production. This process has included sectoral, organizational, and locational transformations (Tokman 1978). Thus, the growth of the informal sector in advanced industrial countries is but one of the symptoms of reorganization of productive activities on a global scale.

Third, from the vantage point of large investors and service providers, the preference for and reliance on subcontracting and, by extension, on the expansion of the underground economy, can be seen as part of an offensive against formal workers and organized labor. Not surprisingly, the expansion of underground activities in the United States and other advanced industrial economies has paralleled the massive reduction in union membership, the disappearance of large numbers of skilled jobs, and a general decline in the standards of living for many workers in the formal sector.

Finally, there has been a tendency to consider participants in the informal economy as a relatively homogeneous mass. An in-depth inquiry shows that at least two classes must be distinguished within this sector: (1) informal workers who operate without contractual arrangements or legal protection and (2) informal entrepreneurs and middlemen who organize this labor and establish its links with the formal sector. According to Portes and Sassen-Koob (1987), the earnings of informal workers are significantly lower on the average than those of their formal sector counterparts. However, earnings of informal entrepreneurs, although erratic, can be much higher.

The preceding points show that considerable advances have been made regarding our understanding of the characteristics and causes of the expansion of the underground economy in advanced industrial countries. Nevertheless, many questions still await an answer. One of the most important of these concerns is the actual relationship between the advanced capitalist state and the growth of the informal sector.

State Agencies, Labor Legislation, and the Informal Sector

During the last decade and a half there has been a paradigmatic shift in the study of the part played by states in relation to economies and societies. This change has not occurred at the same pace in writings of differing theoretical orientations. The structural-functionalist school, for example, has been generally reluctant to view the state as an independent actor involved in socioeconomic processes. Instead, the tendency has been to portray bodies of government as channels for the conciliation of pluralist interests in the larger society. On the other hand, Neo-Marxists have engaged in a debate about the alternative nature and functions of the capitalist state. Some see it as a tool of class domination; others, as a mechanism for ensuring and perpetuating favorable conditions of production; and still others, as a dynamic expositor of class struggle (Skocpol 1985).

One important lesson derived from the current debate is the realization that, by and large, states are not passive reflections of socioeconomic and political processes. Rather, they can act in a relatively autonomous manner implementing policies that often lead to unintended as well as intended consequences. Another relevant lesson concerns the particular nature of state formations as a result of historical events. For example, the modern U.S. state did not grow out of a centralized bureaucratic apparatus typical of preindustrial and predemocratic times. In part for that reason, it is characterized by the dispersal of authority throughout the federal system and the division of sovereignty among branches of the national government. These are factors that often lead to contradictory practices and policies. Relative self-determination of the state as well as fragmentation and dispersal of authority are critical factors in the study of economic informalization.

Previous studies have assumed that deviation from or conformity to federal and state legislation basically determines the formal or informal status of industrial establishments and their labor force. The type of interaction between firms and workers on the one hand and the state on the other are taken to be the main variables separating formality from informality. This view presupposes that government agencies have erected coherent and mutually compatible bodies of legislation normalizing the exchanges between workers and employers.

The reality is more complex. Research shows that the stylized dichotomy between formal and informal sectors is, at best, a simplification. For example, workers often move intermittently between the two sectors, responding to need and opportunity created not only by the economic environment but also by policies emanating from state or federal agencies. Small licensed companies may resort to unauthorized productive arrangements during times of financial crisis. In contrast, law-abiding firms may occasionally engage the services of homeworkers to supplement production during periods of increasing demand. Thus, the formal and informal sectors appear to be divided by a highly porous membrane, not a rigid boundary.

Moreover, the state embodied in specific legislative practices—in agencies, departments, and divisions—can play a role in the expansion of the informal economy. In this respect, the growth of underground activities is being made possible, to a large extent, by three overlapping factors:

1. The type of legislation and legislative changes formulated over time at the federal and state levels, including legislative response to constituencies in differing positions of political and economic strength
2. The capabilities for enforcement in different locations
3. The actions and policies of agencies with varying, and often contradictory, mandates

A few examples are given below to illustrate each of the three aspects.

Legislation and Legislative Changes

Our first example has to do with the origins and implementation of labor legislation through the Department of Labor Standards and Wage Enforcement (generally known as the Wage and Hour Division). The Wage and Hour Division is charged with the supervision and application of the Labor Code, which originated in the Labor Act of 1938. Since that date, this act has been the point of reference for establishing the proper exchanges between employers and their workers, although hardly a year has passed without some modification.

The Labor Act of 1938 was the culmination of a period in U.S. history characterized by the establishment of modern industry, unprecedented labor militancy expressed in the consolidation of unions, and the rise of living standards for American workers. Not surprisingly, the act captures the spirit of protective legislation, making the collective interests of workers a matter of state concern. A close reading of the Labor Act of 1938 and, particularly, of its strong repudiation of homework, suggests that it was written with the garment industry in mind (Weiner and Green 1984). That sector had been the source of some of the most militant outbursts of the preceding period and one of the most viable trade unions: the International Ladies' Garment Workers' Union. It is important to note that the Labor Act specifically bans *all* homeworker garment and textile production (including the weaving of fabric, the construction of garments, and the attachment of appurtenances such as buttons, trim, and lace).

The thoroughness with which garment production is treated in the Labor Code contrasts vividly with its approach to other industrial activities. The prohibition on homework applies to the manufacture of pharmaceutical products, food processing, the assembly of toys, the handling of flammable products, and "all other activities judged to be injurious to the health or wellbeing of individuals and neighborhoods."

It is with the last statement that the law becomes open-ended, allowing for considerable discretionary interpretation and implementation. The results have been an uneven application of the ban on homework and its widespread practice in many industries. The most striking case is found in electronics (an industry that did not exist when the Labor Act was first drafted), in which homework is legal in both California and Florida, but not in New York. From direct interviews with employers, we estimate that over 50 percent of electronics assemblers in Los Angeles, Orange, and San Diego counties make intermittent or regular use of homeworkers, many of whom are Southeast Asian or Latin American immigrants.

From the point of view of field-enforcement officials in the Wage and Hour Division, there is justification for the asymmetrical application of the ban on homework in the positive public image surrounding the electronics industry.[1] However, our examination of records in branches of the same agency revealed that electronics firms are as likely to be cited and fined for violations of wage and hour regulations as garment manufacturers. Moreover, there is no evidence to support the claim that electronics assembly is less hazardous than sewing, especially when it involves the use of chemicals in the kitchens of homeworkers. Thus, the application of the ban on homework has as much to do with the timing of the original legislation, and with the differing political strength of industrialists vis-à-vis the state, as with the actual characteristics of home employment.

More important for the purposes of our argument, the existence of a ban on homework at the federal level is variously modified and even contradicted by local and state legislation and its discretionary application. Consequently, a recent lift on the ban on homework for the knitting industry in Vermont (1984) was greeted by editorials in the *Wall Street Journal* as a welcome indication of nascent respect on the part of government for free enterprise.[2] Others see this measure as a first step in redefining the role of the state with respect to industry, and they look for greater state encouragement for self-employment and individual competitiveness. This possibility raises questions regarding the future definition and meaning of the informal sector.

Nevertheless, it is not necessary to look at cross-industrial applications of federal labor legislation to find the opportunity for the expansion of underground economic activities. The very laws that forbid homework include exemptions. For instance, at least one article in the Labor Code excludes from the prohibition all individuals who must perform wage labor at their homes in order to care for dependents, whether young, elderly, or disabled (Boris 1985).

Few people know about this aspect of the law. For field enforcement agents at the Wage and Hour Division, knowledge of this exemption places them in a curious position. This is particularly true in locations like southern Florida and southern California, where government officials often share the same ethnic background with the people most likely to be involved in the underground economy.

Such was the case of one Cuban field agent in Miami and two Mexican-American agents in southern California, interviewed in 1985. While their official task was to eradicate homework, the three found themselves serving as facilitators for the certification of Cuban and Mexican women working at their places of residence. In the words of the Cuban enforcer:

> Only a week ago I had to confiscate all fabric, thread, and tools from the house of a forty-five-year-old widow. It was like taking bread out of the mouth of someone in my own community or in my own family. She was crying and pleading but I couldn't do otherwise. I have to enforce the law! She had been working at a factory but then her mother had a stroke and she had to stay home. Now I am trying to get her certified. I told her her troubles are only temporary.

This is only one instance showing the extent to which the definition of the underground economy can be altered depending on an imaginative application of labor legislation. Even through the mediation of an enforcing officer, an individual may speedily cross the threshold between the formal and informal sectors. However, whether because of lack of information, fear, or the need to maximize a meager income, most underground workers avoid compliance with the law, in collusion with the employers who frequently abuse them.

Capabilities for Enforcement

A common frustration among field enforcement officers investigating labor violations is the extent to which their jobs are made difficult by budgetary and staff limitations. However, such limitations may be a symptom of deeper structural constraints. An official who has spent four years with the Wage and Hour Division in southern California voiced his concerns in the following way:

> We are supposed to oversee the enactment of the labor law, right? To me that means that it is important to follow up on investigations of workers' complaints, to get to the bottom of the case, and to make sure that fines are paid. But that is very time consuming and there are only five of us in charge of all complaints for the county. The backlog is enormous, and by the time we get around to looking at the case seriously, the employer may have fled the scene, closed up shop and reopened under a different name. . . . If you ask me, government is not that interested in small potatoes like garment.
>
> Once in a while, an order comes from the bigwigs to target a particular

industry. Everything else comes to a halt and the five of us take part in the raid. We know where the violators are. We go into this big display of force confiscating parts, distributing citations, fining people. We get great coverage by the newspapers and by television. Then it all goes back to the same old routine until another politician thinks about the goodness of wage and hour legislation.

These statements reflect an inherent ambivalence in the application of the Labor Code which is partly explained by the contradictory demands and interests of workers and employers, as perceived by state representatives in differing positions of power. On the one hand, a large legal and administrative apparatus has been erected to monitor the protection of workers' rights. On the other hand, through the differential allocation of funds, personnel, and supplementary resources, decision makers implement priorities that may have little or nothing to do with the original intent of a particular agency. Thus, under the conservative administration of Governor George Deukmejian in California, sanctions against employers in general were de-emphasized in the name of greater respect for the free play of labor supply and demand.

Under these conditions, the ability or failure to enforce wage and hour legislation cannot be seen as a random occurrence or as the unwelcome result of scarce resources. Rather, it must be seen as an expression of relative tolerance on the part of state representatives for illegal practices.

Contradictory Mandates of State Agencies

The Commission on California State Government, Organization, and Economy was founded in 1962 as a body to examine questions of policy. In its "Review of Selected Taxing and Enforcing Agencies' Programs to Control the Underground Economy" (August 1985), the commission acknowledged the opinion of experts who estimate that, nationwide, underground economic activities account for between $300 and $600 billion each year. In California the equivalent figure is almost $2 billion in unpaid income tax alone. In looking for the causes of this phenomenon, the commission concluded that "conflicting or dissimilar objectives limit the overall effectiveness of State enforcement activities. Since each agency is most concerned with its own objectives and collecting its own revenue, the overall benefit to the State is often overlooked. Because of this, the State's overall effectiveness in combatting the underground economy may be limited" (Commission on California State Government 1985, 4).

This candid assessment is consistent with the information provided by government officials whose pursuit of narrowly defined, and sometimes contradictory, goals contributes to the growth of underground activities. For example, definitions about what constitutes an employer-employee relationship differ according to the point of view, whether that of the Internal Revenue Service or the Department of Industrial Relations. The debate centers on the characterization of "independent contractors" versus that of "employees."

According to a highly placed official of the Department of Industrial Relations in California, an employee is anyone hired to perform any kind of service in exchange for a wage or a salary. All employees are protected by the Labor Code. While the majority of employers abide by these rulings, others circumvent them by entering into agreements with "self-employed" individuals. Thus, they try to evade responsibilities that may range from the payment of taxes to the provision of benefits, checks on working conditions, unemployment compensation, limits on working hours, and payment in accordance with minimum wage legislation.

This official view has had an impact on practices such as homework. Our interviews with women who assemble garments in their places of residence revealed a general confusion regarding the status of self-employment. In some cases, intermediaries or brokers had suggested that the women obtain self-employment permits from their local business bureaus. Such permits are irrelevant from the point of view of the Wage and Hour Division. Nonetheless, and as a result of ignorance, many women felt they had a better or even a higher status because they were self-employed. Some had been unpleasantly surprised when field enforcement agents paid them a visit and explained that they were working illegally.

While the Department of Industrial Relations has a straightforward definition of the employer-employee relationship, the same is not true of agencies, like the Internal Revenue Service, whose purpose has little to do with the correct implementation of the Labor Code. Contrary to the Wage and Hour Division's view, the IRS endorses the status of self-employed individuals and of *statutory workers*. In the words of a State of California tax auditor: "Our aim is to make sure that monies that belong to the state are paid as they should, whether they are owed by a company owner, a worker, or a self-employed contractor. We are not in the business of determining whether some people are being exploited or not. Our job is simply to determine what is the state's fair share of revenue."

The way in which this view can shape the exchanges between employers and workers is noteworthy. An illustrative example will suffice at this point. In the course of our research on the underground economy in San Diego County, we interviewed a young woman who owned a profitable doll-making factory. While visiting her operation we noticed the presence of only five workers, two men and three women, all undocumented immigrants from Mexico. We asked the owner whether all the sewing took place on factory premises. "We do most of the sewing here," she said, "but a couple of women sew at home. They also attach glass eyes to the puppets, tie ribbons and labels, that sort of thing." We wondered whether that kind of work was not illegal. "Not in this case," the owner told us "those women are statutory workers." She had learned the term as part of the advice offered by her tax auditor.

It was during our conversations with California tax officials that the significance of the category in question became clear. Its relevance to the definition of employer-employee relationships also became apparent. In its Circular E (*Employers' Tax Guide*), the IRS states that "generally, an employer is a person or organization for whom a worker performs a service as an employee. The employer usually provides the tools and place to work and has the right to fire an employee." The document specifically differentiates between "common law" and "statutory" employees. Anyone performing services that can be controlled by an employer, even when allowed freedom of action, falls into the first category. What matters in this case is that the employer has the legal right to control the method and result of the services provided by the employee. In contrast, statutory workers are those not conforming entirely to the definitions given above. They are self-employed individuals providing services for payment outside of an established place of work, but their condition as employees (different from that of the self-employed or independent contractors) has been determined by statute, generally issued by courts of justice examining class actions. This category includes agents (or commission) drivers who deliver food or beverages, full-time life insurance salespersons, traveling salespersons, *and* "homeworkers who work by the guidelines of the person for whom the work is done, with materials furnished by and returned to that person or to someone that person designates."

Three features are striking in this technical distinction. First, it establishes the factors that constitute an employer-employee relationship, regardless of what it is called: "The employee may be called a partner, agent or independent contractor" (Internal Revenue Service 1983, 4). It also does not matter how payments are measured or paid, what they are called, or whether the employee works full- or part-time. Second, the determination of this relationship is made exclusively to assign employers different tax obligations for different types of workers. Thus, the employment of industrial homeworkers in a common law category involves an obligation to withhold taxes and to pay federal unemployment taxes. As a result, there may be advantages in the employment of statutory workers.

Third, the establishment of narrow distinctions for taxing purposes, without taking into account the objectives of other agencies, can have unexpected outcomes. In this case, the endorsement of categories such as *statutory worker* opens a loophole allowing employers to circumvent bans on homework. Thus, the contradictory legislation emanating from taxing and labor-protective departments, as well as their differing mandates, is another mechanism through which the informal sector can grow.

Labor Market Insertion Patterns and Hispanic Women's Employment in the Garment Industry

In the preceding section we have given attention to the part that federal and state agencies are playing in creating a climate suitable for informalization. Now we turn our attention to a complementary process, namely, the differential allocation of workers into segments of the informalized labor force. Because the emphasis of our study has been on Hispanic women, it is necessary first to provide some background information.

A review of the 1970 and 1980 censuses shows that while all other ethnic groups in the United States have diminished their participation in blue-collar employment, Hispanic women have increased their relative share in it. Fully 35 percent of all women employed in manufacturing in the New York metropolitan, Greater Los Angeles, and Greater Miami areas are Hispanic. The contrast between the proportion of Hispanic and non-Hispanic women in manufacturing is striking. In Los Angeles, 35.7 percent of all females in that sector are Hispanic while only 19 percent are Caucasian. The equivalent figures for New York and Miami are 35.1 percent versus 17.5 percent, and 28.6 percent versus 15.4 percent, respectively.[3]

The importance of minority women's employment in assembly is readily apparent in southern California (including Los Angeles, Orange, and San Diego counties), where 67 percent of working women employed as "operators, fabricators, and laborers" belong to ethnic minority groups. Fifty-one percent of these are Hispanic. In Los Angeles County, 74 percent of all female "operators, fabricators, and laborers" (136,937 persons) are members of ethnic minorities. Almost 60 percent of that subgroup (105,621 persons) are Hispanic. Even more revealing is the composition of workers classified as "textile, apparel, and furnishings machine operators." Approximately 46,219 women are employed in those occupations in Los Angeles. Almost 91 percent of these are minorities, 72 percent of whom are Hispanic. Equivalent data for New York and Miami (the two other areas with the fastest-growing Hispanic populations) indicate similar trends.

These results run counter to the impression that Hispanic women's participation in the labor force is not significant or that it is isolated in the services sector. Moreover, census materials may underestimate the actual involvement of Hispanic women in wage labor. Many work in the underground economy, that is, as laborers in small unregulated assembly shops or as unreported homeworkers. We now consider the profile of garment production in California and Florida.

California

The history of the needle trade in this area is intimately related to developments in New York. The growth of garment manufacturing was coterminous with the rise of standardized production. Early garment factories in New England brought about the incorporation of mostly white, rural women into the labor force. By the mid–nineteenth century, the onset of international migration provided a steady supply of workers for the expansion of both markets and production. The role of several waves of German, Jewish, Italian, and Irish workers in this process is well documented (Taylor 1980).

It was against this backdrop that New York assumed a preeminent role as a center of operations for the garment industry. In the latter part of the nineteenth century, California became a center for the manufacture of ready-made wear for mass consumption. In the 1920s, the Los Angeles clothing industry emerged, stimulated in part by the arrival of runaway shops evading unionization drives in New York. From the very beginning, Mexican women were employed in nearly all positions of the industry. Accounts of the time describe the work force in the Los Angeles clothing industry as formed primarily by Mexican females, three-fourths of whom were between the ages of sixteen and twenty-three, two-thirds of whom had been born in the United States, and nine-tenths of whom were unmarried (Taylor 1980).

The Great Depression sent the Los Angeles garment industry into a period of turmoil, but the rise of the movie industry in the 1930s established new guidelines for fashion and fresh opportunities for production. Los Angeles began to specialize in expensive women's sportswear (Perlmutter 1944). By 1944, the number of garment manufacturers in Los Angeles had grown to 900 with a work force of 28,000 people, 75 percent of whom were Mexican women. The value of the product was said to be in excess of $110 million. By 1975, there had been a dramatic increase of plants to an estimated 2,269 with a work force of 66,000 people (Maram and Long 1981).

During this same period alarm over violations of the Labor Code and tax laws and the expansion of homework also grew. The recent history of the garment industry in Los Angeles has been characterized by concern over unregulated home assembly and the negative impact of foreign imports. Throughout the 1980s, there has been continued restructuring of the industry, resulting in decreasing numbers of large firms and the proliferation of small manufacturing shops. Of 2,717 registered apparel and textile manufacturers in Los Angeles County in early 1984, 1,695, or 62 percent, employed between 1 and 19 workers. The number of the total work force in the formal sector hovered at around 81,400 persons (Scott 1984).

Contrary to the widespread impression, garment production in Los Angeles is growing quickly. This is probably due to the expansion of the informal sector. Garment contractors in Los Angeles County generated approximately $3.5 billion in sales in 1983. It is estimated that between 30 percent and 50 percent of that value may have originated in home production and unregulated shops.[4]

Florida

In the early sixties, the Florida garment industry employed fewer than 7,000 persons, specializing in the manufacture of belts, gloves, and purses. This was a highly seasonal industry, depending on the periodic arrival of New York entrepreneurs feeding luxury markets in Europe and the United States.

The advent of several waves of refugees as a result of the Cuban Revolution was seen by many as an opportunity for revitalizing industrial activity in southern Florida. Retired manufacturers from New York who had homes in Miami saw the advantages of opening new businesses and hiring large numbers of freshly arrived Cuban women. At the same time, New York was experiencing a resurgence of union drives. The two factors combined to create a boom in garment manufacturing in southern Florida. By 1973, the industry employed more than 24,000 workers, of whom the vast majority were Cuban women. The same process led to the predominance of Cuban males among middlemen and subcontractors. Thus, from its inception in the early sixties, apparel manufacturing in Miami was an exemplary case of gender and ethnic stratification, with 70 percent of the manufacturers being Jewish men, 90 percent of the subcontractors being Cuban men, and 95 percent of the work force being Cuban and female.

In 1984, the Florida apparel industry employed 355,000 (in the formal sector) and comprised 716 firms located in Miami with a quarterly direct payroll of $64 million. The annual sales volume reached approximately $1 billion. Since the late seventies, there have been labor shortages in the Florida garment industry as a result of several trends, particularly the relatively advanced age of the work force (hovering at over forty) and the absence of a new labor supply. As we will note below, it is the decreasing availability of a free-floating labor supply that has contributed to the expansion of homework in Miami.

A Comparative Sketch

A comparison of garment manufacture in Los Angeles and Miami raises several issues. First, the two sites differ in the timing of the industry's evolution, maturity, and restructuring. In Los Angeles, production is not only older but also rooted in specific events such as the Great Depression, changing conditions for assembly in New York, new definitions of fashion linked to casual wear, and continued reorganization as a response to the impact of foreign imports. The garment industry in Miami has had a shorter history characterized by a less diversified experience.

Second, the expansion of the Los Angeles clothing industry resulted from the employers' ability to rely on continuing waves of Mexican immigrants, many of whom were undocumented. The sustained character of Mexican migration over the last half century ensured a permanent supply of workers for the garment industry. In contrast, the expansion of garment production in Miami was due to an unprecedented influx of exiles produced by a revolutionary upheaval.

Third, perhaps the most important difference between Mexicans in Los Angeles and Cubans in Florida is related to their distinctive labor market insertion patterns. Historically, Mexicans have arrived in the U.S. labor market in a highly individuated and dispersed manner. As a result, they have been extremely dependent on labor market supply and demand forces entirely beyond their control. Their working-class background and the stigma attached to their frequent undocumented status has accentuated even further their vulnerability vis-à-vis employers. In contrast, Cubans have been able to consolidate an economic enclave containing immigrant businesses that hire workers of a common cultural and national background. This enclave partly operates as a buffer zone separating and often shielding members of the same ethnic group from the market forces at play in the broader economy (Portes and Bach 1985, chap. 6). The ethnic enclave does not preclude exploitation on the basis of class; indeed, it is predicated upon the existence of a highly diversified immigrant class structure. However, quantitative and qualitative evidence suggests that commonalities of culture, national background, and language between immigrant employers and workers can become a mechanism for collective improvement of income levels and standards of living. Differences in labor market insertion patterns among Mexicans and Cubans have led to varying social profiles and a dissimilar potential for socioeconomic advancement.

Finally, the two paths of labor market incorporation are significantly related to household composition. Neither proletarian atomization among Mexicans nor participation in an economic enclave among Cubans can be explained without consideration of the role played by households and families in the allocation of workers to different segments of the labor market. It is to this crucial point that we now turn.

Household Organization and Informalization

Both Marxist and non-Marxist writings have tended to portray families and households as entities outside of the economic and political spheres, although passively affected by external processes. Over the last decade a rich literature authored primarily by feminist scholars has redressed this misconception by providing a wealth of ethnographic and historical evidence making clear the extent to which specific modalities in the composition and organization of domestic units are simultaneously the cause and effect of broader conditions (Rapp 1982).

Two lines of thought derived from this literature are relevant from our perspective. First, a conceptual distinction should be made between *family* and *household*. *Family* is a normative, that is, ideological, notion that frequently transcends class barriers. Such an ideal includes marriage and fidelity, the role of men as providers and of women as caretakers of children, as well as the expectation that families so formed will reside in the same home. In this respect, the nuclear family organized according to patriarchal mores continues to prevail.

While the concept of family designates the way things ought to be, *household* refers to the actual manner in which men, women, and children come together as part of observable domestic units. Households represent mechanisms for the pooling of time, labor, and other resources in a frequently shared space. The concept of the family appears "natural" and unchangeable. Households, on the other hand, constantly adjust to the pressures of the surrounding environment. Indeed, households often stand in sharp contrast to widespread ideals regarding the family.

Social class accounts largely for the extent to which notions about the family can be upheld or not. The conditions necessary for the maintenance of long-term stable unions in which men act as main providers and women as principal caretakers of children have been readily available among the middle and upper classes but woefully absent among the poor. Thus, the poor often live in highly flexible households in which meager resources and vital services contantly flow but in which adherence to the norms of the patriarchal family are unattainable.

The evidence from our case studies points in two different directions. In the case of Mexicans, proletarianization appears to be related to a high incidence of female-headed households and households in which the earnings of women are indispensable for maintaining standards of modest subsistence. Underemployment partly accounts for the inability of men to serve as main providers. Above one-third of women working in the Los Angeles garment industry are heads of households. In the case of Cubans in Miami, women's employment was originally a strategy for coping with an unfamiliar environment and the need to restore a middle-class standard of living. This contrasting experience involving the relationship between households and labor markets has occurred in spite of shared values regarding the family among Mexican and Cuban women.

Nowhere are these differences clearer than in the circumstances surrounding homework. Consider the typical experience of Petra Ramos, a thirty-two-year-old from Torreón, Coahuila (Mexico):

> I've worked in several garment shops since I came to California five years ago. At
> first I lived with my aunt and uncle and another Mexican family with whom we

shared the apartment. None of us had papers. But the problem was language; how to make yourself understood when you're looking for a job. . . . So I ended up sewing. A lot of people speak Spanish in the clothing factories. Then I got pregnant. I didn't want to live with relatives then, so I had to work at home.

Similar cases can be found among Cuban and Central American women in Miami. However, a large proportion of female Cuban workers have had a different trajectory. Among the first waves of refugees, in particular, there were many who worked hard to bring the standards of living of their families to the same levels as those they had in their country of origin. The consolidation of an economic enclave was largely predicated on fierce loyalty to the family. While wives toiled in garment factories and in unskilled and semiskilled services, men entered the world of business. Many became garment contractors who employed first their own wives and mothers before they hired outside laborers. Eventually, many moved ahead, purchased homes, and achieved comfortable styles of life. At that point, many Cuban men pressed their wives to stop working outside the home. In the words of a prominent manufacturer in the area:

> Cuban workers were willing to do anything to survive. When they became prosperous, the women saw the advantage of staying at home and still earn some income. Because they had the skill, owners couldn't take them for granted. Eventually, owners couldn't get operators anymore. The most skilled would tell a manager, "My husband doesn't let me work outside of the home." That was a worker's initiative based on the values of the culture. I would put ads in the paper and forty people would call and everyone would say, "I only do homework." That's how we got this problem of the labor shortages.[5]

Interviews with Cuban women involved in homework confirm the general accuracy of this interpretation. By capitalizing on their scarce skills and experience, some Cuban women have even become subcontractors, employing neighbors and relatives and transforming so-called Florida rooms (the covered porches typical of Miami houses) into sewing shops.

Conclusions

Our purpose has been to examine, in preliminary fashion, two convergent processes leading to the growth of the underground economy in an advanced industrial context. On the one hand, we have explored the role of the state as it is embodied in concrete practices and policies, in the creation of a climate suitable for the expansion of unregulated production and industrial homework. On the other hand, we have emphasized the importance of labor market insertion patterns in providing a labor force for informalized production.

The comparison between different experiences among Hispanic women in two social settings shows that involvement in informal production can have entirely dissimilar meanings depending on the type of incorporation into the labor market. The examples considered should reaffirm the importance of studying the underground economy as an uneven and richly variegated spectrum, rather than as a homogeneous phenomenon resulting from the interaction of standard economic factors.

Notes

This essay is based on a research project titled "A Collaborative Study of Hispanic Women in Garment and Electronics Industries." Funds have been provided by the Ford and Tinker foundations. The authors gratefully acknowledge the support and encouragement of Dr. William Díaz and Ms. Patricia Biggers.

1. This assessment derives from interviews conducted in late 1984, 1985, and 1986 with personnel at the Employment Development and Department of Labor Standards and Wage Enforcement in Los Angeles, Orange, and San Diego counties.

2. "Tip of the Ski Cap," *Wall Street Journal*, November 12, 1984. See also "U.S. Again Issues Rules to Let Firms Employ Individuals at Home," *Wall Street Journal*, November 6, 1984.

3. These figures were abstracted from the 1980 U.S. Census and the Census of Manufacturers, 1980.

4. Estimates were provided by government officials contacted during our field research. See also the "Review of Selected Taxing and Enforcing Agencies' Programs to Control the Underground Economy" (August 1985) by the Commission on California State Government, Organization, and Economy.

5. Field interview with an official of the Florida Needletrade Association, January 1986.

References

Boris, E. 1985. "Regulating Industrial Homework: The Triumph of 'Sacred Motherhood.'" *Journal of American History* 71:745–63.

Commission on California State Government, Organization, and Economy. 1985. "Review of Selected Taxing and Enforcing Agencies' Programs to Control the Underground Economy." August.

Gershuny, J. I. 1979. "The Informal Economy: Its Role in Industrial Society." *Futures* 11:3–16.

Internal Revenue Service. 1983. *Employer's Tax Guide*. Circular E of the Department of the Treasury, publication 15. Rev. July.

Leichter, S. 1982. "Sweatshops to Shakedowns: Organized Crime in New York's Garment Industry." Monthly Report. Office of the Twenty-ninth District of the State of New York.

Maram, S. and S. Long. 1981. "The Labor Market Impact of Hispanic Undocumented Workers: A Case Study of the Garment Industry in LA County." California State University at Fullerton. Mimeo.

Peattie, L. 1980. "Anthropological Perspectives on the Concepts of Dualism, the Informal Sector, and Marginality in Developing Urban Economies." *International Regional Science Review*, Spring, 70–88.

Perlmutter, M. 1944. *The Rag Bizness*. Los Angeles: Wetzel Publishing Co.

Portes, A. and R. Bach. 1985. *Latin Journey: Cuban and Mexican Immigrants in the United States*. Berkeley and Los Angeles: University of California Press.

Portes, A. and S. Sassen-Koob. 1987. "The Informal Sector: Comparative Material from Latin America, the United States, and Western Europe." *American Journal of Sociology,* July (forthcoming).

Rapp, R. 1982. "Family and Class in Contemporary America: Notes toward an Understanding of Ideology." Pp. 168–87 in B. Thorne and M. Yalom (eds.), *In Rethinking the Family: Some Feminist Questions*. New York: Longmans.

Sassen-Koob, S. 1985. "Growth and Informalization at the Core: The Case of New York City." Pp. 492–519 in *The Urban Informal Sector: Recent Trends in Research and Theory*. Conference Proceedings. Department of Sociology, The Johns Hopkins University, Baltimore.

Scott, A. J. 1984. "Industrial Organization and the Logic of Intra-Metropolitan Location: The Women's Dress Industry in Los Angeles." *Economic Geography* 60:3–27.

Skocpol, T. 1985. "Bringing the State Back In: Strategies of Analysis in Current Research." Pp. 3–43 in P. B. Evans, D. Rueschemeyer, and T. Skocpol (eds.), *Bringing the State Back In*. London: Cambridge University Press.

Tanzi, V. 1982. *The Underground Economy in the United States and Abroad*. Lexington, Mass.: D. C. Heath.

Taylor, P. S. 1980. "Mexican Women in Los Angeles Industry in 1928." *Aztlán, International Journal of Chicano Studies Research* 11:99–129.

Tokman, V. 1978. "An Exploration into the Nature of Informal-Formal Sector Relationships." *World Development* 6:1187–98.

Weiner, E. and H. Green. 1984. "A Stitch in Our Time: New York's Hispanic Garment Workers in the 1980s." Pp. 107–38 in J. Jensen and S. Davidson (eds.), *A Needle, a Bobbin, a Strike: Women Needleworkers in America*. Philadelphia, Pa.: Temple University Press.

14 Industrial Development, Ethnic Cleavages, and Employment Patterns: Penang State, Malaysia

**T. G. McGee, Kamal Salih,
Mei Ling Young, and Chan Lean Heng**

This chapter addresses a deceptively simple question: What happens to the informal sector when a regional economy "takes off," experiencing a rapid increase in regional product and substantial shifts in the size and composition of the labor force? We propose to explore this question by an analysis of economic and labor force changes in Penang State, Malaysia, since 1947 (see McGee 1973; McGee and Yeung 1976; McGee 1978; Armstrong and McGee 1985). We argue that a particular combination of capital, state, and labor processes operating at the macrolevel (international), mesolevel (national-regional), and microlevel (ethnic group and household) combine in Penang to produce the region's peculiar pattern of informal sector production.

Changes at the international level (most commonly described as the international division of labor) lead to national-level changes, including both the decline of old centers of production in the advanced capitalist economies and the emergence of new production centers in countries such as Malaysia. Stagnation and decline in the advanced economies lead to informalization of employment, and this trend in turn generates changes at the household level, particularly through the incorporation of women in informal production. In the newly industrializing countries, the new production zones create new employment opportunities, especially for women, though both the demand and supply of labor are subject to marked fluctuations. In a recession, workers in newly industrializing countries who have been laid off return to the household until required again; in the advanced economies, wages are depressed and the bargaining power of unions is diminished.

The mix of international, national, and microlevel processes is somewhat different in every case. Thus the conditions that bring about the decline, persistence, or growth of the informal sector are not uniform. The implication is that a broader political economy approach is necessary to explain the bewildering variety of regional informal economies that are described in the various chapters in this volume.

Cross-regional comparisons, of course, must rest upon some generally accepted working definition of the informal economy. Castells and Portes offer such a definition in this volume, and we agree with their view of informalization as a process of income generation that falls outside a regulated institutional environment. However, this definition, while conceptually appealing, is difficult to apply empirically. In this study, we have defined the informal sector mainly according to the scale of production (comprising firms with less than thirty workers). This definition enables us to interpret data from censuses and surveys but gives only a general indication of informalization processes such as the subcontracting processes described by Sassen-Koob, Benería, and Benton in this volume. We recognize that although this definition is useful in the analysis of industrial change in Malaysia, where small-scale units of production are closely correlated with the lack of government regulation, it may not be applicable in other, different, settings.

Our examination of the developments in the informal economy of Penang State is divided into three parts. In the first, we analyze the impact of the processes of labor formation, capital investment, and state policy on Penang State within the context of the Malaysian and international economies.[1] In the second part, we consider the effects of these changes on the informal economy of Penang with particular attention to ethnic differences. The third part illustrates these processes at the level of the workers engaged in both the formal and informal sectors. Finally, in the conclusion, we discuss the implications of these findings for the continued existence of the informal sector.

The Setting: Penang State in the Regional, National, and International Economies

In 1985, Penang State[2] had an estimated population of one million, generated about 6 percent of the gross domestic product of Malaysia, and had the fourth-highest state gross domestic product per capita of the fifteen political units of Malaysia.[3] It contained the major port and acted as the industrial and trading center for the northern region of peninsular Malaysia. Historically, this economic position arose out of the role played by Penang State, and particularly the city of George Town, in the trade of tin, rubber, and other regional commodities. Administered by the British, Penang developed as a state predominantly populated by Chinese. It was the commercial hub of a region inhabited largely by Malays engaged in the cultivation of rice and other cash crops, and Indians employed on the plantations.[4]

In the period after World War II, Penang State experienced slow economic growth, new out-migration, and loss of investment to other parts of Malaysia (Tan 1972). Its gross domestic product was 12 percent below the national average and only sixth highest in the country in 1970. Its economic mainstay was commercial and service activity, which contributed almost two-thirds of the gross domestic product and accounted for 50 percent of employment.

By 1980, this situation had changed significantly. Between 1970 and 1980, the GDP of the state more than doubled. The contribution of manufacturing to the GDP rose from 21 percent to 41 percent, and employment in manufacturing increased from 10 percent to 37 percent of the labor force (Government of Malaysia 1981). This regional "industrial revolution" in Penang was only a microcosm of broader industrial change in the country. The contribution of manufacturing nationwide grew from 8 percent in 1957 to 20.5 percent in 1980 (Jomo 1986).

The state actively promoted industrial development in a number of ways.[5] First, its contribution to industrial development as part of national expenditure increased radically, growing from 1.25 percent of expenditure in the First Five-Year Plan (1956–60) to 4.62 percent in the First Malaysian Plan (1965–70) and up to 20.37 percent in the Fourth Malaysian Plan (1981–85). Second, the Malaysian government adopted a number of investment-encouragement schemes and other measures in support of the growth of both private and foreign investment in industrialization. For instance, the semiconductor assembly operations are almost 100 percent foreign-owned (see Scott 1985; Onn 1986; McGee 1987).

Third, the government accepted recommendations for the creation of industrial estates (developed areas comprehensively planned and provided with infrastructure, subject to some form of centralized management). Between 1962 and 1984 some eighty-six industrial estates were established. They are heavily concentrated in the main urban zones of Kuala Lumpur–Keland, Penang Ipoh Taiping, Johor Baharu Seremban, and Melaka. An important variant in these industrial estates were the free-trade zones (also called export processing zones), which in 1984 consisted of nine zones located in Selangor, Penang, and Melaka.

The Malaysian state's goals in pursuing rapid industrialization stem largely from the state's central concern with restructuring the participation of various ethnic groups in the economy. The goal was set forth in the new economic policy (NEP) and first implemented in the second Malaysian Plan (1971–75). A major component of the NEP has been the encouragement of the growth of a Malay "commercial and industrial" class through the creation of state enterprises that will give Malays majority ownership of the corporate sector (Jomo 1984). By 1983, this share of Malay ownership was estimated to be 18 percent.

The other prong of the NEP was directed at the eradication of poverty and the reduction of income differentials between the major ethnic communities. As indicated in table 14.1, the proportion of Malays in the industrial labor force has grown dramatically, reaching 53.5 percent by 1980. There have also been particularly significant increases in Malay female employment (see Ariffin 1981; McGee 1982, 1985; Daud 1983).

Much of this employment creation occurred in the five main urbanized

Table 14.1 Proportion of Malays and Chinese in
Employed Manufacturing Labor Force

Year	Malay Workers (%)	Chinese Workers (%)
1957	19.6	72.0
1970	28.9	65.2
1980	53.5	45.4

Source: Government of Malaysia, general reports on
censuses of 1957, 1970, and 1980.

regions of Johore Bahru, Melaka, Kuala Lumpur, Kelang, and Penang. New
employment was an important contributor to overall urban growth; the level of
urbanization in Peninsular Malaysia increased from 26.6 percent in 1957 to
37.4 percent in 1980 (see Caldwell 1963; Salih and Young 1981; Salih 1981a,
1981b, 1983).

In 1980 these five urbanized regions accounted for 32 percent of the
total population of peninsular Malaysia, made up of Malays (37%), Chinese
(49%), Indians (13%), and others (1%). Twenty-one percent of the peninsular
Malaysian Malay community and 50 percent of the Chinese lived in these areas.
In 1980 they contained 56 percent of those employed in manufacturing, and
during the seventies they absorbed 55 percent of the total increase in manufacturing employment. Almost 50 percent of that increase was made up of workers
employed in the manufacture of electrical machinery, textiles, and clothing. A
very high proportion of this latter group (100% in the case of semiconductor
workers) were either employed in free-export zones or licensed manufacturing
warehouses located in these urbanized regions.

The impact of these strategies in Penang was very significant.[6] Between 1971 and 1984, eight industrial estates were created, including five free-
trade zones producing mainly electronics and clothing, and three industrial
estates producing a wide array of goods (often protected by import tariffs).
Between 1971 and 1984, the number of factories in such estates increased from
36 to 243, and employment rose from 4,500 to 56,000. The major characteristics of the industrial areas in 1982 were as follows: First, in terms of paid-
up capital, 31 percent of the investments were in the textile and garment
industries; 8.5 percent were in electronics; 8.4 percent, in metal products; and
another 8.4 percent, in industrial gases. Second, in terms of employment, the
electronics and electrical industries were responsible for nearly half (47%) of
the jobs created; the other big employers were in the textile and garment
industries, with 24 percent of the new jobs. Third, almost 62 percent of the
workers were females, of which 82 percent were in electronics and textiles. The
ethnic breakdown of workers suggests that Penang's industrial estates have
been a major source of employment for Malays. In 1982 they made up some 45
percent of employed workers on the industrial estates, compared with 33 per-

cent of the total manufacturing employment in Penang State in 1980.

The implications of these development policies for Penang State and Malaysia have been the articulation of a national industrial policy with structural adjustments in the world economy (Salih 1983) and an attempt to reduce ethnic disharmony over economic inequality inherited from the colonial period. The new divisions of labor in the world economy which have manifested themselves in such activities as semiconductor assembly by transnational capital have been in part a result of "development by invitation." The national state has thus aided this process.

We have some evidence from national employment statistics that the role of the informal economy has changed with this process of economic development, and that this change is reflected in different ethnic-group employment patterns. Census data for Penang State show that employment of own-account workers declined from about 40 percent of those employed in 1947 to 21 percent in 1980. This suggests that the informal sector played an insignificant role in absorbing labor during this period. However, when we analyze the relative absorption by the main ethnic groups, we find that the Chinese have experienced a 33 percent increase in own-account workers, compared with absolute and relative declines in the Malay and Indian communities. While the numerical increase is small, much of it has been concentrated in the commerce and small-industry areas, suggesting that the Chinese have been unable, or unwilling, to move into the wage sector, particularly in industrial activity, as quickly as the Malays. It is this process of ethnic differentiation in informal sector employment which we examine below.

Workers in the Formal and Informal Sectors in Penang

The problem of collecting socioeconomic data on the informal and formal sectors has been discussed at length in the literature (see, e.g., Bromley and Gerry 1979; Salih 1981b). There are difficulties with both longitudinal and cross-sectional data. Some researchers have responded to this problem by limiting themselves to case histories (e.g., Bromley and Gerry 1979). Other researchers concentrate on comparing the formal and informal sectors within a particular economic activity (McGee 1973). In this chapter, we illustrate the processes that have been described at the macrolevel and mesolevel for Penang State and Malaysia as they affect workers in the informal and formal sectors within manufacturing (see Salih et al. 1985).

We selected two residential areas in the Penang urban area, one with a high proportion of workers in informal sector industry and the other with a high proportion in formal industry. The formal sector was defined as comprising establishments with thirty or more workers, while firms in the informal sector were operationally defined as those with less than thirty workers. The study concentrated only on workers in manufacturing. The definition of formal sector workers referred only to operators on the production line, including packers and handlers. Informal sector workers were defined as those engaged in production and processing in manufacturing industries. This definition excluded service-oriented workers, such as servants, hawkers, and washerwomen. Further, respondents had to be currently working and between the ages of ten and thirty-six. The main objective of this research was to study young workers.

Interviews were conducted in two study areas in 1982. Most of the formal sector workers were located in Bayan Baru, a residential area adjacent to the factories of the free-trade zone. The informal sector workers came mainly from Weld Quay, an inner-city zone that had experienced considerable occupational variation. The informal location, Weld Quay, next to the city center, was one of the first areas of Penang to be settled in the early nineteenth century. It consists of jetties and the adjacent foreshore, and it is populated almost entirely by Chinese, who historically provided the labor for the lighters that conveyed goods and passengers to and from ships berthed in Penang harbor (see Chan 1980). Beginning in the 1960s, this economic base eroded as the entrepôt trade declined and new wharves were built. As a result there has been much diversification into other activities including fishing, petty trading, manufacturing assembly in homes, and small industry.

The area of mainly formal employment is Bayan Baru, located eighteen kilometers from the center of town. This area includes the Bayan Lepas Free-Trade Zone, which contains the majority of semiconductor and textile plants. Suburban housing has grown up around this industrial zone, in some cases encapsulating small villages. The housing is occupied both by workers from the free-trade zones, who frequently live together in groups of up to twenty or more, and by middle-class families whose household heads are engaged in government or other service occupations. Many of the workers living in this area are Malay female migrants from outside Penang.

Predictably, the two locations exhibit quite different distributions of workers. Of the 351 workers who responded to the survey in Weld Quay, 210 (60%) are employed in the informal sector; the remainder are in formal sector employment. The population of Weld Quay is 98 percent Chinese. In contrast, the workers in Bayan Lepas are all engaged in the formal sector but are ethnically more mixed, with a population 53.6 percent Malay, 33 percent Chinese, and the remainder composed of other ethnic groups.

Socioeconomic data from the surveys are presented in terms of contrasts between formal and informal sector workers, rather than by area or ethnicity. It must be remembered, however, that the informal sector is made up entirely of Chinese from Weld Quay, while the formal sector includes workers from both Weld Quay (who often commute in company-hired buses to the factories) and Bayan Baru. This spatial and sectoral distinction is a reflection of the manner in which the new Malay migrants to the city have been inserted into the formal labor force.

As noted, many of the surveyed workers in the formal sector are females (90.5%), compared with 55.7 percent in the more heterogeneous informal sector. Most of the workers are young; the average age of the workers in the formal sector is 22.6; those in the informal sector average 22.3 years of age, a finding that reflects the sampling frame as well as the relative recency of the labor force in both sectors. However, closer examination of the age pattern reveals that in the informal sector, where there is no enforcement of the law on the minimum age for work (16), the age range is greater; 9.5 percent of the workers are below sixteen, and the oldest workers are also in this sector.

Education is perhaps the single most important overt sociodemographic factor influencing occupations. It is certainly a prerequisite for most formal sector jobs. In the informal sector, in contrast, personal contacts based on ascribed values play a crucial role in job placement. Thus workers in the formal sector have a higher mean number of years of school (eight years) compared with 6.2 years for those in the informal sector. While 70 percent of formal workers have been to secondary school, the proportion among the informally employed is 44 percent. Those without schooling in the formal sector are mainly Chinese sewing-machine operators employed by a Chinese-owned garment factory (rather than a foreign-owned transnational) producing solely for export.

Why this discrepancy? The main reason lies in the selective process of migration. Young Malay women who migrate to the city tend to be more educated than their peers left behind in the villages.[7] The young women who migrate are responding to the needs of the TNC factories, which require their workers to have a certain level of education. The pattern also reflects the increasing educational opportunities provided to the rural Malays by the government. But, more important, it appears that the Malays in rural areas perceive the importance of education for social mobility. Educational attainment is essential to obtaining government and other corporate sector jobs. In contrast, for many poorer Chinese, while schooling is important, it is not viewed as essential because there are other ways to train for an occupation.[8] However, for the very poor Malaysians, the cost of schooling is also prohibitive.[9]

Other important factors differentiating workers in the two sectors are migrant and nonmigrant status and the history of occupational mobility. There are great differences in migration experiences between workers in the formal and informal sectors. Those living in Penang at the time of the survey, but born outside the state, comprise 45 percent of the formal sector and only 7 percent of the informal sector. This pattern can be explained in part by the labor demands of the two sectors and the more recent development of large-scale manufacturing.

The different types of economic activities in the two sectors are also of importance. Over 90 percent of the work force in the large industries is female. Not surprisingly, the majority of women surveyed work in electronics and electrical companies or in textile and garment firms (71% and 24%, respectively). Females constitute 96 percent and 89 percent of the total work force in these two industrial areas, respectively. While young Malay women are engaged mainly in electronics (70%), the majority of Chinese are in textiles (53%). This may be explained by the fact that all the electronics and electrical companies are multinationals and have adhered to the policy of employing Malays. Further, the electronics industry has more stringent education requirements than the textiles industry and tends to employ older workers.

The homogeneity of occupations in the formal sector may be contrasted with the heterogeneity of informal manufacturing jobs, as shown in table 14.2. The major types of informal work are associated with the manufacturing or processing of food, beverages, and tobacco; tin and steel; paper and cardboard products; and charcoal and wood products. These major headings disguise the myriad of types of work involved. The skills required are easily learned and highly repetitive. Enterprises in the informal sector are usually small and inconspicuous, and often are located in backyards or within other mixed living and working environments. They are characterized by relatively low capital investment, and the "production line" often appears disorganized. The work force is made up mostly of women and children, who are not barred from such employment by age and educational requirements.

Gender is an important factor in the distribution of different tasks within informal enterprises. Females are engaged in the lighter types of work such as grading, sorting, and assembling different products (e.g., cleaning and classifying fish, folding and stacking newspapers, and assembling plastic flowers). Males are employed in heavier work associated with metal industries

Table 14.2 The Informal Economy in Penang

Sector	Number of Firms	Percentage of Sector
Food, beverages, and tobacco	38	18.1
Tin and steel	38	18.1
Paper and cardboard	35	16.7
Charcoal and wood	31	14.8
Agriculture and animal husbandry	22	10.5
Textiles and garments	20	9.5
Footwear and plastics	13	6.2
Sales and advertising	5	2.4
Storage, transport, and construction	4	1.9
Vehicle parts	2	1.0
Electronics and electrical	2	1.0
Total	210	100.0

Sources: Salih, M. L. Young, Chan, Lon, and Chan 1985.

(89% male) and wood and charcoal (71%); the latter represents an important traditional industry of Weld Quay. Child labor (under 16 years old) is found in the more undemanding work such as making paper products (e.g., paper bags), garments (e.g., sewing labels onto shirts), and in the food and beverage areas (grading onions, prawns, etc.) Along with females in the traditional sector, children have the lightest and most unskilled work.

Occupational differences between the two sectors are also reflected in the patterns of job recruitment. Whereas almost 77 percent of the workers in formal employment get their jobs by application, a majority of workers in informal enterprises utilize kin or friends to get jobs. Job histories also reveal differences. Nearly half of the workers in the large firms are in their first jobs—hardly surprising since most of them have recently left school. The remainder show a strong tendency to shift jobs within the same industry, often for only slight improvements in working conditions or hourly rates.[10] Job mobility is less marked in the informal sector, although there is a similar proportion of first-job participants, reflecting the similar age structure.

A common assertion concerning formal and informal occupations is that incomes in the former are higher. This is not supported by our survey, which reveals that formal workers have a mean monthly income of $M225.2 while the informal mean monthly income is $M254.4.[11] However, a higher proportion of those in informal employment—nearly 30 percent compared with 14 percent of formal workers—fall into the low-income category. Also, as anticipated, males tend to receive higher wages than females in the larger firms. The youngest age groups receive the lowest income, but there is no clear indication that increasing age or higher education means higher incomes.

In summary, several major features distinguish informal workers. They have a wider age range, which includes younger workers, while large employers must adhere to the legal minimum age of employment (16). In the formal sector, a minimum education is required for particular jobs, while education is relatively unimportant in informal employment. The nature of recruitment is also different; the corporate sector expects certain formal qualifications and follows established procedures for job applications, whereas informal jobs are obtained through friends and relatives. Finally, although earnings for many workers in both types of firms are comparable, a larger proportion of workers in the informal sector are in low-paying occupations.

Conclusions

This study illustrates the role of various processes, not all of them anticipated in the past literature, in shaping the labor market in Malaysia. First, broad political and economic developments have been responsible for the great increase in female employment in manufacturing. These processes operate at a world level and affect both national policies and household decisions. At the world level, the redeployment of manufacturing industries from the advanced countries to many Third World locations—"capital chasing labor"—has resulted in the growth of multinational companies, especially in the electronics, electrical, textile, and garment industries, which employ mostly female production workers. At the national level, complementary actions of the Malaysian state—particularly measures to support industrialization and the employment of Malays—have encouraged the growth of industries and have spurred migration of rural female Malays to urban manufacturing locations.

Our data also show that family and household strategies remain a crucial component of labor processes involving formalization and informalization. Labor processes are adapted and modified by the ethnic and cultural characteristics of the communities of which households are part. The point is clearly illustrated by the way workers are absorbed into the formal or informal enterprises. The large majority of proprietors of small informal enterprises in the cities are Chinese. The firms tend to be small family enterprises run on a traditional kinship basis in which proprietors often discriminate against non-relatives and Chinese who speak other dialects. Entry into this type of employment is through ascription or, in the case of skilled work, apprenticeship. Malays' lack of social ties to these employers makes it difficult for them to enter these jobs. In addition, Malays also tend to view such work negatively because it lacks security.

Thus, in the last ten to fifteen years, the easier and preferred openings for the Malay population have been formal sector jobs in large export-oriented companies. Traditionally, and even today, Malays have tended to gravitate toward government employment; as with the large private companies, entry into government work is determined by educational qualifications, quota systems, and other formal procedures. While it has been argued that the government bureaucracy is an extension of the feudalistic structure of Malay society (Alatas 1967, 1972) and that the Malay social structure emphasizes loyalty to social mobility rather than entrepreneurship (Tham 1977), the main reasons behind the preference for government jobs are security, regularity of income, and prestige.[12] This preference is borne out by Malay factory workers who view their jobs as stepping-stones to government jobs.

Clearly the informal sector has reacted in a complex way to the growth of the regional economy in Penang. To some extent it represents the "residue" of traditional practices to which new informal activities have been added in the form of household or small-industrial enterprises. Partly, it also appears to be a spin-off of the growth of the formal sector and the regional economy. The result is that informal enterprise still offers significant opportunities for employment for one ethnic community, the Chinese, but has ceased to be of importance for Malays and Indians. Thus different facets of the formalization-informalization process—strategies of TNCs, state policies, and ethnic divisions—are juxtaposed in Penang, and no one factor can be identified that uniquely determines its character. The political economy approach advocated in this and other chapters in this volume is essential to unraveling the changing nature of the informal sector and its role in industrial development.

Notes

1. The impact of the international economy is dealt with more extensively in Jomo 1984, 1986; Salih 1981a; McGee 1987; Lai and Tan 1985.

2. We have preferred the term Penang State to the newer Malaysian name, which is Pulau Pinang. The earlier form is still better known internationally.

3. We use the term *political units* to include the eleven states of peninsular Malaysia, the two states of eastern Malaysia, and the Federal Territory of Kuala Lumpur. Peninsular Malaysia excludes the states of Sabah, Sarawak, and the Federal Territory of Labuan.

4. In 1947 the Chinese made up 55 percent of the population of Penang State, compared with only 33 percent of the population of the other northern-region states, Perlis, Kedah, and Perak. The proportion of Chinese was much higher in Penang Municipality, where it reached 72 percent. At the time of independence, Penang State and its hinterland were very similar to other states in peninsular Malaysia.

5. White (1984) has distinguished three types of government that play different roles in industrialization: (1) state capitalist regimes; (2) intermediate regimes, or those that may use "socialist labels" but closely restrict private capital and expand state ownership; and (3) state socialist regimes, in which the government regulates private industrial capital. Utilizing White's framework, we find that, since 1957, the Malaysian state has moved increasingly toward the state capitalist model.

6. See Salih and Lo (1975) for a discussion of the evolution of industrial policy in Malaysia from 1955 to 1975 with particular reference to Penang.

7. See M. L. Young (1982) and Pryor (1972) for the national pattern, Narayanan (1975) for Selangor, and M. L. Young (1979) for Kedah.

8. Based on research on job preferences and reasons for these choices in six villages in Kedah (M. L. Young, forthcoming).

9. See Young, Bussink, and Hasan (1980, 131–35) and Loh (1975) for a discussion of the costs of education in Malaysia.

10. In some cases workers have been laid off and reemployed, although at the time of this survey this was not yet occurring. See Salih and Young (1985) for a description of the problems of retrenchment in the electronics industry.

11. The U.S. dollar was equivalent to M\$ 2.36 at the time of these surveys.

12. These conclusions are based on findings about job preferences of Malays and Chinese in six villages in Kedah between 1975 and 1977 (M. L. Young, forthcoming).

References

Alatas, S. H. 1967. "The Grading of Occupational Prestige Amongst the Malays in Malaysia." Paper presented at international conference, Comparative Social Research, New Delhi, India, March 27–April 1.

————. 1972. *Feudalism in Malaysian Society: A Study in Historical Continuity, in Modernization, and Social Change.* Sydney: Angus and Robertson.

Ariffin, J. 1981. "Industrialization, Female Labour Migration, and the Changing Pattern of Malay Women's Labour Force Participation—an Analysis of Inter-relationship and Implications." Paper presented at seminar, Population and Sectoral Development, Cameron Highlands, Malaysia, January.

Armstrong, W. and T. G. McGee. 1985. *Theatres of Accumulation: Studies in Asian and Latin American Urbanization.* London and New York: Methuen.

Bromley, R. and C. Gerry. 1979. *Casual Work and Poverty in Third World Cities.* London: Methuen.

Caldwell, J. C. 1963. "Urban Growth in Malaya: Trends and Implications." *Population Review* 7:39–50.

Chan, L. H. 1980. "The Jetty Dwellers of Penang: Incorporation and Marginalisation of an Urban Clan Community." M.Soc.Sc. thesis. Universiti Sains Malaysia, Penang, Malaysia.

Daud, F. 1983. "Women in Industry." *Ilmu Masyarakat* 1:72–76.

Government of Malaysia. 1957. *1957 Population Census.* Report No. 3, State of Penang. Kuala Lumpur: Government Printer.

————. 1970. *General Report, Population Census of Malaysia, 1970 (1).* Kuala Lumpur: Department of Statistics.

————. 1980. *1980 Population Census, Penang State.* Kuala Lumpur: Department of Statistics.

————. 1981. *Fourth Malaysia Plan, 1981–1985.* Kuala Lumpur: Government Printer.

Jomo, K. S. 1984. "Malaysia's New Economic Policy: A Class Perspective." *Pacific Viewpoint* 25:153–72.

————. 1986. *A Question of Class: Capital, State, and Uneven Development in Malaya.* Singapore: Oxford University Press.

Lai, Y. W. and S. E. Tan. 1985. "Industrialization Patterns and Economic Growth in Malaysia." Pp. 291–324 in P. H. Hauser, D. B. Suits and N. Ogawa (eds.), *Urbanization and Migration in ASEAN Development.* Tokyo: National Institute for Research Advancement.

Loh, F. S. P. 1975. *Seeds of Separatism: Educational Policy in Malaya, 1874–1940.* Kuala Lumpur: Oxford University Press.

McGee, T. G. 1971. *The Urbanization Process in the Third World.* London: Bell.

————. 1973. *Hawkers in Hong Kong.* Hong Kong: Centre for Asian Studies, University of Hong Kong.

————. 1978. "An Invitation to the 'Ball': Dress Formal or Informal?" Pp. 3–27 in P. J. Rimmer (ed.), *Food, Shelter, and Transport in Southeast Asia and the Pacific.* Canberra: Australian National University.

————. 1982. "Women Workers or Working Women? Some Preliminary Thoughts on the Proletarianization Process in Export Processing Zones of Southeast and East Asia." Paper presented at conference, Women in the Urban and Industrial Workforce in Southeast and East Asia, Manila, Philippines, November 15–19.

————. 1985. "Mass Markets, Little Markets. Some Preliminary Thoughts on the Growth of Consumption and Its Relationship to Urbanization: A Case Study of Malaysia." Pp. 205–234 in S. Plattner (ed.), *Markets and Marketing.* Monographs in Economic Anthropology, no. 4. New York: University Press of America.

————, ed. 1987. *Industrialization and Labour Force Processes: A Case Study of Peninsular Malaysia*. Research Papers on Development in East Java and West Malaysia, no. 1. Canberra: Research School of Pacific Studies, Australian National University.

McGee, T. G. and Y. M. Yeung. 1976. *Hawkers in Southeast Asian Cities Planning for the Bazaar Economy*. Ottawa: International Development Research Centre.

Narayanan, S. 1975. "Urban In-migration and Urban Labour Absorption: A Study of Metropolitan Urban Selangor." M.Econ. thesis, University of Malaya, Kuala Lumpur.

Onn, F. C. 1986. *Technological Leap: Malaysian Industry in Transition*. Singapore: Oxford University Press.

Pryor, R. 1972. "Malaysians on the Move: A Study of Internal Migration in West Malaysia." Ph.D. dissertation, University of Malaya, Kuala Lumpur.

Salih, K. 1981a. "Malaysia and the World System: A Perspective Essay on Incorporation, Social Groups, and the State." Universiti Sains Malaysia, Penang. Mimeo.

————. 1981b. "Man and Work in the Informal Sector: Implications for Policy and Industrial Relations." Paper presented at the Ninth Asian Regional Conference on Industrial Relations, Tokyo, Japan, March 16–21.

————. 1983. "Urbanization in Malaysia: Impact of the New Economic Policy." Paper presented at Parliamentarian Seminar, Kuala Lumpur, Malaysia, October 5–6.

Salih, K. and F. C. Lo. 1975. *Industrialization Strategy, Regional Development, and the Growth Centre Approach: A Case Study of West Malaysia*. Report presented at seminar, Industrialization Strategies and the Growth Role Approach to Regional Planning and Development, The Asian Experience. Nagoya, Japan, UNCRD.

Salih, K. and M. L. Young. 1981. "Malaysia: Urbanization in a Multiethnic Society— the Case of Peninsular Malaysia." Pp. 117–47 in M. Honjo (ed.), *Urbanization and Regional Development*. UNCRD Regional Development Series, Vol. 6. Singapore: Maruzen Asia.

————. 1985. "Employment, Unemployment, and Retrenchment in Malaysia: The Outlook and What is to be Done about It?" Paper presented at workshop, Industrialization and the Labour Force in Malaysia, Research School of Pacific Studies, Australian National University.

Salih, K., M. L. Young, L. H. Chan, K. W. Loh, and C. K. Chan. 1985. *Young Workers and Urban Services: A Case Study of Penang, Malaysia*. Final Report of Urban Service Project submitted to IDRC, Ottawa. Penang: Universiti Sains Malaysia.

Scott, A. J. 1985. "The Semiconductor Industry in Southeast Asia: Organization, Location, and the International Division of Labour." Working Paper 101. Department of Geography, University of California, Los Angeles.

Tan, H. C. 1972. "Industrial Development in Penang State: Rationale for Industrial Development." *Geographica* 8:56–63.

Tham, S. C. 1977. *Malays and Modernization*. Singapore: Singapore University Press.

White, G. 1984. "Developmental States and Socialist Industrialization in the Third World." *Journal of Development Studies* 22:97–120.

Young, K., W. C. F. Bussink, and P. Hasan. 1980. *Malaysia: Growth and Equity in a Multi-Racial Society*. Baltimore: Johns Hopkins University Press.

Young, M. L. 1979. "Migration and Employment: A Case Study of a Rural Settlement within a Development Scheme in Peninsular Malaysia." Pp. 416–41 in K. Salih (ed.), *Rural-Urban Transformation and Regional Underdevelopment*. Nagoya: UNCRD.

————. 1982. "Migrants and Niches: Economic Structure in Peninsular Malaysia, 1965–1970." Discussion Paper no. 7. School of Social Sciences, Universiti Sains Malaysia, Penang.

————. Forthcoming. *Internal Migration in Peninsular Malaysia: A Structural Analysis*. Ph.D. dissertation, Australian National University, Canberra.

15 The "British Experiment": Structural Adjustment or Accelerated Decline?

Guy Standing

In Britain, as in many other parts of Western Europe, the post-1945 era was marked by a broad social consensus. It was based on the general commitment to "full employment in a free society" and the creation of a comprehensive welfare state. In the late 1970s this social consensus was shattered. Underlying that consensus was an essentially corporatist model that recognized class conflict and that accepted the need for institutional mediations and active state involvement in economic and social affairs. From the 1940s onward, for over thirty years, the determination—among all serious public figures—not to return to the mass unemployment of the 1930s was coupled with the institutionalization of a range of labor rights, which together constituted an integral part of the social consensus. These were

1. labor market security, or state-guaranteed full employment;
2. income security through minimum wages (wages councils), the incorporation of trade unions into the state, national insurance-based social security, and a tax system designed to check the growth of income inequality;
3. employment security through regulations on hiring and firing, prenotification of redundancy, costs imposed on employers for dismissing workers, and restrictions on "unfair dismissal";
4. work security through health and safety regulations, limits on working time, unsociable hours, and so on; and
5. job security through the tolerance of demarcation practices and union-backed barriers to skill dilution.

This last right was less accepted than the other four, but was nevertheless tolerated and fairly common among technically skilled workers and the "middle-class" professions.

These various rights always represented costs to employers, although, to a large extent, such costs were passed on to workers in the form of lower wages. Their consensual acceptability depended not only on stable and positive economic growth but on an approximate consensus on income distribution. It also depended, and most crucially, on what was in effect a "closed international economy," whereby the bulk of trade in manufactured goods and services was conducted between countries with essentially similar levels of labor rights. Full employment in a "mixed economy" and the continuation of other rights depended finally on quid quo pros between employers, unions, and workers, which meant that neither side in the labor process could push for excessive short-term gains without disrupting the consensus.

One can recall the hallmark of that era, a "full employment rate of unemployment," that even Keynes and Beveridge, the two intellectual architects of the social consensus, had thought unlikely—1 percent to 2 percent. That seems a long way off now, but for the better part of three decades the politico-economic framework seemed set, consisting of earnest debate between "little inflationists" and "little deflationists," a conflict of fine tuners.

The Cracking of Social Consensus

Five factors eroded the consensus. What emerged was a society in which a dwindling proportion of the working-age population was in regular, full-time formal employment, which was the overwhelming norm previously. An analysis of the factors that disrupted the postwar system is outside the objective of this chapter. However, it is useful to identify the context in which "the British Experiment" came into existence, for there had to be crisis circumstances for such a departure from preceding social and political norms.

Actually, the five factors were common across much of Western Europe. But in Britain they were particularly disruptive. The first was what is generally described as "de-industrialization," which is more than a shift from manufacturing production and employment to services (Blackaby 1979). For many years after World War II, the United Kingdom struggled to remain in the top league of industrial nations, while slowly untangling itself from its empire. In doing so, the pound sterling was retained as a reserve currency, the value of which was defended on the international currency markets even when clearly overvalued, at lasting cost to manufacturing exports and industrial production.

The problems were compounded by successive governments' resort to "stop-go" policies—periodic bouts of demand deflation to correct the balance-of-payments deficits. That discouraged long-term industrial investment. Then, the entry into the European Economic Community (EEC) threatened great swathes of British industry with intensified import competition and introduced new uncertainties that seem to have led to further investment in the EEC "core" countries rather than the "peripheral" U.K. In a sense, EEC entry represented a first "freeing" of markets, which is the ideological core of the "structural adjustment" package of measures that were to crystallize some years later.

Finally, de-industrialization was accelerated by the changing international division of labor, notably by the industrial emergence of Japan, and the global spread of multinationals, which were increasingly prone to move production to where labor costs were lowest and where governments provided attractive subsidies. Industrialization started to accelerate in the so-called NICs (newly industrialized countries), where there was a flexible, nonunionized, "disciplined" labor supply, without any of the rights institutionalized in the U.K. and in other European economies (McGee et al., this volume). By the 1970s, the "smokestack" industries in the U.K. had begun to crumble, propped up only by steadily growing government subsidies, and labor-intensive sectors wilted under competitive international pressure.

The second eroding factor was inflation. Why inflationary pressures became explosive in the 1970s remains a matter of intense controversy. But to offset creeping de-industrialization and the threat to full employment, governments in Britain, as elsewhere, boosted the nominal gross product by Keynesian demand expansion, which in turn fueled inflationary pressures. The rising price of manufactured goods in industrialized countries such as the United Kingdom worsened the international terms of trade faced by low-income countries producing primary goods, which led to various attempts to form primary product cartels. That trend crystallized in the formation of OPEC, which led to the oil price hikes of 1973 and 1979 and the Great Inflation of the seventies.[1]

In the U.K., inflation and the intensified business uncertainty of the post-1973 years contributed to a drying up of industrial investment and helped undermine the social consensus on income distribution, with employers and unions each trying to increase or retain their share of national income. In response, governments turned to clumsy attempts at prices-and-incomes policy (Henry and Ormerod 1978). And then the goal of full employment was abandoned (Deacon 1981).

A third factor eroding the basis of the social consensus was what seems to have been something like a downswing phase of a long Kondratieff wave (Mandel 1981). This may have started in the late 1960s, when technological change slowed, leading to what has been called "technological stalemate," in which labor-saving process innovations predominated over labor-augmenting product innovations. That contributed to the growing tendency for governments, adhering with increasing difficulty to their commitment to full employment, to adopt an offsetting policy of public sector labor absorption, which in turn strengthened inflationary pressures.

Then in the mid-1970s something like a new long-wave upswing began, with "information technology" becoming a radical new heartland technological development. This development has had four crucial features: it reduced the significance of production economies of scale; it facilitated decentralization of production; it required high levels of capacity utilization; and it made production internationally highly mobile, such that, if least-cost production methods were not feasible or accepted in one region or country, part or all of the production process would be transferred elsewhere (Benton, this volume).

The fourth eroding factor was the tendency for the underlying level of unemployment to rise as a consequence of de-industrialization, import penetration, technological change, inflation, and low levels of industrial investment.

That was also closely linked to the fifth factor, what is commonly called "the fiscal crisis of the state." De-industrialization meant that the public sector had to absorb more and more workers in order to maintain something close to full employment. This meant rising public expenditure, creating budget deficits that required high taxes and interest rates, which tended to impede investment and to reduce employment. This trend, according to a growing minority of vociferous economists, led to a "crowding out" of private investment (e.g., Friedman 1975; Minford 1983). To finance the growing public sector, tax rates as well as interest rates rose, which worsened inflation and almost certainly boosted "black economy" activity and tax evasion.

The halcyon days of Keynesian orthodoxy were gone, and the mid-to-late 1970s were marked by growing social divisions, scrambled late-night holding arrangements, resort to job-saving subsidies to prop up ailing industrial sectors, and a loss of political direction. At the end of 1973, the Conservative government, faced by a national miners strike, put the country on a three-day workweek and called a general election on the issue of "Who governs?" It lost. But laborism's triumph was short-lived and illusory. National humiliation seemed complete when in 1976, the chancellor of the exchequer was forced to appeal to the IMF for credit and to sign a letter of intent to get it, by which deflationary policies were accepted and social reforms postponed (Coates 1980).

Symbolically, one could argue that the "forward march of labor" was halted in that year, and the conditions were henceforth created for a steady crumbling of the "corporatist" apparatus and then the demise of labor rights. For a while, subsidies and defensive "nationalization" of declining industries and firms, coupled with deflation of domestic demand, kept the demand for imports from accelerating. Ad hoc attempts to resurrect a so-called social compact had some temporary success, at least in keeping the level of unemployment down in the face of steady de-industrialization and accelerating inflation. But few people had much faith in such agreements as an economic strategy for industrial regeneration. Everybody waited for North Sea oil, being found in growing quantities and practically given to multinationals to start generating revenue as quickly as possible. It was presumed that the profits and taxes from oil would allow the country freedom from balance-of-payments constraints and would provide a surplus for industrial investment (Department of Energy 1978; Singh 1979).

The bitterness and wrangling of the 1970s, however, led to a suitably shabby end in the so-called winter of discontent in 1978–79, marked by a long strike of public sector dustmen and hospital auxiliaries, which left the streets of London strewn with litter and the hospitals with piles of soiled linen. Time had run out for the old social consensus, and politicans on the far Left and far Right drew comfort from their own specific blueprints.

The political right wing of the Conservative party had been preparing itself for this moment. In the mid-1970s, under the intellectual guidance of Milton Friedman, Friedrich Hayek, and others, monetarism had been resurrected politically (Friedman 1975; Hayek 1975). Long regarded as an outdated doctrine inhabiting the fringes of the economics profession, this was slowly to evolve into the new orthodoxy of the 1980s. In 1979, one of the adherents of this market-oriented school of thought was elected prime minister. What leading members of the new government subsequently described as "the British experiment" was launched. Few people called it that at the outset. However, by the early 1980s, as the supply-side strategy crystallized as a wholesale attempt to transform the socioeconomic structure of Britain, its practitioners, its proselytizers, and observers alike were calling it "the British experiment."[2]

The ideology and general outcomes of this experiment have been reviewed in detail elsewhere (Standing 1986b). In the remainder of this chapter, I will focus on what has been described as the "informalization" of the economy. However, to do so, it is necessary to indicate the main elements of the new supply-side strategy. It was launched under auspicious circumstances, for not only was there a public mood of disillusionment with neo-corporatist social bargaining and alarm at the rate of inflation, but profits from North Sea oil were beginning to flow. Oil created a massive increase in tax revenue which allowed the experiment to be launched without an immediate check via a balance-of-payments crisis (the bane of previous governments).

The British Experiment

Once the magical powers of control over the money supply were recognized to be rather weak, the supply-side economic strategy was buttressed by a desire to restore market capitalism and reverse long-term institutional trends toward "welfare capitalism." This basic policy amounted to a reversal of Keynesianism. In the previous era, governments had used macroeconomic policy (monetary and fiscal mechanisms) to preserve full employment while using microeconomic policy to control inflation. Under the new supply-side strategy, macroeconomic policy was to be set to control inflation, *not* employment or output. This meant that microeconomic policy was made responsible for influencing but *not* determining the level of employment. As the chancellor of the exchequer put it, "It is not sufficiently understood that it simply isn't within the Government's power to determine the level of unemployment."[3]

Supply-side economists believed there was a natural rate of unemployment which could be reduced by removing institutional rigidities that prevented the labor and capital markets from operating effectively. The role of government was criticized as distorting, which led to a crusade to cut public expenditure and subsequently to wholesale privatization. Most crucially, the new orthodoxy questioned all the labor rights established as part of the previous social consensus. What were rights before were now presented as rigidities and costs (Friedman 1975; Minford 1983; Department of Employment 1985).

Thus, the government launched a campaign to promote "labor flexibility." It was believed that wages had to be lowered and that unions had to be weakened. This meant a debilitation of minimum wage regulations, which also meant a weakening of wages councils, traditionally used to provide the weakest groups of workers with some semblance of protection. Government representatives (Tomkins 1985) and supporters (Forrest 1984; Institute of Directors 1984) used more polemic than evidence to attack wages councils and succeeded in 1985 in getting the government to deratify the ILO's Minimum Wage-Fixing Machinery Convention.

Another theme, which gathered force in the mid-1980s, was the removal or dilution of employment protection legislation on the grounds that the new policy would encourage hirings by making it less costly to fire workers. Similarly, job security rules were to be dismantled to allow more efficient and flexible use of labor. And efforts were started to reduce nonwage labor costs, seen again as a general deterrent to employment. The policy translated into fewer benefits for ordinary workers. Symbolically, the most revealing measure was the abolition in 1980 of maternity benefits for women in small-scale firms (Marsden 1986).

Supply-side economists also placed great emphasis on tax reduction, particularly direct income tax and corporate tax. Most of all, taxes paid by high-income earners were to be cut. It is but a slight exaggeration to depict the underlying argument as saying that high-income earners needed more income to give them the incentive to work, whereas low-income earners needed less income to give them the same incentive. Subsidies were granted to entrepreneurs, particularly small businessmen, who were portrayed as bulwarks of the capitalist regeneration of Britain. Finally, the institutional machinery to maintain the social consensus was gradually dismantled, with trade unions pushed from center stage politically and economically.

The evolution of the neoconservative strategy had two phases. In the first, monetarism dominated until intervention in the currency markets had to be dismissed as unworkable. At that point, all macrolevel indicators pointed to failure. Subsequent nonintervention led to a dramatic revaluation of the pound sterling, as North Sea oil converted it into a "petrocurrency." Between 1979 and 1981, the exchange rate rose in real terms by over 40 percent on average against other major currencies (Central Statistical Office 1982). Thus, ironically, market forces "priced out" British manufacturing exports. As capital controls were also abolished, there was a massive outflow of capital, encouraged by the high value of the pound. De-industrialization accelerated.

Manufacturing output fell by an extraordinary 15 percent in 1980–81 (National Economic Development Council 1987). Above all, unemployment shot up. And it did so by much more than anyone advocating the supply-side strategy had predicted—more than doubling between 1979 and 1981. To some, this was evidence enough that the strategy had failed. The government retorted that "there is no alternative," that the unemployment was a temporary necessity, and that it was engaged in a "medium-term strategy" designed to create the conditions for increased economic growth.

The experiment then evolved into its second phase, in which supply-side measures came to the fore. The supply-side economists dismissed concern over what seemed to many critics to be the demise of the "real economy." Manufacturing output had fallen to below what it had been a decade earlier, and two million jobs in manufacturing had disappeared in two or three years. As far as Britain's trading position was concerned, by 1983, for the first time in the country's history, there was a balance-of-trade deficit in manufactured goods. Government supporters argued that this did not matter, because if left to market forces, the balance of payments would always balance and services would pick up the gap. The official argument identified two major obstacles to the success of the experiment. First, remaining regulations and institutional mechanisms were impeding the free play of market forces. Second, public expenditure remained stubbornly high, making it hard to cut taxation.

As far as public expenditure was concerned, the government faced what amounted to a prisoner's dilemma. Severe cutbacks in public sector employment and social services, along with other deflationary policies, had not only reduced tax revenue but had raised the demand for transfer payments from the huge army of unemployed and the growing number of working poor. The government's "short-term" remedy for unemployment consisted of a growing array of so-called special measures, mainly carried out by the government's Manpower Services Commission (MSC). These measures mushroomed after 1979—a highly interventionist part of a strategy designated as "noninterventionist." The MSC budget rose steadily and rapidly, to two thousand million sterling per year by 1986; its staff increased to well over twenty thousand, and the numbers employed in its various programs, to nearly one million (Standing 1986b, chap. 5). Some of these activities were designed to put downward pressure on wages (through subsidizing low-wage jobs, for example), while others were developed to take the unemployed off the register, either into temporary jobs or out of the labor force altogether. Finally, others were developed to give short-term training or to subsidize and encourage self-employment and small-scale businesses.

The persistently high level of public expenditure hindered tax cuts. But in the second phase, beginning in 1982, the government produced a temporary solution to this dilemma. At a gathering pace, there was an unprecedented sale of nationalized corporations—a literal rolling back of the state. In a bookkeeping sense, privatization yielded a huge gain to the public exchequer, even if it meant considerable loss in future income. With that and North Sea oil tax revenue at a peak, direct taxation and the government's structural budget deficit were reduced, though one former conservative prime minister, Harold

Macmillan, just before his death ruefully likened the exercise to "selling the family silver."

The "Medium-Term" Outcome: Labor Market Fragmentation and Unemployment

Any summary assessment of the consequences of the British experiment must do injustice to the nuances of recent developments. Socioeconomic inequality has grown; household income distribution has worsened (Central Statistical Office 1985); the divide between the "rich" south and the "poor" north has expanded; the health of the rich has improved while that of the poor has deteriorated; and so on. All of these trends are practically uncontested (see table 15.1). The most outstanding outcome was, however, the huge loss of jobs, reflecting the accelerated decline of manufacturing and a reversal of the earlier pattern of public sector absorption of the surplus (see table 15.2). Despite some job creation, and the effect of special measures, by early 1987 the total number of unemployed claiming and entitled to benefits was still over three million, well over three times what it had been before the experiment was launched and despite no less than seventeen administrative changes in the way that statistics were calculated, every one of which had had the effect of lowering the total number of unemployed.

It is instructive to realize that for years the official forecasts of what would happen to unemployment proved consistently too optimistic, as shown in table 15.3, which gives the official forecasts of registered adult unemployment and the actual outcomes, *not* taking account of the removal of certain categories from the unemployment count between 1980 and 1983. Thus, in March 1980, the Treasury forecast that in 1981–82 unemployment would *peak* at 1.8 million; the outcome was a figure in excess of 2.6 million, despite measurement changes. The figures simply did not behave as predicted. By the mid-1980s the probable figure was about 15 percent.

Table 15.1 Houshold Income Distribution, 1977–1983

	Before Tax and Benefits		After Tax and Benefits	
Percentile	1977 (%)	1983 (%)	1977 (%)	1983 (%)
1–10	0.00	0.00	3.21	3.12
11–20	1.76	0.36	5.15	4.75
21–40	12.27	9.54	14.00	12.93
41–60	18.08	17.91	18.18	17.52
61–80	25.50	25.93	23.43	23.00
81–100	41.78	46.27	36.04	38.68

Source: Morris and Preston 1986.
Note: Households were adjusted for household size.

Table 15.2 Changes in Employment, 1966–1985

	1966–74 (%)	1974–79 (%)	1979–85 (%)
Manufacturing	−8	−8	−25
Public services	+25	+8	−1
Other	−6	+6	0
Total employees	−2	+2	−8
Self-employed	+19	−5	+38
Employed labor force (incl. HM forces)	−1	+1	−4
Changes in thousands	−225	+245	−1,135

Sources: Date for employed labor force from Department of Employment *Gazette*, London, HMSO, March–April 1986, and *Supplement*, April 1985, table 1.1, p. 4. Sectoral breakdown from National Institute for Economic and Social Research data base.
Note: Figures relate to the second quarter of each year.

Table 15.3 Government Forecasts of Unemployment Compared with Subsequent Actual Unemployment, United Kingdom (in millions) (excluding Northern Ireland), 1979–1985

Date Forecast Made	Date Forecast					
	1979–80	1980–81	1981–82	1982–83	1983–84	1984–85
March 1980	1.25	1.6	1.8			
March 1981		1.81	2.5	2.7	2.7	
March 1982			2.6	2.9		
February 1983				2.74[1]	3.02[2]	
February 1984					2.85[1]	2.85
Actual	1.26	1.82	2.6	2.77	2.85[1]	2.93[2]

Source: *Guardian*, Oct. 25, 1984.
[1]Change in official definition reduced unemployment by about 170,000–190,000.
[2]Average for first six months.

The situation is actually much worse than implied by these figures. The reason is that during the past decade the labor process has indeed become far more "flexible," that is, far more precarious and informal, to the extent that fewer workers are in full-time regular employment covered by the range of labor rights accepted as the norm in the 1970s. This is partly a reflection of government efforts to deregulate the labor market and to encourage the use of temporary and "self-employed" workers. It also reflects industrial restructuring, the new types of technology, and corporate management strategies.

One development has been the shift away from employment in large-scale enterprises, partially reflecting the shakeout of workers from manufacturing after 1979. The largest manufacturing enterprises reduced their work forces very substantially indeed (see table 15.4). In the same period, the size distribution of firms changed such that far more workers were in small establishments (see table 15.5).

Table 15.4 Employment in Large Manufacturing Companies, United Kingdom, 1977–1983

	1977	1983	Percentage of Decline
British Steel	209,000	81,100[1]	61
GEC	156,000	136,944	12
British Leyland	171,943	81,261	53
Courtaulds	112,009	56,336	50
ICI	95,000	61,800	35
British Shipbuilders	87,569	62,583	28
GKN	73,196	33,600	52
Lucas	68,778	49,042	29
TI Raleigh	61,777	25,100	59
Dunlop	48,000	22,000	54
Vauxhall	30,180	20,527	32
Talbot	22,800	7,109	69
Massey Fergusson	21,486	13,066	39

Source: Financial Times, June 11, 1984.

[1] 1982–83 figure. In some cases (British Leyland, British Steel, and TI Raleigh, principally), the full scale of the reduction reflected partially a sale of subsidiaries to other firms.

Table 15.5 Establishment Size in Manufacturing, 1979–1983

Number of Employees	1979 (%)	1983 (%)
1–10	4.0	4.5
11–19	3.5	6.5
20–49	6.0	7.5
50–99	6.8	7.7
100–199	9.5	10.1
200–499	16.1	16.9
500–999	13.2	13.3
1000+	40.9	33.5

Source: U.K. Census of Production.

The outcome of these processes has been labor force fragmentation. At the top there is a small elite, whose salaries, job security, and benefits are tied to the international labor market and "best offer" conditions of multinationals. They have often gone without employment security in the interest of high income. Their living standards on average have risen enormously in the past few years and have gained through "privatized" benefits. Second, there are those in competitive but protected jobs, whose wages or salaries have at least kept pace with inflation, in part due to monopolistic bargaining power of unions or professional restrictive practices. These first two strata were shielded from the post-1979 labor shakeout and have gained in relative employment, job, and income security in the 1980s (Standing 1986b, chap. 3).

The third stratum consists of manual workers in declining labor-surplus sectors, the traditional blue-collar proletariat, whose skills have become increasingly obsolescent with the decline of manufacturing. This has always been a male-dominated group, and despite rearguard actions by its unions, it has become highly vulnerable to the erosion of income and employment security. Many of the new poor in the 1980s have come from this traditional backbone of British industry.

The fourth group might be described as the precariously employed stratum. For the most part, this group consists of those in traditionally labor surplus, low-productivity services. Many are low-paid and as a group have lost with the weakening of wages councils. Many have no statutory or negotiated rights to fringe benefits, corresponding to one operational definition of informal labor (Portes and Benton 1984). Many of these jobs are part-time, temporary, or casual. Many who hold them are self-employed, even if often they are disguised wage workers in reality. In total, while the third stratum above has shrunk, the number in this precarious category has risen very considerably, accounting for all the growth in jobs over the past four or five years. This is the stratum that is expected to continue to grow, just as it has done in the United States (see Sassen-Koob, this volume).

The fifth group consists of what is best described as a *detached stratum,* effectively cut off from the labor market—those unable to enter the employed work force, mostly youths, and those pushed into long-term unemployment or economic inactivity. This segment also multiplied from 1979 onward. By the mid-1980s, there were more people recorded as having been unemployed for more than a year than the total number of unemployed in 1979, and they accounted for over 40 percent of the total. Although this heterogeneous group was somewhat cushioned by the plethora of special measures, its income deteriorated during the experiment (Dilnot and Morris 1983).

According to the influential Institute of Fiscal Studies, between 1979 and 1984 the average unemployed married man lost about 15 percent more of his weekly income as a result of changes in the tax structure, while employed company directors gained 43 percent; senior managers, 19 percent; and middle managers, 7.5 percent. A growing proportion of the poorest households consisted of those with working-age members, and if taxes and benefits are excluded, the share of income going to the poorest 20 percent of households fell by about 60 percent between 1975 and 1983 (Central Statistical Office 1984). In short, not only did the detached stratum grow very substantially but its relative and, in many cases, absolute living standards deteriorated acutely (Low Pay Unit 1986).

Another way of looking at labor force trends is by tracing the shift away from regular full-time employment. By the mid-1980s, only about 40 percent of the adult population in the United Kingdom were in full-time employment, and only just over *half* of the adult male (16+) population were in full-time jobs, a rate lower than in any other EEC country. About one in five wage earners were in part-time jobs, and such jobs were accounting for *all* the net growth in employment by the mid-1980s (see table 15.6). As most were occupied by women, it was not surprising that male unemployment rose above the female rate. Even in 1987, a projection by the University of Warwick's Employment Centre forecast that full-time employment would fall by a further one million by 1990, while part-time temporary jobs and "self-employment" would grow by nearly as much (*Financial Times* 1987).

Official Department of Employment figures issued in February 1987 estimated that the newly called "flexible" labor force—part-timers, temporary workers, homeworkers, and the "self-employed"—expanded by 16 percent between 1981 and 1985; by the latter year, it accounted for 34 percent (8.1 million) of those in employment (*Financial Times* 1987). Meanwhile, the number in full-time regular wage employment had fallen by over a million, a decline of 6 percent over four years.

There has been a very substantial shift from wage- to self-employment since the beginning of the decade, a sustained reversal of the previous long-term trend. Part of the growth of self-employment reflects the informal "survival activities" of unemployed people not entitled to unemployment benefits, and therefore not counted as unemployed. Part of the growth reflects the subsidized support program funded by the government through the MSC, notably its Enterprise Allowance Scheme, which gives small subsistence allowances to unemployed people prepared to invest savings in self-employment work activity. And part of the growth, so widely proclaimed as heralding the emergence of an enterprise economy, turns out to be fictitious. In March 1987, the results of the 1986 Labour Force Survey revealed that the guesstimated growth of self-employment had been vastly overstated in 1985–86 (Department of Employment 1987).

Table 15.6 Employment Changes in Great Britain, 1983–1986

Year[1]		Employees (in thousands, seasonally adjusted)				
	Male	Female Full-time	Female Part-time	Self-employed	Hm Forces	Employed Labor Force
1983–84	−37	+5	+221	+275	+4	+468
1984–85	+46	+3	+174	+108[2]	0	+332
1985–86	−59	−30	+172	+122[2]	−4	+199

Source: Chancellor's Autumn Statement, November 7, 1986.
[1]Figures refer to changes from June one year to June the next.
[2]Figure for self-employment over the last year is a projection based on self-employment growth over the previous 4 years.

So, although self-employment has grown during the time of the experiment, it is difficult to know quite what the figures mean. Many firms appear to have dispensed with employees and then reacquired their services as "self-employed" workers. The workers concerned are thereby put in a difficult position because, while they remain economically dependent on an employer, they are not protected under labor laws that only cover employees. Thus the concept of self-employment in the modern "flexible" labor process should always be treated with skepticism. The image of a self-employed person as a small-scale entrepreneur or an independent craftsman is often deceiving.

In sum, the labor process in the United Kingdom at present can be characterized as increasingly precarious, informal, and flexible. Labor surplus is chronic. And it is much worse than the conventional, official unemployment statistics reveal. In order to identify the appropriate politico-economic strategy for the next decade and beyond, it is essential to recognize the extent and form that this labor surplus is taking.

Statistical Manipulation

The British unemployment figures have been repeatedly redefined downward, as noted earlier. The most crucial change was the administrative decision, in the early 1980s, to exclude from the official count all those without work and seeking it who were not entitled to unemployment benefits. Subsequently, older workers (60+) were largely excluded from the count and, in 1986, more workers of all ages were eased off the register by being denied benefits for failing to adequately answer the new "availability for work" questionnaire. Others no longer qualified for benefits because the waiting period before entitlement for "voluntary" job quitters was extended. Still others were excluded because reduced-rate benefits were abolished for those short-time workers who were hitherto entitled to partial benefits.

Additional workers have been eased out of the labor force, including those long-term unemployed who, in a government exercise called Restart, were persuaded to reclassify themselves as sick or were excluded because they failed to turn up for the interview. Finally, some 700,000 unemployed people have been put into special measures, many of whom have thus been artificially reclassified as either employed or as outside the labor force.

By these numerous means, the real rate of unemployment, which is much greater than the official rate, has been effectively disguised. In the 1980s, the gap, even excluding "discouraged workers," has steadily grown, as indicated in table 15.7. The official rate has thus become a less reliable barometer of the actual state of the labor market. However, precisely because the labor process is becoming more "flexible" and informalized, one needs something like a full-time labor underutilization index that takes into account, for instance, the fact that the employment rate is not the same when over a third of the

Table 15.7 Underlying Unemployment Trends, United Kingdom, 1983–1987 (in thousands of workers)

	March 1983	March 1984	March 1985	March 1986	March 1987	Change: March 1983– March 1987
Official series for U.K. unemployment[1]	2,820	2,964	3,095	3,199	3,043	223
Effect of job creation program[2]	54	114	126	185	241	187
Effect of other administrative changes[3]	69	81	64	39	148	79
"Underlying" level of unemployment	2,943	3,159	3,285	3,423	3,432	489

Source: Charter for Jobs 1987.

[1]Excluding school leavers, seasonally adjusted.
[2]Excluding Youth Training Scheme.
[3]Including Job Release Scheme.

employed are only working part-time or intermittently, or have a job but no work (another growing category). An approximation to such an index has been made elsewhere (Standing 1986b, chap. 1). What it indicates is that—even ignoring the number of people put on special measures and the administrative changes—the official unemployment rate should be multiplied by about 1.3 to get a full-time real equivalent figure.

I have dwelt on this issue at some length because it highlights what has been happening to the principal losers in the British experiment. Above all, there has been a growing dependence on—and need for—state transfers for subsistence survival. There has been a rapidly growing number of people chronically dependent on transfers, that is, welfare benefits in one form or another. There is also a growing number, including many part-time and casual workers, intermittently dependent on transfer benefits. And there are many more people in insecure jobs, including many of those classified as "self-employed," who do not have fringe benefits and income stability.

At the same time, there is evidence that a strengthened form of household dualism has emerged, with multiple-earner households coexisting with multiple-unemployed-person households. While total employment in the country fell by about 750,000 in the first seven years of the experiment, the number of "double" jobholders increased very rapidly—and these are counted twice in the official figures on employment (Charter for Jobs 1987). The haves have been gaining by access to more jobs as well as higher incomes and more fringe benefits, while the have-nots have been losing relatively and absolutely.

Conclusion: Options for the Nineties

Where lies the best hope for the future? Four possible routes may be outlined. First, according to those adhering to the existing course, the past eight years have not been a failure, but a great success. A radical transformation takes time, and if there is mass unemployment, it merely indicates the need for even more labor flexibility, even more deregulation, even more decentralisation, and even more financial assistance for entrepreneurs. In May 1986, a government white paper was published stressing the need for further deregulation and announcing plans to make it easier for small firms to dismiss workers and to charge workers a fee, for the first time, if they wished to bring a case for unfair dismissal before an industrial tribunal (United Kingdom Government 1986).

At the same time, great emphasis is being placed on making the pay system more flexible, notably by giving tax relief to profit-sharing and profit-related pay (PRP) schemes and by discouraging national-level pay bargaining. Such moves promise greater inequality between those in formal full-time jobs and those outsiders who are intermittently employed or more or less permanently detached from the labor market. Meanwhile, the supply-siders persist in arguing that much of the recorded unemployment is voluntary because welfare benefits encourage idleness and discourage risk taking. So, according to them, benefits for the unemployed should be cut in real terms, conditions for their receipt should be tightened, and youths refusing places in short-term "training or community-work schemes should be excluded from benefit entitlement" (Burton 1987).[4]

A second route might be called old labourism, represented by the Labour party and the Trades Union Congress. This would mean an attempted return to neo-corporatism and a re-creation of the social consensus of the 1950s and 1960s. The most atavistic aspect of this route is the desire to return to full employment in the old sense of the term. This path seems overgrown with weeds and impossible to re-create. Regular full-time employment for a growing proportion of the working-age population is not a realistic possibility. As perceptive trade union leaders are recognizing, labor flexibility and informal employment relations are growing. As the Transport and General Workers' Union, the largest union in the country, put it in early 1987, "A new employment pattern is emerging. We either accommodate it or we suffer by it."[5]

A third proposed route out of the labor market crisis is work sharing. If hours of work were cut, if older workers were encouraged to take earlier retirement, if full-time jobs were "split," and if all teenagers were induced to stay at school or in full-time training, it is argued that there would be a sufficient cut in labor supply to radically cut unemployment. Unfortunately, this route is less promising than it seems at first, as most analysts have soon realized (see Standing 1986b, chap. 7). Moreover, it is both arbitrary and potentially inequitable, leading to discrimination against those who are expected to be out of the labor market. Work sharing on a voluntary, equitable basis is a desirable social objective but not an easy cure for mass unemployment.

A fourth, just conceivable, route out of the crisis is one that makes a virtue out of the informalization of the economy. One might call this the social dividend route, though it could also be seen as the nucleus for a new socialist strategy. The premises are that labor process flexibility is growing and, to foster accumulation and economic growth, should be encouraged in ways that also reduce inequalities of income and insecurity. As inequalities in the production process have been growing, so the need has grown to institutionalize mechanisms for sharing out the wealth by means *other than wages*.

Two mechanisms that would reduce economic insecurity and reduce the growth of income inequality are collective profit (or surplus) sharing and the provision of a guaranteed basic income paid by the state to each individual. The former is necessary so that the payment system is made more flexible, an objective behind the rapidly spreading profit-sharing schemes in private corporations. But if it is to be reasonably equitable, it must be collective so that the least-secure workers are less likely to be omitted from profit shares. Problems with implementation of collective profit sharing can only be tackled in the practical application of such schemes, as is being realized in Sweden.

The really important need, however, is for the social security system to be transformed into a means of providing individual income security while allowing and promoting genuine labor flexibility. One way of reconciling flexibility with individual security would be a "social dividend" scheme under which every individual would receive a state-guaranteed basic income. The idea has a long history, but it is one whose time may be coming, partly because stable, full-time "formal" employment (with all the security associated with it) is no longer the norm.

The social income guarantee would be a right of citizenship. The objective, to which all political parties and all governments have been ostensibly committed, is to ensure that everybody has at least enough to cover primary living costs. The principles are straightforward, and the means of implementation, quite feasible. A basic income transfer would be guaranteed to each person as an individual, with a lower amount for those under sixteen but otherwise provided regardless of age, sex, work status, marital status, duration of paid work, or past tax paying. Whether introduced by stages to replace the existing social security system or, much less likely, in one radical reform, the social dividend would replace all existing means-tested benefits, though supplements would be provided to those with special needs that impose intrinsically higher costs of living. Such a system would require an integration of the tax and benefit systems, made technically feasible by computerization. The basic income would be tax free, but all income earned above it would be taxable.

There are three objections to a social income scheme, which have been discussed in more detail elsewhere (Standing 1986a). The first objection is cost. Against that, one can point out that social security already accounts for a third of the GDP and has been the most rapidly growing component of public expenditure. Most extraordinary, about 40 percent of all households in the country already rely on state transfers for well over half of their income, and many more who are entitled to them do not claim them. The second objection is the supply-side response, with the claim that a guaranteed basic income would be a disincentive to work. It would also involve, it is claimed, a huge increase in tax rates, which would represent a further disincentive. There are several replies to this argument. One fact will suffice here: currently, many of the working and nonworking poor face marginal tax rates of 80 percent or more, that is, those in poverty and unemployment traps. With a social income scheme, nobody would face such high rates.

The third objection, coming from old labourism, is that a social income scheme would break the link between income and the labor market and would thus lead to a lowering of wages. Against that, one can merely reply that the link between income and the labor market has already been disrupted by the chronic labour surplus conditions and the precarious nature of many new jobs. Moreover, individuals with a guaranteed income would be better able to resist sweatshop conditions and would have their bargaining position strengthened.

There are many advantages of a social dividend system, which could make it the central feature of a new social consensus. Across Europe, the attractiveness of such a reform and the realization that it is feasible are spreading. There are many points to be settled. But this program would provide a secure basis for a new social existence, in which individuals could pursue various work activities in a flexible manner. In the wake of the supply-side experiment, it offers the chance of putting human concerns and a sense of the future back onto the political and economic agendas.

Notes

Views expressed herein should not be attributed to the International Labour Office.

1. It is important to realize that the establishment of OPEC was not an exogenous event that created the international upheavals, but was, rather, a consequence of the inflationary pressures and international restructuring of the time.

2. Perhaps if the expensive escapade in the South Atlantic had not intervened in 1982 it might have been short-lived. Just before that, the government was most unpopular.

3. Interview, *Observer* (London), March 17, 1985.

4. Significantly, the new Job Training Scheme for those eighteen to twenty-four years old, which provides six hours of training per week for a few months—during which time most participants receive benefits of about $40 per week—has been attacked for having a "workfare" character. If they do not go for "training," they may lose their entitlement to any benefit. Several large unions have urged their members to boycott it (*Independent*, February 14, 1987).

5. *Financial Times*, February 27, 1987.

References

Blackaby, F. 1979. *De-Industrialisation*. London: Heinemann Educational Books.
Burton, J. 1987. *Would Workfare Work?* Buckingham: Employment Research Centre, The University of Buckingham.
Central Statistical Office. 1982. *Economic Trends*. London: HMSO.
———. 1984. *Economic Trends*. London: HMSO.
———. 1985. *Regional Trends*. London: HMSO.
Charter for Jobs. 1987. "Declining Unemployment: A Statistical Illusion?" *Economic Report* 2 (May).
Coates, D. 1980. *Labour in Power?* London: Longmans.
Deacon, A. 1981. "Unemployment and Politics in Britain since 1945." Pp. 59–88 in B. Showler and A. Sinfield (eds.), *The Workless State*. Oxford: Martin Robertson.
Department of Employment. 1985. *Employment: The Challenge for the Nation*. London: HMSO.
———. 1987. *Gazette*. March.
Department of Energy. 1978. *The Challenge of North Sea Oil*. London: HMSO.

Dilnot, A. and C. Morris. 1983. "Private Costs and Benefits and Unemployment: Measuring Replacement Rates." *Oxford Economic Papers* 35:321–40.

Financial Times. 1987. Feb. 27.

Forrest, D. 1984. *Low Pay or No Pay? A Review of the Theory and Practice of Minimum Wage Laws.* London: Institute of Economic Affairs.

Friedman, M. 1975. *Unemployment versus Inflation? An Evaluation of the Phillips Curve.* London: Institute of Economic Affairs.

Hayek, F. 1975. *Full Employment at Any Price?* London: Institute of Economic Affairs.

Henry, S. G. B. and Ormerod, P. A. O. 1978. "Incomes Policy and Wage Inflation: Empirical Evidence for the U.K., 1961–1977." National Institute for Economic Research *Review* 85:31–39.

Institute of Directors. 1984. *Wages Councils—the Case for Abolition.* London: Institute of Directors.

Low Pay Unit. 1986. *Low Pay Review* 23.

Mandel, E. 1981. "Explaining Long Waves of Capitalist Development." *Futures* 13:332–38.

Marsden, E. 1986. "Small Firms and Labour Markets in the U.K." International Institute for Labour Studies, Geneva. Mimeo.

Minford, P. 1983. *Unemployment: Cause and Cure.* Oxford: Martin Robertson.

Morris, N. and I. Preston. 1986. "Taxes, Benefits, and the Distribution of Income, 1968–1983." *Fiscal Studies,* November 1986, 18–27.

National Economic Development Council. 1987. *Capacity and Investment.* Memorandum by the Director General. June.

Portes, A. and L. Benton. 1984. "Industrial Development and Labor Absorption." *Population and Development Review* 10:589–611.

Singh, A. 1979. "North Sea Oil and the Reconstruction of UK Industry." Pp. 202–24 in F. Blackaby (ed.), *De-industrialisation.* London: Heinemann Educational Books.

Standing, G. 1986a. "Meshing Labour Flexibility with Security: An Answer to British Unemployment?" *International Labour Review* 125:87–106.

———. 1986b. *Unemployment and Labour Market Flexibility: The United Kingdom.* Geneva: ILO.

Tomkins, W. 1985. *Consultative Paper on Wages Councils.* London: Department of Employment.

United Kingdom Government. 1986. *Building Business . . . Not Barriers.* White Paper. London: HMSO.

Conclusion: The Policy Implications of Informality

Alejandro Portes, Manuel Castells, and Lauren A. Benton

The Changing Geometry of Informalization

The multiple manifestations of the process of informalization in different settings may discourage even the boldest analyst from attempting a comprehensive set of propositions. It seems as if every study contradicts the conclusions reached by the previous one and is questioned, in turn, by the ones that follow. And yet it is clear that, behind all these differences, there is a common core of social and economic reality which all serious studies on the topic highlight. Thus, the negation of a universal process and the return to a case-by-case approach as a way out of bewildering empirical diversity will not do. Instead, we must face the challenge posed by this heterogeneity by reflecting on what empirical inquiry tells us about its origins.

Variations in the form and effects of the informalization process are not random, but reflect the character of the specific social and economic order in which they occur. The changing geometry of the formal-informal relationship follows the contours delineated by economic history as well as the character of state authority and its interaction with private interests. The development of the unregulated sector depends very much on the form adopted by the regulated one, for each, mirrorlike, reflects the other, or, to suggest an alternative analogy, both fit as parts of the same puzzle.

There is thus no great secret in the diversity of the formal-informal interface. Every concrete situation has in common the existence of economic activities that violate or bypass state regulation, but what these are varies according to the history of state-society and state-economy relations. Hence, what is informal and perhaps persecuted in one setting may be perfectly legal in another; the same activity may shift its relative location across the formal-informal cleavage many times; and, finally, the very notion of informality may become irrelevant in those cases in which state regulation of economic relations is nil.

Such cases are rare indeed, however, and their very scarcity supports our assertion in the first chapter about the universality of the informal economy. Reasons that account for the observed heterogeneity of the process also help explain its second feature—a global character. The complexity of modern economies requires some sort of state regulation; this regulation is likely to be extensive, even in those cases in which authorities are imbued with laissez-faire ideology. From issuing the currency and regulating the financial system to monitoring the supply and training of the labor force to arbitrating disputes among private interests, the presence and interference of the state in economic life is not a contingency but a structural requirement of modern civilization. This fact ensures that a "formal sector" of some sort will exist even in the least-developed nations and, therefore, that its elusive counterpart will also be present.

It is but a slight exaggeration to assert that formality begets informality, insofar as one is meaningless without the other. The process actually takes three distinct forms: First, economic activities may be informalized *passively,* through no fault of the participants, as it were. This occurs when state regulation extends to new, previously unmonitored areas converting practices that were, until then, part of the normal economy into underground activities. Thus the decision of the Soviet state, described by Grossman, to forbid almost all independent artisanal production for the market turned this previously legitimate activity into an informal and even criminal one (see chap. 8).

Second, informality may come about through the efforts of firms and other private interests in a regulated economy to gain market advantage by avoiding some state controls. This second path may be labeled *competitive,* insofar as it is the lure of higher profits or the threat of loss, because of internal or foreign competition, which drives the process. The bulk of case studies reported in the empirical literature on advanced and newly industrialized countries reflects this trend. The rapid decentralization of the garment industry in New York City, described by Sassen-Koob, provides a notable contemporary example (see chap. 3).

Finally, there is a process of informalization which takes place precisely because formal rules and controls exist, through manipulation of their application for private gain. The causal role of formal regulation in the origins of informality is nowhere clearer than in these instances, because it is the very existence of state-imposed controls which generates a "market" for exceptional treatment with respect to them. Official corruption represents an informalization *of privilege,* insofar as sellers are usually members of the very state apparatus entrusted with the application of rules, and buyers are those who can afford profitable exemptions from compliance. The trade in selected posts within the Bolivian state bureaucracy, described by Blanes, offers a poignant illustration, insofar as the price commanded by an office is in direct relation to the "gatekeeper's rents" available to its holder (see chaps. 7 and 8).

The near-universal presence of state regulation and the informal arrangements that it fosters pretty much guarantee that the global character of these practices will not be temporary. Instead, they may be expected to remain a resilient feature of the world economy. In addition, the extraordinary diversity in manifestations of this process should not obscure the existence of several typical situations with identifiable profiles and consequences. Capecchi makes the point by distinguishing situations in which informal arrangements are required for sheer survival; those in which they interlock, in a subordinate role, with institutions of the formal economy; and, finally, those that offer the potential for autonomous growth (see chap. 10). We follow his lead below by examining consequences of these practices for both individuals and collectivities and the conditions under which the informal economy can function in ways other than as a reservoir of overexploited labor.

Exploitation and Growth

The political discovery of the informal economy has led to sweeping and contradictory evaluations of its significance and effects. In answer to the question—What are we to do with the informal sector?—figures of the political left have roundly condemned these practices as a throwback to the nineteenth century and have called for greater government and trade-union vigilance against unscrupulous employers. On the opposite side, the informal sector is celebrated as a reassertion of the entrepreneurial spirit, and its achievements are extolled as an example of what could be accomplished if the entire economy would follow suit. In Latin America, for example, a well-orchestrated and well-financed campaign has promoted wholesale informalization as the best solution to these countries' endemic economic crises.[1]

More serious research on the character of the informal economy and its relationship to the regulated sector casts doubt, however, on these laissez-faire advocates' rosy predictions. The weight of empirical results is much heavier on the negative side, which makes questionable the viability of a development strategy based on informalization. These results indicate that negative consequences of the process are endured not only by workers—who must cope with low wages, insecure jobs, and lack of occupational safeguards—but also by entire industries in which resort to backward and exploitative labor arrangements creates a strong disincentive for technological innovation. As Benería points out, the naïveté of a developmental policy for Third World countries based on informal enterprise lies in ignoring the poor capitalization and backward technology of most of these initiatives and their dependence for survival on inputs and demand from the larger firms (see chap. 9). Thus, the true engine of economic growth in many countries, including industrialized nations, continues to be the large-scale formal firm, in relation to which informal enterprises play mainly a supplementary and subordinate role.

Yet an a priori position against the informal economy would also lack empirical support. In some selected instances, we find nonideological accounts of positive effects of informalization for households, communities, and even entire regions. For example, Roberts describes the close fit between informal employment and particular stages of the life cycle among working-class households of Guadalajara; in a similar vein, Fernández-Kelly and García, Ybarra, and Fortuna and Prates document the situational advantages of informal home-work for women laborers compelled to balance income-earning activities with household tasks (see chaps. 2, 4, 11, 13). At a higher level of inclusiveness, Sassen-Koob portrays the significance of informal enterprise for the viability and growth of ethnic neighborhoods in New York City, and Stepick relates how modest informal initiatives laid the groundwork for the vigorous emergence of a Cuban enclave economy in Miami (see chaps. 3, 6).

Two different types of positive assessments of informalization must be distinguished, however. The first contrasts the availability of unregulated enter-prise and employment with *the absence of alternatives*. In these instances—in which the reference point is usually the individual, household, or immediate neighborhood—the advantages of the informalization process emerge only when these activities are compared with the closure of opportunities in the regulated economy. Formal work is seen as preferable but, given its scarcity, irregular occupations—even when insecure and poorly paid—are better than nothing. Similarly, stable working-class neighborhoods based on a regular-wage labor force remain the norm, but given accelerated de-industrialization and the consequent loss of good jobs, informal enterprise is seen as a better alternative than total destitution.

Such relative evaluations are not particularly encouraging because they uphold implicitly the superiority of the model based on absorption of the labor force into the formal economy. There are a few exceptional instances, however, in which the process of informalization appears to have consequences superior to those of a model of development based on large-scale enterprises and a fully regulated labor market. Such instances are usually regional in scope; that is, the advantages of the process extend well beyond the worker and his immediate circle to encompass an entire local economy.

The archetypal example is central Italy, where informal artisanal enter-prises have evolved into a complex network of small-scale firms specializing in different facets of high-tech and high-fashion products. Advantages for indi-vidual workers, in terms of income and realization of their creative potential, are matched by regional gains, in terms of lower-than-average rates of unem-ployment, a more egalitarian income distribution, and high export earnings. This successful experience has gained much attention in recent years and has prompted enthusiastic arguments in favor of the model of "flexible specializa-tion" (Piore and Sabel 1984). As Capecchi points out in this volume, however, the origins of the Emilian industrialization experience are complex and include several sui generis circumstances not easily found elsewhere (chap. 10).

A second exceptional example is that of Miami, where the exodus of the Cuban middle class following the Cuban Revolution prompted the growth of informal enterprise in some sectors and the informalization of others. Mak-ing use of their past business experience and of the peculiar solidarity fostered by a common past, informal entrepreneurs were able to expand and move in force into the regular economy. Their success opened opportunities, in turn, for later arrivals. The development of this ethnic enclave—from informal enterprise to present large-scale firms—has had positive consequences for participants as well as for the overall urban economy, which has expanded rapidly in recent years (Boswell and Curtis 1984; Botifoll 1984). However, as Stepick makes clear, the benefits have not reached all members of the local population; in particular, recent immigrants—such as Haitians—remain marginal to the growth sectors and to integrated entrepreneurial development (chap. 6).

A third example is that of Hong Kong. As noted in chapter 1, an extraordinarily successful export economy has been built in this island on the basis of networks of small and informal producers who market their products through specialized import-export houses. Wages paid to workers, often recent refugees from the mainland, are low, but this is somewhat compensated by an extensive system of free or low-cost public services provided by the Crown government. The condition of the Hong Kong working class thus lacks the features of extreme poverty and vulnerability to overexploitation characteristic of informal workers elsewhere, while the very dynamism of the export economy generates opportunities for individual moves into self-employment (Castells 1984; Sit, Wong, and Kiang 1979).

Instances of informal economies of growth are clearly exceptional and do not justify the celebration of "flexible specialization," enclave economies, or small-scale export production as generalizable solutions to economic underdevelopment. As noted previously, the existing research literature leads to a definite rejection of predictions concerning the benefits of wholesale informalization, particularly in the Third World. At the same time, successful experiences are sufficiently important and have proven resilient enough to deserve careful attention. The central questions are what features, if any, these historical experiences have in common and to what extent they are transferable to other settings. Depending on the answers, such instances may be considered fortunate, but irreproducible, accidents or may, alternatively, provide a basis for cautious optimism about implementation of decentralization policies at least in some areas.

Characteristics of Informal Economies of Growth

There are several features that successful instances of informalization possess in common. First, small enterprises in these instances are not limited to production of labor-intensive, low-technology goods, but at least some of them have been able to capture a niche in upscale segments of the market. In the Italian and Chinese cases, this was accomplished through the innovative adaptation of imported production technology. Given the particular characteristics of the south Florida economy, Cuban small-scale enterprise has moved toward the provision of a wide variety of both consumer and producer services (Portes 1987).

Second, goods and services produced by small informal enterprise are not limited to the supply of the local market but possess a strong "export orientation." As described by Capecchi, Brusco, and others, the system of flexible specialization leads many small firms to concentrate on the production of components rather than final products. The latter, however, are generally destined for the export market. Similarly, production of clothing, footwear, furniture, food products, cigars, and the like by small firms in Miami meets a sizable local demand, but also reaches beyond it to the broader U.S. market; producer services in this setting are also strongly oriented toward the export sector (see Brusco 1982; Piore and Sabel 1984; Capecchi and Pugliese 1978; Boswell and Curtis 1984; Botifoll 1984; Portes 1987).

Third, small enterprises in each of these instances are relatively independent, rather than integrated into vertical hierarchies of subcontracting, as those documented by Benería in Mexico City and Fortuna and Prates in Montevideo (see chaps. 4, 9). Although extensive subcontracting does occur in every case, the absence of large formal firms that dominate the process and impose their own terms on smaller ones means that the latter possess greater flexibility both in the organization of production and in final marketing.

The three features of technological advancement, export orientation, and relative autonomy highlight similarities in descriptive accounts of informal economies of growth. They do not say anything, however, about what is common to the origins of these experiences or what explains their success vis-à-vis the mainstream logic of large-scale firms and exploited informal labor. In her analysis of the Madrid electronics industry, Benton describes an intermediate case in which technologically advanced small firms that possess many of the features of flexible specialization have emerged without quite achieving the complexity or resilience of the Emilian or Hong Kong models (see chap. 12). This incomplete development provides a useful point of reference for the analysis of causal factors by highlighting systematic differences with instances of successful informalization.

Although differences in the forms adopted in each case are not trivial, it is possible to identify three significant points of convergence.

Government Support

Contrary to the conventional government response to informal activities as a form of tax evasion, the posture of state agencies in each instance of growth has been one of support. This positive approach has not been limited to tolerating informality as a survival mechanism for the poor or as a means to increase competitiveness of formal sector firms; nor has it merely promoted the process for the private enrichment of state functionaries.

Instead, every successful instance registers evidence of an official attitude that downplays the lack of observance of certain rules and actively supports the growth of entrepreneurial ventures through training programs, credit facilities, marketing assistance, and similar policies. To be noted is that general support at the level of national governments seems less important than local actions by regional offices or by municipal and provincial authorities. Thus, for example, Capecchi notes that the beginnings of the Emilian experiment featured a national government indifferent if not hostile to local initiatives, but that early artisanal enterprise received the strong support and assistance of the regional government.

In Miami, as Stepick notes, Cubans were accorded a favorable U.S. government reception as refugees from communism. Subsequently, local branches of the federal government—such as the Cuban Refugee Center under the old Health, Education, and Welfare Department and the Small Business Administration under the Commerce Department—proceeded to implement an extensive program of refugee assistance. Occupational retraining and educational and commercial loans gave Cubans a head start seldom granted to immigrant groups in the United States (Pedraza-Bailey 1985; Díaz-Briquets and Pérez 1981). Although this support alone does not account for the rise of the Cuban enclave economy, the existence of these programs plus official tolerance toward incipient refugee enterprises contributed significantly to their rapid growth.

In Hong Kong, credit and marketing assistance for small producers is supplemented by a vast subsidized network of public services in such areas as housing, education, health, and transportation, which effectively reduces the cost of both skilled and unskilled labor for the enterprises while ensuring basic living standards for the workers (Castells 1986). In Madrid, on the other hand, informal shops initiated by electronics engineers and technicians have developed without effective assistance from the government. This situation explains, at least in part, the precarious state of this otherwise promising initiative.

Entrepreneurial Environment

The remaining points of convergence lack the tangible character of the first, belonging more properly to the sociocultural realm in which economic activity is embedded. In contrast with most situations, there is, in each instance of growth, a concatenation of historical events which leads to unusual receptivity to technological innovation and entrepreneurial opportunities among the people involved. Knowledge of basic aspects of the production process in a particular industry or of the ins and outs of a specific trade is not acquired spontaneously and often requires formal training or extensive periods of apprenticeship.

In each of the relevant instances, an exceptional set of circumstances produced a concentration of entrepreneurial abilities in a given location and the consequent emergence of a strong business culture in which later arrivals were socialized. The exodus of Shanghai merchants and industrialists to Hong Kong and of the Cuban middle class to Miami provided the initial impetus in these instances, creating, at the receiving points of each migration, a critical mass of would-be entrepreneurs. In Emilia-Romagna, the origins of a strong artisanal culture in the metallurgical and textile industries date back to the prominent commercial role of Bologna and its periphery since the Middle Ages and to the establishment of technological schools for workers in the nineteenth century.

As a result of these non-ordinary sets of circumstances, there is, in each of these situations, a sociocultural environment in which the business successes of former workers serve as models for their own employees and in which the small scale of enterprises puts acquisition of requisite skills within reach of would-be entrepreneurs. The business drive to imitate successful others is conceivable in these contexts of numerous and viable small firms. In contrast, it becomes much less credible in communities of wage-workers, dependent on large Fordist-style industries, and even less so in impoverished inner-city areas where both autochthonous enterprise and apprenticeship opportunities are nearly absent.

Bonds of Solidarity

The least-tangible factor characterizing informal economies of growth is the existence of a common identity that binds together participants, somehow distinguishing them from members of the surrounding population. The significance of such ties is that they provide the basis for an overarching solidarity that facilitates, in turn, cooperation among small firms and nonconflictual relations with workers. Well-defined communities with a common history create a set of rules of conduct and obligations which can alter, in significant ways, what would otherwise be pure market relationships. Thus, complementarity rather than cutthroat competition may come to characterize relations among small entrepreneurs, and relationships of "complicity," rather than exploitation, may become the norm between employers and employees.

In Italy, the basis for solidarity stemmed from a common class ideology that isolated the "red" central provinces, and in particular their working class, from the Christian Democratic national government to the south and large-scale industry to the north. Cooperatives of small producers thus emerged as a peculiar case of "proletarian" capitalism, guided by the conscious intent of regional leaders and the independent artisan traditions of the region. This kind of flexible and cooperative specialization among enterprises is absent, for example, in the Madrid experience in which neither trade unionism nor common political socialization provides a basis for transcending atomized market relations among small firms and their workers.

In Miami, the basis for solidarity is a common language and culture plus the experience of a major political upheaval. As numerous accounts of the rise of this ethnic economy emphasize, its common national origin underlies every aspect of internal economic relations—from the unsecured access to credit by Cuban entrepreneurs on the basis of their pre-exile business reputation to the particularistic preferences of Cuban employers in hiring and promotion.

Like the emergence of an entrepreneurial environment, the presence of a communal basis of solidarity underlying economic activity is the result of exceptional circumstances. The normative situation is one in which participants in informal enterprise—workers and employers alike—are no different, nor do they see themselves as different, from the rest of the local population. A female homeworker in Mexico City and the middleman who gives her work seldom share anything that sets them apart from, say, factory workers and their bosses in the same industry. In both cases, market relations are predominant, and informal ties tend to be characterized, more often than not, by exploitation rather than "complicity."[2]

Policies toward the Informal Sector

The evidence presented in this book suggests that the processes and profile of the informal economy are historically specific, depending upon the relationship between the state, capital, and labor in each country. Therefore, it is not possible to formulate, even at a very general level, policy guidelines that would be applicable everywhere. We can, however, extract some lessons from the processes observed and enumerate their basic implications for policymakers attempting to deal with informal restructuring of their economies. The identification above of different types of informality yields several important conclusions. First, despite the enthusiasm awakened by experiences such as that of central Italy, attempts to "transfer" experiences elsewhere must be regarded with skepticism. There are unique features of history and culture underlying each successful experience which can not be easily reproduced in other settings.

Even more dangerous are ideological campaigns that portray these instances as examples of what "getting the state out of the economy" can accomplish. As seen above, a necessary if not sufficient condition for dynamic informalization is precisely getting the state *into* the economy in support of small-scale entrepreneurial initiatives. A positive official posture toward these activities, plus training, credit, and marketing support programs, emerge, in every instance, as a sine qua non for their development. Arguments that advertise wholesale informalization as a cure for the ills of underdevelopment, such as those currently promoted by the "Freedom and Democracy" movement in Lima, are doubly wrong. First, the laissez-faire capitalism that would follow could seriously weaken the formalized sectors of industry and the working class, the demand from which is the only source of dynamism for such informal enterprise as exists in Third World countries. Second, the argument suggests that such reform is all that is needed to unlock the energies and creative capacities of informal entrepreneurs; as empirical studies repeatedly indicate, even the most promising informal initiatives cannot go very far in the absence of solid outside assistance.

A second, related conclusion is that state policies that have proven so far most beneficial to informal economic growth are those implemented at the local level. Such policies have shown greater effectiveness perhaps because regional agencies are not embroiled in the types of policy debates which often paralyze national-level initiatives. Nor do regional policymakers have to consider implications of their efforts for macroeconomic objectives. The latter concerns may help explain the slowness with which most national governments have adjusted economic policies to respond to decentralization and informal sector expansion.

Finally, in those exceptional instances in which sociocultural conditions favor the development of informal economies of growth and in which state agencies are able and willing to promote them, support must go well beyond exclusively economic measures. More important than access to large sums of money, as the cases reviewed in this book suggest, is the central role of an environment in which entrepreneurial opportunities are both visible and within reach of persons of modest resources. Albeit few in number, informal economies of growth demonstrate the creative potential of common people once threats to their very survival are removed and once they are enmeshed in contexts that promote autonomy while protecting them from unbridled competition.

In summary, the findings underscore the need for innovative state responses to a novel economic trend, rather than a return to earlier models of either rigid planning and control or simple deregulation. The process of informalization generates simultaneously pitfalls and opportunities for local labor absorption and economic growth. Effective action to promote the latter requires a shift in the style of government intervention, but not its abandonment.

Proletarianization and the Class Struggle

Having examined the various forms assumed by the informal economy and characteristics of regional success stories, it is time to return in this last section to the more global consequences of the process. Regardless of their specific form, the real-life events described in this book question the tenability of a basic assumption in theories of modern industrial development. This is the belief that economic development leads inexorably to the incorporation of the working-age population into regular labor relations dominated by the wage bond. As noted in chapter 1, the assumption of progressive incorporation of the labor force into modern wage and salary relations is enshrined in both orthodox liberal and neo-Marxist theories of development. Depending on the school, the belief is labeled "full" labor utilization or "proletarianization."[3]

The assumption has many consequences, of which the most important is an image of class structure composed of a mass of organized wage and salary earners, on the one hand, and of managers and owners, on the other. Class struggles, confrontation, and bargaining are expected to proceed along this basic divide. Academic theories of these processes as well as state actions toward them rely on the same imagery. The consequence of informalization, regardless of the form that it assumes, is to subvert the logic of the proletarianization process by introducing multiple arrangements that defy incorporation into a regular mold. In the advanced capitalist countries, industrial workers cease to be workers to become self-employed artisans, part-time home laborers, odd-jobbers, or small entrepreneurs; in the capitalist periphery, the expected absorption of labor into formal relations fails to materialize, as modern firms continue to rely on multiple subcontracting arrangements. Finally, in those most apparently formalized structures—the socialist command economies—ingenious informal initiatives continuously bypass and subvert state regulation.

To the extent that informal relations persist and expand, their most general consequence is to blur the profile of the class structure and alter expected patterns of class relations and struggle. There are still dominant and subordinate groups, to be sure, but their interactions adopt a multiplicity of forms at variance with the model of increasing homogeneity portrayed by conventional theories of industrial development. Industrial unions can not be organized when factories cease to exist; proletarian mobilization becomes more difficult when the formal proletariat represents a shrinking component of the labor force and its remaining members fear for their privileges; employers can not be easily confronted when they remain well-concealed under multiple layers of subcontracting.

The advantages that informalization holds for employers must figure high among the forces promoting the process in capitalist countries, for it is certainly more effective to weaken the organized proletariat through plant closures and decentralization than to dissolve its rallies with police. The new geometry of class relations created by these developments confronts trade unions and other organizations of the working class with a challenge that, so far, has not been met effectively. In command economies, on the other hand, informalization is ironically a tool in the hands of urban workers and peasants to confront the all-powerful state. In certain national instances, such as that of Hungary, the informal economy has proven strong enough to compel state managers to gradually yield to its logic (Rev 1986; Sabel and Stark 1982).

Informalization may be seen from this position as an instrument wielded by different participants in the class struggle, depending on the overall organization of the economy. The outcome, in all cases, is to alter the original class structure and blur the lines demarcating its points of cleavage. More broadly, informality, as the obverse of proletarianization, has expanded rapidly because of the increasing obsolescence of the model of triangular relationships between capital, labor, and the state institutionalized in most countries during the last half century or so. When institutions fail to reflect the changing reality of social and economic organization, this reality emerges through the cracks with singular force, sometimes as social movements but most often as novel adaptive mechanisms.

In the past, the assumption of relentless proletarianization has been defended with the argument that reversals in the process are but "blips" in a long-term trend.[4] Economic downturns are particularly propitious for such reversals and for the return to backward labor practices. During upswings, however, these practices are likely to fall by the wayside as incorporation into modern labor relations restarts and expands. As noted in chapter 1, it is true that the recent global expansion of the informal economy coincided with and was partially due to the world economic recessions of the mid-1970s and early 1980s. It is doubtful, however, that the events that took place during this time and that are documented at length in the above chapters represent only a passing phase to be reversed in future years.

Unlike the results of past global downturns, the main outcome of the last one was not the mere expulsion of part of the proletariat into the ranks of the unemployed but the *reorganization* of economic activities into decentralized arrangements that have acquired their own momentum. Interests of firms in less rigid and more profitable forms of production combine with those of former proletarians in personal survival and, at times, in economic autonomy to promote these novel practices. New entrants in the labor force—such as women, the young, and immigrants—tapped to fill the less-skilled, lowest-paid category of occupations in informalized enterprise can not be easily returned whence they came. More important, new technological innovations—primarily those in informatics—make possible decentralization of industrial activities on an increasingly routinized basis going well beyond the initial impulse provided by the economic crisis.

If the process of informalization is here to stay, and if its principal practical consequence is to alter the character of class structures and struggles, the obvious final question is how to confront this reality. The analysis of informal economies of growth above indicates how, under certain circumstances, the process can be turned to the advantage of direct producers and small entrepreneurs. In the vast majority of cases, however, the process in capitalist economies serves to strengthen the hand of the dominant class and to weaken labor's organizations. The challenge then is how to develop new organizational forms as flexible as the new arrangements and which respond to the emerging needs and interests of participants.

As Standing notes in the case of Great Britain, a return to the past through the use of state police powers is no longer feasible. The task under these circumstances is how to redefine the struggle for equality in terms other than wage levels, working hours, and benefits attached to conventional employment. A key policy issue in this respect is finding means to break the direct link between social benefits and employment in private firms. A new Social Contract in which governments would guarantee minimum living standards and security to people as people and not as workers, would do away with the most socially wrenching consequences of decentralization and informality. A guaranteed social wage would remove the burden of benefits financing from payroll taxes and thus reduce much of the incentive for concealment and exploitation of workers. The successful Hong Kong informal economy begins to approach this model of economic reorganization.

The ultimate lesson to be learned from the evidence has, therefore, a double character. First, the conventional image of industrial development on which past policies and struggles were based must give way to a new one that reflects a world made more complex by the strategies of owners to reassert hegemony and those of workers to survive and gain autonomy under the new conditions. Second, the regressive features of the process which threaten to do away with decades of social progress can only be reversed by a new contract between the state, business, organized labor, and the new social actors (women, ethnic minorities, youth groups, etc.). Such agreement would reinforce the features of flexibility and dynamism in the new model of economic organization, while breaking its reliance on vulnerable labor. Until then, the Janus-like profile of informality will endure as a promise of growth and individual liberation marred by the threat to living standards and painfully gained social equality.

Notes

1. This campaign is centered in an organization called the Institute for Freedom and Democracy in Lima. Through a series of pamphlets and articles, the institute has conducted an active campaign in recent years in defense of full informalization of the economies of the region. See DeSoto 1987.

2. The above sets of special features characterizing informal economies of growth are clearly interrelated. Distinctive group identities underlie the creation of measures that are specifically tailored to meet local needs; thus successful implementation of government policies to support informal enterprises occurs in the political "space" created by regional or ethnic differentiation. Similarly, entrepreneurial culture owes its emergence in these cases as much to political and economic conditions as it does to cultural proclivities. Under other conditions, would-be entrepreneurs may choose to apply their energies differently (for example, by emigrating or by working their way up inside formal enterprises) or they may, in the absence of a strong basis for group solidarity, face insurmountable obstacles to forming successful small enterprises.

3. On this point see the classic treatise by W. Arthur Lewis (1959). See also García and Tokman 1985; Wallerstein 1974, 1976; and Portes and Sassen-Koob 1987.

4. See, for example, Wallerstein (1974) and Hopkins and Wallerstein (1977) who describe proletarianization as the principal "secular" trend of the world economy.

References

Boswell, T. D. and J. R. Curtis. 1984. *The Cuban-American Experience*. Totowa, N.J.: Rowman & Allanheld.

Botifoll, L. J. 1984. *How Miami's New Image was Created*. Occasional Paper no. 1985-1, Institute of Interamerican Studies, University of Miami.

Brusco, S. 1982. "The 'Emilian' Model: Productive Decentralization and Social Integration." *Cambridge Journal of Economics* 6:167–84.

Capecchi, V. and E. Pugliese. 1978. "Due Citta a Confronto: Bologna e Napoli." *Inchiesta* 9.

Castells, M. 1984. "Small Business in a World Economy: The Hong Kong Model, Myth and Reality." Pp. 161–223 in "The Urban Informal Sector: Recent Trends in Research and Theory." Conference Proceedings. Department of Sociology, The Johns Hopkins University. Mimeo.

———. 1986. "The Shek Kip Mei Syndrome: Public Housing and Economic Development in Hong Kong." Working Paper. Centre of Urban Studies, University of Hong Kong. Mimeo.

DeSoto, H. 1987. *El Otro Sendero*. Buenos Aires: Sudamericana.

Díaz-Briquets, S. and L. Pérez. 1981. "Cuba: The Demography of Revolution." *Population Bulletin* 36:2–41.

García, N. and V. Tokman. 1985. *Acumulación, Empleo y Crisis*. Santiago de Chile: PREALC.

Hopkins, T. and I. Wallerstein. 1977. "Patterns of Development of the Modern World-System." *Review* (Fall):111–45.

Lewis, W. A. 1959. *The Theory of Economic Growth*. London: Allen and Unwin.

Pedraza-Bailey, S. 1985. *Political and Economic Migrants in America: Cubans and Mexicans*. Austin: University of Texas Press.

Piore, M. and C. Sabel. 1984. *The Second Industrial Divide*. New York: Basic Books.

Portes, A. 1987. "The Social Origins of the Cuban Enclave Economy of Miami." *Sociological Perspectives*.

Portes, A. and S. Sassen-Koob. 1987. "Making it Underground: Comparative Material on the Informal Sector in Western Market Economies." *American Journal of Sociology* 93:30–61.

Rev, I. 1986. "The Advantages of Being Atomized." Working Paper. The Institute for Advanced Study, Princeton University.

Sabel, C. A. and D. Stark. 1982. "Planning, Politics, and Shop-Floor Power: Hidden Forms of Bargaining in Soviet-Imposed State-Socialist Societies." *Politics and Society* 4:439–75.

Sit, V., S. Wong, and T. S. Kiang. 1979. "Small Scale Industry in a Laissez-Faire Economy." Working Paper. Centre for Asian Studies, University of Hong Kong. Mimeo.

Wallerstein, I. 1974. "The Rise and Future Demise of the World Capitalist System: Concepts for Comparative Analysis." *Comparative Studies in Society and History* 16:387–415.

———. 1976. "Semi-peripheral Countries and the Contemporary World Crisis." *Theory and Society* 3:461–83.

Contributors

Lourdes Benería is Associate Professor, Department of Economics, Cornell University.

Lauren Benton is Assistant Professor, Department of Urban Studies and Planning, Massachusetts Institute of Technology.

José Blanes is Senior Investigator, Center for Study of Society and Economy, Bolivia.

Vittorio Capecchi is Professor, Department of Education Sciences, University of Bologna, Italy.

Manuel Castells is Professor, Department of City and Regional Planning, University of California at Berkeley.

Maria Patricia Fernández-Kelly is Research Scientist, Institute of Policy Studies, Johns Hopkins University.

Juan Carlos Fortuna is Senior Investigator, Center of Research and Information of Uruguay.

Anna M. Garcia is Investigator, Center for United States–Mexico Studies, University of California at San Diego.

Gregory Grossman is Professor, Department of Economics, University of California at Berkeley.

Monica Lanzetta Pardo is Investigator, Department of Political Sciences, University of the Andes, Colombia.

Terry McGee is Professor, Institute of Asian Research, University of British Columbia.

Gabriel Murillo is Professor and Chair, Department of Political Sciences, University of the Andes, Colombia.

Alejandro Portes is John Dewey Professor of Sociology and International Relations, Johns Hopkins University.

Susana Prates was, until her death, Professor, University of the Republic, Uruguay.

Bryan R. Roberts is Professor, Department of Sociology and Population Research Center, University of Texas at Austin.

Saskia Sassen-Koob is Associate Professor, Graduate School of Architecture and Planning, Columbia University.

Guy Standing is Chief, Employment Planning and Population Branch, International Labour Office.

Alex Stepick is Associate Professor, Department of Sociology and Anthropology, Florida International University.

Josep-Antoni Ybarra is Associate Professor, Faculty of Business and Economics, University of Alicante, Spain.

Index

Circular E (Employers Tax Guide) (U.S.), 256

Cities: and informal sectors, 74; of peasants in Bolivia, 139

City of New York, 62, 74

Class, 32; and gender, 248; and household organization, 261; identity in Uruguay, 92; and informality, 307–10; struggle, 307–10

Co-ethnic: alliances between capital and labor, 125; firms, 115

Coates, 282

Coca: allocation of earnings in Bolivia, 143; cultivation, 136; movement through state structures, 144

Coca-Cola, 45

Cocaine: banking of revenues, 144; in Bolivia, 135–49; and formal sector, 138–39; and inflation in Bolivia, 139; and informal economy, 135–49; and labor market in Bolivia, 137; production and marketing of, 136–39; revenues and national development, 143, 147

Colbert, 127n8

Collier, 27

Colombia, 16, 17, 95–110

Colombians, in New York City's informal sector, 67

COMIBOL (state mining company) (Bolivia), 140

Command economies, 150, 308

Commerce Department, 304

Commercial classes, 44

Commission on California State Government, Organization, and Economy, 254, 263n4

Common law and statutory employees (U.S.), 256

Communist parties: in Emilia-Romagna, 190, 196, 198, 199, 203, 305; in Madrid, 239

Community characteristics (Malaysia), 274

Comparative advantage, 136

Comparative political economy, new, 6

Competition, international: and complementarity, 305; in Great Britain, 280–81; and informalization, 28, 73, 125, 179, 299; in Italy, 207; in Madrid, 229–30, 239

Complementarity among small firms (Italy), 199, 202, 305

Complicity: definition of, 193; and exploitation, 192–93, 197, 203, 210, 211, 306

Computers, personal, 192; production in Italy, 207, 208; programming work in Italy, 210

Connections (personal), importance of (USSR), 153, 161, 163

Connolly, 173

Conservative party government (Great Britain), 282–83

Construction: in Colombia, 104–5, 108; firm size in, 64; in Guadalajara, 49, 50; industry, levels of informal employment, 49; in Miami, 114, 118–20, 124; in New York City, 63–65; in Spain, 218; in USSR, 168n7; wages in, 51

Consumer durables industry (Mexico), 176

Consumption patterns (Bolivia), 139

Continuing Survey of Households (Bolivia), 142

Contraband imports (Bolivia), 137, 139, 140–46

Contracts and informalization: in Colombia, 105, 107; in Madrid, 224, 234–35; in U.S., 249–50; in USSR, 168n7

Control over work process, 50

Cooley, 117

Cooperativist movement: in Madrid, 238–39; role of, in informalization, 305; and solidarity, 305–6; and worker control in, 241

Cordera and Tello, 173, 174

Corni Institute (Italy), 195

Corruption, 299; in Bolivia, 143, 144, 146; in USSR, 150–51, 153–54, 164

Cosmetics industry (Mexico), 176, 177

Costs: of capital reproduction, 95; of production in Spain, 224

County Business Patterns, 21

Courtaulds, 288

Craft skills, 43

Credit: informal arrangements, 71; lack of access to, 185; markets of, in Bolivia, 144, 145; and small firms in Madrid, 236–37, 243n6

Criminal activities, 60

Cubans: banks, 114; construction firms, 119; enclave economy in Miami, 114, 248, 301; entrepreneurs, 114, 248, 302; family income, 113; and Miami's informal sector, 111–31, 301, 306; U.S. government's reception of, 113–14, 304; women, 114, 259

Cultural diffusion (USSR), 152–53

Currency traders, ambulatory (Bolivia), 145

Customized products, 75

Dade (Miami) County, Florida, 21, 22, 111–31

Data, problems with, 269

Daud, 267

Day care, informal: in Italy, 203, 206; in Miami, 123. *See also* Children

De la Peña, 44

De Oyarzábal, 243n6

De-skilling, and informalization, 92
Deacon, 281
Debt service: of Bolivia, 147; of Mexico, 174
Decentralization, 29, 33; in Italy, 200; in Madrid, 233–42
DeGrazia, 223
Dejean, 127n7
Delorozoy, 221
Delpirou and Labrousse, 146
Demand for informal production and distribution, 73
Democracy, and class dislocation (Uruguay), 93
Departmento Aministrativo Nacional de Estadística (DANE), Colombia, 96–101
Department of Cochabamba (Bolivia), 148n2
Department of Employment (U.S.), 284, 290–91
Department of Energy (U.S.), 282
Department of Health, Education and Welfare (U.S.), 304
Department of Industrial Relations (U.S.), 254, 255
Department of Labor Standards and Wage Enforcement (U.S.), 251, 252, 253, 255, 263n1
Dependent development, 5, 183
Deregulation of small enterprises (Italy), 206
Desirability of types of informalization, 74
De Soto, 310
Detached stratum, 289
Deukmenjian, Governor G., 254
Development: strategies, 239–42, 298–311; theory, 4, 225
Díaz, 127n4
Díaz-Briquets, 114; and Pérez, 304
Dilnot and Morris, 289
Disarticulation: of labor markets, 139; of society, 135
Diversification (Colombia), 108
Doeringer, 186n8
Domestic units, 79–82. See also Households
Dominicans, in New York City's informal sector, 67
Donoso, 141
Doria Medina, 137, 140, 144, 145
Downgraded labor, 26
DPD, 42, 44, 49, 50
Dressmakers, Haitian (Miami), 122
Drink industry, 49
Drug trafficking: attempts to control in Bolivia, 136; government agents and complicity in cocaine trafficking, 137; and informal sector in Bolivia, 135–49
Dualism: economic, 12, 78; in Guadalajara,

55; in household types in Great Britain, 293; in industry, 230
Dunlop, 288
Durand, 117

Eastern Europe, 2
Ebel, 225
Economic restructuring, and informalization, 61–62
Education and informalization: in Colombia, 100, 105–7; in Italy, 207; in Malaysia, 271, 273, 274n9; in Spain, 224; in Uruguay, 81–82
Edwards, 6, 33n4, 229
Electronics industry: in Guadalajara, 50; in Italy, 207; in Madrid, 228–44; in Malaysia, 268, 271–72; in Mexico City, 176–78; in Miami, 124; in New York City, 64, 67–68; unionized labor in, 67–68
Elson and Pearson, 181
Elwell, Keeley, Fragomen, and Tomasi, 127n7
Emigration, and labor supply, 79
Emilia-Romagna, Italy, 23–24, 189–215, 304–5
Employer-employee relations, 305–6; in U.S., 254–55
Employer's Tax Guide, 256
Employment and informality: in Bolivia, 147; in Britain, 290–91; in Guadalajara, 41–55; in Malaysia, 265–78
Employment Development Department (California), 263n1
Enforcement of labor legislation (U.S.), 247–56
Engineering sectors, 45
Enterprise Allowance Scheme, 290
Enterprise zones (U.S.), 75. See also Free-trade zones
Entrepreneurship: in Colombian transportation, 106; and Communist parties in Italy, 190, 199, 203; entry costs for, 73; environment for, by Haitians in Miami, 122, 304–5; in Italy, 198–201, 208–10; in Madrid electronics, 233–34; in Mexico City, 182, 184; and modernization in Valencia, 224–25; in New York City, 68, 70; and recycling in Uruguay, 90, 91, 92; regulations and, 75; subsidies for, in Great Britain, 284; in USSR, 153
Environment, entrepreneurial, 304
Environmental controls, 28
Escobar, 43, 46, 49–51, 57nn17, 20
Establishment size and employment (Great Britain), 287–88
Estevan, 233, 234, 242n5, 243n6

Ethnicity: antagonism in Miami, 111, 119; cleavages and restructuring in Malaysia, 265–78; difficulty in making distinctions in U.S., 127n10; and employment in Miami, 116, 117, 119; enclaves, 114, 248, 257, 260, 301, 307; and informality, 26, 32; neighborhood, 301; in New York City, 63; and U.S. garment industry, 259
European Economic Community (EEC), 280
Evans, 183, 243n8; and Stephens, 6
Exploitation: and complicity, 192–93, 197, 203, 211, 300, 306; definition of, 192; and economic growth, 300
Export orientation, 302–3
Export-led growth, 229
Export-processing zones. *See* Free-trade zones
Export-related industries, role of female labor in, 181

Falkland Islands/Malvinas war, 296n2
Families: definition of, 261; firms in Bolivia, 140; labor, in Guadalajara, 46, 48; labor, in Italy, 189; labor, in Madrid, 234–37; in Uruguay, 81, 87. *See also* Households
Faría, 17
Fascism (Italy), 190, 196
Feige, 20, 60
Female employment: in Alicante, 219–24; in Mexico, 46, 180–81; and Third World industrialization, 181
Ferman, Berndt, and Selo, 12
Fernández-Kelly, M. P., 26, 29, 175
Fernández-Kelly, M. P., and A. M. García, 5, 20, 41, 47, 73, 113, 116, 118, 228, 247–64, 300
Fiat, 28
Filgueira and Geneletti, 81
Financial Times (Great Britain), 288, 290, 296
Firm size: and employment of women, 181; and industrial capacity, 232; and informalization in Guadalajara, 51; and informalization in Malaysia, 272; and labor markets, 183
Flexibility of labor force, 284, 287, 290–91; immigrants and New York City, 71; and subcontracting, 175, 182–84
Flexible research strategy, 3
Flexible specialization, 30, 302–3; and entrepreneurial mobility, 202; and Fordist models of industrialization, 201–2, 204–5; in Madrid, 240; in the semiperiphery, 241–42; spread throughout Emilia-Romagna, Italy, 189–215; and worker skills, 202

Flores-Blanes, 136
Florida, 21, 22, 302; garment industry in, 259–62; Needletrade Association, 263n5; southern, 247–64
Food and drink industry: in Guadalajara, 49–50; in Malaysia, 272; in Spain, 218
Footwear industry: in Colombia, 102; female labor, 50; in Guadalajara, 45, 49; in Malaysia, 272; in New York City, 69; in Valencia, 217–18; wages in, 51
Fordist model factories: as contrast to flexible specialization, 305; in Italy, 201–2, 205–6
Foreign capital, and Mexican industrialization, 174, 176
Formal sector: links with informal sector, 12, 13, 30, 119, 173, 298; mixing employment within households, 82, 138–40, 169n10
Forrest, 57n18, 284
Fortuna, J. C. and S. Prates, 5, 7n2, 13, 78–94, 99, 103, 108, 146, 224, 300, 303
Fouron, 127n7
Franco regime, 230–31
Freedom and Democracy movement (Peru), 306, 310n1
Free enterprise economy, and informal sector, 185
Free trade zones: and female labor, 181; in Malaysia, 267–70; in the U.S., 112
Frey, B. S., and Weck, 212, 213
Frey, L., 212, 213
Friedman, M., 282, 283, 284
Fröbel, Heinrichs, and Kreye, 180, 181
Fua and Zacchia, 214n2
Fuel production (Malaysia), 272
Full, working (F-W) households, 165
Full employment (Great Britain), 279, 290
Furniture and fixtures (New York City), 64, 68–69

Gallo, 65
Garbage collection and recycling industry (Uruguay), 86–88
García, A. M. *See* Fernández-Kelly, M. P., and A. M. García
García, B., Muñoz, and Oliveira, 174
García, N., 16; and Tokman, 310n3
García de Blas and Ruesga, 217, 219
García Meza, General, 146
Garment industry: in Colombia, 102, 106–7; in Malaysia, 272; in Mexico, 53, 176; in U.S., 114, 116–18, 247–64
Garofoli, 182
Garreau, 112
Garza, 44, 56n8

U.S., 60–61, 111, 113, 119, 304; and local economic growth, 113; in New York City, 68, 69, 73, 79

Import-substitution industrialization, 229, 233

Income distribution, 301; and drugs, in Bolivia, 139; in Mexico City, 173–74; of poor in Guadalajara, 53

Income-pooling units. *See* Households

Incomes in informal sector (Malaysia), 273

Independence and informal sector participation, 223; of small firms, 303

Independent (Great Britain), 296n4

Indians in Malaysia, 268, 274

Indirect wages, avoidance of, 30

Industrial Board of Appeals, 68

Industrial capital and informal sector (Bolivia), 139

Industrial development, 28–29; in Malaysia, 265–78; systems of, 204–5; theories of, 189; women and, 173–88

Industrial Reconversion program (Spain), 243n6

Industrial restructuring, and the informal sector, 27, 171–244

INE, 141, 142

INEGI, 45, 46, 51

Inequality (Great Britain), 286

Inflation: and dollarization of Bolivian economy, 145; in Great Britain, 281; in USSR, 164

Informal, use of term, 3

Informal economies: debate over, 1; definitions, 11–15, 265–66; deregulation and, 193; economic dualism and, 12; employment in Italy, 189–215; and flexible specialization, 189–215; of growth, 192, 195, 203, 211; integrative, 192, 195, 203, 211; internal heterogeneity of, 249; marginality and, 12; methods of estimating size of, 218–20; in Miami, 111–31; permanence of, 92, 299; and poverty, 12; subsistence, 192, 193, 211; as strategy, 49; types of, 192; universality of, 298; in Valencia, 218–20. *See also* Informal sector

Informal economies of growth, 302–7, 310n2

Informal expenditures (USSR), 162

Informal household (or individual) income, 155, 166

Informal incomes: centrality of, 223–24; types of, in USSR, 153

Informal labor force, 19

Informal management practices, 195

Informal monetary economy (Italy), 192

Informal sector: alternatives to, 301; and automation, 30; and collapsing legal sector, 216; criminal activities, 14–15; definitions of, 41, 148n6, 266; desirability of, 74; difficulty in gathering information on, 175; genesis of, 27–29; and government regulation, 12; heterogeneity of, in Malaysia, 272; household relations and, 225; integrated (Cuban) in Miami, 116–21; isolated (Haitian) in Miami, 121–25; linkages to formal sector, 95–109; and marginality, 26, 31, 102, 185; official reports and, 1; and organized labor, 31; as parasitic, in USSR, 152; and productivity, 30; and regional economies, 265; size of, in Spain, 242n3; size of, in U.S., 254; structure of, 25–27; theoretical status of concept, 78–79; views of, 185; vitality of, 75

Informal sector participation, and gender (Italy), 212–13

Informal workers, 81, 270

Informalization: and avoiding organized labor, 249; causes of, 220–24; causes of, in USSR, 152; and class struggle, 307–10; consequences of, in Valencia, 224–25; definition of, 127n6, 217; as diverse strategy, 42; effects of, 29; and the future, 32–33; and immigration in Miami, 119; impact on urban economies, 4; importance of historical conjuncture to, 301; limitations to generalizing solutions, 302; and long-term adjustment, 232; and marginality, 248–49; momentum of, 309; negative consequences of, 300; pattern of, in Miami, 116–25; policy implications of, 298–311; positive consequences of, 300–1; and profit levels in Valencia, 221–22; in semiperiphery, 229–33; and technological innovation, 225, 232, 300

Innovation: in Spain, 225, 232; and successful informalization, 302; in Uruguay, 83

Institute of Directors, 284

Institute of Fiscal Studies, 289

Internal Revenue Service (U.S.), 254–56; definition of employee by, 256

International Labor Office Minimum Wage-Fixing Machinery Convention, 284

International Ladies Garment Workers Union, 66, 251

International Monetary Fund, 186n9, 282

Irish workers, in U.S. garment industry, 258

ISFOL-CENSIS, 212, 213

Israel, survey of Soviet emigrants in, 155

ISTAT, General Census of the Italian population, 190, 191

Italian workers, in U.S. garment industry, 258

Italy, 24, 25, 28, 176, 301, 302, 305, 306; *autunno caldo* of 1969, 28; Bologna, 23; "black" labor, 23; central, 23; Emilia-Romagna, 23, 24; funding of small firms in "red" belt, 239, 242n1; labor unions of, 28; Modena, 23

Jaffe, Cullen, and Boswell, 127n4
Jalisco, Mexico, 41–55
Janjic, 224
Japan, 178, 280
Jean-Barte, 127n8
Jenkins, 174, 186n3
Jewish workers and owners, in U.S. garment industry, 258, 259
Jews, Soviet, 157
Job Training Scheme (Great Britain), 296
Jobbers, 179
Johns Hopkins University, 3, 7n3
Johor Baharu Seremban, Malaysia, 267, 268
Jomo, 267, 275n1
Jorge and Moncarz, 113

Kazakhstan, USSR, 156
Keeley, Elwell, Fragomen, Tomasi, 127n7
Kelang, Malaysia, 268
Keynesian economics, 282, 283
Kinship: and contracts in Colombia, 105; income exchange within groups, 103; ties, 55
Kondratieff waves, 281
Kritz and Ramos, 219
Kuala Lumpur, Federal Territory of, Malaysia, 268, 275n3
Kuala Lumpur-Keland, Malaysia, 267
Kugler, 96
Kurzban, 127n8

La Paz, Bolivia, 135–49
Labor absorption, 16, 30, 41, 174, 281
Labor Act of 1938, 251
Labor and health code violations, 75, 81
Labor aristocracies, 28
Labor Code, 248, 251, 253–54, 255, 258
Labor costs: and informalization, 125; and subcontracting, 179; and underground operation, 179
Labor exploitation, and informal sectors, 75
Labor flexibility, 295
Labor force: ethnic composition of, 116, 119; fragmentation of, in Uruguay, 92; reproduction of, in Colombia, 102–4; segmentation in, 17; skilled, 46; split in, 31

Labor legislation and informal sector (U.S.), 247–56
Labor market: fragmentation in Great Britain, 286–91; insertion in Colombia, 108; insertion patterns by Hispanic women in U.S., 257–62; segmentation in Mexico, 42, 46
Labor relations, and informalization, 305–6
Labor rights (Great Britain), 279
Labor supply and informalization: in Bolivia, 145; in Great Britain, 291; in Spain, 222–23
Labor unions. *See* Unions; Unionization
Labor-capital relations, integration (Uruguay), 79, 82–92
Labour Force Survey, 290
Labour party (Great Britain), 294
Labourism, old, 294, 295
Laenz, 81
Lafuente, 242n3
Lagos and Tokman, 29
Laguerre, 127n7
Lai and Tan, 275n1
Land tenure: and gender roles, 194; and genesis of informal economy in Italy, 194; and housing market, 44
Landes, 83
Lanzetta de Pardo, M., G. Murillo Castaño, with A. Triana Soto, 5, 7n2, 33n3, 95–110
Latin America, 5, 16, 17, 18, 19
Latvia, USSR, 156
Laundering of drug earnings, (Bolivia), 139
Laverdiere, Tremblay, Lavallee, Bonny, Lacombe, Boileau, Lachapelle, and Lamoureaux, 117
Lawless, 127n7
Leather goods manufacture, 69
Lebergott, 19, 33n2
Legality of operations (Spain), 222
Legitimate socialist income of a household or individual, 155, 166
Leichter, 62, 66, 247
Leningrad, USSR, 151, 156, 157, 159, 160, 161, 162, 163, 169n12
Levine, 112
Lewis, 16, 311n3
Life chances, 41–45
Life cycles, 41–55; and formal-informal divide, 51, 52–54
Linz, 243n7
Lithuania, USSR, 156, 157
Little Haiti, Miami, 121–25
Little Havana, Miami, 121
Little Miami, La Paz, 145
Llosa, 186n9
LNY (last normal year), 165

Speculation, inflation, and cocaine in Bolivia, 139
Spitznas, 20, 60
Sportswear, 258
Squatter settlements, 27
Standing, 5, 26, 27, 279–97, 309
Stark, 6
State: and classes in Bolivia, 145–47; contradictory mandates of agencies, in U.S., 250–56; and economy, 306; and economy in Bolivia, 135; encouragement of self-employment in U.S., 252; fiscal crisis of, in Great Britain, 282; and industrial development in Malaysia, 267, 275n5; and informal firms in Spain, 230–33; interference in economy, 298–99; legitimacy and informality in Bolivia, 146; misappropriation of property in USSR, 152; need for innovation in, 307; ownership, in USSR, 150; regulations, 28, 79, 97; relative autonomy of, 250; role in informalization, 5, 247; in the semiperiphery, 241–42, 243n8; transfers for subsistence survival, 293; weakness in Bolivia, 143, 146, 148n1. *See also* Government
Statistical manipulation of unemployment figures in Great Britain, 286, 291–93
Statistical sources (USSR), 150
Status, and informal employment, 49
Status of labor, 13
Steel sector, 45
Stepick, 5, 7n2, 20, 23, 28, 60, 73, 111–31, 301, 302, 304; and Portes, 126n2, 127n9
Stevenson, 127n4
Stonecutters, masonry and plastering workers (New York City), 65
Street peddlers: in Bolivia, 141, 142, 145; in New York City, 70
Strike of public sector workers (Great Britain), 282
Struggle, class. *See* Class struggle
Subcontracting, 42, 43; and avoiding risks, 182, 249; and avoiding union labor, 249; in Brazil, 183; and employment in Mexico City, 173–85; family businesses and, 182; flexibility and, 183–84; hierarchies (or chains) of, 174–86, 236, 303; and industrial dynamism, 228; insecurity of, 236; and labor costs, 249; and quality, 1, 236; and productivity, 180; reasons for, 179–85; in Spain, 222, 228–44; and transportation costs, 182; views of, 228–29. *See also* Contracts and informalization; Informal sector

Submerged economy, 3. *See also* Informal sector
Sub-subcontracting in Madrid, 236
Supply-side strategies, 283–85, 293, 296
Survey on Conditions of Life and Work in Spain, 232
Survival strategies, 75, 290
Sweatshop activities, and gentrification, 63
Sweden, 294

Tailors, Haitian (Miami), 122
Talbot, 288
Tallin (USSR), 159
Tanzi, 13, 20, 60, 247
Taxes, 28; evasion, 75, 139, 254, 289; and income distribution in Great Britain, 289; and informality in USSR, 152–53
Taylor, 258
Technical schools for workers, 305; role in Italian flexible specialization, 195–96, 197, 207
Technological change, and production costs, 180
Technological developments, lack of access to, 185
Technological innovation: and decentralization, 309; and informalization, 207–12, 300; and production costs, 180; in Uruguay, 83, 84
Textile industry, 44, 50, 203, 268. *See also* Garment industry
Tham, 274
Tin economy, collapse of (Bolivia), 135, 146
TI Raleigh, 288
Tlaquepaque municipality, Mexico, 56n56
Tokman, 13, 16, 19, 249
Tomkins, 284
Torreón, Coahuila, Mexico, 261–62
Total personal income of a household or individual, 155, 166
Total private payments and consumption per household, 155
Tourism: in Italy, 209–10; in Miami, 111, 120–21
Toy manufacturers: Mexico, 64, 176; Spain, 217, 220; U.S., 252
Trades Union Congress (Great Britain), 294
Trade unions. *See* Unions
Traditions and informality (USSR), 152
Training, and informalization (Italy), 200, 208
Transcaucasia, USSR, 152, 157, 162
Transferability of solutions, 302
Transport and General Workers' Union, 294
Transportation: costs and subcontracting, 183; Haitians in Miami, 122–24; industry

Transportation (*cont.*)
in Colombia, 104, 106–8; industry in
New York City, 70; in Malaysia, 272
Treml, 154
Triana Soto, A. *See* Lanzetta de Pardo, M.
Turkish worker in Germany, 27
Turner and McMullen, 229
Types of informalization, 299

Ukraine, USSR, 151, 156, 157, 159, 160,
161
Unemployment, 301; in Bolivia, 287; in
Great Britain, 281–82, 285–87; and in-
flation, 283; and men, 261; persistence
of, in Third World, 78–79; policy alter-
natives, 293–94; statistical manipulation,
291–96; taxes, in U.S., 256; in USSR,
154
Underdevelopment and informalization: in
Bolivia, 143; in Uruguay, 78; in Valen-
cia, Spain, 216–27
Underground economy, 3. *See also* Informal
sector; Informalization
Uneven development in Mexico, 173
Unformalized labor relations, and informal
sector, 78–94
Union membership, and wages, 51
Union of Construction Contractors, 65
Unionization: and electronics industry, 67–
68; and footwear industry in New York
City, 69; of garment industry, 117, 118;
and informalization in Madrid, 238–39;
and subcontracting, 182, 249
Unions, 26, 27–28; in Bolivia, 141; in Great
Britain, 289, 294; future of, 308; in
Miami, 118, 119; in Spain, 230–31; vig-
ilance of, 300
United Kingdom Census of Production, 288
United Kingdom Government, 293
United Nations Economic Commission for
Latin America (ECLA), 29
United Nations' Regional Employment Pro-
gram for Latin America (PREALC), 16
United States, 2, 16, 18, 19, 20, 22, 29,
33n2, 289; Bureau of the Census, 64,
263n4; Florida, 116, 128n14; Department
of Labor, 116, 118; Hispanic women in,
247–64; multinationals in Guadalajara,
51; temporary migration to, 52; New
York City, 60–77
University of California, Berkeley, 1
University of Warwick Employment Centre,
290
University research centers, and flexible spe-
cialization in Italy, 204–7
Unprotected wage workers, 18
Upscale markets, production for, 303

Urban marginality, 4
Urban Survey on Migration and Employment, Bolivia, 142
Uruguay, 18, 78–94, 146
USSR, 2, 5; emigrants in U.S., 150–70;
informal sector in, 150–70; irregular
methods of obtaining goods, 167; locational categories in, 165; personal income
in, 159–62; representativeness of, 157;
state, 300
Uzbekistan, USSR, 156

Valencia, Spain, 216–27
Valle de México, 46
Value of informal production in Valencia,
Spain, 219
Vauxhall, 288
Vázquez and Trigo, 220, 242n3
Veltz, 225
Vending (Bolivia), 141
Venezuela, 17, 18
Vermont, 252
Vertical integration, 5
Vertical methodology, 2
Vertical perspective, 95–96
Very small establishments (VSEs), 20, 21
Vilanova and Vicedo, 225
Vilnius, USSR, 159
Vocational training. *See* Technical schools
Vodka, importance of (USSR), 154

Wages: costs of and informalization in
Madrid, 240; and informalization in
Guadalajara, 51; in Mexico City, 180;
in USSR, 154
Waldinger, 23, 28, 30
Wallerstein, 311nn3, 4
Wall Street Journal, 252, 263n2
Walsh, 127n8
Walton, 29, 44, 56n7
Warren, Stack and Corbett, 127n3
Washing plastic recyclables, 88–91
Watanabe, 175, 178, 186n2
Wealth, and informal economy opportunities
in Italy, 212–13
Weaving (Italy), 195
Wedel, 168n5
Weiner and Green, 251
Weld Quay, Malaysia, 270, 273
Welfare coverage, 50
Welfare state, 28; in Great Britain, 279;
dismantling of, in Bolivia, 146; women's
labor and in Italy, 206, 211
West Astoria, New York, 72
Western Europe, 25
White, 275n5
Williamsburg, Brooklyn, New York, 72

Williamson, 30
Wilson and Portes, 114
Woldemikael, 127n7
Women, 26, 32, 50, 55, 309; in Colombian
    garment sector, 106; education and em-
    ployment, 224; Haitian petty vendors in
    Miami, 122–24; Hispanics in U.S., 247–
    64; and homework in Uruguay, 81, 85,
    91; household labor of, 52, 54; informal
    food production in Miami, 122; and in-
    formal production in Malaysia, 265; and
    informal housework, 300; and informality
    in Italy, 193–95, 197; and plastics home-
    work in Mexico, 179; sectoral differences
    in employment in Italy, 202–3; in Uru-
    guay, 85; wages of, 186n4; welfare state
    services in Italy, 206, 211. *See also*
    Female labor
Wong, 29
Wonsewer and Notaro, 80
Wood and paper products (Spain), 218
Worker control over work process: in
    Guadalajara, 41–51; in Madrid, 235–37,
    241
Worker independence, and skills, 43

Working class: polarization in, 51; reproduc-
    tion of, 109
Working conditions, in small firms, 183,
    235
Work sharing, 294
Work situations, 31
World Bank, 174, 186n9
World economic adjustment and national
    economies, implications for Malaysia,
    269, 273–74
World economy and informalization, 228.
    See also Competition
Wortham, 127n8

Ybarra, J-A, 5, 24, 25, 26, 28, 30, 107,
    186n5, 216–27, 228, 232, 240, 242n3,
    300
Young, M. L., 275nn7, 8, 12; with Bussink
    and Hasan, 275n9. *See also* T. G.
    McGee
Youth, 26, 32. *See also* Age, and informal
    sector participation

Zucker, 127n8

CPSIA information can be obtained at www.ICGtesting.com
Printed in the USA
LVOW12s2201291014

411182LV00001B/77/P